THE BELIEVER BOOK
OF WRITERS TALKING
TO WRITERS

THE BELIEVER BOOK OF WRITERS TALKING TO WRITERS

Edited by VENDELA VIDA

BELIEVER BOOKS

a tiny division of

MᴄSᴡᴇᴇɴᴇʏ's
which is also tiny

BELIEVER BOOKS
a division of
McSWEENEY'S

826 Valencia Street
San Francisco, CA 94110

books.believermag.com

Cover design by Alvaro Villanueva. Illustrations by Charles Burns.

Printed in Canada by Westcan Printing Group.

ISBN: 1-932416-36-6

TABLE OF CONTENTS

Notes and Apologies:

★ The interviews are arranged alphabetically, by last name of interviewee.

★ There are many writers we would have liked to have included in this collection. Interviews with these writers may appear in future issues of the *Believer* magazine and perhaps a second edition of this book.

★ Whenever possible, the conversations took place in person. Sometimes, when this was not possible, they took place via email, on the phone, or through the mail. One took place at a cricket match; one in the methamphetamine capital of the world; one at the Scientology Celebrity Center in Los Angeles.

★ Authors interviewed in this book are primarily writers of fiction. Also included are playwrights, memoirists, journalists, and poets—but it's mostly fiction people.

★ Though many of the conversations have appeared in the pages of the *Believer* magazine, a third of them appear here for the first time.

★ In all cases, the interviewers proposed the writer they would like to interview. "I'd like to have a conversation with _____," they said.

★ Some of the interviews in this book are shorter than others, but all of the interviews are long.

TAYARI JONES

TALKS WITH

CHRIS ABANI

"I AM IN EXILE, BUT NOT ENTIRELY IN EXILE.
THE WHOLE THING ABOUT BEING AFRICAN
IN THE TWENTY-FIRST CENTURY IS THAT
YOUR IDENTITY OCCUPIES A LIMINAL SPACE
THAT IS DIFFICULT TO ARTICULATE
TO A WESTERN AUDIENCE."

Rites of passage, fictional and real:
Participating in a pro-democracy movement
Writing a third novel
Killing a chicken
Learning to wrap the cocaine

I n 1985, the Nigerian writer Chris Abani was arrested and imprisoned on suspicion of masterminding a political coup. The evidence: his first novel, a political thriller written two years earlier, when the novelist was just sixteen years old. Since then, Abani has been imprisoned twice more, sentenced to death, and tortured by electric shock; he has also thwarted assassins, published four books of poetry, written eight novels (published three), and won numerous literary awards. His latest novel, GraceLand, was published by Farrar, Straus & Giroux in February 2004.

Though Abani's history makes for titillating copy, he should be best known for his detailed, nuanced, and haunting prose. GraceLand is a *sprawling coming-of-age tale that explores the underground world of the slums of Lagos, Nigeria. The author of this beautiful and searing novel, which explores the kidnapping of children for their organs, vigilante justice, civil war, incest, and Elvis impersonation, is not a world-weary and embittered man. Instead, Mr. Abani is thoughtful and soft-spoken—the parlance of California fusing with his British-Nigerian English.*

This interview was conducted by phone from Abani's Los Angeles home. He spoke of hard subjects: colonialism, exile, and war, yet he laughed at the interviewer's jokes and made a couple of his own.

—T.J. (Winter 2003)

I. "ONCE, SOMEONE USING A STONE OR BRICK TRIED TO CRACK MY SKULL BECAUSE HE WANTED TO SEE IF MY BLOOD WOULD BE RED OR WHITE."

TAYARI JONES: I noticed how many of the references in *Grace-Land* are American. For example: Hugh Hefner, Elvis. Nigeria being a British colony, I was surprised that the British references were so few. Why does the United States figure so prominently as opposed to Great Britain?

CHRIS ABANI: I think it's a combination of two things. One has to do with the notion of assimilation. There is the old joke we postcolonials have—*Q: What is the difference between the French colonials and the British? A: While the French would see a native African on the street as an animal, or try to civilize you or assimilate you, the British would simply not see you.* British culture is not about assimilation. It is about maintaining the status quo. The whole thing about American culture—because it is driven by capitalism—is this sense of global whiteness through global assimilation. It's sort of a new wave of empire—so I think that was why America had more of an appeal. And also the advent of television and movies. I mean, these were in existence long before I was born. But with my coming into awareness of them, the heroes—even black—were like Shaft.

And Superfly. It was the first time we encountered people of color who had any kind of power. Omar Sharif was a big hit for us. It was easier to sort of find yourself or frame yourself in a global context because of American films.

TJ: I read somewhere that your mother is English and she would call you for tea every day at four p.m. How did your bicultural experience shape your thoughts and ideas about Nigeria and your thoughts about colonialism? How does that figure into your equation?

CA: Well, that's kind of curious. It might have been a slight exaggeration to say "every day." The thing is, my parents met in the '50s at Oxford. In those days the big thing was for every Nigerian to claim that he was the son of a chief. My father was very clear with my mother that he didn't come from that kind of stuff, that he came from working-class people. In fact, my father was the first graduate from his town and the first one to go abroad. And he knew there would be resistance to his bringing a white wife back, and he prepared her in every possible way for the poverty and the differences. So much so that when my mother went there she was surprised that she could buy everything that she could buy in England. Like her marmalade and her tea.

But certainly the thing is that my father was very insistent that I be raised as a Nigerian. And, more importantly, that we be raised as Igbo men. [The Igbo people are an ethnic group who live mainly in southeast Nigeria. Their traditional language is one of the Benue-Congo subfamily of West African languages.] So I went through every single rite of passage, every initiation, and I speak the language inside and out.

But when you grow up with a mother who is English, you're usually learning to read Western texts and comic books. I grew up on Marvel Comics and things like that. It's confusing being biracial in Nigeria. You get treated with a fair degree of specialness and part of it is that you are seen to be weaker and not as strong as everyone else. Once someone using a stone or brick tried to crack my skull because he wanted to see if my blood would be red or white. [*Chuckles*] This was back in 1971.

TJ: Wow.

CA: It was a strange balance. Growing up, I remember listening to all the stories of the Mau Mau uprising [A '50s tribalist guerrilla movement in Kenya]. As a seven-year-old I hated these Mau Mau Kenyans who were killing all these white settlers because I thought they were going to come and kill my mother. And yet, I did not fully understand the implications of white settlement in East Africa until later.

You have the ability to individuate your mother from the rest of whiteness. And then you are more a product of your environment than race. So I do have the same uneasiness that every other Nigerian would have with colonialism and global whiteness and with racism or white power. It is a very difficult thing to negotiate at home with a mother who has never seen you as "black," but to have to say to her, "Oh, did you realize that what you just said might be construed as racist?" That kind of stuff.

TJ: I feel like you're almost anticipating my questions. You mentioned Kenya and Mau Mau and I was thinking about contemporary African writers and liberation movements. These are two of the themes I noticed in *GraceLand*. And also because I am an African American, I was thinking about liberation struggles here as well. I was wondering if you saw any link between the liberation movements on the African continent and civil rights in the United States. Earlier, you were talking about global whiteness. Do you have any ideas—

CA: About global blackness? I am glad that you picked up on this. All these subtle things that you do as a writer, you think that no one is going to get. Even when Elvis [the protagonist of *Grace-Land*] wakes up, the book he is reading is Ellison's *Invisible Man*.

TJ: Yes, it is!

CA: The book falls and cracks apart down the middle. The actual, physical book. That is very interesting. I grew up conflicted about this whole notion. Especially about Pan-Africanism. Especially since Nigeria's independence came quickly and was inspired a lot by Ghana's independence, which was led by [the Pan-Africanist] Kwame Nkrumah. Also in Nigeria was Nnamdi Azikiwe, who was very into Pan-Africanism. But it is interesting that these guys were educated mostly in America. These guys had contact with Du Bois and Marcus Garvey long before they came back. You can see this link much more in music. Enslaved Africans brought the roots of the blues with them to the United States and it made its way back to us in Africa. Sailors would come back and teach kids on the docks of Accra and Mali all the American guitar movements, which later produced people like Ali Farka Toure, who plays this hybrid Malian music that sounds so much like the blues. And he influenced people like Fela Kuti. There's that dialogue going on there all the time. And I see a lot of it happening in literature as well. *Invisible Man* becomes such an icon. In the opening of *GraceLand* there's that metaphor of the book falling off Elvis's chest and splitting open. This not only represents the splitting of the diaspora but the ability to enter the text in a way that he wouldn't be able to if he didn't share that fundamental racial heritage.

II. "THERE IS A PARTICULARLY BAD SCENE IN MY FIRST NOVEL WHERE THE GUY GOES TO A RESTAURANT AND SEES A WOMAN HE REALLY LIKES... HE DOES THIS AMAZING SKETCH OF HER AND PASSES IT TO THE WAITER TO GIVE TO HER, TO GET HER ATTENTION. I WAS SIXTEEN."

TJ: I spent a year in Nigeria in 1983, the year the civilian government of Shagari was overthrown, and the military regime took over. I was there with my parents—my dad had a Fulbright. But I was only in ninth grade. Where I was in the north was a quiet town. I was very young. But I remember that people were excited because the coup d'etat gave us three days of uninterrupted NEPA [electricity].

CA: [*Laughs*]

TJ: It was a big thing. And the currency was all changed to a different color. This is what I remember. But what did 1983 mean to you, both in general and with your writing?

CA: Well, I was sixteen at that point. I was just finishing form five, the equivalent of high school. And I had just had my first novel accepted for publication. It won the Delta Fiction Award. My novel actually opens up with a civilian president in power. A mimicry of Shagari. He is overthrown and all this kind of stuff. But how the country was taken over in my novel was not internal, but by neo-Nazis, of all people—don't ask me why; I was sixteen and fascinated by a lot of subjects.

I was born in Nigeria, but left for England halfway through the civil war and returned at the civil war's end. I have memories of the soldiers always being in control of the country. The Igbos were considered the rebels. And there were army cantonments everywhere you went. Roadblocks and such. The Shagari moment (1979–1983) was the first time, for many of us, that we considered the idea that the country had not always been under military control. That the stories our fathers had told us about democracy from 1960 to 1966 actually were true and we had this capacity to return to it. Unfortunately, Shagari's corrupt government led to the sort of disillusionment of that dream, but the subsequent coup sort of marked the beginning of the notion of something we could fight for. I think the seeds for most of the activism were planted then. It's not just myself but a whole generation of people who are now my age who, in one form or another, were involved with anti-government and prodemocracy movements that will never be catalogued, their stories never told. And this is part of the sadness of it all. But that moment, whether we were fully conscious of it or not, marked us. So 1983 was kind of a dark time, and inversely a moment of power.

TJ: What was the title of your first book, the one you wrote at age sixteen?

CA: It was called *Masters of the Board,* because the structural grid of it was a chess game. I sort of had a Nigerian James Bond trying to solve this web of international intrigue.

TJ: Is it available now?

CA: It's out of print. The Library of Congress has a copy, but I'm not very sure how the Library of Congress works.

TJ: Me neither.

CA: The blurb on the back of the book describes me as "Africa's answer to [British political-thriller writer] Frederick Forsyth." [*Laughs*] Crime thrillers were my thing. The novel is very male, very sixteen-year-old. Lots of guns. There is a particularly bad scene in my first novel where the guy goes to a restaurant and sees a woman he really likes and she is across the room. He does this amazing sketch of her and passes it to the waiter to give it to her, to get her attention. [*Laughs*] I was sixteen.

TJ: Not bad for sixteen.

CA: It's still a sophisticated book for that genre, but it's not something I'm really proud of and I hope it never gets reprinted.

TJ: OK, then I won't look for it. You mention your generation quite a bit. I want to know: who are the writers that you feel are doing important work in your generation? Who are the writers who you think paved the way? Since you do playwriting, I think of Wole Soyinka, the Nobel laureate. And: what do you think is the duty of your generation that is different from those who came before you?

CA: Well, I'll start from the back and work my way to the front. The beautiful thing about being an African writer of my generation is that there is already a rich tradition to mine and build upon. People like Chinua Achebe and Wole Soyinka created a presence for African literature. It's impossible to grow up in that country and not be marked by those books, by those texts. It's sad—I teach here in the United States and I teach young African American men and women who don't realize that they are part of a tradition.

I think for my generation the duty is not just to stand on the shoulders of that tradition but to further it. Like with craft and with language, exploring different forms. For example, a contemporary of mine, Chimamanda Ngozi Adichie, wrote a novel, *Purple Hibiscus,* which is a wonderful book. She does the opposite of what I do. She focuses in on a very detailed portrait of a family, while I try to cover a whole generation of people. There is also Helon Habila, whose narrative structure in *Waiting for an Angel* is highly innovative and original. Someone who I think is very underrated is a writer called Festus Iyayi. I'm not sure if he's my generation or if he bridges my generation and the one that came before. His novel *Violence* inspired what I did with *Grace-Land.* He was writing about poor people in a way that is non-voyeuristic. It's just solid and real. His novel *Heroes,* which is about the Nigerian-Biafran civil war, is probably way up there with the Vietnamese book *Novel Without a Name,* written by Duong Thu Huong. It's about character, not about political ideology. Because for a long time what has driven a lot of African literature has been protest against colonialism or internal strife, so the political ideology has sometimes overshadowed the craft and the art.

III. "IN EUROPE YOU ARE GIVEN YOUR FIRST TWO NOVELS TO FAIL AND FIND YOUR VOICE AND BY YOUR THIRD BOOK, YOU ARE READY TO STAND. BUT HERE IN AMERICA IF YOU DON'T COME OUT WITH THIS AMAZING MASTERPIECE AS YOUR FIRST NOVEL, THEN THAT'S IT. YOU'RE DONE."

TJ: As you know, right now in the United States, many creative writers—myself included—come through M.F.A. programs. I want to know about the way that you came to study writing and what you think of this idea of teaching writing in the university.

CA: I am a self-taught writer in many ways. This may have been a good thing. I learned by reading as well as writing. I teach at the M.F.A. program at Antioch University. It seems that people come with the idea that by taking a workshop they are somehow miraculously going to become good writers. And they don't need to read and they don't need to study. They say they don't want to be read because they "don't want to be influenced by it." I want to tell them that they should be so lucky as to have someone read their work and say, "Wow, this is like Toni Morrison," or something. I want to tell them, "You should be so damn fortunate." [*Laughs*]

Personally, I don't think that you can teach people to write. I think you can teach people to read in a more nuanced way. For instance, to look at one of Toni Morrison's books as a writer, say, and not as a cultural critic. To look and see how you can manipulate the body and objects and devices in ways you wouldn't have thought about. My class is bizarre in that I do things like give them a deck of cards and say, "Build me a poem." They look at me like I'm crazy. But I want to teach the idea of convergence and simultaneity. I do that rather than the traditional workshop where people say things like, "I don't like this line," or, "That didn't, like, work for me." Who cares what works for you! [*Laughs*] I don't care

17

what you like. I had one of my students read a book, and she said, "I didn't know what life lesson I was supposed to learn from this book," and I thought, "You're here as a writer. This is not a book club!" It's not about life lessons. It's about taking this book apart and looking at the characters and seeing how it's built. It's very difficult to get my students to see themselves as craftspeople. The only way I can think of to do it is to trick them.

Because I have been censored in my life and I am very leery of censoring anybody, I am very suspicious of this hierarchical rendering of experience—of whose experience is more fascinating than someone else's. I just think that people are not pushed to go to the places where their stories are, so they just write generic stuff. What professors want, what publishers are looking for, what agents are looking for. But there are plenty of writers in this country who are writing things that will rip your guts out. Percival Everett, for example.

TJ: Yes!

CA: His new book that's coming out, *American Desert,* is about someone who has the DNA of Jesus and is trying to reproduce Jesus and each model fails because when they kill him, he doesn't resurrect. [*Laughs*]

TJ: That's so Percival Everett.

CA: He's incredible. And I must say, having come to the United States, the whole point of my journey here was to meet Percival Everett. Because he turned *GraceLand* from a verbal description into a novel in nine months. He's my most amazing teacher.

TJ: This summer, I met Minnie Marie Hayes, who edits *Story-Quarterly,* one of my favorite journals. She is a great fan of your work. She said that she likes to publish you because you have something to write about. She commented specifically on an excerpt from *GraceLand* when a little boy has to kill a chicken as a rite of passage. She said, "Now *that* is a story."

CA: Minnie Marie often says to me, "I can't stand another cancer story." But I think there may be a cancer story out there that she hasn't seen yet. I don't think that you can overwrite any given topic. Otherwise, we would have all been out of business after the Bible.

But I do think that writers here need to be pushed to find their own raw edges. I think the problem of the M.F.A. is that it smooths things over too much. I think that the pressure on a first novelist in America is too much. In Europe you are given your first two novels to fail and find your voice and by your third book, you are ready to stand. But here in America if you don't come out with this amazing masterpiece as your first novel, then that's it. You're done. It just seems so ridiculous to me. Writing is about growing. In *GraceLand* there are a lot of rough edges.

IV. "I CONSIDER MYSELF TO BE IN EXILE. BUT THAT'S JUST ME. I WENT TO A CONFERENCE ON EXILE AND PEOPLE WERE TALKING ABOUT *BRIDGET JONES'S DIARY* AND BEING EXILED FROM THEIR FEMININITY!"

TJ: Is it right to consider every African writer who is not on the continent to be "in exile"? What does that mean? And I was thinking about Ngugi wa Thiong'o. He writes in Kenya, right? He's home, right?

CA: Actually, he's in Irvine.

TJ: California? Since he writes only in Gikuyu, I just assumed that he must be based in Kenya.

CA: This is part of the dilemma of just being African. He was in exile. He still is in exile. Part of his project has been to recoup an essential Africanness that might have survived colonialism. In Kenya and South Africa it is very different from Nigeria. We were never occupied in West Africa. Our language was never banned as theirs was. And also you have to understand that Ngugi is a Marxist and part of his belief is that your art has no consequence if it can't speak to everybody. Part of his endeavor has been to create his art in his own language so everyone can have access to it. Then it is translated into English as a secondary project. And part of the irony of being African is that he lives in Southern California and does this.

And this brings us to exiles. You have a lot of your intellectuals, writers, doctors, and professionals of all sorts who have had to leave—for economic reasons—to the West, and can't return on a full-time basis to Nigeria because they cannot be sustained creatively, professionally, or economically. And so they have to live in exile in a way. Then you have a second generation born outside of the country whose African-ness, Nigerian-ness, or Igbo-ness is just a received narrative. And who have a sense of exile because they are not accepted by the mainstream community or by the home community. I was a political activist who had to leave Nigeria for my own safety, but there was never a government bulletin saying, "Chris Abani has to go into exile." And even in Soyinka's case—you just leave because you know if you stay any longer, you will die. So in this sense, I am in exile, but not entirely in exile.

The whole thing about being African in the twenty-first century is that your identity occupies a liminal space that is difficult to articulate to a Western audience. If you are in exile, you can apply for a special grant because you are in exile. So you have to navigate through the expectations of these terms. And then there is the resentment at home from people who think that you are benefiting from occupying this liminal space and then you have to make clear in your own head who you are, where you come from. And what your writing will reflect. I consider myself to be in exile. But that's just me. [*Laughs*] I went to a conference on exile and people were talking about *Bridget Jones's Diary* and being exiled from their femininity! [*Laughs*]

TJ: Let's talk about *GraceLand* a little bit more.

CA: You've read it. Tell me. I know you have had some experience of being in Nigeria. But how would you relate to this book, just reading it as an African American?

TJ: So now you're interviewing me?

CA: In a way.

TJ: Actually, it reminded me of *Linden Hills*, a Gloria Naylor novel. The mingling of the recipes with the narrative. I think that part of my culture as an African American is to identify with the struggles of African or dark-skinned people everywhere. Even if I hadn't lived in Nigeria, I would have been able to relate to it. This fear of the police, this is rife in the world that I live in. I've been terrified of police since I was three years old. But on another level, many of the relationships between the characters were just sort of—I hate to use the word "universal," because it usually means something else—but the idea of the son trying to please the father. I read that you consider this book to be a love letter to your father. Could you elaborate on that?

CA: Well, my father died in 2001. I had a very difficult relationship with my father, from when I was, like, six or seven. When I was a kid, Nigeria was still so steeped in tradition and the notion of masculinity as being trained to be a warrior, in many ways. Even though your fight may be a symbolic one in the Ministry of Education. So to have a son who wrote poetry, who was reading Baldwin at nine, and read about homosexuality and tried to defend the idea that love, no matter what kind of love it was, was acceptable— I'm not gay so he couldn't beat me up for that. So my version of masculinity was something he couldn't accept. And he totally hated the idea of my writing. He burnt my first draft of my first book. We had a lot of domestic violence. He really kicked the crap out of us.

In 1991, when I left Nigeria, it was the last time I ever spoke to him. I went from hating him to pitying him to finally being able to understand that in some perverse way, there was actual love between us. I think that occurred when he died. One thing I tried to do in *GraceLand*: even though it is set in a ghetto and all sorts of terrible things happen, I tried to show a level of love in all of the interactions between the characters. For example, when Redemption [one of Elvis's friends] is showing Elvis how to wrap the cocaine, you get the real sense of tenderness, that Redemption is teaching him something. Terrible thing, but there is not just the homoerotic thing, but a big-brother thing, like the Artful Dodger teaching Oliver Twist.

TJ: That's exactly what I thought when I read it.

CA: Yes, he has a very protective tender way, but they are preparing drugs. They are going to kill people. And Redemption goes out of his way to protect Elvis from the Colonel, but doesn't tell them that they are moving dead bodies—people killed for their organs and body parts. And yet at every single point in that book, there are moments of frustrated love. Love that can't find any way of expressing itself.

V. THE INVISIBLE WHITE MAN IN THE ROOM

TJ: I remember when I was growing up in Nigeria, there was all this vigilante justice. Someone could point at you and yell, "Thief," and you could be killed by a mob. One of the most devastating scenes in *GraceLand* is when the carpenter is accused of being a thief and the crowd sets him on fire. There are at least five people who get burned alive in this book.

CA: It's not just about the fire and the reality of what the fire does. Apart from that, it has to do with the symbolism of fire. We sort of set ourselves on fire. We sort of self-immolate every time we engage in those kinds of actions.

   I grew up in a very violent culture. It's violent because it was colonized violently. Then there was the violence of colonial occupation itself. Intertribal wars and conflagrations. All of this stuff building up to a society that had just come through a civil war.

I went to primary school with people—nine, ten years old—who had been soldiers, who had shot people. People would place bets—"Give me twenty kobo and I will stab myself in the leg." You give them twenty kobo and they would do it.

TJ: Twenty kobo? That's less than a quarter.

CA: You put it in the context of when Nigerian currency had value. It was a little bit of money. Enough for a Coke and a snack. But I grew up watching this. And then there is corporal punishment at school, corporal punishment at home. There's an old Fulani custom: before you could get married you had to have a hundred slashes with a whip. If you cried, you weren't man enough. The book is soaked through with it. But the real question is how come at least 70 percent of our population seems to be immune to this violence.

TJ: I noticed this with Elvis. He is walking and he hears someone screaming and he doesn't stop walking.

CA: If you live outside of it, you wonder how people carry on. You wonder how people live in Sarajevo, but they do. I wanted to sort of explore that. It is painful for me to write about it. You're torn between representing what you know to be true and worrying how it will be perceived by a Western reader. Will they think that we are all savages?

TJ: Ah, that. What we call the invisible white man in the room. Peeking over your shoulder as you write.

CA: And sometimes it becomes a censor. And that is disingenuous. What I do is similar to what Ngugi is doing, operating under that notion that African art must exist in an appreciative context that is outside of the power of Westernization to reduce or empower. We allow access to the Western reader but also say we don't care about what you think. This is what we are trying to show you. If you get it, fine. If you don't get it, we don't care. ✯

JONATHAN LETHEM

TALKS WITH

PAUL AUSTER

"IT'S CERTAIN THAT THE WORLD'S LARGE
ENOUGH AND INTERESTING ENOUGH TO
TAKE A DIFFERENT APPROACH EACH TIME
YOU SIT DOWN TO WRITE ABOUT IT."

Things novels have swallowed:
Paintings
Songs
Fax machines
Fat women gesturing operatically

Paul *Auster began as a poet, essayist, anthologist, and
translator, but since* City of Glass *(1985) he's been recognized above all for being one of our most spare, lucid,
and elegant novelists. The protagonists of many of his
books, including* The Music of Chance *(1990),* The
Book of Illusions *(2002), and* Oracle Night *(2003), are pensive but
gentle urban everymen, and some are writers or other artists. They're easy
for Auster's many young admirers to identify, rightly or wrongly, as both
themselves and the author who put them on the page. In my twenties,
when I was becoming a writer, I was certainly one of those young admirers. When I was lucky enough, years later, to have the chance to know
Paul, I wasn't disappointed.* —J.L. *(Winter 2004)*

I. MUSIC

JONATHAN LETHEM: What were you doing today before I appeared in your house?

PAUL AUSTER: The usual. I got up in the morning. I read the paper. I drank a pot of tea. And then I went over to the little apartment I have in the neighborhood and worked for about six hours. After that, I had to do some business. My mother died two years ago, and there was one last thing to take care of concerning her estate—a kind of insurance bond I had to sign off on. So I went to a notary public to have the papers stamped, then mailed them to the lawyer. I came back home. I read my daughter's final report card. And then I went upstairs and paid a lot of bills. A typical day, I suppose. A mix of working on the book and dealing with a lot of boring, practical stuff.

JL: For me, five or six hours of writing is plenty. That's a lot. So if I get that many hours the other stuff feels satisfying. The other stuff feels like a kind of grace. But if I have to do that stuff when I haven't written—

PA: Oh, that's terrible.

JL: That's a terrible thing.

PA: I've found that writing novels is an all-absorbing experience—both physical and mental—and I have to do it every day in order to keep the rhythm, to keep myself focused on what I'm doing. Even Sunday, if possible. If there's no family thing happening that day, I'll at least work in the morning. Whenever I travel, I get thrown off completely. If I'm gone for two weeks, it takes me a good week to get back into the rhythm of what I was doing before.

JL: I like the word "physical." I have the same fetish for continuity. I don't really ask of myself a given word or page count or number of hours. To work every day, that's my only fetish. And there is a physical quality to it when a novel is thriving. It has an athletic component. You're keeping a streak going.

PA: Writing is physical for me. I always have the sense that the words are coming out of my body, not just my mind. I write in longhand, and the pen is scratching the words onto the page. I can even hear the words being written. So much of the effort that goes into writing prose for me is about making sentences that capture the music that I'm hearing in my head. It takes a lot of work, writing, writing, and rewriting to get the music exactly the way you want it to be. That music is a physical force. Not only do you write books physically, but you read books physically as well. There's something about the rhythms of language that correspond to the rhythms of our own bodies. An attentive reader is finding meanings in the book that can't be articulated, finding them in his or her body. I think this is what so many people don't understand about fiction. Poetry is supposed to be musical. But people don't understand prose. They're so used to reading journalism—clunky, functional sentences that convey factual information. Facts... just the surfaces of things.

JL: This relates to the acute discomfort of publicity, so much of which consists of requests to paraphrase the work. Which inevitably results in something unmusical. It's as if you've taken the body away, then drawn its outline and described its contents.

PA: I don't know why the world has changed so much that writers are now expected to appear in public and talk about their work. It's something I find very difficult. And yet one does have some sense of responsibility toward one's publishers, to the people trying to sell the book.

I've tried to pick my spots. I don't do it that often. But every once in a while I'll come out and do it as an act of good faith. Then I hope I'll be left alone again for a while. For example, with the last novel I published, *Oracle Night,* I just simply refused to go on book tours. I just didn't have the stamina for it.

JL: Kazuo Ishiguro has a funny way of talking about it as if it's a giant, consensual mistake all authors made together, by agreeing to this. And then suggesting we need to end it together. It's like a version of the Prisoner's Dilemma. If one of us tours, we all have to tour. If everyone refuses…

PA: He's speaking from deep experience. He did something that no one else I know ever did. He was on book tour for about two years. He went everywhere, to every country in the world where his book was published. In the end, it probably nearly killed him.

JL: Did you read *The Unconsoled*?

PA: I've wanted to.

JL: It's one of my favorite novels by a living writer. An epic Kafkaesque account of a pianist's arrival in a city to give a recital which never seems to happen. One possible description of it is as the longest and bitterest complaint of a book-touring author ever written.

PA: There's a great entry in Kafka's diaries in which he describes an imaginary writer in the process of giving a public reading. So-and-so is up there onstage, and people are getting restless and bored. "Just one more story," he says, "just one more…" People start getting up and leaving. The doors keep slamming shut, and he goes on begging "just one more, one more," until everyone is gone and he's left alone at the podium, reading to an empty room.

II. FILM

JL: It does seem that lately you've managed to reinstate your primary relationship with novel-writing. I mean, judging from the degree of concentration evident in the two recent novels and from your testimony that you're already deep in another one, which is nice news.

PA: Yeah, deep, deep in it.

JL: When you talk about the exclusivity that the novel demands, I'm very much in agreement with you. So I wonder about the years when you were apparently happy in the world of film. Did you feel that you had to retrench?

PA: I stumbled into filmmaking by accident. I've always been passionately in love with movies, to such a degree that even as a young person of about nineteen or twenty I thought maybe I would try to become a film director. The reason I didn't do it was because I felt I didn't have the right personality. At that time in my life, I was mortally shy. I couldn't speak in front of other people, and I thought: if I'm going to be this silent, morose, brooding person, I'm not going to be able to communicate effectively with the actors and the crew and so on. So I gave up that idea. And then ironically enough, it was only after I started publishing novels that I got involved with film—because people started calling me about potential film rights, writing original screenplays, and eventually I got lured into it.

JL: In your recent novels I imagined I'd spotted a subtle turn from film toward fiction—that is to say, the last two books both portray artists. In *The Book of Illusions,* your main character is a filmmaker, and the reader encounters extensive—and beautiful—descriptions of his films. In *Oracle Night* the main character is a novelist, and we read a portion of his novel-in-progress. Does this match a turn in your own attentions?

PA: I want to disentangle this a little bit. During the years I was making films, I never believed I was abandoning the novel. The two films with Wayne Wang took two years of my life. It was a wonderful experience. One of the great pleasures was getting out of my room for a while, working with other people, opening up my mind to new ways of thinking.

Lulu on the Bridge was an accident. I wrote the screenplay for Wim Wenders and then he had a conflict; he wasn't able to direct the film. At his urging, I decided to take on the job myself. And so, boom, there went another two and a half years of my life. But, then again, it was an irreplaceable experience, and I'm glad I did it. Then came the promotional tour which was far more exhausting than making the film itself. You think books are hard—films are deadly. I can remember doing forty interviews in two days in Japan. Long interviews, one after the other, one after the other. I was so worn out, I got sick and wound up in the hospital. That was when I came to a decision: as much as I enjoyed making films, and as much as I thought I was beginning to get the hang of it, I understood that it's a full-time job. You can't do it as a hobby. In order to go on making films, I would have been forced to give up writing, and that was out of the question. There was no doubt in my mind that what I'm supposed to do is write novels. So, very happily, without any regret at all, I retired. I'm not in the movie business anymore.

But to get back to *The Book of Illusions,* to Hector Mann and his film career: the fact is that Hector was born inside me long before I got involved with the movies myself. He came to me one day in the late '80s or very early '90s, full-blown in his white suit with his black mustache, and I didn't know what to do with him. I thought perhaps I would sit down at some point and write a book of stories that would describe his silent films—each story a different film. I walked around with him for years before the book finally coalesced into the novel it is now. People have said, "Oh, this is a result of Auster's foray into filmmaking," but it really predated all that.

The last thing to say about this little adventure into moviemaking is that it's rare that a person gets a chance at a somewhat advanced age—I'm talking about my mid-forties—to learn something new. To get involved in something you've never tried before. In that way it was good for me. It was good for me not to write a novel for five years. The only piece of prose I wrote during that period was *Hand to Mouth,* my little autobiographical essay about money.

JL: This is something I wrestle with. I am actually in the middle of the longest break from novel-writing of my adult life. I began trying to write novels when I was eighteen.

PA: Me too.

JL: They weren't any good, of course, but I've never been away from the activity since then. But in the past two years I've done a tremendous amount of promotion, and then worked on assembling two collections—a book of stories and a book of essays.

PA: Nothing to be ashamed about.

JL: Thank you. But it means that this body that's been accustomed to this practice for twenty years, as an athlete's body is accustomed to showing up at the clubhouse and putting on the cleats and running, my writer's body is—

PA: Atrophied a little bit.

JL: Yes, atrophied. It's a bit dismaying. I have a friend, a novelist with a delightfully unembarrassed sense of ambition. He's got a bit of that Norman Mailer–getting-into-the-boxing-ring-with-Tolstoy thing. He says a thing that haunts me: "If you look at the record, with very few exceptions novelists are at their best between the ages of thirty-five and fifty. The crossroads of youthful energy and experience." And here I am kissing off a couple of years at the start of my forties.

PA: Just to reassure you, I'm a firm believer that there are no rules in art. Every trajectory is different. My French publisher once told me that a novelist has twenty years, that all his best work will be done in that span of time. I don't necessarily buy that. But the interesting thing is how easy it is not to work. Yes, writing is a necessity and often a pleasure, but at the same time, it can be a great burden and a terrible struggle.

JL: I'm glad to hear you say that.

PA: In my own case, I certainly don't walk into my room and sit down at my desk feeling like a boxer ready to go ten rounds with Joe Louis. I tiptoe in. I procrastinate. I delay. I take care of little business that I don't have to do at that moment. I come in sideways, kind of sliding through the door. I don't burst into the saloon with my six-shooter ready. If I did, I'd probably shoot myself in the foot.

III. PLACE

JL: You've reminded me of another thought I had when you mentioned going to your little apartment. I hope you don't mind me saying you have an extraordinary house. The sort of house which, in my fantasies, I would never leave. There'd be a beautiful office in it and I would write in that office. But in fact, you've actually arranged to slip out of this house. That slippery, crabwise kind of movement is one the writer thrives on. Or, anyway, another thing I identify with.

PA: It's complicated. When we lived in a crowded apartment with children, there was nowhere for me to work, so I found a little studio apartment for myself. I worked there for six or seven years, and then we bought this house. In the beginning, there were tenants downstairs, but eventually they left and I decided to move my operation here. For quite a number of years, I contentedly worked downstairs. But last year we started doing work on the house. We were invaded by contractors, carpenters, plumbers, electricians, painters. There was so much noise. The doorbell was ringing all the time. The phone was ringing all the time. I realized I wasn't able to concentrate. And I thought, maybe I should go back to the old way. I found a little apartment in the neighborhood about nine months ago and I find it good, very good. This is a magnificent house. It's the product of Siri's [Siri Hustvedt, Auster's wife] tremendous aesthetic sense, her brilliant eye for harmony and order. But I think working in a rougher, meaner environment is good for me. I've always been a kind of Caliban. I feel happier in a bare space.

JL: My equivalent, perhaps, is that I enjoy an indirect relationship to place. People understandably think I moved back to Brooklyn in order to write about it, but the odd truth is that I've written the majority of these Brooklyn books in Toronto or Saratoga Springs or German hotel lobbies. I seem to write most happily about Brooklyn from a little distance, glancing back, yearning for it.

PA: Like Joyce and Dublin. As it happens, I'm writing about Brooklyn now, as well. The last book, *Oracle Night,* was Brooklyn twenty-two years ago. Now I'm writing about the Brooklyn of today. I can tell you the title of the new novel because I'm not going to change it: *The Brooklyn Follies.* It's an attempt to write a kind of comedy. I've never been in this territory before, and I'm having a lot of fun with it, doubting every word I write, and yet finally, I think, producing something that's interesting. I hope so, anyway.

JL: I can't wait.

PA: You try to surprise yourself. You want to go against what you've done before. You want to burn up and destroy all your previous work; you want to reinvent yourself with every project. Once you fall into habits, I think, you're dead as an artist. You have to challenge yourself and never rest on your laurels, never think about what you've done in the past. Just say, that's done, now I'm tackling something else. It's certain that the world's large enough and interesting enough to take a different approach each time you sit down to write about it.

JL: Anyway, your voice is going to be helplessly your own. And so the books will be united despite your attempts to ignore your own earlier work.

PA: Exactly, because all your attempts to flee from yourself are useless. All you discover is yourself and your old obsessions. All the maniacal repetitions of how you think. But you try. And I think there's some dignity in that attempt.

JL: I'm laughing, because now, as I'm about to begin a new novel at last, the only thing I'm certain of are the exclusions, the things I'll refuse to do again. I'm avoiding Brooklyn. I'm going to avoid writing about parents and children. And I've noticed that each previous book, as different as I thought they were, had mortal stakes attached. Someone was capable of pulling a gun on someone else. So I decided to restrict myself to emotional stakes.

PA: Well, that's good. When you become aware of what your limits have been so far, then you're able to expand them. And every artist has limits. No one can do everything. It's impossible. What's beautiful about art is that it circumscribes a space, a physical and mental space. If you try to put the entire world into every page, you turn out chaos. Art is about eliminating almost everything in order to focus on the thing that you need to talk about.

IV. TECHNOLOGIES

JL: Do you find it difficult to include certain technologies, now deeply imbedded, such as email and cell phones, in your fiction? I find that technologies invented beyond a certain date—for me it might be 1978, or 1984—don't seem to belong in the realm of fiction.

PA: That's a very interesting question. In *The Book of Illusions,* which is set in the late '80s, there's a fax machine. Something very important happens through a fax machine. So, I'm not, per se, against talking about technology. In the book I'm working on now, there's a reference to email. Also to cell phones.

I'm one of the few people left without a computer. I don't write on a word processor, and I don't have email and I'm not really tempted to get it. I'm very happy with my pen and my old portable typewriter, but I'm not against talking about anything, actually. I think the glory of the novel is that you're open to every-thing and anything that exists or has existed in the world. I don't have any proscriptions. I don't say, "This is not allowed because..."

JL: Not an ideological boycott, of course, but more a tendency to flinch from including those things. I email frequently. But if I include it in fiction I begin disbelieving the fiction instantly. It seems to disqualify the reality of the page.

PA: But this leads to a much larger and more interesting question that I've debated with various people over the years. You know, there are the enthusiasts for technology, and they always say—and this has been happening now for probably 150 years—they say that new technology is going to change the way people think and live. It's going to revolutionize our lives. Not just our physical lives, but our inner lives as well. I am not at all a believer in this view for the simple reason that we have bodies. We get sick. We die. We love. We suffer. We grieve. We get angry. These are the constants of human life whether you live in ancient Rome or contemporary America. I really don't think that people have changed because of the telegraph or the radio or the cell phone or the airplane or, now, computer technology.

Seven or eight years ago, I was invited to Israel by the Jerusalem Foundation and stayed at an artists' center called Mishchanot. A wonderful place. I was fifty years old, and I'd never been to Israel, a Jew who had resisted the idea my entire life. I was waiting for the right moment, and when the letter from Teddy Kollek came and he said they wanted to invite me for three or four weeks to stay here and live in this building and write and do whatever I wanted, I thought it was the appropriate moment to go. Siri and Sophie [their daughter] went with me. At one point, we took a tour around the country. We visited the town of Qumran, where the Dead Sea Scrolls were discovered. There's an extraordinary museum there with the scrolls and other artifacts that were found in the cave and around the site. These artifacts are so fascinating because there are plates that look like plates you could buy in a store today, with the same patterns, the same design, or baskets that any French or Italian person would use to take to the market today. And I had a sudden revelation about the extraordinary sameness of human life through the ages. That's why we can read Homer and Sophocles and Shakespeare and feel that we're reading about ourselves.

JL: I spent my early twenties in the Bay Area during the late '80s. I was witness to this extraordinary boom in the ideology of computing, the birth of *Wired* magazine and all that gave it context. There was a tremendous excitement at the idea that human life would never be the same once virtual reality existed. But if you read Dziga Vertov, the great Russian theorist of cinema, a hundred years earlier he was making the same claim for film. And then, if you search just a decade or so earlier, the advent of radio was surrounded by the same rhetoric.

PA: It must have seemed revolutionary then. The world—people from distant places, were suddenly in contact. This isn't to say that there aren't dangers in technology. We're all too aware of teenagers today spending their lives in front of their computer screens, dulling their senses, not living fully anymore. But, I think as they grow up and life begins to impinge on them, they're going to join the rest of us.

JL: The sweet irony is that so much of the online world takes a written form. What was meant to be a postliterate or visually literate culture is now obsessed with epistolary exchange. Letters. Or diaries.

PA: Exactly. That gets us back to the question of fiction. Over the generations, countless people have predicted the death of the novel. Yet I believe that written stories will continue to survive because they answer an essential human need. I think movies might disappear before the novel disappears, because the novel is really one of the only places in the world where two strangers can meet on terms of absolute intimacy. The reader and the writer make the book together. You as a reader enter the consciousness of another person, and in doing so, I think you discover something about your own humanity, and it makes you feel more alive.

JL: I like your emphasis on the privacy of the experience. No matter how enormous a novel may become, the physical act of reading determines that there's no way it can become a communal experience. To read is intimate. It's almost masturbatory.

PA: There's only one reader of a novel. That's, I think, the crucial fact about all this. Only one person. Every time, only one person.

V. EKPHRASIS

JL: I'm also fascinated by this notion of the novel's capacity for extensive descriptions of other art forms. It seems to me one of the novel's defining strengths: that it can swallow a song, a poem, or a film—

PA: Or a painting.

JL: Or a painting. It has a scope that other art forms are denied, because a novel can't be recapitulated in some other art form.

PA: I think the word is *ekphrasis,* which is a rhetorical term meaning the description of imaginary works of art. It's so interesting to me that one of the things that novels have tended not to concentrate on over the centuries is the fact that people read books. I show books and the experience of reading as part of the reality of the world. And the same goes for film. Why not describe movies? After I published *The Book of Illusions,* I sent a copy to my friend Hal Hartley, the filmmaker. And he said to me, "You know, I think maybe written films are better than real films. You can see them in your head and yet everything is exactly as you want it to be."

JL: Novelists get to direct the perfect films. We get to cast every part. We dress the set exactly as we wish.

PA: With a book you can read the same paragraph four times. You can go back to page 21 when you're on page 300. You can't do that with film. It just charges ahead. It's often difficult to keep up, especially if you're watching a film you admire very much. Good films demand to be looked at several times in order to be observed completely.

I think one of the mistakes I made with *Lulu on the Bridge* was that I wrote the script too much as if it were a novel. I think the film has to be seen several times before you can really penetrate what's going on. There's a moment early in the film when Harvey Keitel is walking down the street and there's a little graffito on the wall that says "Beware of God." I had seen this on a T-shirt and liked it very much. It's the dyslexic "Beware of Dog." Later on, I very consciously put a barking dog in the distance. That dog, to me, was a deity. And that's when Harvey's character discovers the dead man in the alley. Nobody, nobody could possibly understand what I was trying to do.

JL: A reader, encountering a sentence about a barking dog, would have to dwell on why that choice was made at that moment. Everything in a novel is explicitly chosen, whereas some of what a film captures feels incidental, according to the vagaries of photography and sound recording.

PA: Exactly.

JL: Meanwhile, I just can't help noticing that while you described that, a dog was barking in the distance, here in Brooklyn.

PA: Yes.

JL: So what's your fondest example of ekphrasis—the work of art depicted in another work of art?

PA: There's a great moment in *War and Peace* when Natasha is taken to the opera and Tolstoy deconstructs the whole experience. Rather than write about it from an emotional point of view or an artistic point of view, he depicts it simply from a raw, physical point of view. You know, "Then some fat woman came onstage and started gesturing, and then a gong sounded in the background, and then lightning struck, and then a skinny man sang an aria that no one understood." And I think that's probably the funniest description of a work of art I've ever read. But, probably the best and most beautiful, and I'm doing this right off the top of my head—

JL: That's ideal.

PA: I hate to bring this so close to home, but I think it's Siri's last novel, *What I Loved*. The painter's artworks are of a sublime profundity, and the artworks are part of the novel. It was so beautifully articulated. I don't know that I've read another novel in which art has played such an integral role in the story.

JL: I'm remembering the description of a painting in which the artist's presence is shown, just barely, at the edge of the frame.

PA: A little shadow.

JL: Yes.

PA: Over the years, I've been intensely interested in the artificiality of books as well. I mean, who's kidding whom, after all. We know when we open up a book of fiction that we're reading something that is imaginary, and I've always been interested in exploiting that fact, using it, making it part of the work itself. Not in some dry, academic, metafictional way, but simply as an organic part of the written word. When I was a kid, I'd pick up a novel written in the third person, and I'd say to myself, "Who's talking? Who am I listening to here? Who's telling this story?" I can see a name on the cover, it says Ernest Hemingway or Tolstoy, but is it Tolstoy or Hemingway who is actually talking?

I always loved the books in which there was some kind of excuse for the fact that the book existed. For example, *The Scarlet Letter*, where Hawthorne discovers the manuscript in the custom-house and then proceeds to print it in the subsequent pages. It's all a ruse. Art upon art upon art. And yet it was very compelling to me. I think that's why most of my books have been written in the first person rather than the third.

JL: When you first started out, did you think that would be the case? I, too, gravitate towards the first person, but when I was a young reader, I thought of third person as the more pure. It seemed to me in some way the higher form of fiction.

PA: Perhaps, but I like the low. I'm very interested in the low, the close to the ground, something that's almost indistinguishable from life.

JL: At what point in a project are you certain of which form you'll choose?

PA: I think in every case, I've known from the beginning. The only time I was confused was when I was writing a book of nonfiction, *The Invention of Solitude*. The first part of that book is written in the first person, and then I started the second part in the first person as well. But there was something that I didn't like about it. I couldn't understand why I was dissatisfied. I wrote, I wrote, I wrote, and then I had to stop. I put it away, meditated for several weeks, and understood that the problem was the first person. I had to switch to the third. Because in the first part I was writing about somebody else—my father. I was seeing him from my point of view. But, in the second part, I was mostly writing about myself. By using the first person, I couldn't see myself anymore. By shifting to the third person, I managed to get a certain distance from myself, and that made it possible for me to see myself, which in turn made it possible for me to write the book. It was very strange.

JL: You use the word *distance*. And it seems to me one aspect of your work—omnipresent, but very elusive, and difficult to speak of—is a quality of reserve.

PA: This might come as a surprise to you, but I tend to think of myself as a highly emotional writer. It's all coming out of the deepest feelings, out of dreams, out of the unconscious. And yet what I'm constantly striving for in my prose is clarity. So that, ideally, the writing will become so transparent that the reader will forget that the medium of communication is language. So that the reader is simply inside the voice, inside the story, inside what is happening. So, yes, there is a certain—I wouldn't call it reserve, but precision maybe, I don't know. At the same time, I'm trying to explore the deepest emotional questions I know about: love and death. Human suffering. Human joy. All the important things that make life worth living.

JL: Yes, I certainly didn't mean to suggest I experience the books as dispassionate. I found *Oracle Night* a wrenchingly emotional book. I'm not surprised by that. I do think you're right, that what I'm trying to characterize proceeds from the precision of the prose, its exacting quality. The effect is one of timelessness.

PA: I want to write books that can be read a hundred years from now, and readers wouldn't be bogged down by irrelevant details. You see, I'm not a sociologist, and the novel has often concerned itself with sociology. It's one of the generating forces that's made fiction interesting to people. But that's not my concern. I'm interested in psychology. And also certain philosophical questions about the world. By removing the stories from the morass of things that surround us, I'm hoping to achieve some kind of purer approach to emotional life.

JL: What's lovely is that you grant that same imperative to the characters themselves. They are often looking to purify their relationship to their own lives.

PA: I suppose in a way most of my characters are nonconsumers, not terribly interested in all the little baubles and artifacts of contemporary life. Not to say that there aren't many specific things mentioned in my books; it's just that I don't dwell on them excessively.

JL: Yes, even the most contemporary references in your work seem to float off into a timeless place.

PA: I'm very concerned that every word, every sentence in my book is pertinent. I don't want to indulge myself in the luxury of writing beautiful paragraphs just for the sake of making beautiful writing. That doesn't interest me. I want everything to be essential. In a sense, the center is everywhere. Every sentence of the book is the center of the book. ✫

BEN EHRENREICH

TALKS WITH

JOHN BANVILLE

"I AM OLD-FASHIONED ENOUGH
TO USE THE WORD 'BEAUTY'
WITHOUT BLUSHING OR GIGGLING."

Art originates in:
Thought
Feeling
Earthy things like flesh

It is not:
Self-expression

It becomes:
A sudden access of self-awareness

There is a long-dead painter who pops up in more than a
few of John Banville's thirteen books, a Nabokovian
wink of a character whose name, Jean Vaublin, is roughly
anagrammatic with the author's own, and whose work
inspires Banville's cast of unfortunates to frequent reverie
and occasional murder. "He is the master of darkness, as others are of
light," Banville wrote of Vaublin in 1993's Ghosts. "Even his brightest
sunlight seems shadowed, tinged with umber from these thick trees, this
ochred ground, these unfathomable spaces leading into night." It's hard not
to read this as jokey self-portraiture, so apt a description is it of the gloom-
ful world of Banville's novels, with their less-than-heroically doomed

protagonists wriggling desperately about for a glimpse at something that might resemble rest. They sometimes catch it for a moment or two, but more usually the only light to be found is the stuff gleaming through the wit and polish of Banville's nearly perfect prose. That's plenty light enough.

In a body of work stretching over thirty years, Banville has taken read-ers from his early Birchwood *(1973), in which a boy runs off with a tattered circus in famine-plagued Ireland; through a trio of historical novels about Copernicus, Kepler, and (sort of) Newton, in which the famed cos-mologists do their best to eke a little harmonic order out of a world where it is far from immediately evident; through another triad of books chroni-cling the repentant flailings of a maid-murderer named Freddie Mont-gomery; to 2000's* Eclipse, *about a defeated actor returned to his child-hood home in search for self among "the jumble of discarded masks"; and at last to* Shroud *(2002), his most recent, about a vicious drunk of an academic superstar with his share of nasty secrets. Banville's themes are the big ones—the shifting grounds of truth, time, and the ever-shaky self—and he digs at them with doggedness, ambition, and a vocabulary that will bring even the most casual logophiles to their knees in bliss.*

This interview took place over two months and two continents (Banville lives in Dublin), and employed two technologies of communica-tion (email and phone).   —*B.E. (Spring/Summer 2003)*

BEN EHRENREICH: Do you find that you're able to like any of your books?

JOHN BANVILLE: No. I hate them all. With a deep, abiding hatred. And embarrassment. I have this fantasy that I'm walking past Brentano's or wherever and I click my fingers and all my books on the shelves go blank. The covers are still there but all the pages are blank. And then I can start again and get it right. I hate them all. They're all so far below what I had hoped they would be. And yet one goes on. Here I am starting a new book. This is the absolute best stage of it, because when you're writing the opening pages of the book, anything is possible, you might actually get it right this time. In my heart, of course I know that I won't. In a couple of years' time when I finish the book, I'll hate it just as much as the others. I won't deny that every now and then I write a sentence and I can hear a chime, I can hear that ping that you get when you hit your fingernail on the side of a glass, and I think, "Yeah, that's right." Why would I sit here day after day doing this stuff? I certainly don't get any money for it.

BE: Your protagonists are generally a pretty wretched lot—broken by time, by the lies they've told themselves, by their weaknesses and fears, but struggling desperately, even when they know better, for some form of redemption. And they do find it, not any lasting sort with harps and hymns, but shards of transcendence, brief salvations. And these transitory redemptions seem to come almost exclusively from art or from sex.

JB: I have an elderly friend who holds that he is like the census form—broken down by age, sex, and religion (he's the same corpulent friend who adapted Connolly's famous dictum to "Outside every thin girl there's a fat man trying to get in"). I suppose one might say the same of my sorry lot of marionettes. They do seek some form of redemption for themselves, although I'm surprised you see so much sex in my work (not half enough, my publishers feel). Art offers them brief moments of transcendence, but they always come crashing back to earth, usually making a messy landing in something soft. I'm acutely aware that "redemption" and "transcendence" are more of those big words that so troubled Stephen Dedalus, and as such one must beware them. Art, in one formulation, is transcendental play—with an equal emphasis on adjective and noun—and play should always involve earthy things, such as clay, flesh, human beings, as well as dice, of course. I like your "not any lasting sort with harps and hymns, but shards of transcendence, brief salvations." Brief salvations is nice, implying as it does that there is more than one way of being saved.

BE: Why "dice, of course"?

JB: Well, play involves chance, of course, hence the dice.

BE: Your characters are very conscious of the role chance plays in their lives, of the degree to which they are marionettes to what Freddie Montgomery (in *The Book of Evidence*) calls "the ceaseless, slow, demented drift of things." They are often quite stubbornly dismissive of any notion of responsibility or volition, of any substantial self capable of making choices. But their narratives are largely confessional—stabs at selfhood, blunderings towards forgiveness for crimes they recognize as theirs. Would you allow that in this sense, your novels are highly moral creatures?

JB: I don't think—in fact I'm sure, in my case, at least—that artists ever set out to make art with a moral purpose in mind. It simply would not work. One can only make art for its own sake, otherwise there is adulteration. This is what makes Orwell, for instance, such a good political satirist and such a dreadful novelist. However, the artist's intentions are not everything—in fact, they may be negligible, once the work is finished—and it's perfectly possible for a work of art to have a moral force, even a moral direction, of its own devising, as it were, even of its own volition. My characters twist and turn, reel and writhe, not out of moral anguish, but in the awful, salt-on-the-snail's-back agony of trying to be authentic. It is this—vain—quest for authenticity that drives them all, I think.

But this is the artist taking on the role of critic in regard to his own work, which is always dangerous. I look on my books with a mixture of bafflement and shame; half the time I don't know what I'm doing when I'm doing it, and the other half I am in doubt that I should be doing what I'm doing. What is it Kafka says?—I do not speak as I think, I do not think as I should, and so it all goes on in helpless darkness (in German he would not have set two "ess" endings in sequence).

BE: Yes, I don't mean moralistic or moralizing at all, just that their concerns are moral ones, are the most basic moral ones—the possibility of choice, of becoming, to paraphrase Nietzsche (and I won't dare to speculate on his German), an animal capable of making promises. I suppose I want to push you to unravel for me the notion of "art's own sake," because it seems that you do have your purposes, conscious or not, which are not adulterating but actually fundamental, that you grapple with the same problems in different ways in different books, and do so with such precision and grace that I can't believe it's entirely unconscious.

JB: Well, I read a lot of philosophy, for the beauty of the thought if not for the rigor, and I suppose some philosophical concerns must seep into my literary thinking. I do like fiction to have a "mind," I mean, to have a sense that it originated in thought as well as in feeling. Kundera is disparagingly good on the present-day hegemony of feeling over thought, emotion over reason; he remarks somewhere that far more and far greater crimes have been committed for heartfelt than for rational reasons. Probably it is not possible to be a thinking being without a concern for the moral.

But any question of the moral inevitably raises—for the artist, at least—the question of the beautiful. I am old-fashioned enough to use the word "beauty" without blushing or giggling. Yet one has to be suspicious of what one might term "unattached" beauty. Hermann Broch held that to say "art for art's sake" is not much different from saying "business is business" or "war is war." I'm not sure I agree with him—in fact, I'm not sure I understand him—but the remark has been lodged in my mind for many years. Certainly one has to beware the overly burnished surface.

Recently I came across again a wonderful observation by Proust, I don't know from where, in which he contrasted Flaubert with Balzac. Flaubert's style, he said, replaces the object, the "mere" object, with a highly polished metaphor, so that his work is everywhere uniform, seamless, gleaming; Balzac, on the other hand, leaves all kinds of bits and pieces of things lying around, and consequently his work has the rawness and roughness of real life. I hasten to add that of course I greatly prize Flaubert over Balzac; but one knows what Proust means (indeed, Proust would most likely have detested Scott Moncrieff's daintified translation of *À la recherche…*). As to Nietzsche ("Nietzsche I loved, and after Nietzsche, art…" Sorry), I wonder if you know this wonderful aphorism from *The Gay Science:* "I fear that the animals regard man as a creature of their own kind which has in a highly dangerous fashion lost its healthy animal reason—as the mad animal, as the laughing animal, as the weeping animal, as the unhappy animal."

What were we saying…?

BE: I'm not sure exactly, but Nietzsche and other unhappy animals provide a convenient transition—in *Shroud,* your latest novel, philosophy is more in the forefront than ever. It's set in Turin against the backdrop of Nietzsche's famous breakdown, and its protagonist, Axel Vander, has a little Althusser in him and more than a little Paul de Man. What about those men grabbed your interest, and what brought them together for you?

JB: All my books since *The Book of Evidence* have been more or less concerned with the quest for authenticity. I wrote about a murderer, an actor, a spy. De Man had been in my mind for a long time, ever since I became friendly with the Belgian scholar who unearthed de Man's wartime journalism, Ortwin de Graef. Then I read Althusser's marvelous, frightening memoir, *The Future Lasts Forever* (I recommend it to you, if you don't know it already), which begins with his account of murdering his wife. (Recently I met an old friend of the Althussers, who gave it as his opinion that the only moment of true sanity in Althusser's life was when he killed "that woman.") So I blended de Man/Althusser into a kind of Frankenstein's monster, and came up with Axel Vander, a man who has lived a lie for decades, who has stolen another man's identity, who denies even his Jewishness, for no good reason that he can think of. The quintessential Banville protagonist, no?

In Vander I think I at last expressed all my thinking about the problem of authenticity—now I can move on.

BE: There were a few moments in *Shroud* in which you seemed to be—and this may be a simplistic way of putting it—explaining Vander's theoretical work, which in some ways echoes Paul de Man's, through his life. So of course he felt that "every text conceals a shameful secret," as he put it, because he saw his own shameful secret everywhere he looked. Is it right to read into the book an implicit critique of the sort of literary criticism that de Man engaged in?

JB: No. I mean, it's a travesty of de Man. I'm surprised I haven't had hate letters from de Man scholars. Fiction is absolutely conscienceless and cannibalistic. It gobbles up material wherever it can find it. I suppose I wanted to find an emblematic figure from that period. I have no interest in commenting on the great issues of our time. I just wanted to find a public figure, so I blended these two together, shamelessly, and made a fictional character.

BE: So you weren't interested in engaging with de Man's work?

JB: I find de Man's work very interesting. I think it is very... shrouded. It's written in an extraordinarily guarded, obtuse style. Frequently it is extremely difficult to find out what he's talking about, and I'm not sure whether that's intentional or not. Certainly after Ortwin de Graef discovered these anti-Semitic pieces, people leapt on de Man's work and said, "Oh, the whole thing is an elaborate smokescreen." I find that extremely hard to believe. These were pieces that he wrote at an extraordinary time in twentieth-century history, an extraordinarily dangerous time. Everybody's loyalties and politics were obscure, and I can't imagine that a man of his intellect would lead his life and erect critical systems on a peccadillo from during the war. Certainly one of the pieces he wrote is pretty disgracefully anti-Semitic. He famously said that if the Jewish element were removed from Europe, European culture would lose nothing, which is disgraceful, no doubt about that.

But so many people did so many appalling things—look at the early books of Graham Greene, which are dripping with anti-Semitism. And one only has to mention Eliot. Most of the modernists with the great and notable exception of James Joyce were fascistic in tendency and most of them anti-Semitic.

So I don't see that de Man would have felt all that guilty. He did have something to hide, but who hasn't? Certainly if you lived through the period that he lived through in Europe and then went to America, it would be extremely difficult not to have something to hide. And I don't like to think what I would have done if I had been invited to write for a collaborationist newspaper in Belgium in the early '40s, but that doesn't mean that I don't reprehend the stuff that he wrote. Anti-Semitism always seems to me an extraordinarily *stupid* attitude, and extraordinarily dim. I'm always amazed that people with such delicate and finely honed sensitivities, an Eliot or even a Graham Greene, would be anti-Semitic. I just don't know how they could do that. But I didn't live through the period that they lived through. Everybody in the '30s seem to have been casually anti-Semitic.

But this is going wildly off the subject, because I had no intention of writing about these subjects in *Shroud*. From my point of view, a book manifests itself and then the only task I have is to get rid of the damned thing, throw it away. Someone once asked Joyce why did he use Homeric parallels in *Ulysses,* and he looked at him as if he were mad and said, "Well, it was a way of working." In other words, it didn't mean any more than that it was a method of working. I think that's true of practically all art that's real. I don't think art has a conscience of any kind.

BE: Let me ask you a hopelessly nineteenth-century High Romantic question of the sort that you're not supposed to ask (or, God forbid, try to answer) with a straight face these days. What do you believe is the task of literature? The word *task* is perhaps a bit didactic. Maybe *mission* would be better, or *end,* but among the many things that literature does and can do, is there any one thing that you can pinpoint that it must do to be worthy of the name?

JB: As usual, it's easier to say what literature is not than what it is or should be. Certainly it's not self-expression, as so many imagine, including some writers who should know better. I'm rather inclined to agree with Auden, that poetry—all art—makes nothing happen. Real art is perfectly useless, if by useful we are thinking of politics, morals, social issues, etc. Cyril Connolly put it well and simply when he declared that the only business of an artist is to make masterpieces. And yet the work of art is always moral, even though the artist harbored no moral intentions in making the work. The moral quality arises from the fact that the work of art represents the absolute best that a particular human being could do—perhaps even a little more than he could do. I realize, of course, that the same can be said of science, which is all right by me—but what about sport? Does the ephemerality of the sporting moment somehow make it less significant than the work of art?

You ask me what a work of literature must do in order to be worthy of the name. I suppose I would say it must have a quality of the transcendent. I do not mean metaphysical transcendence, but a kind of heightening. In the work of art, the world is made for a moment radiant, more than itself while at the same time remaining absolutely, fundamentally, mundanely, utterly itself. So the artistic act is almost like the sexual act: In the glare of its attention, the Other, in a sudden access of self-awareness, takes on a transcendent glow. High talk, I know, but we are, I take it, talking of high art.

BE: You said earlier that several of your novels addressed what you called "the problem of authenticity," which in a way surprised me, because so many of your characters seem to reject the whole notion of authenticity. Freddie Montgomery at one point in *The Book of Evidence* says, "To place all faith in the mask, that seems to me the true shape of refined humanity." Do you agree with him?

JB: I don't know. I don't know that I have any opinion. And I don't know that my opinion counts very much. I don't either agree or disagree with the feelings and the thoughts of the characters that I invent. I don't think fiction works that way. I don't think art works that way. Again I would with Joyce say that that was a way of working. I spent I suppose ten years, damned near twenty years, following that vein of writing. I've now finished it. *Shroud* is the last book I'm going to write like that. (I'm now writing a book about childhood and the seaside!) I felt that in *Shroud* I had gone as far as I could go in that direction. Many people would say I've gone at least one book too far. But I had to try to get it right, and I didn't get it right. I think that the problem of authenticity for characters like Freddie Montgomery and Axel Vander is in a way precisely what you say, that they don't believe in authenticity. And yet, if one doesn't believe in the possibility of authenticity, then how is one to live, literally—how is one to find a solid piece of ground to put one's foot on? This is the question that they all are following, all those characters from Freddie Montgomery right through to Axel Vander. How does one find a solid place to stand?

BE: About the new book, I was about to ask, "What could be more quintessentially un-Banvillean than childhood and the seashore?" but then the protagonist of *Birchwood* was a young boy, wasn't he?

JB: He was, but this is a much simpler book. I've only started it, so God knows what it will become. It may turn into some horrible, dark, monstrous thing, as they usually do. I hope not. Again I suppose I will be writing about an essential inability to absorb reality. I think this is the predicament of all artists, that they stand outside the world looking on in amazement. The only passage in fiction that I've ever written that I thought came close to a direct statement was in *The Book of Evidence* where he says, "I've never felt at home on this earth. I feel that our whole presence here is a sort of cosmic blunder, and the people who were meant for here are out at some other planet on the other side of the universe, and," he says, "they'd be extinct by now in the world that was made to contain us."[1] I suppose if you wanted to extract a testament from the books, that would be it. I'm constantly astonished by the world. I have been since childhood and I've never got used to it.

I'm sitting here looking at clouds going across the sky. Clouds have always fascinated me. They seem the most unreal things. Skies always look to me like things out of a science fiction movie. And yet I've been looking at skies for the past fifty-seven years. I should've got used to them by now, but I'm not. I look at people in the same way. People do the most extraordinary, outlandish, bizarre things quite ordinarily. I've always felt that if you were a Martian and you came to earth, and you'd coped with everything—half the population scraping its face with a blade every morning and things like that—and thought you had it all down pat, and then somebody sneezes, or somebody yawns and stretches their arms in that sort of silent howl. You'd say, "Oh no, I've got to go back and rethink this whole thing. Obviously these human beings are far stranger than I thought they were." I find the world constantly an astonishing place. Not because of the mysterious things, but because of the quite ordinary things.

BE: I suppose there's a real Martian quality to childhood.

JB: Yes, I think that's why I'm going back now to do this book, which is probably the one I've been practicing to do for the last forty years.

BE: In what sense do you mean that?

JB: I'm pushing sixty now. I find it hard to believe, but I am. One

[1] The exact quote is: "I have never really got used to being on this earth. Sometimes I think our presence here is due to a cosmic blunder, that we were meant for another planet altogether, with other arrangements, and other laws, and other, grimmer skies. I try to imagine it, our true place, off on the far side of the galaxy, whirling and whirling. And the ones who were meant for here, are they out there, baffled and homesick, like us? No, they would have become extinct long ago. How could they survive, these gentle earthlings, in a world that was made to contain *us*?"

starts to look backwards and try to see clearly one's beginnings, and I feel that I was formed very much by, for instance, those pre-pubertal loves. To fall in love at the age of eleven is one of the most extraordinary, tender, and anguishing experiences that one can have. One never forgets them. There are girls that I fell in love with seaside summers when I was a child whom I still remember as vividly as people that I was in love with last year, perhaps even more brilliantly. Of course the danger is that our friend Proust has been there already, and it's going to be very hard to do it, not to mention Nabokov in *Lolita,* which has the quintessential seaside adolescent love affair in the opening pages. I don't know if there's much to do after Nabokov and Proust, but one does one's little bit. One scribbles one's little sentences and hopes for the best.

BE: Many of your novels are interconnected. The story of Freddie Montgomery was told in three volumes published over six years, and Cass and Alexander Cleave reappear in *Eclipse* and in *Shroud.* Do you conceive of your novels as complete works in themselves or do you look at the broader picture?

JB: I think in general there is a Book and all of the books that one writes are volumes in it. When I finally drop off the twig, what will be left will be a work. Each one grows out of the previous one. I planned to write a quartet of books when I did *Copernicus* and then *Kepler* and then *The Newton Letter.* I never got around to writing the fourth novel, about a twentieth-century physicist, which is what I wanted to do in the first place.

BE: Who would that have been?

JB: It would have been an amalgam of Heisenberg and Einstein and Niels Bohr and people like that. In the '70s I read a lot of sci-ence. I have no training in it whatsoever—I was purely fumbling my way in the dark—but I was fascinated by the ideas that science was throwing up then. I haven't kept up with it. It's practically impossible now; things change so quickly. I still feel a quickening of the pulse when I hear talk of superstrings and things like that.

I planned to write those four "science" books and I set out intentionally to do that, but I didn't intend there to be any more books about Freddie Montgomery than *The Book of Evidence*. The next one, *Ghosts,* started off and suddenly, there was Freddie speaking again. I hadn't got his voice out of my head, and I don't think I got the voice out of my head until I had written *Shroud*. It's the same tone throughout. I'm surprised that people hadn't thrown up their hands in despair and said, "Is he ever going to speak in any other kind of voice than this one? We're getting sick of it." And maybe they do. Since I don't read reviews anymore, it may well be that they're all saying that. But I do think that each book grows out of the previous one.

That's one of the reasons that I'm so interested in this little book that I'm starting now, because I can't quite see where it came from. It may be a transition book; it may be a radical shift; I don't know.

BE: It's a very different voice?

JB: It is. It's a much simpler voice. It's a much less malign voice. It's a much more forgiving voice, I think. But let's face it: every writer has only one voice. Even Joyce, somewhere behind all those styles there is a style, there is a voice. Because we can't be more than ourselves. We can't be more than one, no matter how hard we try.

BE: How fully do you plot out a novel when you start?

JB: I used to plan books. *Kepler* is the most extraordinarily planned book. I based the whole thing on Kepler's notion of the five perfect solids in geometry. Each section has the same number of sides as a cube or a dodecahedron or whatever, and I planned it practically to the number of words in each chapter and each section. I knew when I wrote the first line what the last line was going to be and how far away it was going to be. I don't do that anymore. I think *Mefisto* was a transition book for me. It was an extremely difficult book. It took me five years. It almost killed me. My wife insists I had a nervous breakdown when I was doing it. I didn't know where to go with it, I didn't know what to do with it, and I think it was a kind of breakthrough. I don't think that the book was successful in formal terms but I think it has a kind of peculiar coherence that I didn't intend. I wrote about a lot of things and I didn't know why I was doing them. I still don't know why I did them. So now I don't really plan at all.

Eclipse and *Shroud* started as one book. I spent a year or two writing it, and Axel Vander was in that book, in *Eclipse.* I just couldn't get anywhere and it was getting worse and worse and I was thinking of abandoning the whole thing and I suddenly realized there were two books in it and I went ahead and wrote *Eclipse* and then *Shroud.* They were each written quite quickly, in the space of about two years. So there was an instance of something that certainly wasn't planned. It was a bore to be stuck with Cass Cleave in *Shroud* and try to accommodate her fate in that book, but I quite liked writing about poor Cass. It was a relief from writing about these filthy old monstrous woman-killers that I've been writing about since the '80s. So maybe Cass is the one that sent me—this thought has suddenly occurred to me—maybe Cass is the one that sent me back to childhood. That may well be. Maybe this next book is Cass's book.

BE: Are you still editing?

JB: No. I was the literary editor of the *Irish Times* for about ten years but I gave it up about two years ago.

BE: So now you're freelancing?

JB: Yes. I still review for the *Irish Times* and I review for the *New York Review* and the *New York Times* and various places.

BE: It seems like I see your name at least once a week.

JB: [*Laughs*] It's terrible. I remember there was a used-book dealer in

London many years ago. He said he was going to open up a special section of his bookshop devoted to books recommended by Anthony Burgess. When people ask me for blurbs now, prepublication, I say, "My name is such a debased coin, you're better off without it." But I like the discipline. It's so different from writing fiction. You sit there and you do it, like a piece of Zen archery or something. You do it and if you get it right it can be quite satisfying, and it's not as shaming as fiction.

BE: Shaming?

JB: I can write a review in a day. It would take me a day to write a couple of lines of fiction and even then they wouldn't be right. It's an entirely different discipline. And I suppose I feel that if I have any public duty it's to keep people reading, keep people interested. I had an extraordinary experience a couple years ago when Louis Menand's book *The Metaphysical Club* came out. It had been published for about six months and I read it and I said to the *Irish Times,* "Look, I want to review this." We gave it a full page. The book became a best-seller here, just on the strength of that review. I was astonished. I always assume, and I suspect that most reviewers assume, that nobody ever reads reviews.

BE: Or maybe the first and last paragraphs.

JB: Exactly. Before I gave up reading reviews that's what I used to read, the first and the last, because you knew that in the middle it was just the plot summary.

BE: Do you find it difficult to balance writing novels and writing as a critic?

JB: No. In the matter of fiction and criticism I have a split personality, although no doubt each pursuit informs the other, in superficial ways. I was a newspaper copy editor for nearly twenty years; it must have taught me something about precision, clarity, punctuation, etc. Reviewing—and I consider myself a reviewer, not a critic—is a kind of knack that one develops. When one is young one expects to be able to say everything in a review that one feels and thinks about the work under consideration, but rapidly one comes to realize that the demands imposed by word length and deadline and so on mean that one must choose a couple of ideas and reactions and concentrate on them. Fiction—making art—is an altogether more mysterious business, which involves and invokes everything one has to give.

I might put it this way: For me, reviewing is done while I'm awake, and thinking as far as possible in a straight line; art is done while I'm in a form of hypnagogic state that is not quite dreaming and not quite waking. I know all this sounds hopelessly nineteenth-century High Romantic, but there you are.

BE: What is the distinction for you between a reviewer and a critic?

JB: It's quite simple. A book reviewer reviews new books that the public has not seen yet. My job is to introduce people to the book and say, "Look, this is worth your attention." I'm in the happy position now that I can choose what I want to review, so I don't review books that I don't like. My wife always says to me, "You're giving an entirely false image of yourself, because you seem like the nicest person in the world. You like everything you read. It's only because you only review books that you like." She says, "You should take a book now and then that you don't like and take a flying kick at it." I say, "What's the point of that?" There are enough critics around, enough book reviewers around, who are tearing the guts out of books. What I try to do is get people enthusiastic about books. ✻

DAVE EGGERS

TALKS WITH

JOAN DIDION

"I'M INVISIBLE SCARLET O'NEIL
IN WASHINGTON. I MEAN,
IT DOESN'T HAVE ANY CURRENCY.
BEING JOAN DIDION MEANS NOTHING."

Unfortunate decisions California citizens have made:
Electing two movie-star governors
Building prisons to create jobs
Neglecting the public school system in favor of short-term gains
Committing a lot of sane people to mental institutions

his interview took place in San Francisco, in the fall of 2003, as part of a series of onstage interviews sponsored by City Arts and Lectures. The venue was Herbst Theater, which seats about 900. Didion had done interviews at Herbst before, and while watching her previous event, I'd learned that she seemed to prefer chatting over being asked to expound. Ponderous, open-ended questions—"Why do you write, Ms. Didion?"—were not going to work. So on this night I tried to keep the mood buoyant and conversational, especially given that the subject matter of her then-latest book, Where I Was From, *is not sunny.*

That book, by the way, is no less brilliant than The White Album and Slouching Towards Bethlehem, *the collections of her pieces—part journalism, part cultural critique, part memoir—that established her as a writer of uncommon acuity and a voice that spoke to and about a certain generation at a critical point. Like those early books,* Where I Was From *showcases her perfectly calibrated style, and like all of her recent work, including* Political Fictions, *it stands up to her reputation-making books of the late '60s and '70s. As always, her prose is precise and fluid, cruelly accurate while often revealing the vulnerabilities of its author.*

Didion has, of course, written great novels too, and has said that each time she starts writing a novel, she rereads Joseph Conrad's Victory. *Though the style of that book is a bit more rococo than Didion's minimalist prose, it's evident why it would seem to inspire books like* The Last Thing He Wanted *and* A Book of Common Prayer. Victory *concerns intrigue among travelers in the islands of the Far East, a cast of misfits of whom most are wanderers, abandoners. They leave husbands, children, their countries, and they get involved in very tricky business. These are the characters that populate Didion's fiction, and her heroines are among the most complex, even opaque, in contemporary fiction.*

Because Didion's prose is so extraordinarily sharp, some expect that in person Didion would be a kind of raconteuse, a spewer of devastating bons mots. But she's far more personable than that. She is a person, actually, very much a person, even though her name now has about it the sound of legend. The Legend of Joan Didion—*that could be a western, or a book by James Fenimore Cooper.* "The Ballad of Joan Didion"—*maybe a song by Bob Dylan? It means so much, that name,* Joan Didion, *even if she denies it.*

—D.E. (Fall 2003)

DAVE EGGERS: So we're going to just get started. I have the questions printed on blue cards.

JOAN DIDION: It's beautiful type, too. [*Laughs*]

DE: That means they're going to be good. [*Laughter*] So we met about six or seven years ago when I interviewed you for *Salon*.

JD: Yes. And I didn't even—I wasn't on the net at the time. And I did not know what *Salon* was. As a matter of a fact, I wanted to cancel the interview because I had so many things to do and I thought, "What is this? Why am I doing this?" [*Laughs*]

DE: Yeah, and there were many years after that when people were still wondering. [*Laughter*]

JD: That was 1996. It was only seven years ago.

DE: At the time, one of my favorite answers that you gave was when I asked what you missed most about California. Do you remember what you said?

JD: No.

DE: Driving. You talked about how you missed that uninterrupted line of thought that you had when you drove. And you've written about it, about L.A.

JD: My husband and I moved to New York in 1988, and to negotiate going to the grocery store meant you had to go out on the street and deal with a lot of *people,* you know? You had to maybe run into a neighbor—certainly run into somebody in the elevator, run into a doorman. It took you out of your whole train of thought. Whereas if you walked out of your driveway and got in your car and went to the store, not a soul was going to enter your mindstream. You could just continue kind of focusing on what you were doing.

DE: You still have a California driver's license.

JD: I do.

DE: With a New York address on it.

JD: Yes, it does. Mm-hm. [*Laughter*] You know how I got it?

DE: No. How would that work?

JD: Well, my mother was living in Monterey and I was visiting her.

I had to renew my license, so I went up to—I think it was Ocean-side. And I said, "Uh, you know I'm not *actually* living in Califor-nia right now; I'm living in New York. Can I put that address on?" She said, "Put wherever you want us to send it." [*Laughter*]

DE: And another thing, when we talked then, we talked about a book called *Holy Land*, written by D. J. Waldie, about Lakewood, California. And then shortly around that time you wrote about Lakewood yourself, and that would become the first piece—

JD: Part of *Where I Was From*. And in fact, when I wrote about Lakewood, it was 1993. It was a piece for the *New Yorker*—Tina Brown was then the editor and she was interested in this. When I said I wanted to do Lakewood, she was crazy for me to do Lake-wood because there was this group of high school boys called the Spur Posse who were all over shows like *Montel* at the time. They did this totally predictable and not very unusual thing for high school boys: they kept a point system on girls they had slept with, right? And for this, this somehow gained them all this notoriety. But anyway, what interested me about Lakewood was that it was a defense industry town, and the boys gave me a reason to go into a town where there was a Douglas plant that was clearly the only employer in town. And it was during the middle of the defense cutbacks, and so I thought that would be an interesting thing to do. And I met D. J. Waldie then, and he was doing this series of pieces—not *pieces,* they were pieces of a *novel,* it turned out—which he was publishing in little literary magazines. And he gave them to me and I was just *stunned*—I mean, they were so good.

DE: *Holy Land* is an incredible book. And the Lakewood section is one of the primary elements in *Where I Was From*.

JD: Well what happened is, I finished that piece, and I realized that, even though it was 18,000 words long or whatever—I mean, it didn't run that long in the *New Yorker,* but that's how long I'd written it—that I hadn't *answered* the questions I had. That it'd raised more questions about California than I'd answered. I hadn't even thought of it as about California when I started it; I thought of it as about the defense industry, right? The kind of withering of the defense industry in Southern California. But then it turned out to raise some kind of deeper questions about what California was about. So then I started doing some more reading and started playing around with the idea of doing—of trying to answer those other questions about what California was about. And finally— I didn't realize—it was only quite late, when I was writing this book, that I realized that was what Lakewood was about. The person who would explain what Lakewood was, was Henry George, who had written this before the Southern Pacific, when everybody in California was excited about the glories the railroad would bring. He wrote this piece—it was the first piece he ever wrote—for the *Overland Monthly,* called "What the Railroad Will Bring Us." And Lakewood was really an answer to what the railroad had brought us. I mean, it was the answer to what the ideal... It's too complicated. [*Laughter*]

DE: Lakewood was like a Levittown. And it was supposed to be bigger than that, and it went up overnight and all the houses were identical.

JD: They all went on sale the same day. It was bigger than the original Levittown, actually. And it was designed around a regional shopping center. If you look at the *Thomas Guide* book—this is what got me excited about it—to this day, you see the shopping center in the middle of town. You see a public golf course, nine holes, over on the corner of the town. And then down below, you see the Douglas plant. This is a kind of really simple town. And the houses were all identical. I mean, I think there were something like eight basic models, but they were all pretty much alike. They came in various colors and you couldn't have two of the same color next door to each other.

DE: They had a choice of colors and models—

JD: Yeah, but you had to rotate them on a block. And they were really quite small. They were two- and three-bedrooms, but they were nine hundred and fifty to eleven hundred square feet, which is—I mean, I've lived in apartments which were eight hundred and fifty square feet, and it's not a lot of, you know, space. For a three-bedroom house.

DE: But the piece about Lakewood crystallized a lot of the issues that you've been writing about.

JD: *Opened* a lot of the issues. Yeah. I mean, really, it raised all these questions. That's why I started writing this.

DE: So in this book—you've been writing about California for so long, but never with such, I think, *finality*. You know, you really come to conclusions here. Basically, you mentioned the Southern Pacific Railroad and how California has this history of selling itself out for the short gain—you know, short-sightedly—selling its land to the Southern Pacific Railroad, for example. And in some ways, your book is fatalistic, because California hasn't changed that much. Can you talk about that, about the process of realizing that the state has always sort of been this way?

JD: Well, all these things kept happening. I kept thinking that this was evidence of how California had changed. I mean, one of the things that really deeply shocked me was when I realized that California no longer had a really functioning public school system. That its scores were now on a par with *Mississippi's*. And that the University of California system was no longer *valued* as it had been. And that the investment at the state level was not being made there. And yet we were building all these new prisons. I thought this was evidence of how California had changed, but it wasn't. I mean, I finally realized it was the same deal. It was selling the future, selling the state, in return for someone's agreement—short-term agreement—to enrich us. People want prisons in their town because they think it'll bring jobs, right? Well it doesn't even bring jobs, and what does it bring for the future?

DE: But now everything's changed. We had a recall, and we have a new governor, he was an action star—I think we've been really far-sighted about that, at least. [*Laughter*] So you must be thinking optimistically, now. Finally there's a break, and we're thinking of the future—looking ahead. [*Laughter*] But you commented on Arnold's election somewhere, I think. I didn't see it firsthand, but didn't you say, "Nothing good can come of this?" [*Laughter*]

JD: I probably did. [*Laughter*] I was so sort of thrilled over the weekend: I saw in the *Los Angeles Times* that part of the way the budget had been balanced by Gray Davis included getting rid of a huge number of state jobs. But as things progressed, he didn't— Gray Davis didn't—have a chance to get rid of those people. I mean, he could do it now, but he's not going to. And so it will fall to Arnold Schwarzenegger, who will have to make a decision: either to follow through on the job cuts or to find that money someplace else. Where will that money come from? And he keeps talking about bringing *new business* in. Where is this new business coming from?

DE: Well, it was interesting: You talk about how California has this history of individualism and self-reliance, but from the beginning the state has depended pretty heavily on federal money.

JD: Yeah.

DE: And here, Bush came to the state, and Arnold was crowing about how George will come back and give us some money and he'll bail us out. He called himself the Collectinator.

JD: And he himself was deeply into that individual effort, yes. He's almost an exemplar of the kind of error that we've seen over the years in California. [*Laughs*]

DE: Well, the whole map is right here in your book, the blueprint for how this state is run. It's amazing that—well, I don't know. If everybody had read this, I think we might have had a different result with the whole recall effort. It's all there.

Let's back up a little bit and talk about the writing of your book. California has always been a very personal thing for you, and you've woven the two together, the state itself and your upbringing here. And at the same time, this book is sort of about the loss of a certain California that you knew.

JD: Yeah, well, I don't think I could have written it before my parents died. I don't mean that we would have had a fight about it— we wouldn't have had a fight about it at all. But I just couldn't have done it, because it was not their idea. That's one thing. The other thing is that the death of my parents started me thinking more about what my own relationship to California was. Because it kind of threw it up for grabs. You know, when your parents die, you're not exactly *from* the place you were from. I don't know, it's just an odd—it's an odd thing.

DE: Early in the book you trace the paths of many of your ancestors in coming to California. And it connects a lot with the heroines in many of your novels. I think you find sort of the DNA for them in this passage that describes many of your—[*DE gives JD the passage in question*]

JD: Everybody in my family moved on the frontier. I mean, they moved on the frontier, through several centuries. Wherever the frontier was, that's where they were. [*Reading*]

> These women in my family would seem to have been pragmatic and in their deepest instincts clinically radical, given to breaking clean with everyone and everything they knew. They could shoot and they could handle stock and when their children outgrew their shoes they could learn from the Indians how to make moccasins. "An old lady in our wagon train taught my sister to make blood pudding," Narcissa Cornwall recalled. "After killing a deer or steer

you cut its throat and catch the blood. You add suet to this and a little salt, and meal or flour if you have it, and bake it. If you haven't anything else to eat, it's pretty good." They tended to accommodate any means in pursuit of an uncertain end. They tended to avoid dwelling on just what that end might imply. When they could not think what else to do they moved another thousand miles, set out another garden: beans and squash and sweet peas from seeds carried from the last place. The past could be jettisoned, children buried and parents left behind, but seeds got carried.

DE: And when we spoke many years ago we talked about connections between the heroines in *A Book of Common Prayer* and *Run River,* and that passage connected a lot of them together, these women that were—

JD: Even the woman in the last novel—Elena McMahon, in *The Last Thing He Wanted*—she was similar in some ways.

DE: Right. When you were writing *Where I Was From,* did you realize the connections between all those characters in your novels, that their DNA was that of the frontier women in your family's history?

JD: No. No. No, I didn't.

DE: So we just, right now, we just did it. We just figured it out. [*Laughter*] Wow, that was good. That was easy. [*Laughter*] But so there's this idea of, "I'm debunking the myth of California," that runs throughout the book, and in many different ways. But you've also said that you see this book as sort of a love letter to California. Can you explain that?

JD: Well, you don't bother getting mad at people you don't love, right? I mean, you just, you don't. I mean, why would I spend all that time trying to figure it out if I didn't have a feeling for it?

DE: There's a passage near the end, when you're driving from Monterey to Berkeley and your mother's asking, "Are we on the right road? This doesn't look familiar, are we on the right road?" And you keep reassuring her that you're on 101 North, that this is the correct road. And then she finally says, "Then where did it all go?"

JD: Mm-hm.

DE: And there's also a passage, way back, from *Slouching Towards Bethlehem* that went, "All that is constant about the California of my childhood is the rate at which it disappears."

JD: Yeah. Well, at the time I wrote that line, very little of it had disappeared compared with the amount that has disappeared now. I think I was thinking specifically about the *one subdivision* that had been built that was visible from the road between Sacramento and Berkeley. Well, now it's a little bit more built up than that. [*Laughs*] What Mother was talking about when we were driving up from Monterey, that had happened just in a few years. I mean, suddenly, suddenly, suddenly everything had disappeared—suddenly all the open space on 101 south of San Jose was gone. I mean, it had been gone north of San Jose for some time. First Morgan Hill went. Then Gilroy went. Salinas may be next. We were just north of Salinas, when Mother was so troubled.

DE: There's a man that you cite in one of the pieces, Lincoln Steffens, who talks about deep ecology, the belief that humans are inevitably going to destroy themselves, and so we shouldn't worry so much about things like recycling. Are you fatalistic about the future of California?

JD: Well, you know, if you extrapolated from the history, you would not be optimistic. But I keep thinking that we're all capable of learning, you know? That somehow we will, we will see—we'll realize the value of what we have and actually make a commitment to invest in the university, keep some open land, you know, just some basic things.

DE: Switching back: tonight Michael Moore is speaking at San

Francisco State, and you and I talked a little bit before about the political climate right now. You've always been—to I'm sure everyone here—an exemplar of someone who can find nuance and who doesn't necessarily look for the black and the white and the easy answers in your political writing. But right now we're at a point where there is a shrillness to the debate. You turn on the TV and find MSNBC and Chris Matthews and everything else, all so loud and abusive. What's your political diet? What do you watch? What do you read?

JD: Oh, I read a lot. You know, I get five newspapers. But in order to follow what's going on, you actually have to look at television at certain points, because otherwise you don't realize how *toxic* it's become. You get no sense of the confrontational level of everything. I don't know what it is. The obvious answer is it's 24/7 television, it's cable. But how cable took the form of people shouting at each other, I don't know.

DE: In a way, it's a positive thing that Michael Moore is being read so widely, and that Al Franken has a No. 1 book. But then these books keep reacting to each other. I don't know when it's going to end. And I don't know who's *buying all of the books*—

JD: But somebody is. There's a secret there. Ann Coulter's book, for example—Is she the *Treason* or the *Liar* one? I can't—

DE: There's a *lie* somewhere in there.

JD: Yeah.

DE: And her face on the cover, which is nice.

JD: It has a little—there's a little code icon next to it on the best-seller list in the *New York Times*, which indicates that a lot of its sales have been in bulk. [*Laughter*]

DE: Oh, that's true.

JD: And so that's where some of it's coming from. But who the bulk is, I don't—[*Laughter*]

DE: No, that's how it works. But now, *Fixed Ideas,* which is your short book that New York Review Books put out, begins on the stage we're sitting on, when you were here in 2001, in September.

JD: Yeah, it was just after. It was like a week after the event.

DE: Right, and it talks about you touring in the weeks after 9/11 and fearing the quality of discourse. And the people that you met along the road were all afraid of the inability to speak out after that and—

JD: I don't know if they were afraid. They were speaking out, they were absolutely speaking out. I mean, I was amazed. I had sort of arrived from New York like a zombie to do this book tour, which seemed like the least relevant thing anybody could possibly be doing, and to my amazement, everyplace I went people were making connections between our political life—which is what the book was—I was promoting *Political Fictions.* There are many connections between our political life and what happened on September 11. Connections I hadn't even thought to make. I was still so numb. And so then I got back to New York after two weeks, and I discovered that everybody had stopped talking in New York. I mean it was—everybody had flags out instead. And the *New York Times* was running "Portraits of Grief," which were these little sentimental stories about—little vignettes about the dead. I mean it was kind of—it was a scary, scary thing.

DE: In *Fixed Ideas,* you wrote that the people you spoke to recognized that "even then, with flames still visible in lower Manhattan… the words 'bipartisanship' and 'national unity' had come to mean acquiescence to the administration's pre-existing agenda— for example, the imperative for further tax cuts, the necessity for Arctic drilling, the systematic elimination of regulatory and union protections, even the funding for the missile shield." Do you feel that the quality of debate has gotten better since then?

JD: No. I mean, the president is still using—is now using September 11 when he's asked about *campaign funding*. [*Laughter*] No, it's true. He was asked why it was necessary for him to raise *x* million dollars, or whatever it was, for his primary campaign when he was unopposed, and he said that he remembered the way this country was, that he'll never forget September 11. [*Laughter*] And that it was important for him to remain in office, too. [*Laughter*]

DE: Do you have plans to cover the next campaign?

JD: I don't have any plans to cover it. No, I just don't have the heart to cover it. I mean, I might read about it and then write about it, but I'm not going to get on those planes now. [*Laughs*]

DE: No?

JD: No.

DE: Was there a point in your career when being Joan Didion got in the way of your being a reporter? When you couldn't hide anymore, you couldn't just observe?

JD: I think I can usually hide. Especially around politics. I'm Invisible Scarlet O'Neil in Washington. I mean, it doesn't have any currency. Being Joan Didion means nothing. [*Laughs*]

DE: There's a great passage in *The White Album,* in a piece you were doing about Nancy Reagan. And who was that for? And why?

JD: I had a column every other week for the *Saturday Evening Post,* a magazine that no longer exists. So I decided to go to Sacramento, to interview Nancy Reagan, who had become the governor's wife.

DE: And there was a camera crew there, and you were there, and there was a lot of discussion of how to make her seem like she was having a normal day.

JD: Yeah, the camera crew was there to see what she was doing on an ordinary Tuesday morning in Sacramento. This was, like, her first year in Sacramento. And I was there to see what she was doing on an ordinary Tuesday morning in Sacramento. [*Laughs*] So we were all kind of watching each other. And then she said, "I might be picking... I might be picking..." and the cameraman asked her if she might be picking roses. And she said, "I might be *picking* them, but I won't be *using* them!" [*Laughter*]

DE: I never got that part. Did you get it? I never understood what that meant.

JD: It was just—she wasn't having a dinner party. She didn't have dinner parties in Sacramento. She only had them in the *Pacific Palisades,* so she wouldn't be *using* the flowers. I think that's what *she* meant, but what I heard was, it was, you know, sort of a bad actress's line. [*Laughter*] More animation than was required.

DE: You wrote about a trip with Bush Sr., when he was vice president, going to Israel and Jordan. They would always have to have the right backdrop. In Jordan, Bush's people made sure that there was an American flag in every frame, and a *camel.*

JD: A camel. [*Laughter*] I guess that was to clarify the setting, you know?

DE: And at one point they said they wanted Bush to be looking through binoculars at enemy territory. Who knows why. So they give him a pair of binoculars, and then they realized the direction he was looking was Israel. [*Laughter*] When you were following Dukakis, and when they had him playing ball, you wrote that it was "insider baseball." That was also a title of one of the pieces.

JD: "Insider baseball," yeah. It was astonishing.

DE: Yeah. Because they wanted to make them seem real so everywhere they would go, Dukakis and one of his guys would play baseball—play catch outside the airplane.

JD: On the tarmac, yeah.

DE: And then you would be invited to watch—

JD: Right, and then if anybody missed it—I don't mean if *I* missed it, I could have missed it and they wouldn't have even noticed, but if one of the *networks* missed it, they wanted everybody to film it, right—if anybody missed it, they would do it again. [*Laughter*]

DE: And why does everybody—you're astonished by it when you're covering these campaigns, but everybody goes along with the same sort of events. "OK, now we're going to go out, and the candidate is going to eat broccoli, and that's going to lead the next day's news." But everybody goes along with it. They're trading access; they want the access and then in exchange, the campaign gives them this moment.

JD: Yes. You don't want to get thrown off the campaign. That's the key thing about covering a campaign, for people who cover them, is you can't—

DE: You don't want to get thrown off the plane.

JD: Right. You want to be there. So it's a trade for access. In case something happens, right? But nothing is going to happen—

DE: Well, somebody's going to fall off a platform one of these days, right?

JD: Somebody did, remember?

DE: That was Dole.

JD: Yeah, in Chico.

DE: OK. Now we're going to do a quick speed round. With these questions, you're allowed to answer only *yes* or *no*. [*Laughter*] OK, here we go. Will there be another recall, this one of Arnold?

JD: No.

DE: Should there be one?

JD: No, I don't believe in recalls.

DE: Just yes or no, please. [*Laughter*] Will you ever move back to California?

JD: I can't answer that *yes* or *no*. [*Laughter*]

DE: Can you believe how well this interview is going? [*Laughter*]

JD: Yes.

DE: Have you written a screenplay where you were happy with the final product?

JD: Yes.

DE: What was that? You're allowed to answer.

JD: *True Confessions.*

DE: Is that the one with—

JD: De Niro and Duvall.

DE: Oh, right. And—

JD: And it was directed by... I know him as well as I know my own name: Ulu Grosbard. We had a good time on it, and I was happy with it. In fact, I see it on television and it still makes me cry.

DE: So it was written by just you and your husband?

JD: Yeah. In fact, we did all the changes during shooting; we did them on the weekend. Ulu would come over—we were shooting in Los Angeles and he would come over and we would make the changes while he sat there on Sunday afternoon. It was really easy.

DE: So you were on set the whole time?

JD: No, we weren't on set. We were at a house in Brentwood. [*Laughs*] But Sundays they had off, so he would come over on Sunday and we would do it.

DE: OK, a few more in the speed round. Can Wes Clark beat

George Bush?

JD: If he were nominated, yeah.

DE: Can Howard Dean beat George Bush?

JD: I doubt it.

DE: And finally: Really, though, can you believe how well this is going? [*Laughter*]

JD: Yes.

DE: There's a line in the new book where you say, "Not much about California, on its own preferred terms, has encouraged its children to see themselves as connected to one another." Can you explain that?

JD: People in Northern California grew up with the whole founding myth of California, the whole crossing story, etc. Southern California was founded on a different story. The only time when I felt, really, a big connection between Northern and Southern California—and I've lived in both—was when PSA was flying. [*Laughter*] No I mean, literally, PSA connected the state where you could fly—

DE: Explain what PSA is.

JD: Pacific Southwest Airways. You weren't here then, probably. They had these planes with these big smiles painted on them. And you could fly from Sacramento to Los Angeles for I think sixteen dollars, and you could fly from Los Angeles to San Francisco for twelve. And there was what they called a Midnight Flyer, so you could fly up for dinner, in San Francisco, and then fly home, to Los Angeles, or vice versa. I mean, it gave a great sense of mobility around the state which has been—which we never had before, and I haven't felt it since. I mean, going from Los Angeles to San Francisco on a plane now is so unpleasant that my brother always drives—you know, he does this all the time.

DE: So you're talking mostly regionally there, between coastal, inland, north, south.

JD: There were a lot of things I was thinking about there, I suppose. I was also thinking, the idea, the ethic that everybody kind of believed represented California, was one of extreme individualism, and we did not feel very responsible for others in the community. Community wasn't a big idea.

DE: And that's something you feel is prevalent throughout this state? Is that something grounded in the myth of California?

JD: In the way it was settled, yeah. I mean the kinds of people who settled it. The idea was, basically, California was settled by people who wanted to strike it rich, in a way, at the simplest level. And *as* individuals. This ethic kind of took hold; it became a big point of pride even though everyone in the state was heavily dependent on federal government. We didn't feel very responsible for those around us. One of the things that really knocked me out when I was writing this book was the thing about the committal to mental hospitals in the early days of the state. And right into the early twentieth century, people were committed at a higher rate than almost anywhere else in the country. And it was explained that they were kind of unhinged by the ups and downs of life on the frontier, in the gold camps... This wasn't it, I don't think. It was just an extreme disregard for, and a refusal to tolerate, the people around them. I mean, people were being committed in San Francisco for—one older woman was committed by her sister. This was a study done by somebody who had gotten hold of all these records. One woman was committed by her sister because she had lost all interest in crocheting. [*Laughter*]

DE: And the national committal rate was, what, 3,900 people committed one year. And 2,600 of them were from California, or something like that.

JD: Yeah, I mean huge, huge numbers. And they were committed basically for life. I mean it wasn't one of those forty-eight hour deals.

DE: We talked about a passage that I was going to ask you to read, and you asked me to read it, that I think sums up a lot of what is central—both your love of the state and then ambivalence, and also the sense of loss. After your mother died, you flew back to California, and this occurs late in the book. Do you want to read it, or should I?

JD: You read it.

DE: "Flying to Monterey I had a sharp apprehension of the many times before when I had, like Lincoln Steffens, 'come back,' flown west, followed the sun, each time experiencing a lightening of spirit as the land below opened up, the checkerboards of the Midwestern plains giving way to the vast empty reach between the Rockies and the Sierra Nevada; then *home, there, where I was from, me,* California. It would be a while before I realized that 'me' is what we think when our parents die, even at my age, *who will look out for me now, who will remember me as I was, who will know what happens to me now, where will I be from.*" ✷

SUSAN CHOI

TALKS WITH

FRANCISCO GOLDMAN

"I HAD THIS THEORY THAT I WOULD
SORT OF PUT MYSELF OUT THERE,
AND IT WAS AS IF I WAS THE PEN,
LETTING MY OWN INTUITIONS
AND CIRCUMSTANCES GUIDE ME."

Counterintuitive characteristics of certain Central Americans:
Sandinistas are idealistic teenagers
Honduran reporters have no idea what is happening in Honduras
Aztecs were the first balloon twisters

y the time I met Francisco Goldman at a party in early
1997 I was already insanely in love with his writing,
a condition that had never overcome me before where a
living writer was concerned. I felt then, as I continue to
feel today, that it was my great good fortune to be alive
and writing on the same planet with him; little did I know that later that
evening I would be drunk with him, and the next day extremely hungover
with him, although Frank's version of being hungover resembles most people's version of being intensely enthusiastic. Frank showed up first thing
the next morning to remind me and my boyfriend that we'd promised to
take him to the beach to see seals; this was Cape Cod in February, and

the temperature was something lower than zero. But we went and saw seals, all the while borne along by Frank's unequalled stories, as we've continued to be for the seven years since.

The son of an American father and a Guatemalan mother, Frank grew up with one foot in Guatemala and the other in New England, not unlike the narrator of his extraordinary first novel, The Long Night of White Chickens *(1992), which won the Sue Kaufman Prize for first fiction from the American Academy of Arts and Letters and was a finalist for the PEN/Faulkner Award.* The Ordinary Seaman *followed in 1997 and was among other things a finalist for the PEN/Faulkner, the Los Angeles Times Book Prize, and the IMPAC Dublin. In fall 2004, he published a hilarious, tender, magnificent new novel,* The Divine Husband. *Dan Cryer of* Newsday *says, "His talent is nothing short of astonishing," and I could not say it better.*

Since 1999, Frank and I have been neighbors in Brooklyn. Last summer he came over and sat in my yard for a few hours to talk about his work past and present. —S.C. *(Summer 2004)*

I. "I BASICALLY WENT AND JOINED A VOLUNTEER BATTALION AND HUNG AROUND WITH ALL THESE KIDS EVERY DAY, WAITING FOR THE MOBILIZATION ORDER TO GO UP TO THE FRONT."

SUSAN CHOI: Tell me about the rubber plant.

FRANCISCO GOLDMAN: Oh, how *The Divine Husband* started?

SC: Yeah.

FG: This is really the seed of the book. I was in a bar in Guatemala City called Shakespeare's, in something like 1985 or 1986, and a guy came and sat down next to me. It was the gringo bar, a place I just hated. In *The Long Night of White Chickens* it's called Lord Byron's, and remember, everybody in the book hates themselves for going there too, but they go there. [*Laughs*] It was just a sleazy expat bar, though sometimes interestingly sinister. It smelled like wet dog hair.

SC: Wait, why were you living in Guatemala City then?

FG: [*Impatiently*] I was always in Guatemala City in the '80s! I first went down to Guatemala in '79 because I was trying to save money and work in New York and trying to make the time to write the short stories I needed to apply to M.F.A. school. Finally I saved a thousand dollars, and thought I'd go down to Guatemala. I was completely innocent of all political circumstances. The last I'd been down there would have been the summer of '75. I was completely oblivious to anything that was going on at that point, and the real terror hadn't started there yet. But I do remember the first inkling, the first visceral sensation I had of what was really happening: one night, I was out with my friends, we were out in the streets, and a VW Thing came by, full of Salvadorans, students. They had just fled El Salvador because there had been a massacre in the university there, and they'd shut down the university. I'd never heard about anything like that.

SC: Oh, God.

FG: I remember they had great pot. I'd never smoked such strong pot.

SC: They had fled for their lives with their really great pot?

FG: Well, since the university was closed down, they thought they would go to Guatemala and... party, [*Both laugh*] and tell terrifying stories. In '79 I was down there and I wrote the stories at my uncle's house, to send to M.F.A. programs.

SC: But you didn't end up getting your M.F.A.?

FG: No. I was offered some scholarships, but one of the stories I sent up from Guatemala, I also sent it to *Esquire* magazine, to Rust Hills, and it was bought. At the same time, the war in

Guatemala was really erupting all around us. I led the typical, shel-tered-behind-high-walls life of an upper-middle-class Guate-malan, but obviously I was curious about what was going on. That was the period when bodies were always being found—teenage girls would say things like, "My father doesn't want to go jogging anymore: he keeps running by bodies," as if these bodies were landing from Mars. The newspapers were just full of all these euphemisms. They would always say, "Body found bearing the usual signs of torture and a coup de grâce in the head." That kind of language in the papers every day.

Esquire bought a short story, and then they said, "Do you want to do journalism?" They'd just been bought by new people: they were willing to give young writers a chance. I said, "Yes, I'd like to go back to Guatemala and write about what's happening there."

SC: You'd never done journalism before, ever, right?

FG: Never.

SC: So that's why you didn't go to M.F.A. school.

FG: That's why I didn't go to M.F.A. school.

SC: What did you write about for them?

FG: The first piece I ever did?

SC: Yeah.

FG: It was terrible. I basically wrote about my cousins and their friends. I remember I was so embarrassed by the title they gave it, but it was an accurate title. It was called "The Girls of Guatemala." [*Both laugh*] One typical scene in that piece was going to my cousin's graduation from the private school which, in *The Long Night of White Chickens,* turned into Colegio Anne Hunt. And at the very same time, I knew that down in the city that very day there were these massive student protests. They'd opened fire on the protests and killed a bunch of students, and you could smell tear gas in the air, and here I was, up at this exclusive private school, with these girls draped in pink garlands and carrying candles, doing this ceremony, a lot of CIA-type fathers around. I did contrasts like that.

But one extraordinary thing happened when I was at a party in my uncle's house and the daughter of family friends came up to me. I had mentioned that I was down there trying to write about what was going on in Guatemala but I was completely timid— I didn't really know how to report on anything yet, I hadn't learned how to be a reporter. She said to me, "I'm studying medicine at the public university." Her name was Fabiola. She said, "One of the things we have to do is forensics; we have to go to the morgue twice a week and learn how to do autopsies. You should see what it's like in there. Some mornings there are so many dead bodies they stack them up like logs outside the morgue. And you should see the condition they arrive in. Cigarette burns, fingers torn off, and penises torn off—"

SC: Oh my god.

FG: —All the marks of torture. She said, "I want to take you in there." And I said, "Well, all right." I went to the hospital morgue and she gave me medical whites and said, "Pretend you're a doctor." It was *insane*. I took rubber gloves and a stethoscope, and she took me in there. That was an unforgettable moment. It was like falling into a hole.

SC: What happened after that? You went home, you came back to New York?

FG: Yes.

SC: Then did *Esquire* send you down again?

FG: Yes. The next time I went down to Nicaragua. That was in 1983.

SC: What were you doing then?

FG: This was kind of great. I continued to publish some short stories in *Esquire*. I went down to Nicaragua to do a piece for *Esquire*. I didn't know what to do, and I didn't have a good expense account. I had almost no money to spend. All the fancy television journalists and big *New York Times* journalists would rent jeeps and go up to the frontier, and I was still just a complete novice. I'll always be grateful to George Crile, the famous CBS producer, who gave me the most extraordinary tip. He said, "You know, a story I've always wanted to do, and I haven't had the time, is on the volunteer battalions." At this time the Sandinista war was being fought entirely by volunteers, and there wasn't a draft yet. These volunteer battalions would form out of the neighborhoods, and they'd be mobilized and sent to the front. It was kind of a *Waiting for Godot* piece—I basically went and joined a volunteer battalion and hung around with all these kids every day, waiting for the mobilization order to go up to the front.

SC: Were you going to go up to the front with them?

FG: I did. I went up to the front several times.

SC: Did they know that you were a—

FG: Yeah, they knew I was a reporter. They were fine; they trusted me. It was just a portrait of the kinds of kids who were going off to fight the Contra War at that point. It was a portrait of a kind of young idealism, both moving and ultimately heartbreaking, which in 1983 was still there.

SC: Right, like the sisters in *The Ordinary Seaman*.

FG: Yeah, I met them at that time. Esteban in *The Ordinary Seaman* is partly modeled on my great friend Aldo Aranda, who was a company commander in that very battalion, who became a very close friend, and had been a guerrilla during the war before—just a wonderful guy.

I did that story about that battalion and when I handed it in to *Esquire* they had this very famously right-wing editor who sympathized with Republicans, named—oh, I won't name him. Because [the story] tried to give such a humane portrait of the soldiers, he said to me, "I don't believe this is true. And even if it is true, nobody will believe you, because you're not an authority."

SC: An authority in what way?

FG: To be saying, "These are the Sandinista soldiers, they're not ignorant conscripts and thugs and killers and rapists like the soldiers in other Central American countries—"

SC: How old were they?

FG: Teenagers!

SC: How old was Aldo?

FG: He was twenty-three, because he was a commander, but most were seventeen, nineteen. The editor at *Esquire* said, "No one will believe you." And they wouldn't publish it. At that time *Harper's* and *Esquire* were in the same building and I took it right to Gerry Marzorati at *Harper's*—

SC: Just went to the next floor.

FG: Yeah. And they bought it like that. For the rest of the war, everything I did was for them, pretty much.

SC: At any point did anybody teach you how to be a reporter? Were you worried? Or did you just do it?

FG: Yeah, I just did it. I threw myself into it. Doing stuff exactly like that. I think mainly I began to develop a kind of style. I don't think I was ever particularly good at being a reporter—finally, years later, with the Bishop Gerardi murder pieces, I think I finally got somewhere. My method back then was very much a fiction writer's approach to journalism. I began to think of the way you would start a short story and begin with a character, and you hold that pen in your hand, and push it along, and wait to see what will develop. I had this theory that I would sort of put myself out there, and it was as if I was the pen, letting my own intuitions and circumstances guide me. I would let myself try and find a narrative.

SC: See what story you ended up in.

FG: Yeah, and follow a narrative. Whatever it would be, usually some oblique thing. For example, I was very much aware when I was in Honduras that there were two Hondurases. There was the Honduras of privileged information that *real* reporters had access to—*New York Times* reporters, CBS reporters.

SC: Like their sources.

FG: They had the money to rent helicopters and jeeps and to go down to the border; they knew how to cultivate CIA agents and sources at the embassies; they could trade back and forth—they were a power, and they knew how to address power. Whereas I was just a freelance clown. I noticed that the Honduran reporters were outside of the world of true information about Honduras. Any time they tried to find anything out about what was going on in their own country, they were essentially in a Beckett-clown circumstance. There had been this murder, where an American—or two Americans, I think—had been murdered along with some prostitutes. A local Honduran reporter, Rodolfo, was courageously, like a Don Quixote, trying to investigate this murder as though it really was a CIA, Contra War murder. I wondered if it might be, and I sort of teamed up with him, and eventually realized that, whatever this murder was, we were never going be told anything or ever going to find out anything. We were like two Beckett clowns going around and trying to investigate this murder that probably had no connection at all in fact to the Contra War, though it did have a great connection, probably, to gringo sordidness.

SC: Gringo sordidness?

FG: Possibly sleazy business guys. But I don't want to defame any-body's memory. So I let that become the narrative of the piece, which was called "Lost in Another Honduras." We just drove around, we went and looked at the burnt pickup truck connected to one of them, and he found like a tube with some kind of white boric powder and picked it up and said, [*sniffs*] "Cocaine?" I went, "I don't think so. No, I think it's just... baking powder or some-thing." [*Both laugh*] And he said, [*in a low voice*] "I'm taking it to the lab, have it analyzed." We were both so lost. But a whole other story opened up, which was not a story about CIA maneuvers in Honduras, but a very moving story about this world of young prostitutes and poor women and these incredibly shady criminal slums, which is where we followed the story to find out basically the story of the woman murdered along with these Americans. It opened up a whole vision of the Honduran underworld.

SC: And don't you think you had more access to that world because you were the clown, and not the *New York Times*?

FG: Yeah, because we went there, and I don't think a *New York Times* reporter would've had any interest in that story. They were always around the pool at the Hotel Maya, doing very important, serious things. [*Laughs*] So it was a technique that evolved: it wasn't necessarily discovering news, it was revealing another texture that addressed the political reality of Central America more in a metaphorical way.

SC: Don't you think your novels have ended up taking the same structure?

FG: The first two. Definitely. If you look at Moya and Roger trying to find out what happened to Flor in *The Long Night of White Chickens*, it's clear that it was directly inspired by me and Rodolfo down in Honduras, going around trying to find out who had murdered these Americans. It was: "We're never going to find out [*laughs*], no one's going to tell us anything." So that idea, of two buddy narrators being forced into a kind of clownish investigative role, came directly out of that journalism experience.

II. "WE HAD REALLY ROUGH SEAS—YOU WOULD WRITE A LINE AND YOUR CHAIR WOULD GO SLIDING AWAY FROM THE DESK."

SC: You never even finished the story of how you got the idea for that. That's where we started. You're in Shakespeare's—

FG: So I'm in Shakespeare's, and this guy from my hometown, ten years older than me, who I've never met before—I couldn't *believe* that there was somebody from Needham—this guy was eventually arrested and deported from the country for bouncing bad checks. That's the kind of people who'd wash up down there.

SC: You just figured out you were both from Needham, Massachusetts?

FG: Yeah. And I said, "What are you doing here?" He had fantastic stories about my hometown, about that generation of kids who had grown up like Fonzies in the '50s. My town used to be full of drag racers. And I used to hear them drag racing and, in my near-toddler state, I used to think that they were all the Boston Strangler, speeding off in the night after having murdered somebody's mother. He had been one of those, I guess we used to call them greasers, or grease monkeys, or whatever, always hanging around garages. I said, "So what are you doing down here in Guatemala?" And he said, "My family, my mother and father, both worked at Tillotson's rubber factory." I said, "You're kidding, I grew up right next to Tillotson's rubber factory." Tillotson's rubber factory was this enormous red-brick monstrosity of a building that was like the magical mystery playground of my youth. It was *beautiful*. They completely polluted the pond across the street; you couldn't swim in the pond anymore. There's a swamp behind the factory, and the ice would always be these weird colors from all the things leaking out.

SC: [*Laughs*]

FG: You'd find balloon molds, and black rubber doll molds, and rubber glove molds everywhere, back there in the forest. We used to climb the fence and go back into the yard, and the yard was just *fantastic*, it was full of all these barrels of broken discarded balloons and mucky puddles of multicolored balloon dye. And so we would get high, and I remember before a high school dance all of us really excitedly dipping our sneakers in the pool and making them psychedelic-looking. [*Both laugh*]

I couldn't believe it. He said, "Anyway, my parents said, if you ever get down in life, and need a hand up, go look for Mr. Tillotson in Guatemala." Here I'd been in this house—a hundred yards away from the factory—this half-Guatemalan household, this house always full of Guatemalans, and I'd never known that the factory was owned by a guy who had a connection to Guatemala. Which just seemed the most incredible, remarkable thing. I said to myself, "I'm going to invent my own Mr. Tillotson." I immediately pictured this whole story. Of course the novel doesn't turn out to be that, but that was the original interest. I just loved the idea of inventing this New England balloon family that had this tie with Guatemala. And I remember that I had finished *The Long Night of White Chickens* and I began to research the book and I knew I wanted to begin in the nineteenth century. I knew, also, that I wanted it to involve José Martí.

SC: Why?

FG: Because the most famous poem, maybe, in all of Latin America—certainly the most famous love poem and certainly José Martí's most famous poem and certainly the most famous poem that mentions the word *Guatemala*—is "La Niña de Guatemala" by José Martí. It's not Martí's greatest poem by any means, and he was a considerable poet, although an even better prose writer. He had spent an extraordinarily important year and a half in Guatemala.

One of the things that happened while he was in Guatemala was that he fell madly in love, supposedly, with a young girl who was the daughter of an aristocratic bohemian general from an extremely literary family. Once you learn to read Martí's poetry, and understand the way he communicates with himself in his anguished coded language in his diaries, you see that he was, in a morbid, fantastically remorseful way, forever after obsessed with her. Anyway, he fell in love with her and at some point had to tell her that he was engaged to a woman waiting for him in Mexico. He went back to Mexico to marry her, and came back to Guatemala to resume his classes. Nobody ever—no great man in history—has made a worse choice of a wife than José Martí did.

SC: He really did marry this other woman, Carmen Zayas?

FG: Yeah, a rich Cuban who had nothing but disdain for politics, revolutionary politics, being a poet, everything else. He came back, resumed his teaching. He would soon become a pariah: all of Guatemala would soon turn against José Martí, for reasons you know from the book. And "la niña" dies. In the legend now, which is inseparable from the poem, she died of a broken heart. Clinically, she died of pneumonia or tuberculosis, which of course could easily have been provoked by the depression, accelerated by what was apparently a really serious case of heartbreak.

SC: She's eighteen years old?

FG: Seventeen.

SC: Seventeen when she died?

FG: Yeah. Ethereal, beautiful. Supposedly nobody played the piano more expressively in the whole country. And gorgeous—the perfect woman for him. Daughter of a revolutionary—

SC: Niece of a poet—

FG: Niece of a poet—made for him. And he knew it.

SC: But his sense of duty was so overdeveloped he felt he had to—

FG: In a diary that's held in the Cuban archives to this day, he had confided to a friend that Carmen had given him proof of her love before they were married, meaning that she'd slept with him. So Martí goes into his future, and has this horrendous marriage. And you know, he's a secular saint, he's the husband of Cuba. I mean he's an extraordinary, wonderful man who, when he wrote in his diary as a young man, "good men marry young," meant it. He wanted nothing more than to be good and noble in every single thing that he did—and life kept screwing him up. He just was in anguish forever. His diaries and his poetry are thirteen years of just complete, intimate anguish. He's a kind of secular nun—as you know, that nun theme goes through the book—constantly aspiring to be saintly and constantly failing, and being filled with remorse. So there I am in Guatemala City. I said, "OK, the Tillotsons, nineteenth-century balloon family, José Martí's year in Guatemala. Somehow, I've got to find out what Guatemala was like at that point." I had no idea what I was getting myself into.

SC: But you knew that you had to join these two threads.

FG: Yeah. So I went to the Guatemala City archives: I just had to research and research. And I was also in that flummoxed, post–*Long Night of White Chickens* state. I didn't know what to do with myself, but I just became this obsessive researcher. I'm doing this in 1993, '94, even late '92. I didn't know who Martí was, I didn't have a clue. I just knew there was this poem. I hadn't even really begun to research Martí, I was just trying to get the period. I was kind of stuck. So one way I would fill being stuck was research, and reading about nuns, and reading about, you know, just crazy stuff. Eventually, I just realized that I had no idea how to handle so much information. And everything in my life suddenly falls apart, right? My wife and I break up. I have nowhere to live. The war in Central America comes to an end, certainly a good thing for Central

America, but that had defined my life since 1980. It was always how I got work. All of a sudden, I was cast into this void. I went down to Mexico to live, and I realize I can't deal with all the research, I don't know how to deal—I'm just drowning in research, I want to put all that stuff aside. There was so much disillusionment in my own life, a sense of being abandoned, a sense of, you know, everything you feel after divorce… a deep sense of political disillusionment as well, with the way things had gone in Central America, a kind of disgust. All this. I felt shipwrecked. Finally, I had an emotional connection to *The Ordinary Seaman*. Suddenly I knew—

SC: This idea that's been sitting around for a decade, more than a decade—

FG: Yeah. It actually had an emotional heart; it wasn't just a story anymore. And so I—*blblblbl* [*sound-effect for writing quickly*].

SC: Like that?

FG: Yeah, in two years I wrote it. And of course I took a great trip, I went on a ship, but anyway—

SC: Wait, where'd you go on the ship?

FG: The most extraordinary thing happened. I was already well into the book. Álvaro Mutis is a great Colombian writer who writes the Maqroll books about an itinerant sailor-adventurer with a Borgesian erudition who travels the world and has adventures. Mutis is a great poet, and he's of course Gabriel García Márquez's best friend, and a legendary Latin American literary figure, and he had become kind of my father-figure in Mexico. I love him like a second father. Through my incredible good fortune he was a fan of *The Long Night of White Chickens,* and we had become good friends.

I was sitting in a restaurant in Mexico City, reading, actually, an English-language version that I had of the Maqroll books that had just come out up here, which he had signed for me, and there was a guy having a really terrible date at the next table. He was sitting there having a terrible date, and he turns to me, and he goes, "Hey, is that a Mutis book?" I go, "Yeah," and he goes, "I've never seen that edition, can I see it?" And I hand it to him and he read the inscription, and he says, "Oh, you know Mutis." I go, "Yeah," and he goes, "My cousin—*mi primo hermano*," which is a cousin you grew up with like a brother, "mi primo hermano worships Mutis." And I go, "Who's your primo hermano?" He goes, "Well, he's the maritime lawyer for Transportación Marítima Mexicana, the Mexican shipping line."

SC: No way.

FG: Yeah, and I go, "You're kidding." And he goes, "Can you arrange a meeting between my cousin and Mutis?" And I go, "Can you get me on a ship?" [*Laughs*] That was fantastic, sailing on this Mexican freighter to Europe. Foreigners weren't allowed to travel on their ships as passengers so they pretended I had a job. On the ship's manifest I had the title "Writing Technician." It was really funny because I did try to write, and they gave me this room with a desk, a little tiny closet of a room, an engineer's room, except— the chair had wheels.

SC: [*Laughs*]

FG: We had really rough seas, so—you would write a line, and your chair would go sliding away from the desk. [*Both laugh*]. And you'd go sort of like paddling back with your feet, and so after twenty minutes of this I'd inevitably want to go throw up. It was really an incredible experience.

III. "IF YOU COULD IMAGINE A FIGURE LIKE LINCOLN, WHITMAN, WASHINGTON, EVEN SOCRATES, ALL FORMED IN ONE PERSON— THAT'S WHAT MARTÍ IS TO CUBANS."

SC: And then you finished *The Ordinary Seaman* and it came out when? 1997?

FG: Yeah. '97.

SC: Because that's when I met you. I met you right after *The Ordinary Seaman* came out.

FG: Yeah. My god. So *The Ordinary Seaman* was five years after *The Long Night of White Chickens*.

SC: Yeah.

FG: And this new book took me seven years. That's a long time.

SC: Does it seem like a long time?

FG: Yes. It was crazy.

SC: So when did you go back to *The Divine Husband*?

FG: After *The Ordinary Seaman*.

SC: Right away?

FG: Well, what I had hoped would happen happened. All that stuff that I had been writing down in notebooks now took on a poetry of its own. It seemed like a part of my own memory. It had been transformed into something other than just historical research. It had become some kind of strange, odd dream of the past.

I mean, maybe this will never happen to me again. I just immersed myself in this book for years, in a way where I really, slowly discovered where the book was going, always through writing, letting the book dictate things to me, and of course at the heart of it was this deep ongoing seven-year dialogue with José Martí. You'll see that Martí's not even in the book all that much. He's not. But he's the emotional and intellectual center of the book; the book really does coalesce around him.

One of the things that moved me about Martí's life, of course, is that it would now be impossible to do a real biography of José Martí. Later on, after he died, and became the great Cuban hero-martyr, everybody collaborated in creating that hero, which meant that they even silenced their own personal memories of him. They weren't necessarily negative memories of him, but they were human—they often repressed even those in order to collaborate in the creation of this verbal heroic statue. Of course if he'd been a North American or British artist or political figure of that stature, no aspect of his life would have been left unturned by biographers within fifty years. By the 1950s biographers would have gone and ransacked everybody's memory. You would really have an account of what had actually happened in his life.

Because there's no great tradition of biography writing in Latin America, and because Martí occurs at a moment in which, unlike North America, Latin America sort of throws a switch and tries to become modern overnight, this creates this enormous void. Those countries felt inferior. They didn't know who they were. They didn't know where they were going. So there was an extreme need for idealized heroes—even to replace God in a sense. If you could imagine a figure like Lincoln, Whitman, Washington, even Socrates, all formed in one person—that's what Martí is to Cubans.

SC: You said you came to him through the "Niña" poem.

FG: I wanted to know what story was behind it.

SC: Did you know anything else about him?

FG: Nothing.

SC: You knew nothing?

FG: Nothing. I had no idea what I was getting myself into. His collected works fill twenty-nine volumes. He was a champion sufferer and explorer of the inner life. The mistakes he made, he just suffered over them so much, from an overload of sensitivity and sensibility. He's kind of like a male Virginia Woolf. You almost feel like his skin has no—what protects the poor man? Yet he's this driven indefatigable dynamo at the same time. The more you read about him the more easily you understand how people spend their whole lives just studying Martí. Easily. Yet there's no solid record of his life. You find a book like *They Knew Martí* [*Así fue Martí*], a compilation of anecdotes by people who knew him, and you see there that they're all editing their memories to just talk about how glorious he was. All those memories of the real Martí were lost.

SC: Who's Paquito? Every once in a while in the book, you let him suddenly turn to the reader and say, "Is this what happened? I don't really know."

FG: Yeah. Exactly. He's me, or a narrative shadow of me.

SC: He's you. That's interesting. Why? Why on the one hand suggest to the reader that the narrator doesn't really have full authority over the subject but on the other hand freely invent, too?

FG: It's both a game and very serious. It's a novel that allows itself to take the form it wants to take in a playful way. Another way to put it is it's not so much about Martí but about the way people lived their lives and later shaped their memories around him.

IV. "BALLOONS ARE A VERY DIFFICULT THING TO RESEARCH. JUST GO TRY IT. ALMOST NOTHING IS KNOWN."

SC: How would you work? Would you just sit down and write a couple of pages in a day and then maybe be surprised at what had happened?

FG: Well, the book just totally surprised me. It really was about writing deeply into, not just the characters, but this completely fictional world. I knew I was trying to make something beautiful, what I thought was beautiful. That was probably the most conscious understanding I had of what I was doing in a lot of those early pages. I simply wanted it to be beautiful.

Well, what do you mean by that? It's looking for a sense of surprise. You're trying to surprise yourself. You're trying to satisfy a certain ambition for your book to read and feel a certain way. I knew that, for instance, I wasn't looking for historical detail; what I was interested in was taking particular details and giving them a kind of poetics of their own, and having them work like characters in the book. Things like wool and umbrellas, the art of mercantile packing. There's all this debate and argument about how you're supposed to pack things. Things I'd come across in my research that I'd let become like characters to me. It's a completely artificial reality comprising these elements that keep repeating. I was constantly letting the book guide me.

SC: So you started this whole book by deciding to fictionalize the Tillotsons and then you totally lost track of the rubber balloons until the very end.

FG: I knew eventually, without understanding exactly how, that there would be a balloon factory at the end, and it's definitely there in the book.

SC: There was always this balloon with cat ears floating around.

FG: In my research I found out that balloons are a very difficult thing to research. Just go try it. Almost nothing is known.

SC: What were you trying to know?

FG: The history of balloons. I knew there was going to be a balloon factory, so if you want there to be a balloon factory to begin in the nineteenth century then you have to find out the history of balloons. Eventually I ran into a few things. I found out that the first known balloon twister had been this Señor Lopez who did an act of tying balloons into little animal shapes at the Lido Theater in Paris.

SC: He was Mexican?

FG: He was called Señor Lopez the Mexican.

THE BELIEVER BOOK OF WRITERS TALKING TO WRITERS

SC: Did you ever, when you embarked on your balloon quest, have any idea that a Central American would turn out to be a pioneering balloon figure?

FG: No. I mean, there were others.

SC: That's kismet.

FG: Well the book was constantly guided by kismet. I think that one of the ways this book took shape was by opening myself up to those kinds of coincidences. Separately I read that the Aztecs and other Mesoamerican peoples used to tie inflated animal bladders into cat shapes—the first balloon twisters.

SC: Why cat shapes?

FG: Because they were holy. Particularly the jaguar.

SC: They would make balloon cats. So balloons are completely a Central American legacy.

FG: I think they are. And lo and behold, it turned out that the first known person to have a balloon-twisting act was a Mexican. Señor Lopez.

SC: Were you even surprised by all of these compounding coincidences? It just seems as if the symbolic and metaphorical structure of your novel started building itself.

FG: It started building itself, but it's not that these things arrive and they're not in competition with anything else. You have to be incredibly patient. These things are coming to you out of *gads* of information. To find these things you have to look at thousands of things you're going to discard before suddenly you go, "This one. Ah!" That was miraculous for me when I look back on it now. For four years I had no life but this book. You know that. I wasn't seeing anybody really. I would have these sort of impossible loves. Now my friends from Mexico say, "You really chose impossible loves during those years because you were really only interested in your book." For years I was sort of inhabiting this alternative parallel universe.

SC: Was writing this book so different from writing the first two books?

FG: Completely. The past itself is fiction. We can never really know what it was like. That's why I completely agree with the famous Henry James line about the historical novel being humbug and condemned to a fate of cheapness. He saw the novel as a realist form. A historical novel that aspires to realism is a fraud. I completely agree with him. What's beautiful about the past is that it's pure fiction. For me, the only way to answer that, to live in that past, was almost to be living in a world of pure imagination. It was just wonderful to inhabit a novel like that. I had never done that before.

SC: How did you feel when you were finishing or when you knew you were done, after twenty years? Not twenty years of writing but twenty years of—

FG: Twenty years of being in pursuit of it. I felt like it was about time. As I say, I was living almost too solitary a life. I think there's a certain loneliness in the book. Everyone in the book is looking for love. I think that in some weird way—it sounds crazy and I'll certainly never do that again—the loneliness I had in my own life was part of writing that book, part of the heart of that book and why I was able to write about María de las Nieves in the way that I was.

SC: Do you worry when your friends say to you, "You were single the whole time you were writing this book, because you couldn't have been writing the book if you weren't single"? You're not single now. So now what?

FG: I think that I've learned that I'm ready to be more whole in some way.

SC: Do you mean living less in your books?

FG: Maybe now I can live in my books in a healthier way. I think that I learned how to really write novels, writing this book. I think because I wrote a novel in which I didn't use my own life, and because I walked away from certain things that obsessed me in the past and I took a different approach to novel writing, I feel like I taught myself to write fiction. ✶

VENDELA VIDA

TALKS WITH

SHIRLEY HAZZARD

"I AM FULL OF LINES OF POETRY, IMPRESSIONS, EXPERIENCES, WORDS."

Things that seem implausible, either in books or in life:
Two people reading the same book at the same time
Undesired flinging-together
Distant rocks visible only in July

hirley Hazzard was born in Sydney in 1931 and left Australia in 1947. She has since lived in Hong Kong, New Zealand, Britain, and France. Now an American citizen, she divides her time between Italy and New York. Between the years 1952 and 1962, Hazzard worked in the United Nations as a clerical employee, an experience which led her to write not only People in Glass Houses (1967), a satirical collection of character sketches, but also Defeat of an Ideal (1973), a nonfiction book that detailed the weakness of the UN, and Countenance of Truth (1990), about the United Nations and the Kurt Waldheim case. She is also the author of the nonfiction books Coming of Age in Australia (1985) and Greene on Capri (2001).

It's fiction for which Hazzard is best known. She is the author of the short story collection Cliffs of Fall *(1963), and the novels* The Evening of the Holiday *(1966),* The Bay of Noon *(1970),* The Transit of Venus *(1980), and* The Great Fire *(2003). She was awarded the National Book Critics Circle Award for Fiction in 1980 for* The Transit of Venus; *in 2003, more than twenty years after her last novel was published,* The Great Fire *was shortlisted for the PEN/Faulkner award, and went on to earn her the National Book Award.*

Many have compared Hazzard to Henry James, perhaps because like James, Hazzard peppers her novels with clues for the astute reader. In The Transit of Venus, *it's left to the reader to piece together the circumstances of Ted Tice's suicide. Throughout* The Great Fire, *repeated references are made to a thick book Aldred Leith is reading, but Hazzard never blatantly states that it's* War and Peace. *Indeed, Hazzard herself—in her treatment of love and war and the burden of history—is perhaps the closest thing we have to Tolstoy.*

This interview took place shortly after Hazzard won the National Book Award. We met on a snowy afternoon in the Manhattan apartment she shared for many years with her late husband, the translator and biographer Francis Steegmuller. —V.V. (Winter 2003)

I. "THE ONLY CARD I HAD
TO PLAY WAS LITERATURE."

VENDELA VIDA: In *Greene on Capri*, you recount how you started a friendship with Graham Greene essentially through poetry. He and a friend were sitting at a table next to yours at a café in Capri. Greene was reciting a Robert Browning poem, "The Lost Mistress," but he couldn't recall the last line. As you left the café, you recited the elusive line of the poem to him. In *The Great Fire*, the protagonist, Leith, is reading a book on a train, and when he arrives at his destination he's greeted by a soldier who is reading the same book. In fact, in a lot of your books it's poetry or literature that brings people together.

SHIRLEY HAZZARD: Yes, it's quite intentional. You see, books were a theme of life, a lifetime, for whole populations who grew up before the 1950s, when television broke on the world. In one of his novels, *Travels with My Aunt,* Graham's protagonist remarks that one's life is more formed by books than people. "It is out of books," he says, that "one learns about love and pain at second hand." He once said to me that we—those of my generation and of his—had known a world where poetry cut across the classes and the generations. It was true. People spontaneously invoked lines of poetry without self-consciousness, and weren't considered to be showing off or eccentric. A single allusion, to a familiar book or poem, could create affinity.

My novel *The Great Fire* is set in the late 1940s, before television came on the scene. I've noticed that some reviewers question whether the young people in my story could be so well read. This reflects a generational gap. Critics don't realize that books were central to millions of lives, and were a predominant pleasure and a chief form of education.

Years ago, John Bayley, the British literary critic, wrote of "the solace that great language brings." In my childhood and early youth, men and women who read were all beneficiaries of the comfort derived from a great range of human expression. Through authentic expression, we recognized ourselves and one another, and were no longer isolated. This is a sense of sharing that we can enjoy through all the arts.

Through reading, I grew up. I am still hoping to grow up through reading, through music, through experience. When I was sixteen, living in Hong Kong, I went to work in an office of British Intelligence. The young English officers there knew Asian languages, had fought in the war, were clever and amusing. The only card I had to play was literature. They were all full of poetry, and so was I. We were walking anthologies. That was a great happiness and, in those times, not unusual.

VV: As readers, we find our expectations challenged so frequently when reading your work. One of the things we're continually surprised by is how funny so much of it is. One of my favorite scenes in *The Transit of Venus* is when you write: "The country bus lurched over an unsprung road. The girl thought that in novels one would read that he and she were flung against each other; and how that was impossible. We can only be flung against each other if we want to be."

And then a page later you write: "The bus plunged and bucked, determined to unseat them. We are flung against each other." I thought that was such a beautiful synthesis between life and art, and how what may seem far-fetched or unlikely in novels can actually be true.

SH: In that same book, I say a similar thing: that one wouldn't dare put into a novel the amount of coincidence that occurs in life itself.

VV: Yes, one of the characters says: "I've thought there may be more collisions of the kind in life than in books." Maybe the element of coincidence is played down in literature because it seems like cheating or can't be made believable. Whereas life itself doesn't have to be fair or convincing.

SH: Life doesn't have to prove itself. Life happens; we have to accept it. Reading fiction, the disbelieving, skeptical critic likes to feel in control. Yet his own existence, all existence, is subject to the accidental element, to the inexplicable or magical, or dreadful intervention that cannot be justified by logic. A friend of mine who knew the Shetland Islands told me that in the long light of the northern summer there comes a moment, in July, when a rock becomes visible that lies between the Shetlands and Norway. If the weather is favorable, a watch is kept from a certain promontory, and the rock can be seen. This phenomenon was denounced by scientists as wishful thinking, and quite impossible, but the rock has continued to manifest itself irrefutably: the thing is standing there, indifferent, or perhaps laughing to itself, unaccountable.

VV: That reminds me of the scene in *The Great Fire* that I mentioned before, when Leith gets off the train—I just love that scene. He gets off the train and the soldier who meets him has a book. And as a reader you're thinking, "It's not going to be the same book," and at the same time you're kind of hopeful that it is. You think, "It's a novel, she can't do that," and then you do it. It's wonderfully surprising, and surprisingly rewarding.

SH: That was important to me. Leith is on the train. He has his father's book. Arriving, he apologizes for the long wait the driver has had. And the young driver says, "It's all right. I had a book." Nowadays the young driver might of course have his cell phone, or an audio tape, or a Walkman. In those days you read a book— which in this case turns out coincidentally to be the book by Leith's father. All that would have been completely natural.

II. "I FEEL THE SURF OF THE CITY BEATING ON MY WINDOWS."

VV: I thought it was interesting that in *Greene on Capri* you put the explanation of why you wrote the book at the end, instead of at the beginning, as a foreword or preface.

SH: It just seemed to fit better.

VV: Did you experiment with it?

SH: No. You shouldn't start a book by telling the reader, "Here is how I feel, and therefore how you ought to feel." Let readers form their own conclusions. At the end, you can say, "Here is how it came about." In some measure, my memoir of Graham Greene was an opportunity for me to write about the life I shared there with my husband. In that sense, it is really a memoir of our own lives. Of course, Graham rampages about the book, just as he did throughout those years when he was a strong element of our Italian times, when we saw him frequently in spring and autumn on Capri, although our own temperaments and days were distinct from his.

VV: As you describe it, your marriage with Francis Steegmuller was an extremely literary marriage.

SH: Yes, that was an indivisible part of the whole.

VV: Was there a great deal of exchanging of work at the end of the day, or what was your typical work pattern?

SH: People often expect—I don't know why—that two writers living together must generate some hostility or friction. With us, it was the contrary; each understood what the other was up against: the need for seclusion, silence, and a need also for stimulus, sociability, sharing. Even the need for interruption, but only if one could dictate the interruption on one's own capricious terms. I had the study there [*she points*], and Francis had the study near the door. In a New York apartment, no room is really distant from another, so that tact and a sense of privacy are involved. Each of us understood that behind the closed door, on some particular day, the other might be going mad over a recalcitrant paragraph. And then, it always does fall to the woman to come and make the dinner. However, I should add that—and in this, as in much else, I was very spoiled—Francis did nearly all of what I call the administration of our lives: documents, taxes, leases, all those things that now fall heavily to me.

As we were fond of each other, we wanted to be reasonable. We didn't have to make an issue of every small thing that came up. That sort of running resentment can become, I think, an outlet for other forms of discontent between couples. We didn't feel like that, didn't hew to that line.

Looking back, I realize what a great change came over our world. When we were first married, over forty years ago, New York was certainly not a quiet place, but there was space for leisure. In the mild evenings, when there was long light, we might walk out after dinner, walk over to Madison Avenue and look into the windows of antique-furniture shops, of which there were many more in those days, or peer into the displays of the art dealers, and stroll home by some roundabout route. Now, one never has any such time. I feel the surf of the city beating on my windows. Whatever I'm doing, I feel I should be doing something else; should be catching up on some insurmountable backlog.

VV: You address the issue of memory, and the dangers of note-taking, in *Greene on Capri*. You write: "Over our years of Capri meetings, I seldom made 'notes' after our conversations with Graham and Yvonne. An underlying intention to record changes the nature of things, blighting spontaneity and receptivity: an imposition, like a snapping of photographs."

I love that description of how our need to record a conversation (surely these present words included) alters the conversation. I felt, when reading this book, that if someone had just given me a transcript of your conversations with Greene, it would have somehow rung less true.

SH: Of course. I didn't keep what would be called a record. And then, I have a good memory for what interests me. Not so good, I admit, for what is useful. We kept, I still do, a little appointment book for each day. I might write "Dinner, Gemma, with Graham and Yvonne," perhaps adding four or five words to recall some matter touched upon: a word or two that evoked the whole evening. Yet sometimes I might clearly recall whole exchanges of conversation long after.

VV: A lot of your novels are rich with detail and place. Do you ever take notes or do you work purely from memory?

SH: Memory. I think I have a fairly remarkable memory. I've always reserved what gave me pleasure, what interested me. Also, what has been poignant: the nature of sadness, the private anguish of tragedy, regret. I am full of lines of poetry, impressions, experiences, words. If remembrance were all pleasure, that would be too easy. I keep hold of matters that can't be resolved—why something went wrong, who was at fault, or how the difficulty was shared. These remain with me—no doubt as they do with many people. I see, too, looking back from that early youth I kept a reserve of what was beautiful, pleasurable, even sad, as a capital to draw on, and perhaps as evidence of a better self that I could consistently summon before the world.

III. "I'M ONE PERSON NOW IN THREE PLACES IN THE WORLD."

VV: I was reading an interview you did with Michiko Kakutani after the publication of *The Transit of Venus,* in which you said, "I think there is a tendency to write jottings about one's own psyche, and call it a novel. My book, though, is really a story. And that might have contributed to its success."

All of your books are stories. They often commence with a big event, or in the wake of one—whether it's in *The Transit of Venus,* which starts with the capsizing of a boat in which the girls lose their parents; or in *The Great Fire,* which begins in the aftermath of a war and the bombing of Hiroshima; or the first sentence of *The Bay of Noon,* when a military plane crashes on Mount Vesuvius. Is there something in those tragedies that embodies the seeds of a story? Or in your mind, does the story begin with a tragedy?

SH: I think my books often start out with the arrival of a loner. Ted Tice is "arriving" at the beginning of *The Transit of Venus*; Leith is arriving at the start of *The Great Fire.* The circumstances are obviously quite different, but the loner is appearing on the scene. In *The Bay of Noon,* the lonely girl is arriving at Naples. So there has been a break with previous experience; something new is beginning. The protagonist is in each case relatively young. So the future is before them.

VV: Both *The Bay of Noon* and *The Evening of the Holiday* take place in Italy, where you still spend some part of the year. Where do you go in Italy?

SH: In the south of Italy. On Capri and at Naples. In my early twenties, I spent a year in Naples, and have loved the city ever since. It is a complicated place—but all great cities are difficult now. Its street dangers are intimidating to outsiders. The dangers are far less than those of New York City, but they are of unfamiliar kind. Naples retains its strange, singular, ancient ways.

VV: I think it's the only place I've been in Italy where I felt a little wary.

SH: It requires time. For the last twenty years I've had the use of a pied-à-terre on the property of friends in Naples, right on the sea, very near where I lived in my first Neapolitan incarnation in the late 1950s. In *The Bay of Noon* my heroine lives in the district of Posillipo in Naples. And that is where I now stay when at Naples. However, there is also Capri. For many years we rented a dear shabby old place in an old building of Capri. It was never for sale, and, after my husband's death in 1994, the owners wanted it for their daughter. So I sold a painting that we had here in New York and bought a tiny old habitation on a Capri hilltop, and fixed it up. It has a huge view of the sea and sky, and of the green central mountain of the island.

Thus, New York is my headquarters, and I have the two outlying nests in the Bay of Naples. I'm one person, now, in three places in the world, only one of which I own. Perhaps absurd—financially and otherwise. But continuity—habit, and the memories of habit—are precious to me.

VV: Can you tell me a little about where you lived when you were growing up? Your books are set in so many places, and you, as the writer, seem so knowledgeable about and equally familiar with these various settings.

SH: When I was twenty-five, I looked around and realized that I'd lived in six completely different parts of the world for substantial periods: Australia, the Far East, and New Zealand; in Britain, with repeated returnings; New York; and Italy. In the 1960s and early 1970s, we lived half the year in Paris. Wonderful. My husband was writing on Jean Cocteau.

VV: Which won him the National Book Award.

SH: Yes. He had it twice—the second time for translating. [*The Letters of Gustave Flaubert,* 1981]

VV: It must have been fun, for lack of a better word, when you won the National Book Award, too.

SH: Of course. I thought the other evening [at the National Book Awards ceremony] how we would have shared the pleasure—the fun, as you say. I thought, when I was required to say a few words, that I would talk about him, but then—

VV: At the dinner?

SH: Yes. Well, everyone had been talking about their spouse—how helpful, how devoted. So I said to Francis, on the quiet, "Forgive me, but I won't join the crowd. I'll make it up to you in some other way."

VV: [*Laughs*]

SH: He was lovely.

IV. "YOU DON'T KNOW WHAT YOU WILL DO THAT MAY PLEASE YOU MORE, LATER ON."

VV: This might be a hard question, but which book are you most proud of?

SH: I don't think I can separate them just like that. Perhaps I can touch on it by invoking William Maxwell, who, as the chief fiction editor of the *New Yorker,* took my first work out of a slush pile and published it. Divine intervention. He was a marvelous man, who became, with his wife Emily, a great friend to me.

I wrote a number of short stories rather quickly at the time. And then suddenly I was writing a novel. I said to Maxwell, "It's markedly different from my previous work. Perhaps I've grown up as a writer, or the material's different, but I begin to wonder whether some of my first stories will eventually seem quite juvenile to me."

Maxwell said, "I wouldn't count on that. Rather, you'll look back on them as things absolutely fresh and spontaneous, with a kind of innocence that you will only rarely recapture in later work. Your later work may be more mature, riper, more imaginative, more inventive perhaps. But there will always be the freshness about the first work."

I'm aware of the truth in this. A very early story—the second story, really, that I ever wrote, called "The Worst Moment of the Day"—continues to please me, just for a mood or a feeling, or a sentence or two that stand on their own. You don't know what you will do that may please you more, later on. Of course an entire novel exists differently: to bring it all together, you feel, yes, that you've achieved something. But what is that something?—it's hard to know. On occasion, the authentic moment can be conveyed in just a sentence.

All the same, I like my novels. If I reread one of them, with a lapse of years, I don't wish it away. The later books—*The Transit of Venus* and *The Great Fire*—are closer to the way I feel now. But I have an attachment to *The Bay of Noon*; and to some particular stories in *People in Glass Houses*—satirical stories that are on the side of truth. People in power, even if it's only petty bureaucratic power, are rarely good news. They become unreachable, unless by satire. Alexander Pope sees them as "Safe from the Bar, the Pulpit, and the Throne, / Yet touch'd and sham'd by Ridicule alone. / O sacred weapon! left for Truth's defence, / Sole Dread of Folly, Vice, and Insolence!"

VV: I've read that you're an avid reader of Elizabeth Bowen. Who else do you think has been an influence? Do you read D. H. Lawrence?

SH: Elizabeth was a great friend of ours, an incomparable person. The best of her writing is singular, inimitable. As an influence— I really don't know. So many poems and novels have influenced me, have developed my ear. Too varied to discuss here. Browning was the first perhaps, when I was nine or so. The great poems of Hardy, first read at sixteen when I was in Hong Kong; and, later, his excruciating novels. Conrad, whom I first read at school in his stories, remains a companion. His novel *Victory* travels with me.

And one of the greatest of all short stories, "The Secret Sharer," told on so many levels that the reader has to wonder—are there two men here, or is there only one? Consummate. Graham Greene said that the spell of Conrad over him in youth was so powerful that he sometimes avoided rereading him. Greene himself broke on me early, in adolescence: *The Heart of the Matter* was the first for me, perhaps the best. D.H. Lawrence?—I haven't read him in years. I appreciate him, but I don't turn to him eagerly. There have been particular books—Nigel Balchin's *The Small Back Room,* Jean Rhys's *Wide Sargasso Sea,* Nabokov's *The Defense,* Muriel Spark's *The Girl of Slender Means*—many others—that eccentrically touch the imagination.

Whether any of this amounts to "influence," I can't really say. It's just that certain books moved you, and you never forget them. They become intimate, indelible. I'm often linked to the influence of Henry James, yet I had written for years before I settled in to read James, as in youth I'd never really liked him. He has some greatness, but there are even now reservations in my feelings about Henry James. Similarly I'm told that Patrick White has influenced me. He hasn't; but I consider his *Voss* one of the greatest novels of the twentieth century. God help us, the other day someone wrote that I was influenced by Somerset Maugham. Maugham was a splendid writer; he told a fine story. It's true that some sympathy is lacking in his work, but he is a master of narrative language and its deployment. I see nothing in my work that reflects Maugham. But once someone says it, it will go on being said.

VV: Right. [*Laughs*]

SH: In the same vein, people will tell you that you clearly had this or that happen to you at an early age, and you consequently respond in such and such a way. But they don't know what else may have happened, since what is most important for you, you keep to yourself. The greatest literary influence lies in arousing us to words, to expressive speech. That comes through reading, through the pleasure and excitement of reading that creates receptivity. These are wide impressions, not narrow particular ones. Such matters can scarcely be critically addressed. As I consider our modern lives, I feel that, due to the growing uncertainty of the world, people anxiously want to believe themselves on top of things, in control. Especially in the United States just now, at the height of world power, there is the impulse to settle on what is attestable, to pronounce and explain; to exclude mystery, imagination, the intuitive powers of individual existence. What about the *unattestable,* that informs all that most matters to us? What about the accidental nature of our life? The salient events of private life are always tinged with the accidental. If I hadn't gone to a party that Muriel Spark gave down the road here in the Beaux Arts Hotel, I would never have met Francis Steegmuller.

VV: Which brings us back to the coincidences and collisions in your work.

SH: From the psychiatrists and sociologists, we never hear a word about the accidental, the unattestable. Max Beerbohm said, of this era of explanation, "They explain because they can't understand." Which is perhaps why, with so much elucidation, we're still in the dark. ✶

THISBE NISSEN

TALKS WITH

SIRI HUSTVEDT

"I'VE NEVER THOUGHT OF BEAUTY
AND TRUTH AS EQUIVALENT IN ANY WAY.
SOME TRUTHS ARE UGLY, SOMETIMES
BEAUTIFUL, VERY OFTEN AMBIGUOUS
AND INVISIBLE. IT'S THAT AMBIGUOUS
AND INVISIBLE REALM I'M ALWAYS
REACHING FOR IN MY WRITING."

Things our brains do naturally that writers try to do better:
Create order out of the bombardment of sensual data in the world
Combine information in different ways to create diverse meanings
Create narrative wholes from fragments
Dynamically edit past memories
Consolidate numerous voices, images, and stories into one organic whole

Spring break of my senior year in college, in a bookstore in *New York, a paperback cover caught my eye. It was Siri Hustvedt's* The Blindfold *(1992). I bought it, started reading on the crosstown bus, and didn't stop until late into the night when I finished. That semester at school I was taking "Introduction to Literary Theory," and my head was aswirl with Derrida and Barthes, no doubt coloring my reading to such a degree that, when I returned from break, I begged my professor to let me write my final paper on* The Blindfold. *A good sport, he agreed; I bought him a copy and went to work on the last paper of my college career. A paper which, as Hustvedt may well remember, I presented to her, like a groupie,* *at a reading she gave in Iowa City after the publication of her second novel,* The Enchantment of Lily Dahl *(1996).*

Hustvedt's books include a third novel, What I Loved *(2003), a collection of poems,* Reading To You *(1983), and a book of essays,* Yonder *(1998). A new book,* Mysteries of the Rectangle: Essays on Painting, *was published last summer by Princeton Architectural Press, and in January 2006, Picador will publish another collection of her essays,* A Plea for Eros. *In the course of this interview—which took place over email between mid-April and mid-May 2005—Hustvedt never so much as mentioned her forthcoming books. Nearly thirty years living in New York City (where she moved in 1978 to do a Ph.D. in English Literature at Columbia University), and Hustvedt's voice and sensibility still retain an honesty and deliberateness I can't help but attribute to her Minnesota upbringing. They are subtle qualities of which I—a New Yorker transplanted by choice to the Midwest—will always be enormously appreciative, and a little bit in awe.* —T.N. (Spring 2005)

I. IN WHICH THE ABYSS OFFERS COMFORT, ALBEIT UNWITTINGLY

THISBE NISSEN: With college more than a decade behind me now, I look back on that Lit Theory paper with a sort of nostalgically tickled mortification. It's printed in Helvetica. I titled it "Thisbe Nissen, Siri Hustvedt, and *The Blindfold:* An Encounter," and began with a string of disclaimers: "I wish to make no claims to *what is,*" I wrote, "only to *what I perceive to be,* realizing concurrently that my vision/version cannot be asserted without invariably appropriating support from the two other forces I have engaged to participate in this encounter: the text and the author," which I think might have been a complicated way of saying *I read this book and thought about it.*

"In my interpretation," I wrote, with that ubiquitous qualification, "I read the text as Hustvedt's attempt, within a piece of fiction, to create a dialogue with the theorists she has grappled with in the academy, the same theorists I am grappling with, using her work to help me do so… I am engaging in an interrogation of Hustvedt, claiming that she is engaging in an interrogation of the very theories I am using to frame my interrogation of her alleged interrogation of these works." Does this make you cringe? Laugh? Shudder in horror? Nod sagely? Bang your head against the wall? Regret agreeing to this interview…?

SIRI HUSTVEDT: No, I wasn't at all mortified by your paper. I was flattered, and *The Blindfold* is a translation of a period of my life that included an immersion in theoretical and philosophical books, some of which stuck, as they say, and others of which evaporated. What I used in the book, however, was mostly about language and identity. I've always felt the gap between words and things, the impossibility of articulating what's really out there in the world, the strangeness of naming everything, including the self, how completely arbitrary it all is, and yet, at the same time, how it determines identities. The theoretical or philosophical bottom line? It was then and is now the dialectical relation between self and other and the often fragile threshold between them.

When I was a student, the writers that fascinated me particularly were Hegel on self-consciousness through his interpreter Alexandre Kojève, Roman Jakobson on language, M. M. Bakhtin, especially his book *The Dialogic Imagination,* Freud and always Freud, and Jacques Lacan's rereading of Freud. As much as I admired Foucault, I found him oddly Romantic, and Derrida is someone I've understood only through secondary sources. Deleuze I found brilliant but also rather neo-Romantic. And yet my first novel isn't directly about any of these writers. It's about confusion, poverty, eroticism, and fear, and much of what's in there just came from the nowhere or somewhere of my unconscious…

TN: I think I respond so strongly to your work in part because that gap has always felt very real to me as well. Or, rather: I have also always been obsessed with naming, and the awkward impossibility of naming, and the degree to which that which is named is shaped by its name. When I first encountered the theorists who, it turned out, had already put my feelings into words, I was enormously comforted. To be given the words "signifier" and "signified" was to put a signifier on the notion inside me that had always gone unnamed. To grapple with the "abyss" between them—that realm of infinite play and interpretation between the thing and its name, between the idea and the word for the idea—was suddenly not just the existential angst I'd been feeling all my life, but something real and almost tangible in its articulation. I feel a similar gratitude for your novels. They give voice to something I've only explored internally, and that's both a comfort and a challenge at the same time.

SH: I agree with you entirely about the relief offered by theory and by literature. It is ironic that by naming the gap, philosophy or fiction offers the same comfort a person feels when she's walked around for years with vague or acute pains, and suddenly a doctor gives her a diagnosis. Her pains may be exactly the same, but the name organizes the symptoms into a *disease* or a *syndrome* or a *disorder,* and despite the fact that nothing has changed, everything has changed. Perception is determined by language to a large degree, but our perceptions aren't the same as the Real—the stuff of the world out there. I think in my work, I've always wanted the sense that both underneath and beyond our perceptions, our feelings, our thoughts is the unknowable.

George Makari, a psychiatrist, psychoanalyst, and medical historian, described Freud's idea of consciousness beautifully in his essay "In the Eye of the Beholder: Helmholtzian Perception and the Origins of Freud's 1900 Theory of Transference": "For Freud consciousness was surrounded; it was a feeble, faulty lamp stranded between the unconscious and the darkness of outer reality." (Makari began his life as a poet.) This articulates precisely my sense of living in the world. For me writing is an activity that allows me to push at both dark sides—the *in here* and the *out there*. Recently, I've been reading a lot of neuroscience, which has been steadily confirming many of Freud's intuitions about the mind. First, that most of what the brain does is unconscious, and second, that perception is shaped by internal representations, both pictorial and verbal, which act as screens and create expectations in memory that allow us to order the bombardment of sensual data beyond us.

II. BEAUTY, SIGNIFIED, OR IS MY FLY UNZIPPED?

TN: In all three of your novels you contend with that act of imposing order through naming—putting a signifier on a signified—with regard to people and objects and emotions and ideas. You're also in constant interrogation specifically with acts and artifacts of artistic representation. There's a very similar gap, it seems, between a photograph of a person and the actual person, between an artist's portrait and the portrait's subject. Do you want to talk about that gap?

SH: Despite my ongoing fascination with philosophy and my more recent incursions into medicine and neuroscience, I feel that art of all kinds gets closer to presenting the gap, the truth (with a small *t*), than any intellectual system or framework. Good art always treats the particular, and I believe it is always ambiguous. In good art, it's possible to recognize something true that one couldn't have recognized without the work. Bad art uses truisms.

Photographs and paintings of people are different. The first is mechanical and the latter is corporeal, but both represent the human body. I think of both of them as ghosts. Still, a painting bears the trace of the painter's body, his or her hands and arm, the gesture. The painter is the ghost as much as the subject, and the painter could have invented the subject. In a photo, the trace left is of a single moment in the actual world (forgetting about doctored images and digital stuff). It is haunting because it's entirely empty except for the appearance that was. I continue to look at pictures of my dead father these days, awed by his presence and absence in them. The picture gives me only his flat appearance in a photograph at various moments in his life, but I look at his image far more now than I used to. It makes me think of Roland Barthes, staring at the picture of his dead mother...

TN: Much of your work revolves around artistic representations of beauty—particularly female beauty—and the relationship between art and life. You make art that deals with Beauty's representation in art. There's no author photo of you on my paperback copy of *The Blindfold,* just the black-and-white cover image that I think a reader can't help but associate with the narrative-driving black-and-white photo of the book's narrator, Iris Vegan, whom the reader can't help but associate with you, Siri (Iris backwards) Hustvedt (whose mother's maiden name is Vegan). It wasn't until I got my hands on a copy of your book of poems, *Reading To You,* that I found out what *you* actually looked like, and could see very easily how a photo as striking as the one on the back of *Reading To You* could provoke the kind of furor and obsession that the photo of Iris provokes in *The Blindfold.* Is this a question you dread being asked?

SH: I don't mind this question, and it is very complex. I can tell you this: around the age of fourteen, I realized that people were staring at me, and I kept checking the zipper of my fly! I'm fifty years old now, and I feel much more vain and protective of my work than I do about my face and body, and I am vain about how I look, but it's secondary. I've felt for some time that my aging face belongs to me more than my young face did; it's as if my face is finally revealing something of who I am. I also think in terms of external perception, my fifty-year-old face gets more respect than the younger one did. Those are the travails of being a woman. Ideas are often more acceptable in a male or stereotypically school-marmy package... I've never thought of beauty and truth as equivalent in any way. Sometimes truths are ugly, sometimes beautiful, very often ambiguous and invisible. It's that ambiguous and invisible realm I'm always reaching for in my writing.

III. THE GAP: BRIDGED, FLOODED, AND REVEALED (BUT NOT NECESSARILY IN THAT ORDER)

TN: And there's that gap again—between what one looks like on the outside and what one feels one *is* on the inside. It's interesting to me that there's a comfort in the alignment of those two, of feeling that your outside is revealing the inside. It's like the comfort of finding the right word, of pinning the signifier to the signified as closely as possible. I'm curious as to why or how or where along the way you found yourself reaching across that gap through prose rather than poetry?

SH: I wrote poems not only because I loved poetry, but because its many short forms were easier for me to deal with than long forms. In high school I wrote poems all the time, pretty terrible ones. In college I wrote lots of imitations of formal poems, sonnets, alexandrines, heroic couplets, etc., mostly short. I started a novel, too, but after a couple of pages, I had no idea where I was going. In graduate school, I finally wrote a poem I liked and sent it out to the *Paris Review,* which to my amazement published it.

Not so long after that, I was stuck, really stuck. I hated what I was doing, and David Shapiro, the poet, and a teacher of mine in graduate school, told me to try automatic writing as the surrealists practiced it: just sit down and write whatever comes to mind. I wrote thirty pages in a single evening, spent the next three months editing, and discovered I had a prose poem called "Squares" that was published in my little book of poems, *Reading to You.* The revelation was lasting, and I never returned to poems in lines again. The flood technique, as I call it, seemed better suited to the unconscious material that I have always wanted to tap.

I still write like this, but now I am better able to hold a long narrative in my mind, to shape a story, than I was when I was young. Historically, unlike poetry, the novel has mostly been a form for older people. It may have to do with a connection between experience, time, and volume. It may be linked to auto-biographical memory and the fact that by the time you're thirty, there has simply been more life lived. I don't know...

TN: How does the practice of automatic writing work exactly? Do you allot yourself a time frame? Challenge yourself not to remove pen from paper? Set yourself a task, or write "I don't know what to write" until something pops in to replace it? Do you actually write dramatized scenes in this way? It's interesting to hear your process—starts to make the sometimes dreamlike quality of your work make a lot of sense...

SH: No, I'm not at all strict like that, assigning myself a method, but when I'm deep inside what I'm doing, I let the words come and don't work on the prose until later. Some of the best prose seems to come that way, in fact. It's a kind of looseness or open-ness that I can feel, and for me, the most important part of it is rhythm, a physical beat that seems necessary to the process. For me, a book is an organism, not a machine.

In dramatized scenes, I feel that I'm just listening to the people talk and writing it down. Is that what you feel? Of course I change and cut and alter, but once you know the characters, they just seem to talk.

IV, CRITICISM CRITICIZED:
A CAREER RETROSPECTIVE

TN: What's your feeling when you look back on the work you've done so far?

SH: I think it has taken me some time to master a long form. I've been building slowly. *The Blindfold* started as a short story, and after

I had finished the first one, which I called "Mr. Morning," I decided I wasn't through with Iris and wrote more about her, and the final result was a fractured novel. Each part began with some seed of inspiration, usually something that had left me with a feeling of dread. For *The Enchantment of Lily Dahl,* I decided on a more classical novelistic structure, a third-person narration that takes place over a summer and is organized by Lily's menstrual cycle, during which she misses one period, a traumatic absence. The blood shed is Martin Petersen's when he kills himself. The book is entirely overdetermined, to use a psychoanalytic word, and everything relates to everything else. I wasn't at all conscious of some of it as I wrote it, but in the end, I discovered that I'd kept only material that somehow relates to other material. In other words, there are never any isolates.

The book was inspired by an anecdote from my neck of the woods—the twin brother of someone I knew walked into a restaurant, ordered breakfast, ate it, and blew his brains out. That event of a public suicide, self-murder as theater, became the seed for all the doublings in the novel—between play and town, Lily and her doll double, etc. In that novel, I was extremely careful to hide references, to embed everything in the story itself. After it was published, I realized that intellectuals (mostly in Europe) loved the book, but a great many people didn't understand any of the undercurrents… I remain very proud of that novel, however, and formally, it is the most perfect of my books.

TN: You say you think *Lily Dahl* is "overdetermined," but you don't use the word pejoratively. That formal perfection sounds like it's something that pleases you and can still please you even if the average reader doesn't see what's in operation in the book on that level at all. But is it upsetting if readers don't clue into such important guiding themes? Is it OK with you if the European intellectuals get what you're doing and average readers relate to it in a very different way? It seems to me that your work often exists on those two planes at once: a story plane and a coded, theoretical plane. I'm curious as to your relationship to reviews and reviewers, and to criticism—and to praise, for that matter—of your work. Do you read reviews? Are you affected by them? Do you need to find a place inside your head to put those thoughts and words in order to get back to writing, or do you try to put them *out* of your head when it comes to getting your work done?

SH: I did feel sad that so many reviewers, especially here, had no idea how to read *Lily Dahl,* but I also realize that a writer has to keep a healthy distance from what is said in the press about a book because it might interfere with writing in the future. For me, a good book always has an underneath, a deep associative subtext that resonates in the reading. It isn't necessary to explicate that subtext in order to feel it. Reviewing, after all, is not literary criticism. It's journalism, and as such, is necessarily superficial. A reviewer has to say something, and if the work escapes the quick read, then chances are it will create perplexity and annoyance rather than pleasure. This isn't true of just plain readers, however, who don't have to write anything, and I did hear from a number of readers who loved the book... When I published my first novel, I found it incomprehensible when older writers told me they didn't read their reviews. I was so curious! Now it makes perfect sense to me. I often file them without looking; it's an efficient form of self-protection.

TN: And *What I Loved?*

SH: *What I Loved* was influenced by writing essays. I am very comfortable with the ranging, free-wheeling form of the essay, which is all about trying out ideas. It was my most ambitious project, and I really had no clue how to realize it. It started with an image in my mind of a very fat woman lying on a bed in a room, dead. I wrote *What I Loved* four times from scratch over the course of six years, and it nearly drove me out of my mind. Finally I found it. I wrote the fourth draft in eight months. It is much more articulated than the two other books, by which I mean that there is more speculation and meditation than in my earlier novels. It is less hidden. The form was purely organic and imitated the story, which is something like: 1. *Paradise* 2. *Paradise Lost* 3. *Inferno plus Coda.* I understood that only later, however. The novel I'm writing now, *The Sorrows of an American,* is entirely different again, organized by leaps... Perhaps because I won't write that many novels in my life, slow as I am, I always want to push myself and do something entirely different. Of course it's never that different. My obsessions return, in spite of myself.

V. ONE MIGHT ARTICULATE FEAR AS AN AWARENESS OF AMNESIA HOLES

TN: This is my chance to ask a writer what it really means to write a book over from scratch four times. I've certainly heard people talk about working this way, but there's something that just doesn't penetrate my comprehension as to how it really works. Do you mean that you literally have a full draft of a novel, hundreds of pages, that you put away, open a new file, and begin anew from, say, a different point of view, or a different narrative stance, a different place in time? Do you really not use material from the previous draft(s)? In the end, do you go back and cobble in pieces from all four drafts? It is astounding to me to imagine being so devoted to a story that I'd be willing—or able—to go through that much to get it told the right way.

But maybe it's just a very different process of writing. I'm much more of a collagist about the whole process: I write by hand, then type it into the computer, then print it out and start in on it with scissors and tape, hacking it apart, Scotch-taping pieces to yellow legal pads, scrawling in between, winding up with a big thick collaged mass of paper and tape and smudging pen, and then take it to the computer and transpose the new and shifted material. And then I do it again and again and again. People tell me I'm nuts, but I feel like I'm always working from *something* after that very first handwritten chunk, and it seems infinitely easier to work from something than from a blank page or screen. Is there actually something liberating for you in that blank page? I'm determined to try to understand this phenomenon once and for all!

SH: Yes, I really did start on a blank page four times, and yes, I don't think any of the sentences were the same. I always had the same narrator and essentially the same story, but in some versions much more of the story, and I did make some plot changes. The book grew and shrank, depending on the draft. I honestly think that for me it's a drama of finding the tone and rhythm more than story—of feeling the urgency of the telling as real. In *What I Loved* it meant becoming Leo fully, not partly. I relied on my husband as a reader. I gave him complete drafts and he would say, "it's not there yet," and I'd start again, sometimes pretty miserably, but I don't have a gift for revision. I rewrite. This is not to say that I don't edit until the very end. I do. I fix sentences, but it's hard for me to push things around like a puzzle. The only part of *What I Loved* that I skipped over until the very end when I was rewriting was the death of Matthew. I found it unbearable.

The bad first three drafts, I believe, were the product of my fear. I am usually afraid of what I really want to write.

TN: Do you mean that you're afraid it won't come out the way you intend—that the outside representation won't match the inner idea—or is it some other kind of fear?

SH: Oh no, I mean a deep inner fear of myself, of something in me, something amorphous and frightening that is always lurking beneath the act of writing. I have an abiding terror of what's *in* there.

TN: I feel that hearing people talk about something I've written is like undergoing intense psychoanalysis, that they can see through what I've written and into me. I feel simultaneously terrified by what people might find and grubby for that information. It's not a fear of getting it from my brain onto the page; it's the fear of the critical interpretations that come later, from outside, showing me potentially painful or difficult reflections of myself. And at the same time, I'm dying to see those interpretations so I can know something of what's happening as my words cross the gap between me and the world. Is this at all what your fear is about, or is it different?

SH: You are very articulate about your fear in a way that I'm not. Every act of writing is a form of communicating to some other. It may be a generalized other, but it's still an imaginary dialogue of a kind. While I'm writing I don't consciously think about what other people will discover about me or criticize about me. Sometimes after I finish a book, I think about that. The connection to psychoanalysis, however, is real, since in that dyad of analyst/analysand, free association can lead to wounds that the speaker wants to protect or cover because the pain is too great. My fear, I believe, is something like that, fear of pain, but when I aim at the fear, when I'm brave, I find it liberating, and the best material comes from it.

This is why fiction can often provide an avenue for greater truth-telling than nonfiction. The characters and story become translations of deep emotional truths that couldn't be told in a strictly autobiographical way. Sometimes by becoming another, you become more yourself, or you find the fluidity of your many selves. It's a kind of attunement or sensitivity to real experience that is reinvented in a book, not very different from how we reinvent our own memories, put them in some kind of narrative order, and create a biography for ourselves with lots of forgotten parts and a good deal of distortion, but we must have a story in order to go on. Narrative is essential for life. The fear, I suspect, is in knowing that there are those amnesia holes.

TN: I'm not consciously thinking about it when I write either; it's upon putting a book out into the world that I fear the kind of revelation-of-self we're talking about. But again: I both fear it and crave it, because it does seem that having those raw, unconscious things pointed out in your work and brought to the surface is what raises new questions and necessitates the next plunge into the abyss, and opens up that next realm of discovery. Painful as the discovery process may be, it's undeniable. To deny that process would be to deny life. Because, as you say, that's what drives life. I wonder, though, if the amnesia holes can be as strong a driving force as memory? It seems to me there's a whole world to be explored when someone says, "Look at what you're *not* dealing with here. Look at what you're avoiding, or forgetting, or declining to include in your narrative." There's a story in what's been left out, in the reasons—subconscious or otherwise—that you've *not* gone somewhere, or said something, or even been aware of that omission.

SH: We may or may not be talking about two different kinds of fear: one inward and one outward. I was trying to articulate something about my psychological makeup that has little to do with the response of other people in the world, although it may have something to do with a scary internal other. As for amnesia, I agree with you absolutely. Every story leaps over the forgotten, and every story could be many other stories.

In my last book, I wanted to include both the holes and the sense that Leo's is only one of many possible versions of the same narrative. He has a drawer where he puts objects, most of them meaningless, that belonged to people he loved. At one point, he begins to play a game with those things, arranging and rearranging them to create various associations among them, each of which has a different meaning. I loved the idea of this game, but it wasn't until later that I realized its significance in terms of storytelling. Leo knows that there are whole worlds he has missed.

TN: When you set out to tell a story is it daunting to imagine the infinite number of ways in which that story might be told? To consider who's telling it, and from what vantage point? Deciding which threads of the narrative will be remembered, or articulated, and which will remain untold? What will be the gaps and what will be the bridges?

SH: Yes, I find it terribly hard, and I do think this has been a big problem for me: what to put in and what to leave out? My drafts are a way of closing in on what *feels* essential, and I discover what's essential over time through resonances, echoes, similarities, and doublings in the story. If a passage doesn't amplify the material already there in a deep way, I dump it and try again. When I'm down in the bones of a book, I have a feeling of rightness, that I've descended underground, and that descent is connected to memory and the way memory works. Because when we retrieve a memory, we don't retrieve the original but rather our last retrieval of that memory: we don't walk around with original, pure imprints of our past. We edit them through the present. Neuroscientists call this *reconsolidation*. Freud called it *nachträglichkeit*.

I once wrote that writing fiction for me is like remembering what never happened, and that's precisely how I feel. I see my characters and the rooms and streets they inhabit as mental representations that mimic my memories. As for forgetting, nobody can be blamed for what's missing. What's important is to recognize that no story, true or fictional, can include the forgotten, except to say that we know it exists. Our minds create narrative wholes from fragments because that story is necessary for us to go on living. In some way, I'm sure my need to write is linked to an overwhelming urge to investigate those pieces of my evolving memory.

VI. BOOKS BECOME US:
THE COMPLIMENT IT WAS

TN: What fiction writers awe you?

SH: Oh gosh, there are many, but my earliest loves after fairy tales and *Alice in Wonderland* were Charlotte Brontë's *Jane Eyre,* Emily Brontë's *Wuthering Heights,* Charles Dickens's *David Copperfield,* and Jane Austen's *Pride and Prejudice.* I read them all the summer after I turned thirteen, along with heaps of other books, but those remain shaping passions. I read in a continual fever after that, without much discrimination, anything that was supposed to be "good." In junior high and high school, I read a lot of Americans: Melville, Hawthorne, a writer who had radar about what goes on between people, Hemingway, who struck me (and zillions of other writers) as an amazing stylist, Fitzgerald, Faulkner, Baldwin, and that was when I began my lifelong romance with Henry James. I read Sartre, Camus, and Kafka then, too, although I entirely missed the humor in the latter. That would come later.

In college I read Proust and Joyce for the first time and felt like I had spontaneously combusted, and the Russians, Tolstoy, Dostoevsky, Chekhov, all of whom made me weak in the knees, but Dostoevsky's *Crime and Punishment* turned me inside out, and I would reread it several times. I read *Middlemarch* for the first time then, too, and this book has been vital to me, not only because it is an ambitious and great novel, but because I fell in love with Eliot's sensibility, which I discovered not only in her work, but in her dear, good letters. She was a potent intellectual, an excellent translator, a great novelist, and a tender human being. She remains an idol. I started Thomas Mann's *The Magic Mountain* three times before I realized that it was wonderful. Like everybody, I loved *Don Quixote* because it is like reading the whole world.

In graduate school, I was deeply affected by Djuna Barnes's *Nightwood,* a delirious, baroque little novel that opened a door for me to sexual ambiguity in fiction, a subject dear to my heart. I was so moved, I wrote to her, and over a year later and only weeks before she died, I received a brief reply typed on an Underwood with wavy characters telling me that my letter had given her a great deal of trouble. I took it as a compliment, and I think it was.

I found Genet, too, and fell for him, especially *A Thief's Journal,* not strictly fiction, but close enough, and Beckett, whose novels I love, especially the trilogy and a very late work, *Company,* so tender. Flann O'Brien is a fantastic writer, and Henry Miller needs rehabilitation because his prose is wild and brilliant. Ingeborg Bachmann's poems and prose have stayed with me. Later, when I was an adult, books that seared me are Louis-Ferdinand Céline's *Death on the Installment Plan,* Svevo's *The Confessions of Zeno,* Bohumil Hrabal's *I Served the King of England.* There are really many more that I've forgotten, and that's just dead prose writers, not all the poets and the living people.

Reading is the avenue to writing, and after a while, the sheer bulk of influences begins to eliminate the question of influence. Even when my memory is spotty for a particular work I loved, I think it lives inside me in some form. Books we respond to become us. They don't remain intact, of course, or unedited in our recollection, but nobody really writes alone. There are all those chattering voices and stories and pictures taken not only from the so-called real world but from a world that includes the imaginary realm of books. ✻

ZZ PACKER

TALKS WITH

EDWARD P. JONES

"ALL THE WRITERS THAT WENT UP TO THE
'HOUSE OF SLAVERY' WENT IN THE FRONT
DOOR, WHICH IS BLACK AND WHITE WITH NO
SHADES OF GRAY IN SIGHT; AND I JUST
DECIDED TO GO AT IT FROM THE SIDE, AND
OPEN A DOOR THAT HADN'T REALLY BEEN
OPENED VERY OFTEN, AND THAT WAS THE
DOOR INVOLVING BLACK SLAVEHOLDERS."

The ultimate novel-writing mix tape:
Judy Collins, "That's No Way to Say Goodbye" [Six times in a row]
Opening credits theme, The Life and Times of Judge Roy Bean
[Get up and walk around while tape is rewinding; play again]

dward P. Jones has earned renown as a writer of consummate understatement, control, and unflinching honesty, even as his range extends from the intense ode-like
short stories in his collection Lost in the City *(1992)*
to the Miltonic scope of his novel The Known World
*(2003). His prose style is often so clean as to appear initially neutral, and
yet the cumulative effect is that of an interrogation; Jones tests our moral
hesitancies until we are surprised to find ourselves in an epistemological
corral of our own reckoning.*

Set in Washington, D.C., Lost in the City *forsakes the corridors of
power to funnel the reader through a peripatetic tour of D.C.'s most in-*

digent neighborhoods, its denizens trapped black Washingtonians who cling to their humanity while sometimes questioning the dubious gift of it. In The Known World, *Jones's canvas is grander and his sense of irony keener. The novel begins with the death of Henry Townsend, a black slaveholder in pre–Civil War Virginia whose life and death become a manifest for slavery's more absurdist particularities. Through the novel's scores of characters, Jones artfully widens the focus from race onto all of mankind, suggesting that the question of slavery is the ultimate litmus test of any civilization.*

Jones was born and raised in Washington, D.C., received his B.A. from the College of the Holy Cross in Worcester, Massachusetts, and his M.F.A. from the University of Virginia, Charlottesville. Jones was short-listed for the 1992 National Book Award for Lost in the City, *which went on to win the PEN/Hemingway Award for that year. In 2003, Jones was again shortlisted for the National Book Award, this time for* The Known World, *which went on to win the National Book Critics Circle Award and the Pulitzer Prize. He is a recent recipient of the MacArthur Foundation "genius grant."*

This interview took place over the course of two long phone conversations.

—*Z.Z.P. (Spring 2005)*

I. "MAYBE I'LL WRITE A STORY WHERE A MOTHER JUST ABANDONS HER CHILDREN, BUT I'D HAVE TO DIG DEEP TO CREATE HER. IT'D BE LIKE WRITING A STORY WHERE A HUMAN BEING DECIDES TO EAT ANOTHER HUMAN BEING."

ZZ PACKER: I remember a certain writer came to Iowa to read, and he was praising your collection *Lost in the City*, but he also said, "It's remarkable, he got through a collection of stories and there wasn't one white person in it."

EDWARD P. JONES: How many black people are in Heming-way's stories? How many black people are in Chekhov stories? If there are no Martians in the world you live in, why should you be condemned for writing stories with no Martians?

ZZP: A kind of unconscious racism.

EPJ: One reviewer condemned me for not having many men in *Lost in the City*. People get up in the morning and the world is horrible for them, so they have to find a way to take it out on somebody else. It's as if, if you're an atheist, you have to find your religion by beating up on other people's religion.

ZZP: Family, as a structure, dominates both *Lost in the City* and *The Known World,* particularly the devastating effects of its absence. In what way did your portrayal of families in *The Known World* and *Lost in the City* come from your sense of family and how you grew up?

EPJ: I try to make everything up, but I was quite aware growing up that my father wasn't around. I remember one night when I was in high school; we used to take the trash can and put it up on a table because the mice would get into the trash can at night and cause a ruckus… so we set it up there [on the table], but in the middle of the night one night, the trash can fell and we thought someone had broken into the place. I got up and got this little vase to go out there, and my sister was behind me and my mother was behind her, and I remember thinking, "This is what a father is supposed to be doing—protecting his family." That was the best example of that, but there are probably many others that I've since forgotten.

ZZP: There are quite a few dead mothers in your stories. I'm thinking of "The Girl Who Raised Pigeons," "Young Lions," "A Rich Man"—

EPJ: My mother died when I was twenty-four. After that I thought, "God, I don't know what would have happened to me and my sister if she had died when we were kids." Maybe

THE BELIEVER BOOK OF WRITERS TALKING TO WRITERS

we would have gone to live with an aunt in Brooklyn. There were times when I was a child and she was very ill, and it was a scary thing—there was no one else in Washington that would have taken us in. And probably, though it's not on any conscious level, that's in the back of my mind, and I'm sure it comes up in the work.

But sometimes the mother has to be out of the equation. In order to get where you're going people have to be sacrificed... Being the kind of person I am, the way I lean is toward the great tragedy of life being the loss of a mother.

My own mother died January 1, 1975. Then my father died that March. I was in Philadelphia and didn't learn about it [my father's death] until a couple of months later. Not until my sister and her new baby came down in May and went to where my father had lived; the woman my father lived with said he'd died.

I was glad I hadn't been close to him. I don't think I could have taken two losses in such a short time.

ZZP: How often did you end up seeing him?

EPJ: Over the years, he and I had twenty visits. In '65, we went to visit my aunt in Brooklyn. We came back and my mother had moved. But none of us had telephones and my mother couldn't read or write. Luckily we'd found out she'd moved into this place around the corner; they had condemned the place we'd lived in, so she had to move. We lived in one room and there was a hole in it—you could literally see up to the second floor. We could see the light, we could see the *ceiling* of the second floor. So my mother had moved around the corner to a tiny room. The locks were flimsy and people were always stealing stuff from her. God knows how we all slept those nights in that tiny room. My aunt took it upon herself to find us a new place and went out and saw this place on N Street, and it looked fine, so she said we should live there. Well, it was diagonally across from where my father was living. And mother didn't want to do it, but we were in dire straits and so we moved there. So for several years we lived across the street from him.

ZZP: Did you talk to him? Did it feel odd, after not having had regular contact with him for so long?

EPJ: I went over a few times and talked to him. I was in high school, so in a certain sense he was just a person across the street. Before then, we'd spoken maybe ten times.

He knew absolutely nothing about my life. I didn't go and share anything about my life with him—it would have been like sharing my life with a stranger. If my mother had been the kind of person like my father, who just up and left, I don't know what would have happened to us. So I guess I was writing "The Girl Who Raised Pigeons" with that in mind. The father is alone on the street, and his baby girl can't talk, so the father could have up and left.

Maybe I'll write a story where a mother just abandons her children, but I'd have to dig deep to create her. It'd be like writing a story where a human being decides to eat another human being.

ZZP: In "The First Day," a young girl discovers that her mother is illiterate. You said your own mother couldn't read or write.

EPJ: I saw how hard she was struggling, so I always endeavored to be a good kid, a good student. One of the things I was doing early on was reading comic books; then I graduated on to books. A lot of it came from this understanding that we had that she wanted me to get the most education that I possibly could. [*Starts laughing*] I remember once she came home with this paperback some customer of hers had left at the restaurant. On the cover there was the back of a woman, naked, down about to her waist, and there was a man embracing her.

She didn't know what it was about. She just knew it had words and she wanted me to be involved with words. And she knew I read a lot, and here was another book she could help me have. It wasn't a memorable book, and it didn't have much sex in it, either.

ZZP: When did you discover that your mother couldn't read? Did you ever find yourself in a role of translating for her?

EPJ: Well, I remember when I was very young; my brother was retarded and he lived with us until I was about four—he was a year younger than me. A letter came from the court system, but she couldn't read, so she had to find somebody there to tell her what it was about. The letter said they were taking my brother and putting him in an institution.

ZZP: How often did you see him?

EPJ: We would go out to this place in Laurel, Maryland, at least once a month, sometimes every third week.

ZZP: You were homeless once. Can you talk about what that was like?

EPJ: It wasn't for very long: it was in '76. After my mother died I went to Philadelphia, then I came back [to D.C]. I stayed in this mission downtown. You could get a room free for the night if you listened to this religious stuff. A lot of singing and all that. When you're faced with being out on the street versus a cot in a room with about fifty other men, you sort of choose the latter.

ZZP: What got you out of that?

EPJ: I'd written to my sister and asked her to send me fifteen bucks for the Trailways bus up to Brooklyn. I was going to stay with her. I thought maybe my chances would be better up there.

So my sister sent the money, but that week I got the job at *Science* magazine, and the people in Philadelphia finally forwarded one piece of mail that *Essence* magazine had sent—

ZZP: And that was the first piece that you'd ever published, right? In *Essence*?

EPJ: Yeah. All that happened in one week.

ZZP: What was the story called?

EPJ: "Harvest." My sister for a long time had been getting *Essence* and I would read the stories every month. And I thought, "God, these stories are horrible!" So when I was in Philadelphia, I wrote that story and sent it off. And a year later they were going to publish it.

ZZP: Was that the first time you considered yourself a writer?

EPJ: No. After it came out, I still had the job at *Science* magazine and George Washington University had this thing where writers can teach a course to people with regular day jobs. So I went to a writer's house—Susan Shreve's—and did the writing thing.

ZZP: I wonder if there was pressure to be something other than a writer. Weren't you a tax analyst for quite some time after *Lost in the City*?

EPJ: I got a job after graduate school, and my heart was never really in it, but I had to have a place to live and something to eat. It was a nonprofit organization called Tax Analysts, and they were publishing this esoteric magazine for tax accounts and lawyers. I would summarize two or three pages out of a hundred-twenty pages of really dense stuff—court opinions, tax regulations, articles on taxes. I'd summarize stuff from *BusinessWeek*, the *Times*, the *Washington Post*, the *Wall Street Journal*, things like that. Then I did the same thing for two other magazines on insurance and tax-exempt organizations. But my heart wasn't in it.

ZZP: And you were writing while you were doing that?

EPJ: Off and on. I was never one to get up and do it every day. I suppose thinking of it should also be counted as working.

II. "PEOPLE ARE STILL PEOPLE. AND THEY NEVER IMPROVE."

ZZP: Even before reading *The Known World*, I feared for you because of the possible response; I feared other black readers would be upset by the premise of the novel. Were you ever fearful about such a backlash from black readers? Or providing ammunition for certain white readers?

EPJ: No, I suppose I was kind of blinded. I learned about the black slaveholders when I was in college. It's a known fact—well, a little-known fact, and I think that the fact that there were such people gave me license to create this fiction. If there were no black people in this country whatsoever that owned slaves, then I wouldn't have felt that I could write this. I never thought at all about people coming along and hating what I'd written because it was a fact. People have to live with what was factual and what was real. And that's what I would have thought if people had come along and said something [negative].

I didn't want to give ammunition to the antireparations people, and I did mention that in a letter to my editor—but in the end reparations is not based on a certain people giving to another people—the concept addresses the entire system—no matter who profited from it. This [*The Known World*] was just one more weapon in the hands of those people. But reparations addresses slavery [in general], not the fact that there were white people who owned black people.

ZZP: Did *The Known World* come about as a particular interest in an anomaly, or did it arise from an interest in the universality of what any slaveholder represents: a capitulation to a system in which humans are bought and sold?

EPJ: Yeah. I think I sort of started out with the intention of writing about the slaves who were owned by Henry Townsend; I was going to focus exclusively on those people. Because when you're a storyteller you're trying to come at the story from a different angle. So I decided to go at it from that angle. In all the novels that are written about slavery, all the writers that went up to the "house of slavery" went in the front door, which is black and white with no shades of gray in sight; and I just decided to go at it from the side, and open a door that hadn't really been opened very often, and that was the door involving black slaveholders.

Again, when you're a storyteller, you try to be different, fresh, even if ultimately, of course, we're all dealing with the same issues anyway. People in *The Known World* are doing the same things people said and did five thousand years ago. People are still people. And they never improve. [*Laughs*]

ZZP: I like what you're saying about going around through the side door; it does seem as though when we write historical novels, we feel as though we have to write the story that is going to validate the conditions of our ancestors. But writing more obliquely and less directly seems to be the project of fiction, to tell the ultimate truth rather than just the facts. And perhaps we're less likely to fall back on received wisdom—

EPJ: Yes. Henry Townsend says he's going to be a better master than any white master has ever been. But in the end, he's blind to the fact—the way all the white masters have been blind to the fact—that slavery affects everyone who participates in it. And it's important that he's black, but in the end it's the same old thing. The same old crime.

ZZP: The protagonist Henry grows in thrall to his white master and the power his master wields, but Moses, Henry's slave, never imagines that he could have a black master. Moses eventually begins to want to replace Henry, to be a black master as Henry was—to own slaves himself.

EPJ: The thing about Moses is that, chronologically, the first time you meet him he's radically different from the Moses you get at the end: he's been chained to this woman Betsy, and he's talking about them being one and them not being separated, and through the end he's gone through any number of things that makes him the kind of man who throws his family away. He goes from being a man who believes in family to a man who feels he can get on top by throwing his family away.

ZZP: That loss of family seems to presage the destruction of the community at large. Is this deliberate?

EPJ: Yeah. My editor, Dawn Davis, came back with some very minor suggestions about the manuscript of *The Known World*, which allowed me to go back over the manuscript once again and do some other things.

In the second go-round, I was interested in how people had survived slavery, and I realized that one thing that helped people was that they had family—at the very center of that idea was Elias [one of Henry's slaves]. Here was a single-minded man who had one thought: to be free. He never intended to be close to any human being on that plantation; he wanted to run away and be free. But then, through circumstances, he falls in love with this woman who's crippled and cannot run [away with him]. Then, through his love for her and the family they create, he finds a different kind of freedom.

ZZP: So there are characters who have family, and they survive. What about the people who didn't have family?

EPJ: One of the characters, Stamford, doesn't have family, but he's redeemed because he begins to care about others being redeemed, and in a certain sense he finds a family, which is not what he'd been doing all his life when he was chasing after what I call "young stuff." So once he finds a family in a certain sense, the children—he has an affinity for children—he's redeemed. The people who have a family or develop one are the ones who're ultimately saved.

III. "ABOUT EVERY CHARACTER IN [*LOST IN THE CITY*] IS A GIRL OR A WOMAN, AND I ENVISIONED THE COLLECTION AS GOING FROM BIRTH TO OLD AGE. I WANTED TO GO FROM AN INFANT TO AN OLD WOMAN."

ZZP: Back to *Lost in the City*. In "The Girl Who Raised Pigeons," the father, Robert, finally comes home with his infant daughter after his wife's death. The kids playing on the street know enough to respect his grief. We see these little kids who are poor behaving with dignity and respect—reverence—something that seems missing from the images we see of blacks today. In your stories a number of people have that high level of consciousness despite their poverty.

EPJ: I lived on a street like that. An era when people talked about that maxim "It takes a village to raise a child." Adults looked out for kids who weren't even in their families. And I was really conscious of how all that ended. When those people had to move out of that neighborhood. Because, as I show in the story, it obliterated the neighborhood.

And also, all the adults I knew growing up were born and raised in the South, and they came to the city with a sense of community, of looking out for each other when they came to the North. After one, two, three generations, it's gone. Nowadays you don't dare chastise some child out there in the street that's doing something wrong, but when I was growing up it was all right, some kid would do something wrong and get a spanking by somebody in the neighborhood, then when his parents came home and found out, he'd get another spanking. But all that went away. For some reason.

ZZP: For what reasons?

EPJ: Drugs. Even though the Civil Rights era came along, things didn't improve the way we needed them to improve. We didn't have any money, but it was just a nicer world.

ZZP: In "Marie," the eponymous character is part of that old community. I love the phrase Marie repeats to herself after she's slapped a rather saucy, ineffectual bureaucrat: "You whatn't raised that way." Though the story is contemporary, Marie herself absolutely hearkens back to that pre–Civil Rights era.

EPJ: About every character in that collection is a girl or a woman, and I envisioned the collection as going from birth to old age. I wanted to go from an infant to an old woman.

ZZP: I thought it was really wonderful to show a range of women; I think a lot of men shy away from writing about women, as though it might be beneath them to write about the lives of women. I suspect many men wouldn't admit they thought that way, or even suspect they thought that way.

EPJ: Well, I don't know where they're living.

ZZP: Do you think the black community has gotten to the point where we can write about that loss of dignity you spoke of— abandoning the fairy tale idea of always uplifting, but not, perhaps, recording reality? I'm thinking of Zora Neale Hurston, who wrote using folklore and anthropological observations and the Gulf dialect of Florida blacks—and then Richard Wright says blacks shouldn't write in dialect, that it doesn't uplift the "Negro community."

EPJ: People can write it, but whether or not anyone will ever get a chance to read it—given what publishers want to publish nowadays—is doubtful. And the fact that fewer and fewer people are reading. I mean, you can go forth to the typical black teenager nowadays and they might not be able to name five writers born before 1950, but you ask them about the history of some rap star and they know all about it.

Writers, of course, have always done whatever they wanted to do: the problem is that a lot of people have not wanted to publish them. The range is now so narrow. I don't know if I would be the kind of person I am now if that was all there was to read.

ZZP: I guess I'm saying that Wright's idea was that "Negro writing" had to uphold the race—

EPJ: You have an obligation to tell the truth. I remember when I was thinking about the girl who raised pigeons and her father, and I was writing during a time when more and more stuff was coming out about how bad black men were.

As the story develops, he remains with this child: he becomes a father—but I realize that if the story I was working out in my head had him look down in that carriage and walk away, then that's what I would have had to do as a storyteller. It's good to do things that uphold the race, but sometimes a storyteller has to go down a different path.

But the reaction of black people [to *The Known World*] has been 99 percent positive. Only one or two examples come to mind when that hasn't been the case. Any negative reaction is by people who haven't read the book. "You have to keep in mind that black families who owned slaves often bought their own families…" Well, if this cat had read the book, he would have known I'd written that in the first few pages.

A white woman in Fairfax, Virginia, said, "I've read Toni Morrison, and I wonder where you did the research on how people talk." Essentially she was saying the black people in *The Known World* talk too intelligently. I didn't mention Jebediah who's *I ain't dis, I ain't dere* all over the place; but he's smart enough to know how to get under the skin of Fern Elston, who thinks she knows more than anybody else.

A writer can't sit down and think about what everyone else is going to think—I never thought about what someone in Jackson, Mississippi, might think, or someone in Oakland, California. When I sat down to write *The Known World,* I had only one reader in mind: myself. I was trying to make it as good as I possibly could. So it's best not to sit down and anticipate the reaction down the line. You have to just tell the truth as you know it.

ZZP: Many of the reviews of *The Known World* remark that it is a difficult book to enter, but that once you get going, the reader becomes accustomed to your almost Biblical tone. I found it to be almost the opposite; we're lured in by beautifully written prose that at first appears to be third person, from Henry's slave Moses' point of view, but we soon find ourselves in a kind of naked, objective omniscience that's so unsettling because it's *so* objective, forcing the reader to provide her own moral yardstick. We have to confront ourselves and our own prejudices when we're reading this. Is that lack of commentary your way of forcing the reader to come to her own conclusions?

EPJ: No, I can't say I thought about that, actually. The one notion that I did have was that I was going to be writing such a horrendous story that had its own emotional charge that I didn't need to come along and provide what I often call "neon language." I mean, the thing that you write about in such novels is how people suffered in slavery. The grownfolks. And the children, as well. Everyone, everyone [suffered]. The story itself was emotional enough that all I had to do was simply report.

I was influenced when I was in grad school—twenty-five years before I even thought about writing this book—by this Bible as Literature course. I'd never really read the Bible all the way through like that. The Bible we read was the Jerusalem Bible, which is the Catholic Bible. There was a lot of objective prose throughout that. I remember in particular the description of Jonah in the belly of the whale—it was just flat-out reporting, you know, a sense of "these are the facts." And your heart breaks for the man, without the writer ever injecting any sort of commentary whatsoever.

ZZP: That reportorial device strikes me as very Old Testament, where we get all those stories like those about Jeremiah and Jonah, as opposed to the New Testament, which becomes more parable-based.

EPJ: Yeah. Well, I knew the kind of story I would be telling and wanted to do that with straight flat prose. And I think I tend to do that with everything I do, simply because of the kinds of people I'm writing about. These are not people who go into an antique store and think that their lives are going to end because they don't find the right table. These are people with real problems.

ZZP: Fern, a black schoolteacher, and William Robbins, Henry's former master, inculcate in Henry certain ideas about what it means to be a property owner. Their characters seem to suggest that evil requires a model, that we perhaps need to visualize evil as normal before we can become primed to adopt a system like slavery. Were you thinking of these characters in these terms—as models?

EPJ: Henry's problem is that during his formative years, his only influence was William Robbins, because his parents could only come once a week, and there were many times when they weren't even allowed to see him, or times when Henry wouldn't show up when they came to visit.

And Fern, she realizes that her soul is doomed, but she's standing at the gate—and doing all she shouldn't be doing, nevertheless.

ZZP: I kept envisioning Fern as a Condoleezza Rice character.

EPJ: I was intrigued in the 1980s by all the black conservatives coming out of the woodwork, and they were parroting Reagan's line, "It's morning in America," and that essentially racism was dead, and we all could be judged on what we do with our lives and not the color of our skin, but we know, day after day, that people are still being oppressed. Every other month, I read in the *Washington Post* how testers will go to apartment buildings and see if they'll be rented to, and you find out that black people are still being discriminated against.

Those are the kinds of people who—along with the rappers and all those violent sports players—who, if slavery were legal, would own slaves.

IV. "IF YOU CAN'T WRITE THE PROPAGANDA, THEN YOU AT LEAST SUPPLY THE SAND- WICH FOR THE PERSON WHO WRITES THE PROPAGANDA. YOU CAN AT LEAST EMPTY THE TRASH CANS—WE ALL HAVE TO DO WHAT WE'RE ABLE."

ZZP: I remember reading an interview with E. Annie Proulx where she said that all of the books she'd written were like these parcels that had been delivered to her, wrapped in brown paper, and that all she had to do was unwrap them, so that essentially, when she sits down to write, it feels as though all she has to do is take dictation. Is that what it's like for you?

EPJ: Yeah. It felt that way. It's like taking dictation from yourself.

ZZP: That's sort of scary to me. I don't quite understand that.

EPJ: You've written it out in your head, so it's Annie Proulx tak- ing dictation from Annie Proulx. I was afraid you were going to ask—what is it that people say? [*Begins talking in a whiny author Q & A voice*] "I just sit down and my characters take over..." I think that's such crap! My answer to that is, if all you have to do is let your characters take over, then I guess you can go out, watch three or four movies, then come back and the work is all done! The "characters" have done it.

ZZP: Well, I find that when I'm writing there's a back and forth process—I'll think, then I'll write some, then what I've written influences the next train of thought, and so on. It seems as though people like you and Annie Proulx are doing a lot of that back and forth work in your heads. Do you think that comes from having an extraordinarily analytical mind?

EPJ: I don't know what kind of mind I have, but I tell students that if you're driving (I don't drive) on the Baltimore-Washington Expressway, and if your plan is to end up in Baltimore, and you start off at twelve noon, you might see a road sign for a town you've never heard of, ever. And that is the detour in the writing. The final chapter will never change substantially, but there are detours before you get to that final chapter that are surprises. So you end up visiting this town and end up including something about it that you hadn't prepared for.

ZZP: I remember hearing Leon Uris talk about writing that way. He compared it to setting sail on the open seas, but having a destination port... have you written a story in which the destination was one place and the story ended up in a completely different place?

EPJ: No. Generally not. You're always learning how to do this writing stuff... you work it out—the beginning, the middle and the end—in your head, and you go over it. And that's what happened to me with *The Known World*. I went over it all those years in my head, trying to make sure one chapter led logically to the next chapter. So it was as well laid out as I could possibly get it. So when I actually wrote it, there weren't too many substantial changes. A few things here and there.

ZZP: At the end of "A Rich Man" Horace ends up on his apartment floor, going through all those records that have been smashed by the young people who started crashing at his retirement home apartment. I love the ending, but it's very strange—it's just the names of all those albums: "I'm Gonna Pin a Medal on the Girl I Left Behind." "Ragtime Soldier Man." "Whose Little Heart Are You Breaking Now?" "The Syncopated Waltz."
    I was wondering, was it a matter of starting at the end, knowing here's a man who's going to arrive at this complete dissolu-

tion, or did you actually have an image, specifically, of those broken records?

EPJ: No. I think what had happened was that I could see these two people married for a long time, and they were living in this small space together, and yet they were living separate lives, and I just decided to provide what would happen before then and what was going to happen afterwards.

I do remember actually listening to those records. The penultimate one ["Whose Little Heart Are You Breaking Now?"] said something directly about the entire story: the final one was vague like all the others were. One of the copy editors at the *New Yorker* wanted me to move that one to the end, but I didn't want that. I didn't want the very last one to say anything directly like that.

I tend to collect things. I have this great interest in stuff that's old and in the years before I was born; what records looked like, what the world looked like back then. Time-Life had a series where they did a decade of the twentieth century, and I was able to find this 1920s one. And I remember thinking, *which one should be first on the list and which one should be last?*

ZZP: What kinds of things do you end up collecting?

EPJ: I have a great many 33 $^1/_3$ records that I've picked up since the late '60s. A lot of the things I've been interested in collecting have been speeches. I have Elijah Muhammad; I have a great one by Eldridge Cleaver. I think he's speaking extemporaneously at Syracuse University in 1968. It's just great. He engages the audience and he's funny a lot of the time.

I think I have Jesse Jackson, W. E. B. DuBois speaking sometime in the '50s, a couple of tapes by Lenny Bruce, Dick Gregory…

ZZP: You sort of remind me of James Alan McPherson, with his vast archive of speeches.

EPJ: He had lots. I wish I could get copies of what he has.

ZZP: I know he makes copies of tapes. He's always giving them to me. He'll give me a tape, and I'll ask if he wants them back and he'll say, "Keep it, keep it," but he'll lose one of the copies, and I end up sending them back to him.

EPJ: ... Angela Davis. I have this great one with James Baldwin talking, too—

ZZP: How long ago was that before his death?

EPJ: I think it may have been the '70s. I found it in a remainders bin. Brand-new when I got it. I think it was in Charlottesville. The ones from the '50s and '60s are just great. But that one from Cleaver is just wonderful. At that time I think Huey Newton was in jail and Cleaver's going through this whole thing about the political system, and Averell Harriman—Harriman was part of the Vietnam negotiations at that time in '68. [Cleaver would say] "He's a liar, he's a liar…" When he comes out of the place where they're negotiating, he says, "Oh, they just won't talk right." And goes on: "He's a liar, he's a liar." Both sides of this album, he has this joke, then a standard line, "All power to the people, peace and freedom power to the peace and freedom people. Black Panther Party, power to the Black Panther Party." It's just really moving in certain places. I was very enamored of the Black Panthers, the black power movement.

ZZP: Did you ever think you would join the Panthers?

EPJ: There wasn't a Panther office in Worcester. And I had so many other things to take care of.

You see these black people now, and they have their nice cars and their nice clothes and everything, but you can see a sort of emptiness. It reminds me of something Maya Angelou said, maybe twenty-five years ago, about people being "exiled to *things*."

ZZP: Yes. It's as though we can't escape naked materialism. People talk about America losing some sort of moral center, and politicians are taking advantage of that fear.

EPJ: I don't remember when the great force of the anti–Vietnam War movement started, but now we've got Iraq. By this time with Vietnam, there was a great movement out there already. Right now there are people protesting who are antiwar, but there's not the great force that there was with the Vietnam War—and these [Republican] politicians who come along and just out-and-out lie about the situation, coming out and calling the AARP pro-gay, and antisoldier—and no one will deign to call them on it!

ZZP: Perhaps people feel the need to get back to something basic, but it seems like those people aren't realizing that they're being told they can't dissent or criticize—

EPJ: If you even *look* in a particular direction, then you're accused of being on the wrong side. If they continue to get away with it, then before you know it, it's going to get worse and worse.

ZZP: Many writers suspect that being a [fiction] writer has nothing to do with the political world, that their writing isn't going to change anything. Do you ever feel that same sense of frustration?

EPJ: Of not doing enough?

ZZP: Yeah, or feeling that what you're doing as a writer doesn't directly address what's going on.

EPJ: Sometimes, but I know there's not very much that I can do. When I write fiction it's far removed from everyday events. But you are a certain kind of person: you believe in a certain kind of right, no matter what, so when you're writing, the everyday world is consciously on your mind, so what you know as being right seeps into the writing nevertheless.

ZZP: But do you think that ends up changing people?

EPJ: I don't know. I don't think anyone will read what I write and think, "I should be more involved with the world around me." So you have to do what you can do in other ways. If you can't write the propaganda, then you at least supply the sandwich for the person who writes the propaganda. You can at least empty the trash cans—we all have to do what we're able.

I never set out to write an antislavery novel, even though of course I'm fiercely against it, but my beliefs come out in everything I'm writing.

V. "I DON'T HAVE ANYTHING TO SAY, SO I DON'T THINK PEOPLE SHOULD SPEND THEIR TIME TRYING TO GET ME TO SAY ANYTHING."

ZZP: One of those typical questions: do you have any particular writing routine?

EPJ: No, not really. I get up and fix coffee. I don't even really like coffee, but I've found that psychologically, I wake up more with it, just the smell. And I just start writing.

I have a bit of music that I always use. For about 95 percent of *The Known World* I used this tape—and again, this is the physical writing, not the mental—I had copied, six times in a row, Judy Collins singing, "That's No Way to Say Goodbye," then after that I taped the opening credits to Paul Newman's movie *The Life and Times of Judge Roy Bean*. They're both quite moving pieces and rather melancholy. There's something in listening to those pieces that helps me do what I have to do.

I was plagued—from 1999 until last year—by the people living above me who didn't put carpeting down, so my niece gave me a Walkman, and when I was up in the mornings, I had the headphones on, and the tape lasted for a half hour—first the Judy Collins was on for six times, then the movie music from *Judge Roy Bean,* then, when it was finished, I would get up and walk around while the tape rewound.

I paid a friend of mine to tape the movie on a cassette back and front and Judy Collins back and front, so now, rather than waiting about four minutes for the tape to rewind, I can just flip it over. [*Laughs*]

ZZP: I can't listen to songs with lyrics while I'm writing. Do you ever find that you get distracted by the words?

EPJ: The words don't bother me. They become a part of me.

ZZP: There's a song on a Branford Marsalis album, a chain gang song, "Berta, Berta," that I listen to while working on this novel. It might be from Albert Murray's *Train, Whistle Guitar*. Then again, I think it's August Wilson's *The Piano Lesson*—anyway, it completely makes the mood.

EPJ: Certain chords kind of transport you. Then all of a sudden, the scene you're working out is there. They may not be the songs the characters would listen to.

ZZP: I mentioned Albert Murray; did you read him at all, growing up? Who'd you end up reading?

EPJ: There's so many… I can remember reading McPherson when I was in college. I remember it was a black paperback and the letters *Hue and Cry* were in orange. And on the back he's there with a little picture, and he's in a pea coat. And I remember thinking, "Wow, this guy looks like me!" That's the sort of thing that gives you hope.

ZZP: I have an old *Hue and Cry* with that picture. It's a handsome picture.

EPJ: It was only a few years before that when I was reading *Invisible Man*. I was never thinking I would be a writer: I didn't grow up with that idea in my head, but I would be reading *Invisible Man*, and there was a picture of Ellison on the back, and I would come to a nice passage, turn the book over, and say, "you wrote that." Then I would turn back and go on with the story.

ZZP: Do you read any of your reviews? After a certain point do you stop reading them?

EPJ: Everything came in before this prize thing. Luckily nothing has been very mean.

ZZP: It seems as though writers are increasingly asked to be public figures, or a part of a scene—the conferences and the festivals and the parties—do you end up participating in any of that?

EPJ: I try to stick to the readings. I tell them I don't want to be at some faculty cocktail party; they insist on having those for some reason. I try to read student manuscripts. I read eight manuscripts at the University of Minnesota. I'll go to a class or hold individual conferences. I'll spend a half hour or more with each individual student.

ZZP: That's incredibly generous.

EPJ: I don't want to read and just leave. People invite you to read, and if you're raised a certain way, the least you can do is be a good guest. The last thing I like to do is go to these cocktail parties and schmooze around with a glass of wine or ginger ale and talk.

I'm much better in life when I have a script. You read. You answer questions. You read student manuscripts. You sit down and you talk with them and give them your opinion, however small it might be. But going to a cocktail party or somebody's house for dinner—there's no script there. I can't—I'm not comfortable living my life like that. I'm not much of a social person.

ZZP: Perhaps you'd be more comfortable if there were some sort of purpose to those parties besides the schools showing you off to the benefactors.

EPJ: Yeah, I don't have anything to say, so I don't think people should spend their time trying to get me to say anything.

ZZP: You were sued recently by a woman who claimed you'd shown up at her family reunion and stolen information from her to write *The Known World*.

EPJ: Well, I'm not a social enough person to go to anybody's reunion. The lawyer said she had some pamphlet about her ancestors, and she says I *leafed through it* and got all my ideas. Like, "The ground was soaked with rain," and "the people talked all night and all day." Those are the quotes in my book that I supposedly got from her. [*Laughs*]

It's just so far off the wall. She's reluctant to produce whatever it is she's written.

ZZP: You're working on short stories now?

EPJ: About fourteen of them. I have about two or three left to do [for a collection]. So that's what I'll use the summer for. I've been thinking about them since the mid-'90s, thinking, thinking, thinking, and now I'm getting around to them.

ZZP: How long does it take once you finally decide you're going to write them?

EPJ: It could be weeks. I don't think I ever do anything in less than a week.

ZZP: Some people will take a whole year.

EPJ: If you're doing so many things—if you know you have to get up and go, like I've had to do for quite some time, you can't really relax. But when I can relax…

ZZP: Do you find that people treat you differently after your having won the Pulitzer?

EPJ: People ask if I'm happy about this and that, especially when they talk about the money. I am happy, but there's no car in the world I want—I don't want a car—there are places I want to go, but I'm not hungry to do world travel. There's no fancy house that I want.

I got some crabs the other week, twelve crabs, and that's a feast. That's wonderful. That makes me happy.

I was in graduate school, and I was rooming at this place the first year and we all shared the same bathroom. After I moved I wrote to this one friend of mine, "Finally I got a bathroom all to myself." He said I'd probably always be happy because there were small things that made me happy.

I remember when that basketball player Len Bias died of a cocaine overdose. Now, he's from Maryland, he should have gone right down to the crab-house, bought twelve crabs and an orange soda, and that would have fulfilled him. Why didn't he do that? ✶

ROBERT BIRNBAUM

JAMAICA KINCAID

"I HAD THIS EXPERIENCE WHEN
I WAS THIRTEEN YEARS OLD OR SO,
OF MY MOTHER BURNING MY BOOKS.
I DIDN'T UNDERSTAND AT THE TIME
THAT IT WAS A FAIRLY PROFOUND
THING TO DO TO SOMEONE."

Phrases that take up precious space:
"Really?"
"She said that?"
"He said…"
"I was wondering…"

J amaica Kincaid was born on Antigua, on May 25, 1949, as Elaine Potter Richardson. She was educated in colonial British schools, and in 1965, at the age of sixteen, she was sent to Westchester, New York, to work as a servant. She briefly attended Franconia College in New Hampshire, and her interest in photography led her to New York City and the New School for Social Research. Through some fortuitous circumstances she was befriended by New Yorker writer George W. S. Trow, who introduced her to legendary editor William Shawn. Shawn began publishing Kincaid in the New Yorker's "Talk of the Town" section and encouraged her writing. As Kincaid now recalls, "He always made you think you were the best *writer of all. He was an unbelievable suitor."*

In his introduction to Kincaid's collection of "Talk of the Town" pieces, her good friend and colleague during her tenure at the New Yorker, Ian Frazier, *writes:*

> *A lot of the exhilaration of those years for me was in seeing who could be the bravest, who could be the coolest. I kept a mental score-card of brave and cool deeds: I saw* New Yorker *veterans… come in to the office an hour or two before an issue's deadline and in one draft turn out "Talk of the Town" stories as elegant and effortless as a Will Rogers roper trick… but to me nobody was braver than Jamaica. She didn't try to be shocking or "transgressive" or audacious, those imitations of bravery done mainly for effect: her bravery was just the way she was and it came natural and uninterrupted from inside.*

Jamaica Kincaid, who adopted that name to distance herself from her Antiguan family's disapproval of her writing, has published widely in different narrative forms: four novels, Annie John *(1985),* Lucy *(1990),* The Autobiography of My Mother *(1996), and* Mr. Potter *(2002); a story collection,* At the Bottom of the River *(1984), which contains the highly regarded "Girl"; a book-length essay about Antigua titled* A Small Place *(1988), an illustrated children's story with Eric Fischl called* Annie, Gwen, Lilly, Pam and Tulip *(1986); a memoir about her youngest sibling who died of AIDS in 1996,* My Brother *(1997); a collection of writing on gardening* My Garden (Book) *(1999); and an anthology of her* New Yorker *"Talk of the Town" pieces,* Talk Stories *(2001).*

During my phone conversation with Kincaid to arrange our interview, the discussion drifted to our parental responsibilities (she is the mother of Annie Shawn, twenty, and Harold, sixteen) and how they require us to turn our attention to films such as X-Men *and* The Matrix. *In her sweet, girlish, lilting voice, she confessed she was slightly embarrassed by two things: She likes* The Matrix *and she likes* Eminem.

This interview took place on a sunny day at Kincaid's spacious brown clapboard house near Bennington College in Vermont. Nestled on a gentle rise, the house is surrounded on all sides by her plantings. A brief tour revealed her current fascination with mottled red-brown plants and a digression into the difference between "mottled" and "dappled." Identifying one lilac tree, multiple rose bushes, tulips, and a young magnolia tree was the extent of my knowledge of horticultural taxonomy, but it was clear even to my uninformed eye that Kincaid's garden is a separate and complicated universe.

—R.B. (Spring 2003)

I. WHO WAS I THAT I WROTE THAT?

ROBERT BIRNBAUM: A number of people have pointed me to something you wrote years ago, "Girl." It's usually referred to as a short story, but when I came across it in John D'Agata's anthology, *The Next American Essay,* I read it as a prose poem.

JAMAICA KINCAID: [*Laughs*]

RB: What is your sense of it?

JK: I'm kind of stunned. I'd written it as a short story, and when I wrote it I was just beginning to write, and I was convinced that the way people wrote short stories was outmoded, that it was a silly way to write. That the idea of a narrative with a beginning, a middle, and an end, and a "he said," "she said," was ridiculous. I was very young when I thought this. I no longer do.

I no longer care what people do. But I had this idea. I was at the *New Yorker* and I used to come across these stories of people's ennui, young people having all these [*In a small mocking voice*] "Well, I don't know," "Why should I," "He said," and "I was wondering"'s. I just hated that kind of writing, and I was determined that I was just going to stamp it out. I literally thought that I would write things and that the people who wrote these silly [*Returns to mocking voice*] "I don't know, we were driving up in our old Volkswagen bus..." and all this kind of crap, once they saw a story like "Girl," would go [*Sigh*], "Oh," and they would stop writing. Or they would write something wonderful. Well, not only did none of this happen... [*Laughs*]

Actually people hated my story "Girl." A lot of people liked it when they read it by itself, but when my first book of short stories came out and it was full of stories like "Girl," people just really didn't like it. I remember Anne Tyler said it was "insultingly obscure." [*Laughs*] Which I found a compliment, because I found her writing insultingly clear.

RB: [*Laughs heartily*] So there!

JK: So there! I think of it as a short story, and the kind of energy and interest and boldness I had when I was writing these things were qualities you only have when you're young. I don't feel particularly like that anymore. Absolutely, I don't feel like that anymore.

RB: No more crusading.

JK: No, not at all. Not only not crusading, but I don't really care what other people write. I don't have any theories of the Great Novel and the novel of narrative over the novel of anything. I actually love all sorts of things and see that writers are not doing anything deliberately. A person who writes like Jonathan Franzen—I don't think he can write any other way than how he writes, and it is wonderful how he writes, and there's no need to say anything about it other than you like it or you don't. All of these declarations of what writing ought to be, which I had myself—though, thank god I had never committed them to paper—I think are nonsense... You write what you write, and then either it holds up or it doesn't hold up. There are no rules or particular sensibilities. I don't believe in that at all anymore.

RB: Will you venture a guess as to what contemporary writing teachers might get out of "Girl"? It was written in 1978, a long time ago.

JK: Yes, a long time ago, and why is it still relevant? I don't know why it's relevant to anybody. I must say, when I read it myself I marvel at it in some peculiar way, and I think, "Who was I that

I wrote that? How did I know that could be done? What sensibility was I in?" And the only thing that makes me understand it somewhat is that I was at a place where, for some reason, all that I was doing at the time was interesting to the editor [William Shawn] at the magazine, and so I must have just opportunistically taken advantage of being myself. I just really was myself.

RB: You don't strike me as being able to be other than yourself.

JK: No, no. This is true: wherever I was, I was going to be myself. But at that particular place, at that time, myself was very much appreciated. Whatever I was interested these people and was very much encouraged, and even when they disapproved of it—and there were times when they disapproved of it—they just really couldn't deny that I was young and vital.

II. WRITING THE LAST SENTENCE BEFORE YOU WRITE THE FIRST

RB: When you first came to the United States, you were interested in photography, and you studied it in school. Has that gone by the wayside?

JK: No. I just bought a digital camera and I'm always fooling around with it in the garden. That will never go away.

RB: What did you take pictures of?

JK: I had an interest in photographing children. So it must be something about my own childhood. Now I photograph the garden, or I try to. And I always find that I'm lacking. I used to study photography. I used to knit seriously and sew seriously, and then when I got interested in the garden, I stopped doing all of that.

RB: You thought you wanted to write while you were studying photography, and somehow you were drawn into the wake of the *New Yorker* by some friends, including George W. S. Trow, and you started writing for "Talk of the Town," unbeknownst to you—

JK: The first thing that was published I didn't consciously write. I typed up my notes and observations and handed them to Mr. Shawn, and he published them just as I had given them to him. It was from that moment that I understood the thing that became my writing. And I remember struggling with the "we" voice; I soon stopped using it. I didn't like writing in that voice. And then I just wrote a letter from a friend. Or I would devise ways of not mentioning a person. I would invent dialogue. I would write the "Talks" story in terms of a play.

RB: There isn't much dialogue in your work, is there?

JK: No, I don't like dialogue. I don't like to hear people speaking in my work. I like reading it, and I marvel at people who can do it well. And there's something when you see it done well. It's just so terrific. But I'm not able to do it.

RB: One thing that strikes me about your writing is that it's always your voice, you talking. It's very clear.

JK: Yes, yes. That's interesting. I only have one voice; that has its limitations, no doubt. But no, I don't like dialogue. I think it's very hard to do. When you see it not done well, it's painful.

RB: As in the movies.

JK: Yes. "You mean she didn't come? Well, what did she say?" "Really?" I would never write "Really?" The idea of someone taking up that precious space by someone saying, "Really? She said that?" is just beyond me. I couldn't.

RB: But people talk like that. Some of them.

JK: They do. They do talk like that and fortunately, I don't know many of them.

RB: [*Laughs*] "Those Words That Echo… Echo… Echo Through Life," a "Writers on Writing" piece that you wrote for the *New York Times,* starts with you pondering the sentence "Mr. Potter was my father, my father's name was Mr. Potter." When I read the article, I hadn't read *Mr. Potter*—

JK: It hadn't been written yet.

RB: Isn't that sentence the last sentence of the book?

JK: That's right. I had written the last part of it before I wrote the beginning. And, you know, I have not talked about that book. I wanted to write in the middle. I wanted to begin in the middle and then I wanted to go back and then forward; it doesn't happen enough in writing, where you feel the writer's agile thinking. And I don't know that I succeed in this. I want always to write as if my brain has just woken up, because I want it to be exciting to me. The thing that keeps me writing is that it will be new. I will do something new. I don't say that I do actually do it. But the way I get myself to the typewriter is to say, "This will be new and I haven't done this before. This has not been done before." As I say, it's not true, but it's the way I do it.

RB: How do you end a book? How do you know the last sentence?

JK: Well, this is very interesting. The last story in my first book— the title story, "At the Bottom of the River"—took me six months to end. But at the end of the six months, I had not added one word. During the six months, I read "The Prelude," Wordsworth's great narrative poem. I spent six months reading it, and at the end of it I understood what I had been writing was finished. And that's almost always true of my writing. I know it's finished through some odd way, not by actually finishing it. I go over it in my mind and say, "That's the end." Because it crests in some way that satisfies me. Not that it ties things up. It just ends. You know, Dickens is Dickens. Balzac is Balzac. All sorts of things are all sorts of things. But I don't want to write that kind of great novel, the great family novel. I enjoy reading it, but I myself don't want to write it.

III. THOMAS JEFFERSON
AND HIS HYPOCRISIES

RB: When you are moved to write, when you begin, are there any boundaries at all, any parameters, anything that circumscribes what you are going to do, besides using the English language?

JK: Not as far as I can tell. You mean in terms of people's feelings?

RB: People's feelings. Length—

JK: Nothing, no. I wish I could write longer, but I can't.

RB: I think Thomas Jefferson apologized in one of his letters, saying something to the effect that if he had had more time he would have written a shorter letter.

JK: This is just another one of his many hypocrisies.

RB: [*Laughs*]

JK: Have you ever read his autobiography? It's the shortest autobiography by a great man ever. And he did have the time. Jefferson's autobiography is one of those marvelous things. Sometimes I teach a course on reading Thomas Jefferson. His autobiography is like the equivalent of one of those busts that exist of him. It is stony, compact, artful. And it says absolutely nothing about him.

RB: Iconic.

JK: An incredible work of art, when you think about it. He mentions his mother—that he was born of her. He mentions a little about his father. And then he goes on, and he wrote the Declaration of Independence. He wrote this and he wrote that. And then he went to Paris and he did this, and then it ends. Read next to something like the *Confessions* of Rousseau, it's the other extreme, where he tells you everything. And possibly none of it is true. Except that he was born. Maybe a third of it was true. And if you read it in comparison, it's fascinating. Well, anyway, that's another one of Jefferson's disingenuinities—disingenuineness?

RB: Disingenuinenesses?

JK: It's his hallmark: he's disingenuous, ambivalent, contradictory. All sorts of things that people say about Thomas Jefferson. All of them true.

RB: It would be emblematic of Enlightenment figures to think everything was possible, everything was true. Everything they said was true. Despite the contradictions.

JK: Yes, despite the contradictions. Well, I think he's just an example of a really great human being. No great person would be consistent. I think consistency is a sign of absolute stupidity and weakness. And I think our president is a good example of that consistency. This ridiculous person who doesn't—who persists no matter what.

RB: Nunnally Johnson, who wrote the screenplay for John Ford's film of *The Grapes of Wrath,* said only hacks are consistent.

JK: Oh, that's very good. Well, he's a hack, our president. Yes, I can't imagine why you would be consistent.

IV. DICKENS AND CLIMBING
THE HIMALAYAS

RB: What's the first step on the road to writing something?

JK: I never know. It really is always a revelation to me. I never know. I don't have a sketch of what it should be. I never know what will burble up. And that is, again, one of the great pleasures of just writing something. I just don't know how it will go, where it will lead. I thought *Mr. Potter* was going to be a different kind of book. And then it turned out to be what it was.

RB: What would have been a different kind of book?

JK: Well, I thought it was going to be more like a traditional book. Knowing here he is, he's growing up now, he's going to school now, and here he is putting on his shoes. And here he has made this marvelous transition from a boy to a man, through this tiny detail. And now here he is at the crossroads in his life. I thought I was going to do that. But I realized I have no interest at all in doing that. What I am always, so far, interested in is boiling it down into some essence. It's like sucking something. Or maybe like a bouillon cube. You have to add one cup of water. I don't like a cup of water. I just like the bouillon cube.

RB: [*Laughs*]

JK: So that's what it turns out to be—like the bouillon cube.

RB: In one of our email exchanges, you said something about the world not liking writers so much. This is not, as I'm sure you know, a thought held only by you. Given that other writers feel this, how could the world show its appreciation?

JK: It tends to kill them. Or want to shut them up. I had this experience, when I was thirteen years old or so, of my mother burning my books. I didn't understand at the time that it was a fairly profound thing to do to someone. Writers seem privileged in a way that painters and—you hardly ever stop painters. Well, I suppose the Soviet Union and Hitler did stop painters and composers and so on. Anybody can be a writer readily, and often everybody is, from time to time, in one way or another. But when you set yourself apart from all that and say, "Well, I am a writer," you seem so privileged and special, and say things that nobody wants to hear. Most people will say, "Well, I'm doing something and there's a price to pay for this." Writers say, "I am doing something and I insist that I have a right to say it." And people just don't like that. This should cost you something. Writers don't think it: we all just feel it shouldn't cost us anything. I happen to feel it should cost you something. That it's not worth it if it doesn't cost you something.

RB: That's a consistent theme in Robert Stone's work—that you have to pay for everything.

JK: Yeah, I don't mind.

RB: There's a kind of glamorization of the writer, part of which is that one is one's own boss: no cubicles, no rush hour, all that.

JK: But that's only in America. In America, people want to be recognized for everything they do. Only in America does it seem glamorous to be a writer, as opposed to it being an honor. In some places, in France and places like that, it's an honor. Here, we think that it's a glamorous thing. I think that you want to be known for anything in America. And writers are connected to publicity in some way—a great part of publicity is writing, and a great part of writing has become publicity. You might say I'm publicizing myself by speaking to you. No, I don't think so. But in America, it's really an American thing. We cannot stand to just be and just do the thing. It's not that we just want to make money, we really want to be known. It's more important to be known than to make money. I don't know why.

RB: You're teaching undergraduates writing at Harvard. What do you ask your students to read?

JK: We spent this year reading mountain climbing stories because I'd been in Nepal in October and discovered a whole genre of literature that I hadn't known existed. There's a whole set of literature of people who tried to climb these various peaks of the Himalayas. I found one by a man [F. S. Smythe]—it turns out I had been reading his seed-collecting books but I didn't realize that it was the same person. He'd been on all the attempts to climb Mt. Everest and Kangchenjunga—all the failed attempts. The successful one was Hillary, and then Kangchenjunga was with a group of people that had been with Hillary. So he had been all over the Himalayas, trying to climb these mountains, and I discovered a book he wrote called *The Kangchenjunga Adventure*. It was one of the best things I ever read. I had my students read it, and we read Hillary's account of Everest. Not because it was the fiftieth anniversary. This year we just read adventure things. We read Louise Bogan's *Journey Around My Room,* a wonderful piece of writing.

Every year I do something different. One of the things that young writers often can't do—and I don't know if it's just this generation, but they don't really understand a lot of general knowledge. If they say, "Something took me like a hurricane," they don't understand what a hurricane is. Or what a volcano is. They don't understand natural events. And so often I will have them read nonfiction. I was thinking about next year, and I thought, "We'll read one book. We'll read either *Our Mutual Friend* or *Dombey and Son,* just one big book by Dickens." Basically, I have them read whatever I've liked. And that's something the class reads, and then I make up individual lists of books for people to read. People are often in different modes. And there are things only some people are reading because everyone has a different kind of imagination. I always think of a writer's reading list as a writer's friend. You read the person who is helping you while you write. Not to say that you are going to write like them. It just keeps you in the general bathwater.

RB: Why did you go to Nepal?

JK: Seed collecting or plant hunting.

RB: For how long?

JK: One month.

RB: How long did it take to climb to 16,000 feet?

JK: Two weeks.

RB: And you want to go back. Why?

JK: There are many reasons, but I suspect one of them is I love looking at the surface of the earth. That would be only one of the reasons.

V. ON BAD REVIEWS

RB: Do you read much contemporary fiction?

JK: No, I almost never read it. I started to make an effort to read writers who I think are good but had gotten really bad reviews, and so I read Don DeLillo's new book [*Cosmopolis*] and liked it very much. I was just stunned. That's the last book I read. Robert Stone's book got a bad review in the *New York Times* so I was about to buy it.

RB: I think Stone's *Bay of Souls* is a great book.

JK: Is it? Ordinarily, I don't read contemporary fiction. There are so many things—my contemporaries, I think, I already know what they know. But there are so many things I don't know. I haven't read all of Dickens. I've read most of George Eliot. There are some things I haven't read and I want to read them.

RB: How is it that you come to read reviews at all?

JK: I don't read reviews of my own books. Oh, that's not true. How is it that I come to read reviews?

RB: In the case of DeLillo, for example?

JK: He had a new book and I thought, "I wonder what this is like?" If it hadn't been for that bad review, I wouldn't have bought the book, because I don't read much contemporary fiction. But I was so shocked by it. So I just went out and bought it and loved it. I often do read reviews of other people's books out of sympathy or support. No matter what you say, these things are very painful to read. They often don't sound like reviews, but more like quarrels you're having with someone in a dorm.

VI. ANTIGUAN SLAVE NARRATIVES

RB: Are your students intending to move forward in their lives as writers?

JK: A lot of them are. A lot of them are very serious about writing or about literature or art in some way. I think the wonderful thing about having some time in college when you write is just that— that you have some time. It's a wonderful thing to do. If I never turn out one writer, I wouldn't consider myself a failure for teaching. It's not to turn out writers—

RB: Is it to teach them how to read?

JK: Essentially, a good writer wants to read, and reading actually is the only school you have. Certainly, it was the only writing school I had—reading obsessively. I had no idea that it could lead one to write. But I certainly wanted to read.

RB: This is almost a chant, a mantra, in *Mr. Potter.* I suspect that a lot is made of your dark and angry view of life, but certainly what always shines through is your great belief in the value and importance of reading and writing.

JK: Yes. It's hard to know why that is so for me. In a lot of slave narratives, over and over, slaves are forbidden the ability to read and write, or are forbidden to acquire the skill of reading and writing. I don't have any memory of that as part of Antiguan slave narratives, but it's possible that my attachment to it came from my mother, a maternal connection. My mother taught me to read. And she taught me to read as a way of making me independent of her. She was always reading and I was always interrupting her reading to make her pay attention to me. And she thought that if I knew how to read, I would like books as much as she did, and I would leave her alone and would be independent of her. So it's possible—and I have to say I'm telling you something that I have only just this minute understood—this particular insight. It seemed to me that I must attach to this reading and writing a great power of self-possession. Because it led me to really not need her, to survive without her in ways that she couldn't have imagined. When I was sent away from home I started to write, and this was how I became a person that really was a mystery to her.

RB: You answered a question that I was toying with asking. Here's the question: Why is it that people who appreciate reading—and maybe writing, but certainly reading—are so zealous and convinced about its tremendous value, though not necessarily in a proselytizing way?

JK: Self-possession. I could say my name, and in writing my name I knew who I was, and it made me separate myself from the world. "That was mother. This is me, and that's that, and I am not that."

RB: And Mr. Potter, who couldn't read and couldn't write and who had no knowledge of the world, almost didn't exist.

JK: Yes. It's very interesting to me to see it not read accurately. [*Chuckles*] It was hard. I don't think it was a bad book, but it was interesting to see the level of stupidity. I knew it was in trouble when the first review said, "Who will read this book?" And this was by a person who liked it. The reviewer said, "It's so difficult. It's so this and that and let me tell you what it's about and I love it but who's going to read it?" And I thought, oh well. But actually, it's read. Like all my books, slowly.

RB: What can you say about the title to your novel, *The Autobiography of My Mother*?

JK: I once had the insight that my mother wrote my life. My life as seen through writing comes straight from my imagination even as it is rooted in fact. If my mother can write my life, through my imagination, is it possible that I can write hers also using this same imagination? I almost certainly tried to do so in that book.

RB: I read all your books since *Lucy* in the early '90s as substantial narratives driven by your voice. It's you talking about the world you see and experience, about who you are. It's challenging, of course. Consider this: When a man is difficult, he's a contrarian. When a woman is difficult, she's a bitch or something.

JK: This is very true. You'd be surprised at the things you see playing into it, by all sorts of people. I remember *Lucy* being reviewed by a black woman who said it was a very good book but it was not interested in race and class. How could she [Lucy] not be interested in race and class? I thought it would be false for this girl to be interested in race and class in the American sense. Then other people said it was angry. You could see all sorts of people with their own expectations of how a book written by a black woman should be. I don't think anyone has ever accused John Edgar Wideman of being angry. Wideman's work is very much appreciated—as it should be, for being beautifully, exquisitely rendered. Just "powerful" is what it's called, not "angry." I never heard anyone say, "Wideman's work is angry." But for some reason, my work is angry. And it mustn't be. It mustn't be angry. The truth is, I really don't complain, because I really have lots of readers, and my work is well thought of and respected and appreciated, so I'm not going to whine. It would be beyond inappropriate. It would be silly.

RB: Do you know what's next for you?

JK: Oh, gosh. I don't know exactly what's next. But I keep writing, and the world of writing seems—oh, god—so interesting. I catch a glimpse of myself in the mirror, and I realize I am getting to be an old woman, but when I sit down to write, I just feel so young and wonderful. I just forget that I had two children. I feel as if I had never done this. I went on this trek way up in the Himalayas, just a little under 16,000 feet, walking. I had the most wonderful time. I can't wait to do it again. And suddenly I realize, at fifty-four, how often am I going to...? And then I think, oh, it's just begun, this seeing the world. Yeah. It's just great. I just hope everything holds up. ✷

MICHELLE TEA

TALKS WITH

FELICIA LUNA LEMUS

"I DID LITERALLY HAVE MY GRANDMOTHER SAY TO ME ONCE, 'AY! DIOS MÍO, IS THAT A BOY OR IS THAT A GIRL?'"

Grandma's new vocab list:
Butch
Femme
Androg
Kiki

In the heart of Hollywood, down the trashed and scraggly hill-top where the letters of the Hollywood sign lean together drunk-enly, I wait for Felicia Luna Lemus. For so much of Lemus's debut novel Trace Elements of Random Tea Parties (pub-lished in 2003 by Farrar, Straus & Giroux) the main charac-ter is hopping between those lesbo gender expressions butch (girls who look like boys) and femme (girls who look like girls), I didn't know if I was scanning the coffee shop for a suited-up boydyke or a cherry-lipped ladygirl. Then Lemus appears, adorable. Her hair is inky black like a Hernandez Brothers comic, her dress is a flouncy thrifted thing, her ankles are anchored in giant army boots. She has a teensy, darling bouquet of *flowers plucked from her garden—a yellow daisy, spindly stem sprouting fuzzy purple nubs, a stalk of stinky rosemary—and wrapped in tinfoil.*

Rambling and sugary, Trace Elements *is the story of Leticia, a Latina queer girl with a fluid gender thing going on. It's a first-person tale of punk rock Los Angeles dykedom and of family. Leticia's birth family features a cranky, loving Nana, dramatically deceased parents, and macho street-corner boy cousins; Leticia's hand-selected family of truck-driving, graffiti-tagging butch girls, glamorous, femmed-up rich girls pretending to be from the hood, and swaggering, strapping older dykes. Then there's Weeping Woman, the folkloric spirit-vixen who haunts the text. Leticia prays to Weeping Woman, receives her nighttime visits, and is ultimately abandoned by her when families natal and chosen collapse. The book presents a magical, candy-colored vision of Southern California that brings to mind Francesca Lia Block's* Weetzie Bat *books. Like Block, Lemus summons a bright new language, with occasional sentences composed of practically nothing but adjectives clanking together playfully on the page like gaudy faux jewels strung on tinsel: "My girl Edith: smarty-pants Mission District glamour homegrrrl moved down to Los Angeles on her leopard-print motorcycle… When she entered a room, sweet thick crisp green lilac perfume sharpened the air."*

It was Lemus who suggested we brazenly stroll onto the grounds of the mammoth Scientology Celebrity Center across the street. The Scientologists stared at us, knowing we were not of their people. The possibility of being kicked out for trespassing infused our interview with a sense of urgency that manifested in much giggling. And so we sat amidst the cult's million-dollar landscape job—waterfalls! bubbling brooks! gazebos twined with blooming vines!—to talk about stuff like gender and class, and to keep an eye out for John Travolta. —M.T. *(Spring 2003)*

I. "IT'S A NATURAL TENDENCY TO BE SUSPICIOUS OF PEOPLE WHO HAVE MONEY."

MICHELLE TEA: When I lived in Boston, when I was a teenager, we would get drunk and the Scientologists would always try to lure us back to their compound to take personality tests. Have you ever done that?

FELICIA LUNA LEMUS: No. I think I almost did once, but I thought better of it.

MT: It's fun if you're sixteen and drunk with your friends. Do butch dykes exist in Los Angeles?

FLL: Yeah. They do. [*Laughs*]

MT: I really like the gender identity stuff that's going on in your book. At the very beginning Leticia is going out with Edith, who is super femme. Then she's going out with all these butch girls and she's really girly, and I was trying to orient myself to her gender expressions. I felt like, "Why I am I trying to figure out if she's butch or femme; who cares?" Later in the book she talks about identifying as *kiki* and I loved that. Nobody uses that expression. Did you read *Odd Girls and Twilight Lovers?* It's by Lillian Faderman, who's like a dyke historian, and it's a history of lesbianism in America.

FLL: Is it about the '50s bar scene? It was working-class dykes, right?

MT: Yeah, and they were really intensely butch/femme, and then somebody who was a bit more androgynous would come in and they would all call her "kiki" and make her flip a coin to figure out who she'd be that night—butch or femme—so everyone would understand how to relate to her.

FLL: It's still that way. I've gone back and forth between being very boy and very femme. I'm sure people think I have multiple personalities or something because one day they'll see me and I'll be very boyish. Yesterday I was dressed up high femme—punk drag queen meets Audrey Hepburn's Holly Golightly dolled up for a night on the town. Little black dress, lots of leg, heels, updo, red lipstick—always discreetly touched up and, miracle of miracles, not to be found on my teeth once that night—and super-sparkle audacious earrings the size of a small child. People do have a very hard time with it still. Our peers do. This is something that's still an issue.

MT: I liked that I just didn't understand what Leticia's gender identity necessarily was. I thought it was cool.

FLL: It was important to me also in terms of being Chicana. I don't know many androgynous Chicanas or anyone who plays that line quite like I see people of different ethnicities play it. People who are still very much in touch with their culture, who aren't more assimilated, they still play by the kind of old school rules of butch/femme. And I respect that. There's something about it culturally that works. I did literally have my grandmother say to me once, "Ay! Dios mío, is that a boy or is that a girl?" And *loud*. I mean, the whole neighborhood just kind of stopped for a second. [*Laughs*] I had a tight fade—my hair was shaped and shaved clean with a straight-edge at the nape of my neck, very short hairs tapered up with clippers to about half-inch at crown, alfalfa sprigs sticking up at my crown, slightly longer bangs either parted and slicked down geek-delicious style or fanned up into a little wave, sideburns shaved into tight little points, lots of pomade—up the back and a suit and the whole deal. It was such a huge issue.

It was such an intense moment to realize that a woman who otherwise could be so open-minded, even of her generation she could be so open-minded about so many things, but that was where she drew the line. So I was really curious what would happen if I tried to have a main character who's Chicana, who identifies so much with Weeping Woman and wants to be respectful of her family but still is a part of a larger, more eclectic L.A. scene. And what the impact is of that kind of exploring.

There's still a lot that needs to be thought about and talked about with the butch/femme dynamic. It can serve a purpose. It can be transgressive and quite fierce to appropriate those roles for a time being. There have been times where my girlfriend is clearly getting harassed for being as androg/boy as she is, and if I'm looking more girly that night somehow my presence can smooth things out. It's gendered and it's creepy but it's kind of survival at the same time.

MT: When people talk about butch/femme roles it can end up feeling a bit frustrating, because they are just people's natures. I can't look or dress like a boy. I just feel totally uncomfortable like that. I am a girl and girl-gendered. So it's hard when you come up against those very academic arguments about if they're roles.

FLL: If someone wants to be girly and they choose to date someone who is more boy, why is this somehow antifeminist? It doesn't make sense.

MT: I feel it's ultimately a devaluing of femininity. Why is femininity in feminist communities and queer communities seen as not radical or not strong? If you really want to talk about subconscious patriarchal influences at work, I mean, why is that scary to you? Why is a girly girl scary to you?

FLL: Why do you need to be dismissive of it?

MT: Yeah. And why is neutralizing your gender expression or having a masculine gender expression better? There's a writer out of Seattle, Tara Hardy, who is really great. She's a performance poet and a writer, and she is femme and working class. She writes great stuff about the working-class tradition of femininity, how it's loud and very girly and very in-your-face. And that becomes a really sharp target for women who are uncomfortable with femininity, and it ends up being a class thing at times. You have middle-class women and middle-class academic feminists who have a very toned-down, proper femininity that goes with their class background judging this louder working-class femininity expression, and no one talks about the fact that there's a class dynamic going on.

I love the part in your book where it comes out that the Edith character is rich, or her family is rich, and she has been fronting. I feel like that happens a lot in the dyke communities, like it's

THE BELIEVER BOOK OF WRITERS TALKING TO WRITERS

really prized to be as oppressed as possible, which includes your economic background. It sucks because it makes dealing with class almost impossible; you can't have an honest conversation about it.

FLL: When you're choosing to not be a part of mainstream, corporate society, everyone tries to slum it even harder. Especially since so many people who have the opportunity to get to the point where they have the ability to express their creative minds, to have that as an option, to not just have to work to put a roof over your head… So many people who are in that position are privileged. It is something I've seen a lot. If you do come from a working-class or poor background, I think it's a natural tendency to be suspicious of people who have money because they abuse it. It's that simple. And I think that's where the shame comes in, too. It's like white guilt and slavery. You don't want to be associated with something that your ancestors did that you possibly don't agree with, but it sure as hell has gotten you to where you are historically.

MT: Right. You're still standing on the shoulders of all that racism. Your book is a really working-class book. I appreciated that Leticia is really in touch with where she comes from and it's not a very moneyed place.

FLL: What was the name of that one book… a butch dyke wrote it about her experiences in the '50s growing up?

MT: *Stone Butch Blues?*

FLL: Yes! Thank you.

MT: Leslie Feinberg. She's amazing.

FLL: Yeah, yeah. When I read her book, it made me cry I was so happy. It was the first time I had read something where there was a working-class girl literally struggling to keep herself a place to sleep at night. The issues are so real then. If someone doesn't like you and wants to fire you as a result, it matters. It amplified everything. I was inspired by that. My family took a lot of pride in working hard. It was something I identified with.

II. WEARING PRISTINE VICTORIAN DRESSES, CLIMBING TREES

MT: How did *Trace Elements* come together?

FLL: I started writing it in bits and pieces. I just started writing little vignettes mostly. I was obsessed with this one historical figure named Nahui Olin, who's from the 1920s avant-garde, and she's really amazing. She has these very spooky eyes. If you were to see a photo of her she looks as if she could easily be a contemporary punk rock girl, but she's from the '20s. She painted and she wrote poetry and she wrote these pseudoscientific books that were kind of these explorations of the world around her but in this very poetic way, incorporating all those kinds of modern science. So I became obsessed with her and then somehow those vignettes became the beginning of this book. She in some ways inspired Weeping Woman, the way I used Weeping Woman in this story.

I have a friend who just took my rambling, babbling, hyper-manic, freak [manuscript] and said "OK. You need to have structure. Why would someone want to keep reading this? It might be interesting for a couple pages, but you need to kind of ease them along and invite them in and this kind of thing. You've offered people these truffles but now they need a glass of water. Give them water." [*Laughs*] I think he was kind of saying I was killing my reader. It's like they're dying. [*Laughs*]

MT: I think it's OK to write something that doesn't have this traditional arc like you need in a movie. You can just have people who are living these really interesting lives and things happen or don't happen and there's not necessarily this huge resolution at the end where everything's OK.

FLL: Yeah. Happy endings are overrated.

MT: Your book makes Los Angeles seem really romantic. Do you like living here?

FLL: There are lots of things I like about it. I like the old movie houses. I've been going to a lot of estate sales [*laughs*], which I've really been enjoying. There are these awesome, beautiful houses from the early 1900s, which I know doesn't seem very old to certain parts of the country, but here they're like relics. They're beautiful and they're kind of crumbling. There's basically this generation that bought those homes in the '20s that is now dying, and their families aren't interested in keeping the houses. So these people literally put tags on everything in the drawers and put up tables to sell all the family photos and all these different sorts of things. Basically you can walk into their house and rummage through their things. It's very bizarre. It feels like being a grave robber. But it is allowed so it's kind of perverse. You have permission to do it. It's either just recycling or it's this kind of leaching process: I don't know which. But I've been enjoying that.

MT: Have you found good things?

FLL: Yeah. Jewelry and photos. I'm obsessed with old photos, especially young women, these ones who look like they're very clearly dykes. [*Laughs*] There's these ones of really rowdy-looking girls who always have messed-up hair even though they're wearing very pristine Victorian dresses, climbing trees. They're just these hot images. I found one where there's this girl propped up in a tree and giving this very surly look to whoever is taking the picture. It's so hot. Things like that make me happy. And photobooth photos, also. Often if they're ones that have two women in them, it seems like this romantic friendship.

III. CLASSES ON JOINT-ROLLING AND WICCA

MT: Everyone has really great, interesting jobs in your book. K works painting murals on vans and Leticia is painting dogs' toenails. So I'm wondering what jobs you've had.

FLL: Well, I've had the predictable and boring coffeehouse job which served me well. I can still make really good espresso drinks but it's so cliché. It's so bad. I was shift lead. I was very responsible. I actually was in a teaching credential program for a little bit but I had a shaved head and they didn't like me. The kids liked me a lot. [*Laughs*]

MT: Did they love your shaved head?

FLL: Oh yeah. The funny thing is when I had the shaved head a lot of adults would look at me and think, "Oh dear. Maybe she's going through chemo. I won't talk about it." And I understand that, but it went with the rest of my look so it wasn't like this disjointed conservative dress, right? So anyway, I did that. That was fun because I really liked the little kids, but I hated the system. Acculturating them to be good little Americans... teaching the Pledge of Allegiance was something I could not do. Teaching them to sit and listen and behave and be prepared for their corporate, secretarial positions in the future, it was making me depressed so I stopped. What else have I done? I taught English classes. That's the problem. I wish I'd done things like painting poodles' toenails, but I haven't.

MT: You went through the whole school system and you went to grad school. Did you have to unlearn what they taught you? I feel like your voice is incredibly unique and you do run-on adjectives and I love that. And you're making up words. It doesn't sound like any kind of a voice that came out of an academic institution.

FLL: I went to UC Irvine for undergrad and that was wonderful because I had a mentor who was just incredible. He was so supportive and he just really wanted me to develop my critical mind. He kept pushing me. I'd think I'd be done with a paper and he'd say, "Oh, you could work on this," and I would just hate him for a second and then adore him years later, realizing that he made me go that extra step to research my point more and make it more solid and strong. For graduate school, I know some writers that I really respect that came out of Irvine. Like Aimee Bender I think is really fun and quirky, and she's so smart and has her own voice and she went there. So that worked. For me, I went to Cal Arts, which is incredibly bizarre. Their historical reputation is that they used to have classes on joint rolling and Wicca and you could get credit for these classes. They have a swimming pool that used to be clothing optional, but no one wore clothes. They have these Thursday night openings that are just these… they're just out of control. No one is functional on Friday is what it comes down to, including a lot of the faculty. [*Laughs*]

IV. BIG OLD HONKIN' TRUCK

MT: Who do you read that inspires you?

FLL: I read all sorts of things. I get just as much inspiration from going to see art shows or reading science books. I love going to thrift stores. The books are usually twenty-five cents or so. You can stock up on these weird Time-Life Science series. They're very lowbrow. I love learning science trivia and somehow that sparks ideas for me.

MT: Have you ever seen a Time-Life series that's old, from the '70s, I think… it's all about the occult and superstitions?

FLL: Oh my god, I have that one! [*Laughs*] I learned how to palm read. In eighth grade I could trick my friends into thinking I really knew their futures and so they would actually pay me a dollar to read their palms. They were trying to prove that palm reading was a hoax in this Time-Life series so they said that basically what every palm reader does is work off of this one structure. If you memorize this one paragraph and reshape it, taking visual clues from a person's body language or their dress or whatever, you can convince anyone that you know everything about them from reading their palm. So I memorized that one paragraph and went around and did this.

MT: So it taught you how to be a hoaxster. Was the cliché true for you that your characters really took on their own lives and began doing things that you didn't think they would do?

FLL: No. I've heard about one woman who even says that her characters call her on the telephone. She claims that they call and tell her what to write. [*Laughs*] I figure if that happens to me someone needs to offer me some help. So no, I impose things on them for the most part. I just daydream a lot. I can't change their name after a certain amount of time because it becomes their name and I start to get an idea of what they look like. They're just imaginary friends. Same thing I did when I was a kid. I was a total loner, for the most part. I would go in and out of cliques. After school I was alone at home... It's just daydreaming.

MT: You had imaginary friends?

FLL: I didn't really, but I would kind of imagine these ridiculous situations for everyone that I did know. So it's sort of the same thing except now someone is going to publish it. [*Laughs*] It's really ridiculous. The family structure is similar in some ways to what I grew up with but there are huge omissions and constructions that are just completely not true. Some visual details may be true. Certain props fill scenery, certain objects that I'm just obsessed with.

MT: Like what?

FLL: Like K's big cowboy truck. Her big old honkin' truck. My girlfriend has a good truck. It was so sexy when I first saw her pull up in that truck, I was like, [*sighs*] oh, melt. It's a total gas-guzzler and she doesn't drive it that much because it's just economically ridiculous.

MT: Especially here. I don't even drive. My boyfriend had to take care of the car thing when we lived in L.A. He got us a '69

Monaco. Beautiful. Enormous. It seemed always to be on the verge of dying. We were afraid to go anywhere. We couldn't drive out of the neighborhood without having a panic attack about it just collapsing, so we didn't really stray very far. We ended up feeling very boxed-in and frustrated that we had this big car. And weird things would happen. It would be in park and then we'd get a note from our neighbors saying, "Your car rolled into the middle of the street today. We pushed it back and shoved a rock under the tire."

V. THE CULTURAL HERITAGE HERE IS ABOUT FAÇADE

MT: Your book is so sunny. Are you a really up person?

FLL: I can stay grounded. It's taken me years to figure out how to be that way. I can get through anything. What I was trying to do with Leticia is show that the whole thing is just a learning process, you know? All your life until the day you die is just a learning process. So even if things are horrible and just dreadful and you're feeling miserable, if you can focus on it being a learning process, most likely you're going to wake up the next day. And if you don't, you don't. But chances are you will. Chances are no matter how much it hurts, you're going to get through it.

MT: Weeping Woman is a supernatural character, this mystical, mythical entity who visits and protects Leticia, like a guardian angel but sexy and temperamental. Do you believe in magic personally?

FLL: It's just the way I grew up. For example: I was in New York and it was the first time that I felt very strongly that I needed to meet the person who agreed to be my agent. I need to see people in front of me because otherwise they're sort of abstractions. I don't do well on the phone. I have a really hard time having phone conversations, which no one in L.A. can understand since they have cell phones glued to their ears. I won't do it. Let's talk face-to-face or it may not happen. Anyway, I really wanted to meet him face-to-face so I managed to get out there. We were sitting in his apartment and we were having drinks and were going to go out to dinner, and we were kind of talking shit, not really being disrespectful but kind of just talking honestly about our families, joking around, saying things that weren't entirely polite about our mothers. But lovingly, right? All of a sudden, the light went out. [*Laughs*] And he just kind of looked at me and got kind of nervous and then it flickered and it went back on. I was just calm. He looked at me and he says, "Now that was your fault, wasn't it?" I said that it wasn't me, it was probably my great-grandma. Stuff like that happens all the time.

I know it comes across as being wishy-washy or odd to a lot of people, but it's Mexican, it's the way I grew up. Spirits don't just disappear when the body is dead; there's still some sort of energy. And I'm not Christian-religious—I don't think that there are winged angels watching over me—but I do think there's a source of energy that somehow remains present. And they can be tricky and they can have a sense of humor and all of that sort of stuff. So we were getting scolded for being disrespectful. [*Laughs*]

MT: I was struck by how Leticia's scene is claiming a dyke sensibility in opposition to a lesbian sensibility that's older and less fashionable or whatever. What do you think of that?

FLL: It's the Normandy Room. West Hollywood, on the Santa Monica strip. Smack dab in the middle of Boy Town. My friends and I used to stomp in with our ratty clothes and punk brat dyke attitudes to occupy the place and play pool and throw lots of attitude and flirt—serious flirting—and smoke inside and drink more than our fair share and go home with each other and that sort of thing on Friday nights. There was a bartender who had a sexy gold tooth. She served ridiculously huge shots and rarely charged us. The place has gone to hell now. The Normandy always had tendencies toward being, and has now irreversibly become, the sort of bar that comes fully stocked with bleached lesbian fluff—big blond hair, aerobics-class bodies, fitted jeans worn high up above belly buttons. That is, if you can find any women there at all. Last time I was there, boys outnumbered girls.

In L.A. I think everything is so exaggerated because it's such a body culture here and it is so much about superficiality and surface and façade. It was agricultural to start with, but soon after that it was Hollywood and so it feels that the cultural heritage here is about façade. And you feel it a lot. And you feel it a lot even when you go to clubs, even when you go to bars, there's a lot of posturing.

VI. ANARCHISTIC AGITPROP-GRAFFITI ARTIST–ECOTERRORIST TYPE

MT: I really liked the part in your book where they all go to the art show and Leticia's so pissy about being there. I liked the outsiderness.

FLL: Well my girlfriend's a visual artist. [*Laughs*] We went to every opening for I don't know how many years. It's important to see what's out there and, more than that, it's important to be supportive of other artists' work. To be a visible presence at young artists' openings because it makes such a difference. It can be such a difficult thing to be a visual artist and to not be one of the few people who are selling their paintings for half a million. Where you're having to work a couple of different jobs to support it. So I needed to vent, is what it comes down to.

MT: What's your writing process like?

FLL: [*Laughs*] A total fucking mess. I need things to be visual when I'm working on them, so I actually tape sections and scenes that I'm working on up on the wall. I have one wall that's a good size and it's just basically covered with paper and Post-it notes, images that I xerox from different books and the photographs that I get at estate sales. That's basically how things come together. But it's a complete mess. They're not actually taped directly to the wall, they're little binder clips that I tape to the wall so I can push the binder clip open. I'm a total office supply junkie. It's very neurotic and embarrassing, but it really is a fetish. So I push open the binder clip and I can shuffle things around because I never know where things go to start with. For the life of me I cannot sit down and write an outline. I'm a little bit jealous of people who can do it sometimes.

MT: What are you working on right now?

FLL: I'm working on a novel where the main character is an archivist and her job is to shred duplicates. She's supposed to scan and shred duplicates that the library has in their holdings. She comes across a book that clearly is not of the pulp fiction, paperback category that most of the books are that she's supposed to be processing. It turns out to be a very historic book that probably has something to do with that character Nahui Olin. It gets a bee in her bonnet so much that she becomes this anarchistic agitprop-graffiti artist–ecoterrorist type. So she goes around doing what she calls her "public beautification or improvement" projects. She does them in the middle of the night, rides around on her bike and does all this bad stuff. So that's the main character, and she has a girl-friend. And there's a lot of how cultural memory is constructed, the sociopolitical parts of it, who is included in history and who isn't. This person Nahui Olin is basically nonexistent in history.

I heard someone say once that the strength or truth a political statement has is directly correlated to how much it will be censored. If something is actually quite dangerous to the status quo in that it's truly transgressive and pushing boundaries, chances are that's what's going to be pushed down the most. I want to kind of manifest that in terms of blindness. Her girlfriend in the story is, by choice, blind. She doesn't have the use of her eyes.

MT: By choice?

FLL: By choice. It's a long story. [*Laughs*] So it's about blindness and about the choice of blindness and how that manifests itself in individuals as a result of larger societal choices to be blind to certain historical figures or problems. My main character is very interested in forcing these things into focus, into the foreground. But right now the novel's taped up on my wall.

MT: That sounds great. More cool girl heroes. Anything you want to talk about that I haven't asked?

FLL: I'm quite happy.

MT: Signing off now from the Scientology Celebrity Center in Hollywood, California.

FLL: And we still haven't seen John Travolta. ✶

DAPHNE BEAL

TALKS WITH

JANET MALCOLM

"THE NARRATOR OF MY NONFICTION
PIECES IS NOT THE SAME PERSON I AM—
SHE IS A LOT MORE ARTICULATE
AND THINKS OF MUCH CLEVERER
THINGS TO SAY THAN I USUALLY DO."

Results are not guaranteed with:
Czech wit in translation
Emails
Photographs
Interviews
World War II–era recipes

**E**very journalist who is not too stupid or too *full of himself to notice what is going on knows that what he does is morally indefensible," Janet Malcolm writes at the opening of* The Journalist and the Murderer *in the kind of fierce statement that has earned her a reputation as an unswerving truth-teller. Like many of Malcolm's other nonfiction works, this book, published in 1990, takes a specific event (a murderer suing a journalist) and unpacks it so extensively that the work illuminates a larger topic—in this case, the complex psychological dynamics at the heart of the art of journalism.*

Malcolm, who has been publishing pieces that seamlessly combine essay

and reportage in the New Yorker *since the late '70s, has written eight books, spanning such topics as the politics and pitfalls of the field of psychoanalysis* (Psychoanalysis: The Impossible Profession, *1981), the problem of biography seen through the lens of Sylvia Plath (*The Silent Woman, *1994), and a meditation on the life and work of Chekhov (*Reading Chekhov, *2001). Others include* In the Freud Archives *(1984) and* The Crime of Sheila McGough *(1999), as well as two collections of essays,* The Purloined Clinic *(1992) and* Diana and Nikon *(1980, expanded in 1997). What grabs and regrabs the reader in her writing is its deft commingling of sleuthing and contemplation. Reading Malcolm, one has the sensation of being in the presence of a mind constantly in action on several levels, mediating between external reality (one most often consisting of facts that are at odds with one another) and her own consciousness. With the exception of* The Purloined Clinic, *none of her books is much more than two hundred pages, but the rigor of her writing gives them the quality of murals painted by a miniaturist.*

Malcolm can be unsparing in her portrayals of the people she comes across, but her extraordinary precision does not preclude compassion. Occasionally, Malcolm's subjects damn themselves, but more often they reveal the vanities, obsessions, and desires that we all share—if to a heightened degree.

Currently at work on a book about Gertrude Stein and Alice B. Toklas, Malcolm corresponded with me by email. —D.B. (Spring 2004)

DAPHNE BEAL: It's interesting that we're doing this interview by email, because one of the phrases that's long been in my head is your description from *The Silent Woman* of letters written today on computers as being "marmoreally cool and smooth," in contrast to letters from previous decades written on manual typewriters. Correspondence plays such a large role in almost all your books, not just the content and tone, but often the texture and feel of the letters' pages. Email seems to up that smoothness even further. Do you use it a lot yourself, or are "real" letters still a preferred form? How do you think email has affected the way people communicate by the written word?

JANET MALCOLM: When I wrote *The Silent Woman,* email had not yet arrived—or was not yet in common use. I would not use the phrase "marmoreally cool and smooth" about email. I think of email as messy, both in appearance and in the character of the writing. Email encourages a kind of laxness, a letting down of hair. When I write a "real" letter, I care about how it looks. I will compulsively redo a letter if the indentations aren't uniform or if I've smudged the signature. With email, I don't know what the message will look like on the receiver's screen. I only know it will be surrounded by all kinds of stuff—titles, "headers," numbers, codes, etc.—that I had nothing to do with. So I take no trouble over the appearance of the message. I take some trouble over the message itself, but not as much as I would in a letter.

Doing this interview by email gives me a chance to think of answers to your questions. If we did it in person, I might just look at you in blank helplessness.

DB: Reading your work, it's hard to ever imagine you with such a look! I'm always amazed by the quick turns, the dips and dives through any given moment of interaction, especially when it comes to the psychological underpinnings of things. I read somewhere that your father was a psychiatrist. Did that mean you were very aware of psychology as a philosophy/art/science from an early age? Was that a field you ever seriously considered going into?

JM: No, I never considered becoming a psychiatrist or psychoanalyst, and while growing up I paid little attention to my father's work. He himself was not all that invested in it—for many years he was head psychiatrist of an outpatient clinic of the Veterans Administration. He loved nature, literature, and sports, and he was a gifted comic writer. Unfortunately, he wrote in Czech, and Czech wit does not translate well. This is not to say that he didn't excel in his work as a psychiatrist (and as a neurologist, his second specialty). He just wasn't pompous about it—as many psychiatrists were in those days. He had affectionate regard for his patients and no use for social workers. He was wonderfully satiric about them and their clipboards. A piece of writing of mine that is connected to my father is "The One-Way Mirror," about the family therapist Salvador Minuchin. Would you like me to tell you about that?

DB: Sure, I'm a sucker for anything about families and their influence.

JM: In the late '70s I gave up smoking and, naturally, couldn't write. I decided to do what the *New Yorker* called a long fact piece, which would require many months of reporting. I figured that by the time I finished the reporting I would be ready to try writing without smoking. I remembered something my father had told me about a remarkable man who cured anorectic girls in one session—at lunch with their families, at the end of which the girls would eat, the way cripples would walk at the end of faith-healing encounters. He had seen this man perform at a hospital near his clinic, and marveled at his powerful personality. I had never heard my father speak so enthusiastically about anyone in psychiatry, and decided to make that man, Minuchin, the subject of my piece.

For many months I took the train to Philadelphia where Minuchin had a clinic, and watched him instruct a class of young psychiatrists in his kind of theatrical family therapy. When it was time to write, I found I could write without smoking. This was the first long fact piece I had ever done, and this kind of writing turned out to be congenial to me.

DB: How many years into your writing career were you when that happened? And did that process of choosing Minuchin for your subject matter become in any way a prototype for how you've chosen other topics?

JM: When I wrote "The One-Way Mirror," I had been writing for about ten years. I had done book reviews, essays on photography, and pieces about decorative art. But I had never done reportage.

The way I stumbled on Minuchin as a subject is pretty much the way I stumble on all my journalistic subjects. I hear or read about someone, or someone writes to me. My book *The Crime of Sheila McGough* came out of a letter I received from its heroine, who thought I might be interested in her story of going to prison for a crime she didn't commit. Journalists get a lot of letters like that, but this one had an unusual atmosphere (and wasn't on yellow lined paper), so I wrote back. But why am I telling you this? Because you asked. One of the things that journalists come to understand after doing journalism for a while is the power of the question.

DB: I want to come back to Sheila McGough, but at the moment I'll make a kind of left turn if that's OK. Last fall you had an exhibit of your collages at the Lori Bookstein Gallery here in New York City, a medium (as I understand it) that you've been working in more privately for some time. How did you come to work in collage, and what kind of questions does the medium ask or answer that writing does not? Or is it more related to your writing than I'm supposing?

JM: To try to answer your question, let me quote from a piece I wrote about ten years ago about the artist David Salle:

> Writers have traditionally come to painters' ateliers in search of aesthetic succor. To the writer, the painter is a fortunate alter ego, an embodiment of the sensuality and exteriority that he has abjured to pursue his invisible, odorless calling. The writer comes to the places where traces of making can actually be seen and smelled and touched expecting to be inspired and enabled, possibly even cured. While I was interviewing the artist David Salle, I was coincidentally writing a book that was giving me trouble, and although I cannot pin it down exactly (and would not want to), I know that after each talk with Salle in his studio something clarifying and bracing did filter down to my enterprise.

Quoting this excerpt—apart from telling you something about my attitude toward artists—enacts what I do as a collagist. I have taken something from one place (the Salle piece) and put it into another (this interview). It also exemplifies what I do when I write. I do an enormous amount of quoting—of people and texts—in my books and articles. David Salle is a painter who does nothing but "quote" or "appropriate" in his paintings. But that is another subject. I guess what I have been trying to say is that, yes, collage is "more related to [my] writing than [you're] supposing."

DB: I remember reading about you showing your collages to Salle, but it seems like another thing altogether to show your work in a gallery. How, if at all, has exhibiting your work changed your relationship to it? For one thing, is it as fun?

JM: When I first started exhibiting I was ambivalent about the idea of people buying my collages. When you publish a book, the text remains in your possession, so to speak. When you sell a painting or drawing or collage, you lose it. It goes out of your life. At first, I wasn't ready to let go of my work. Now I am. I am happy when someone buys a collage. There are a lot of them now. I feel I can keep making them. But even as I say this, I feel a little stab of regret about the collages that are hanging on the walls of strangers, and that it is unlikely I will ever see again.

As for whether the work is as enjoyable as it was before I began to exhibit, the answer is no. I work harder. My standard of craftsmanship is higher and so is my idea of what is good enough to show.

DB: It does seem that while your writing and collage share certain qualities, the truth that collage is after is much more open-ended than writing's. I'm thinking in particular of your eloquent (that is, jaw-dropping) opening of *The Journalist and the Murderer*, about the inevitable betrayal by the journalist of the subject in the name of a higher truth.

The theme of betrayal is echoed in much of your writing—

the biographer of the subject, the protégé of the mentor, the photographer of the subject (Diane Arbus especially comes to mind), Gertrude Stein of the Jews around her, etc. I wonder if you would comment on this recurring motif?

JM: I did not set out to write about betrayal, but by writing about journalism, biography, and photography I kept bumping into it. In each of these genres the practitioner has an enormous amount of power over the subject. Apart from the practitioner's use or misuse of this power, the genres themselves have a built-in tendency to be unkind. It isn't only Diane Arbus who betrays the subjects of her photographs. Most people who have their picture taken hate the result. And most people who are the subjects of newspaper or magazine stories feel at least a little wronged if not outright betrayed. As for the illustrious dead...

DB: Being so thoroughly engaged in one of those inherently unkind professions, how do you reconcile the "not-niceness" (to borrow your description of the *Ariel* poems) of the finished piece with the process of asking your subject for his or her trust? Does that person occupy a different place in your thinking by the time you've finished writing than he or she did when you were in the thick of interviewing?

JM: In answer to your first question: You do not reconcile it. That is the moral problem of journalism. But journalists don't ask for the subject's trust—they don't have to. Subjects just give it. They are eager to tell their story and don't seem to realize that they are not invisible as they tell it. Incidentally, the final product of the inherently unkind professions isn't always not-nice. There are photographs in which the subject looks beautiful, and there are biographies and journalistic portraits from which the subject emerges as a great soul. I recently had the pleasure and privilege of writing about Anton Chekhov, about whom it is simply impossible to find anything seriously bad to say. Some of his biographers have tried—and failed.

I'm not sure I understand your second question. Could you put it more simply? (I'm reading Gertrude Stein's *The Making of Americans,* which may explain my difficulty in understanding a sentence that isn't simple and hasn't been repeated a hundred times.)

DB: I think what I'm really asking for is advice. In my own experience I find it incredibly difficult when writing about someone to transition from that human connection that happens in the most fruitful of interviews to the more critical stance I need to take afterward. Because Chekhov seems to be part of a very small minority of people, dead or alive, of whom one can say nothing bad, and because people's contradictions are among their most interesting qualities, the writer has to be able to step back from that intimate place of interviewing (or research)—where practically anyone's reality can seem like the truth for at least a moment—to a more objective point of view. This often feels like an almost painful betrayal to me.

What I wanted to find out (in my thickly veiled previous question) was how do you make the switch from supplicant or equal interviewer to authority writer?

Is this clearer? If not, we can just abandon this line of thinking. I also realize that *The Journalist and the Murderer* addresses this question in booklength form.

JM: I'm glad I asked. What you write is very eloquent. Yes, I wrote about this dilemma in *The Journalist and the Murderer,* but I did not exhaust the subject by any means. You bring something new into the discussion with your comment about the journalist's momentary identification with the subject. Since you are a novelist, you probably have more capacity for this kind of imaginative leap. I am incapable of writing fiction, so I am probably less empathic. But this doesn't seem to make any difference to the subject. He or she assumes your empathy—and then feels betrayed when what you write isn't like something he or she dictated to you.

I put it another way in *The Journalist and the Murderer* (if you'll forgive me for quoting from myself again): "The journalistic encounter seems to have the same regressive effect on a subject as the psychoanalytic encounter. The subject becomes a kind of child of the writer, regarding him as a permissive, all-accepting, all-forgiving mother, and expecting that the book will be written by her. Of course, the book is written by the strict, all-noticing, unforgiving father."

But getting back to your anxiety about the discontinuity between the coziness of the interview and the coldness of the act of writing—yes, it is a problem and no, it can't be resolved. When you make the switch from "supplicant or equal interviewer to authority writer" you are, like every other journalist, committing some sort of moral misdemeanor.

DB: So maybe the adjustment I need to make is simply down-grading my transgression from felony to misdemeanor. I was thinking, too, about your reputation as a writer for being quite exacting toward, or even tough on, your subjects. The same rigor that thrills some of your readers seems to make others extremely uncomfortable. I wonder if you've ever felt that the reception to your work has been colored by the fact that you're a woman. Are women still meant to be "nicer" as writers, less difficult?

I ask because I think of my own interviewing style, at least in person, as incorporating some stereotypical feminine behavior: slightly low-status and deferential, punctuated by ready laughter, and driven by an accommodating attitude. Later, when I'm writing, I feel I've acted as something of a wolf in sheep's clothing.

I remember your description of your "more Japanese technique" in *The Journalist and the Murderer,* in contrast to the more flat-footed *Newsday* reporter's. I have a sense, of course, but wondered specifically what you meant by that?

JM: I really don't know whether the people who don't like my writing don't like it because of their perception of me as a tough, not-nice woman. It seems kind of ridiculous—I think of myself as a completely ordinary, harmless person—but what people think of your writing persona is out of your hands. The narrator of my non-fiction pieces is not the same person I am—she is a lot more articulate and thinks of much cleverer things to say than I usually do. I can imagine her coming across as a little insufferable sometimes. But she, too, is out of my hands—I may have invented her, but she is the person who insists on speaking for me.

As for the wolf-in-sheep's clothing question, perhaps the way to minimize one's feeling that one has not been as straightforward with the subject as one should have been is to be a little more straightforward. To swallow the too-nice thing one is about to say. To remember that the subject is going to say what he or she wants to say no matter what you say or don't say. You can't keep your mouth shut all the time, of course, but you do well to keep it shut a lot of the time. If silence falls, let the subject break it—even though that's a very hard thing to do. By the way, I don't think the "feminine behavior" you describe is limited to women journalists. Men journalists can be just as ingratiating, deferential, accommodating, and laughter-prone.

When you ask what I mean by the Japanese technique, you are not employing it.

DB: Your answer really made me chuckle. I can't say exactly why, except I think it has to do with the endless conundrum of writing—the fact that it *seems* so much in one's control (especially in contrast to, say, theater or visual art), and yet still there is that mystery of: who is this character who insists on speaking for me? The undeniable fact that in the end the work and its effect are out of one's hands.

Maybe then this is a good time to turn to the simultaneously charming and irascible Stein—speaking of being difficult. (I remember during my Midwestern childhood in the '70s confusing Gertrude Stein and Gloria Steinem, because, well, they were both considered impossible by local standards, but that's another story…)

How did you come to write about her and Toklas? Is that *New*

Yorker piece being turned into a book, and have you finished it?

JM: You made me chuckle too with your wonderful mixing up of Gertrude and Gloria. Yes, I am continuing to write about Stein. No, I have not finished. It is an exceptionally beautiful day today, and I am reminded of what Stein wrote (or said she wrote) on an exam paper in a course at Radcliffe given by William James: "Dear Professor James, I am so sorry but really I do not feel a bit like a philosophy paper today." James (according to Stein) sent her a postcard saying: "Dear Miss Stein, I understand perfectly how you feel. I often feel like that myself," and gave her the highest grade in the class. There is reason to think that this didn't happen the way Stein said it did. But anyway, may I be excused from the examination today?

DB: Dear Miss Malcolm, I understand perfectly how you feel. I often feel like that myself. [And a week later...] Your response to the GS question left me unsure of whether you'd rather not talk about her at all right now, but my Malcolm-fan friends have been pressing me to ask why her, why now? I wondered if Stein's larger-than-life personality and work drew you initially to write about her, or if it was the question of her being Jewish and staying in France that began your investigation?

In contrast to Chekhov, she seems to be a more problematic literary figure and her writing arguably less universally loved than his. It made me wonder if the topic of your last book pushed you in a different direction for the next. Or, conversely, I was thinking about the continuity—if there is more pleasure in writing about the "illustrious dead" than living subjects at the moment?

JM: I told you earlier how I stumble on subjects for pieces. I stumbled on the Gertrude Stein–in–wartime piece when the *New Yorker* asked me to contribute to an issue on food. I decided to write about the Alice B. Toklas cookbook. While rereading Toklas's chapter on what she cooked during the German occupation of

France, I became curious about Stein and Toklas's wartime history. The longer piece followed my short piece about trying to cook a weird dish involving artichoke hearts and asparagus and calf brains. (The asparagus spears were somehow supposed to stand erect in a mush of calf brains and béchamel sauce.)

I'm planning to write more about Stein and Toklas, but I can't really say why right now. I may know when I've written the piece. As for whether it's more agreeable to write about the illustrious dead than about the living, I'd say it all depends on which dead and which living.

DB: I laughed again, mostly because I was afraid of what would happen if I thought too much about the idea of "a mush of calf brains."

Re: dead v. living subjects, how did the prolonged Masson suit affect your choice of subjects after that, if at all? I don't mean to belabor this question of choosing subject matter, but again I've been reflecting on how one knows what will make a good topic over a lengthy period of time—satisfying both the need for a certain meatiness and challenge, and for a pleasure in the task.

JM: Until this moment you were the first interviewer who did not bring Jeffrey Masson into the discussion. I guess that isn't possible after all. What you seem to be asking is whether being sued by him has made me leery of writing about people who are alive rather than safely dead. The answer is no. One of the reasons I refused to settle the Masson lawsuit (as the people he previously sued, Muriel Gardiner and Kurt Eissler, had done) was to leave no doubt in the minds of readers and future subjects that Masson's accusations of misquotation were untrue. As it turned out, a year after he lost his lawsuit at trial, my two-year-old granddaughter pulled a red notebook out of a bookcase, in which the things Masson said he didn't say were scribbled in my hand. The notes had been lost for ten years. The jury had decided to believe me anyway. But if the notebook hadn't got misplaced, there would have been no lawsuit.

Your reflections on your desire to find a subject that is meaty and challenging *and* pleasurable to write about interest me very much. They remind me of one experience I had of not taking pleasure in a subject. That was the subject—business crime—of my book *The Crime of Sheila McGough*. To master the intricacies of the con of a certain con man was very difficult for me. I may not have solved the problem of how not to bore the reader with what gave me enormous trouble to understand. The book was not popular. But I have a special fondness for it, though I may be wrong about its merits.

DB: Sorry to be so tiresome as to bring up Masson, just like the rest. I think it's impossible not to because it does sound like it was such an ordeal, and when I think about events or circumstances in my own life that affect my writing, it's hard not to be curious.

My final question is a two-parter.

First of all, I was intrigued by what you wrote about the Sheila McGough book, about your special fondness for it, and I wondered if you would say a bit more. It sounds like it gave you some trouble in the writing. Is that difficulty where the fondness springs from? (Sometimes I think I may have assigned too much value to pleasurability in the writing process...)

The second part is one of my reprise questions, and it has to do with email (just to complete the circle). In the course of our interview, I've often thought about your description of email as a letting down of one's hair and inherently messy, and tried to figure out if I agree. Messy, yes, but is it truly a letting down of one's hair, especially when the person on the other end isn't particularly known? I've often felt that email has a kind of conscious messiness (as in, "Well, this isn't perfectly articulated, but hopefully she'll know what I mean..."), whereas talk seems like the messiest form of communication of all, the way things slip out.

In short, my question is this: at the end of this interview, has your opinion of email changed any since your original answer, and is this the first interview you've done by email?

JM: To answer the first part of your question, about why I am specially fond of *The Crime of Sheila McGough*: I like its oddness. I think it may be the most original of my books. I like the second part where I travel to the South to interview various strange persons, and the coda where I go to Treasure Mountain, where Bob Bailes, the con man, was going to build a fantastic resort, and where I find a peaceful late summer landscape. I like the book's own late summer melancholy. And, of course, I like Sheila McGough, a most unusual and sad person. Finally, I was glad to use some of what being a defendant myself taught me about the law and lawyers. Without that knowledge, I would not have been able to write (or even been interested in writing) the book.

About email. Yes, this is my first email interview, and yes, talk is the messiest medium of all. Any transcript of a tape recording confirms that. Email lies somewhere between speech and proper writing. But I don't consider our interview a true example of email. Knowing that what I write will be published, I naturally take some trouble over it, and I assume you have done the same. No, so my opinion of email hasn't changed because I haven't really availed myself here of its permission to write sloppily.

[*After reading the interview, Malcolm sent the following email.*]

JM: I read the interview in the way one looks at photographs of oneself, and, except for one place, I thought I came out looking OK. But the exception may be the most interesting part of the interview. I'm talking about the place where you ask me about the Masson lawsuit. Until that moment the atmosphere of the interview is friendly and collegial and almost conspiratorial. Now it turns icy. I make an unpleasant observation and then launch into an absurd defense of myself. In defense of my defensiveness, I can only say that for a long time I wrongly assumed everyone would know that the accusations against me weren't true. Now, having

JANET MALCOLM & DAPHNE BEAL

finally learned that accusations must be answered at once, I ridiculously answer accusations that, years later, no one is making.

But what is most interesting about this moment in our interview is the illustration it offers of a subject's feeling of betrayal when he or she realizes that the journalist is writing his or her own story. In my version of the story of my writing life, I wouldn't give Masson any role whatever. But your version—and any other good journalist's—would naturally give him a role. The lawsuit happened and my wish to deny its significance cannot cut any ice with you. My getting all huffy about your natural and not at all badly intentioned question just goes to show that even journalists are not immune to the vanity and self-deception that interviews bring out in their subjects and that journalists, like novelists, lie in wait for. ✱

ZADIE SMITH

TALKS WITH

IAN McEWAN

"I HAVE NOW REACHED THE STAGE
WHERE AS SOON AS ANYONE SAYS LIFE
MOVES AROUND A SINGLE, ORGANIZING
PRINCIPLE I STOP LISTENING TO THEM.
I DON'T FEEL THAT LIFE ORGANIZES ITSELF
AROUND ANY SINGLE PRINCIPLE.
IT'S A RELIGIOUS IMPULSE TO ONLY GRASP
AT ONE THING, ONE EXPLANATION."

Aspects of the "English Novel" to avoid:
Polite, character-revealing dialogue
Stable, linear narrative
Lightly ironic ethical investigation
Excessive amounts of furniture

I *have often thought Ian McEwan a writer as unlike me as it is possible to be. His prose is controlled, careful, and powerfully concise; he is eloquent on the subjects of sex and sexuality; he has a strong head for the narrative possibilities of science; his novels are no longer than is necessary; he would never write a sentence featuring this many semicolons. When I read him I am struck by metaphors I would never think to use, plots that don't occur to me, ideas I have never had. I love to read him for these reasons and also because, like his millions of readers, I feel myself to be in safe hands. Picking up a book by McEwan is to know, at the very least, that what you read therein will be beautifully written, well-crafted, and not an embarrassment, either for* *you or for him. This is a really big deal. Bad books happen less frequently to McEwan than they do to the rest of us. Since leaving the tutelage of Malcolm Bradbury and Angus Wilson on the now famous (because of McEwan) University of East Anglia creative writing course, McEwan has had one of the most consistently celebrated careers in English literature. We haven't got space for it all here, but among the prizes is the Somerset Maugham Award in 1976 for his first collection of short stories,* First Love, Last Rites; *the Whitbread Novel Award (1987) and Prix Fémina Etranger (1993) for* The Child in Time; *he has been shortlisted for the Booker Prize three times, winning the award for* Amsterdam *in 1998. His novel* Atonement *received the WH Smith Literary Award (2002), the National Book Critics Circle Fiction Award (2002), the Los Angeles Times Book Prize for Fiction (2003), and the Santiago Prize for the European Novel (2004). He's written a lot of good books.*

Because of the posh university I attended, I first met McEwan many years ago, before I was published myself. I was nineteen, down from Cambridge for the holidays, and a girl I knew from college was going to Ian McEwan's wedding party. This was a fairly normal occurrence for her, coming from the family she did, but I had never clapped eyes on a writer in my life. She invited me along, knowing what it would mean to me. That was an unforgettable evening. I was so delighted to be there and yet so rigid with fear I could barely enjoy it. It was a party full of people from my bookshelves come to life. I can recall being introduced to Martin Amis (whom I was busy plagiarizing at the time) and being shown his new baby. Meeting Martin Amis for me, at nineteen, was like meeting God. I said: "Nice baby." This line, like all conversation, could not be rewritten. I remember feeling, like Joseph K., that the shame of it would outlive me.

I didn't get to speak with McEwan that night—I spent most of the party hiding from him. I assumed he was a little annoyed to find a random undergraduate he did not know at his own wedding party. But I had just read Black Dogs *(1992)—that brilliant, flinty little novel, bursting with big ideas—and I was fascinated by the idea of an English novelist writing such serious, metaphysical, almost European prose as this. He was not like Amis and he was not like Rushdie or Barnes or Ishiguro or Kureishi or any of the other English and quasi-English men I was reading at the time. He was the odd man out. "Apparently," said my friend knowledgeably, as we watched McEwan swing his new wife around the dance floor, "he only writes fifteen words a day." This was an unfortunate piece of information to give an aspiring writer. I was terribly susceptible to the power of example. If I heard Borges ran three miles every morning and did a headstand in a bucket of water before sitting down to write, I felt I must try this myself. The specter of the fifteen-word limit stayed with me a long time. Three years later I remember writing* White Teeth *and thinking that all my problems stemmed from the excess of words I felt compelled to write each day. Fifteen words a day! Why can't you write just fifteen words a day?*

Ten years later, less gullible and a writer myself, it occurs to me that my friend may have fictionalized the situation a little herself. An interview with McEwan himself, like the one you are about to read, was of course the perfect opportunity to settle the matter, but it's only now, writing the introduction after the fact, that I remember the question. I do not know if Ian McEwan writes fifteen words a day. However, he was forthcoming on many other interesting matters. McEwan is one of those rare novelists who can speak with honest perspicacity about the experience of being a writer; it is a life he openly loves, and talking to him about it felt, to me, like talking with an author at the beginning of their career, not at its pinnacle. The fifteen-word thing may indeed be a red herring, but my friend had intuited a truth about McEwan: he is not a dilettante or even a natural, neither a fabulist nor a show-off. He is rather an artisan, always hard at work; refining, improving, engaged by and interested in every step in the process, like a scientist setting up a lab experiment.

We did this interview in McEwan's house, which is Dr. Henry Perowne's house in the novel Saturday *(2005). It is a lovely Georgian townhouse that sits in the shadow of London's BT Tower. From the balcony of this house Perowne sees a plane on a crash trajectory, its tail on fire. It is a perfect McEwanesque incident.* —Z.S. (Spring 2005)

I. "IT HAD BEEN
A MALEVOLENT INTERVENTION..."

ZADIE SMITH: I'm not good at this. I interviewed Eminem a while ago and when I got home and transcribed it it was more like "An interview with Zadie Smith in which Eminem occasionally says yes and uh-huh." I talk too much. I'm going to get straight to my first question, which I guess is also the biggest one. I thought we could start there and maybe get small afterwards. Because I read all the books so close together—

IAN McEWAN: What order did you read them in?

ZS: Basically chronological.

IM: OK.

ZS: Except *In Between the Sheets,* which I read only a few days ago. Anyway: there is a line in *The Child in Time,* when you discuss the traumatic event in that novel, the abduction of a child: "it had been a malevolent intervention." And much of your past fiction has dealt with that idea, of a malevolent intervention. Then when you read this latest book, *Saturday,* which deals obliquely with 9/11, it becomes clear that something about the nature of what happened on that day was already a McEwanesque incident. Because the burst of the irrational into the rational was your *modus operandi* anyway. And so (this is a strange thing to say to the writer himself) when you see a writer moving into his strongest period, and staying there, or at least not losing his previous strength, then I always figure that either the age has come to meet him or he's come to meet the age. I think it's the previous case with you, and I remember thinking even before I read *Saturday* that if there were to be a 9/11 novel which was integrated and serious and soon—because it is quite soon—it was more likely to be written by you than anybody else. Because your fiction was already *about* the idea of a malevolent intervention. And I wondered whether you knew that consciously or whether you agree with that.

IM: The first thing I remember thinking was that it [9/11] was a heroic moment for journalism. That was my first sense. Perhaps it's because Annalena [Annalena McAfee, McEwan's wife] works in a newspaper I take an interest in the sort of *thingyness* of newspapers, but it happened two o'clock our time, London time. So front pages had to be clear and basically twenty-five pages set out, produced, and this much-hated profession had its sudden noble moment.

ZS: But it was a moment. You talked about that in the two articles you wrote about September 11 for the *Guardian*. The moment turns quickly and depressingly.

IM: But it was a moment that seemed first to demand accurate journalism before anything else. That was my first feeling. And the best things written about it have been journalism, not fiction. I read a lot of what came out and was impressed by it. Actually I think another instance of this on a much smaller scale was the Dunblane massacre. Hit the wires at about three-thirty in the afternoon. By the time of the London evening papers there were ten, fifteen pages. So my first instinct, my first reaction was that journalists rose to the bar that day, and when I wrote I just wanted to write in that public way, expressing my immediate reaction, the same honorable tide that everyone else was on. Not to write fiction. But even as I was doing that I was thinking the human way into it would take more than journalism, would be more intimate than that. The thought of so many of these people announcing their love down mobile phones...

ZS: There was a small paragraph—I think it was in the second article you wrote about it—where you say that if the terrorists had been able to empathize properly with these others, with the very *idea* of otherness, then they couldn't have done what they did. Now, that's something I do believe, and it's a belief I sort of "push" in my fiction—that real empathy makes cruelty an impossibility. But I always assumed when I read your fiction, that that wasn't at all what you believed. Especially in the earlier work, the opposite, much darker truth seems to be being articulated: mainly, that even after empathy people still can and do perform the most terrible acts.

IM: I've always thought cruelty is a failure of imagination. And I know that I include within that the possibility that some people do empathize with their victims very much, in fact, that's the reason they harm them—they get some erotic charge out of harming what they love. But that's a special case. That's still about pleasuring the self and not heeding to the true terror of the child that's being tortured or whatever it might be.

At least since the early '80s, it's began to fill out for me as an idea in fiction, that there's something very entwined about imagination and morals. That one of the great values of fiction was exactly this process of being able to enter other people's minds. Which is why I think cinema is a very inferior, unsophisticated medium.

ZS: Absolutely. Because you get surfaces only.

IM: Right. And with the novel we have happened to devise this form, this very elastic, mutable form that can allow us moments of real human investigation. Milan Kundera says very wise things in this context. He lays a lot of stress on the novel as a mode of investigation. It's an open-ended way of looking at our own image, in ways that science can't do, religion's not credible, metaphysics is too intellectually repellent on its surface—this is our best machine, as it were.

ZS: You use that machine quite differently from your peers. Yours are different English novels than the English novel as I was brought up to think about it.

After I read your back catalog I Googled you and I found this website for kids—because a lot of kids are studying you at the moment, you're on the A-Level list. It was a messageboard of kids freaking out because they didn't know how to read you. It was very interesting. I think the barrier they kept coming across is that they come with their ideas of an English novel, the classic English novel, where character is revealed through dialogue for a greater part of the book, where action is laid out along a basically stable idea of linear time, where the tone is lightly ironic and your job as a reader is to perform a kind of ethical investigation. They particularly rely on a pretty muscular narrator to nudge them in the direction of correct judgement. So Austen never leaves us in any doubt that Mrs. Bennett is not a person to be respected, for example. But your books screw with time, they use very little dialogue, and the narration is ethically ambivalent. It's all a bit metaphysical when you're sixteen and you've got an essay crisis on. They were freaking out.

IM: Why are they freaking out? I don't understand. Because they're being told too much?

ZS: Well, lets take one of those aspects. Time in McEwan. Most of your contemporaries dealt with time in a pretty traditional fashion. If Rushdie was interested in it, if Amis was interested in it, if Barnes was, it was usually historical time. And partly politicized historical time in the case of Rushdie and when Amis spins time backwards. Flashbacks and historical jumps are used to cast the present in a new, challenging light. But the idea of what does it really feel to *be* in time, to exist in it—this is not something that English A-Level students have to face up to very often.

IM: Well, I don't have any conscious design on time, I don't think—except when I was thinking about it as a specific element of the novel, as with *The Child in Time*. But apart from that, if there's anything going on about time in my novels it's really a spin-off of some other concern. Something to do with the fine print of consciousness itself. I mean, I'm interested in how to represent, obviously in a very stylized way, what it's like to be thinking. Or what it's like to be conscious, or sentient, or, fatally, only half-sentient. And how difficult it is to see everything that's going on and

understand everything at one time and how much our recollections can play into what we accept as reality—how much perception is distorted by will. That's something I find very interesting.
The ways in which we convince ourselves, persuade ourselves of
things, either to settle some notion of our own or an intellectual
position. That's why I've liked the evolution of psychology, they
talk a lot of about self-persuasion… In my fiction I've tried to
indicate my sense of how interestingly flawed we are in the ways
in which we represent ourselves and "what we know" to each
other. So if time gets fractured or refracted along the way, that's an
offshoot. I don't do that consciously.

ZS: Maybe it's "the malevolent intervention" that messes with
time. Like the car crash in *The Child in Time,* where a four-second
moment seems to last forever. I thought when I read *Saturday* that
your audience, through 9/11, now has a mass experience to mirror exactly that strange sensation, when time elongates. The tow-
ers fell in slow motion. Time was warped by this insane event, and
we all felt that communally. Prior to that my only experience of
time trauma was when I was fifteen and fell out of my bedroom
window—timewise, that was a deeply surreal experience. I knew
that privately but to share it with anybody was a bit—

IM: You fell out of your bedroom window?

ZS: Yeah.

IM: Sleepwalking?

ZS: No, no, no, trying to smoke a fag.

IM: Oh my God.

ZS: Yeah, comedy story. I almost died, but the point is, that fall and
the slowness of it, literally the *days* of it—I couldn't find a way to
talk about it without sounding a little loopy. But several times in
your fiction that feeling is expressed, very accurately I think.

IM: Yeah, but isn't it also something to do with demands of narrative—so let's say we're looking at a fifteen-year-old, balancing a buttock on a window ledge, doesn't want to breathe smoke back into the bedroom—

ZS: Yeah, that was it.

IM: Suddenly you're dividing the moment with much more intensity. Even in describing it you're slowing the movement. Because you think this is high-value, rich experience, therefore only two seconds are 1,200 words. And you've done it for the reader, already, without having any notion of time, you would have conveyed this slowing instinctively. And probably, one mistake I regret in *The Child in Time* was the way I harangue the reader, telling everybody that "TIME IS SLOW." You don't need to say that. The prose slows it down.

ZS: But I think in the car incident the two are quite well meshed, the description and the feeling, it's a pretty amazing passage.

IM: Yeah, all I need to do is cut away from the bits where it says "time slowed."

ZS: Now, what about repudiating previous work? I've been trying not to read the reviews of *Saturday* because I want to have my own feelings about it, but I presume a few people picked up on *The Child in Time* reference and also the magic realism references in the book. You satirize that kind of writing, and also the magic realism in your earlier work. And actually, reading your back catalog, I realized there's quite a lot of it. More than I remembered.

IM: Yeah. I wouldn't do it now, I must say. And although I never really trusted any magic realist literature, very far, I was at least able to—you know how it is, you give characters views you can't or wouldn't condone.

ZS: Yes, exactly. It's fun to do that. It makes you brave.

IM: Yes. But I suppose I do have a sneaking sympathy with the view that the real, the actual, is so demanding and rich, that magical realism is really a tedious evasion of some artistic responsibility.

ZS: Because the magic is *in* the real. I was trying to pick out some of my very favorite lines in *The Child in Time*—and there's the one about the neck. Do you remember this?

IM: No. Neck?

ZS: Yeah, it's a lady's neck: Emma Carew.

IM: Oh, right. "The fan of tendons round the neck of Emma Carew, a cheerful, anorexic headmistress, tightened like umbrella struts when her name was remembered and spoken aloud."

ZS: Exactly. Now, for me, that brings wonder already, there is no need for the rest. But was there a switch in your mind, a point where you decided to stop writing stories about women in relationships with monkeys, for example?

IM: Well, as I say, I never had much time for it.

ZS: The short stories have quite a bit of it, though.

IM: There's some.

ZS: There's a lot of different approaches: there's hyper-realism, there's allegory, there's the supernatural, the grotesque—there's a whole raft of techniques used to introduce the incredible.

IM: Yes, but those were short stories and I think they're great to try, to "put on," like trying on your parents' clothes. When people ask, "Is there any advice you'd give a young writer?," I say write short stories. They afford lots of failure. Pastiche is a great way to start. But I was never really a great one for that kind of extreme Angela Carter magic realist stuff... although actually I got to know her and admire her and was kind of a neighbor in Clapham.

ZS: Oh, really?

IM: I liked her really on the basis of those stories she wrote in Japan. But then the further she got into fairy tales and then into *Nights at the Circus*—that wasn't for me.

It seemed to me such a narrowing down of all the possibilities. The real, the actual, they place heavy demands on a writer—how to invent it, how to confront it or pass it through the sieve of your own consciousness. So I was never a great Márquez person, I admired the *Tin Drum* but never really admired it the way I did Kundera, say. And it seems to me now that that style has become a bit like the international style in furniture, this sort of lingua franca that really defies the central notion of the novel which is that the novel is local. It's regional, it's a bottom-up process, and somehow these international styles seem to have a top-down process. They are too similar to each other.

ZS: They have trademarks. One of their trademarks is a kind of kinetic energy. Energy at the expense of everything else.

IM: Yeah. It's tennis without the net. There's no fun.

ZS: Nothing at stake.

IM: Yes. But then I thought if I'm taking a sideswipe here at that kind of fiction [in *Saturday*], I'd better include myself!

II. "SOMEONE ONCE ASKED ME 'IF YOUR LIFE COULD BE EXTENDED TO 150 AND YOU COULD START ANOTHER CAREER, WOULD YOU?' AND I SAID 'NO, THANKS, I THINK I'LL STICK AT THIS.'"

ZS: I still feel this technical difference between you and the generation you came up with, not just in quality but in kind. I found a quote of yours:"What drove me was an impatience with the English fiction I read. It seemed like a polite talking shop of which I was no part" and I wanted to think about that in reference to dialogue, because I do think your dialogue is different and serves different purposes than, say, Amis's. There's a lot less of it, for starters.

IM: Well, Martin would have his roots more in Dickens, in a love of the absurd and caricature.

ZS: And dialect plays a more serious role with Amis, as it does for me. Less so with you.

IM: Yeah.

ZS: Only, recently there's more dialect in yours than there was before.

IM: Yeah. Martin used to sit around with his dad and take a lot of pleasure in looking, with some kind of hilarious scorn, at the way people spoke and how these phrases passed into the language, and he would come back with a fresh nugget and say, "Yeah, Kingsley and I were talking about the way people say"—whatever it was— and he'd be able to impersonate it exactly.

ZS: He still does that?

IM: Yeah. Wonderfully accurate, but there is some distancing going on there, too.

ZS: Well, there will always be a little difference in someone like Martin's comfort in the language, his kind of flippant freedom with it, and your own, possibly more hesitant, approach. You spoke a little bit about that in "Mother Tongue," and linked it with class.

IM: There is all that. My mother's hesitancy in language was a cru- cial element of my English class position. But like anything to do with English class, my exact position was complicated. My parents were working class but when I was fourteen my father was com- missioned as an officer… He was one of the British army officers who've come up through the ranks; they're not Sandhurst, they don't have university degrees and they're not posh, and all his friends were similar people. And I know looking back that all the other officers sort of looked down on them. They respected them, too, because they knew an awful lot about the army. And when my father became an officer, we were immediately posted somewhere else, so we went from being part of the sergeants' mess world to the officers' mess world. And that was a kind of rootlessness right there, which was partly about language, the way we spoke and the way we did things.

ZS: It's like you had a kind of impersonality thrust upon you—and of course there's a lot of English criticism about that idea. That the less rigidly placed you are in this society the more conceptual space you have to write.

IM: It's the business of class but also, for me, a question of rootlessness in terms of location. I spent my first three years of life in Aldershot in a garrison town and then it was the Far East and then it was North Africa, so I know, even when people say where do you come from, well, I can say Aldershot, but I know that I'm not rooted in any particular place. And then I went to a strange boarding school, a state boarding school where the kids were largely working-class kids from central London from broken homes, they'd take a few kids from lower-middle-class parents like myself, an officer but not grand, not Sandhurst. The idea was to take those kids from central London, working-class kids, give them the kind of education they would have got at a public school and send them to university. And that's what they did. It was an old-fashioned, ameliorative view which is now long out of fashion. So that was another kind of rootlessness, I was with all these boys, there were three hundred of us in what was once a stately home on the Essex-Suffolk border, beautiful countryside. It was hilarious, a wonderful school in many ways. Everyone stayed in the sixth form, they sent a third of the sixth form to Oxbridge—

ZS: That's pretty impressive.

IM: Yeah, everyone went to university. And then I went to sort of a bright, plateglass type university in Sussex and then another one in East Anglia.

ZS: Were you conscious of wanting to be a writer or of taking it seriously from that early stage? Your first stories are so unerringly confident.

IM: I think I was making a strength out of a kind of ignorance. I had no roots in anything and it was almost as if I had to invent a literature.

ZS: One of the other striking things about your stories is the absence of—I don't know what to call it—let's say a "judging consciousness." The narrator who guides your judgement as you read—that idea is completely evaporated. The reader is absolutely out on a limb. There's no help given, and English readers, like those kids on the internet, are used to at least being pointed in the direction of what they should disapprove of. And that's not there.

IM: I wanted to write without supports. I was very impressed by a quote from Flaubert:

> What seems beautiful to me, what I should like to write, is a book about nothing, a book dependent on nothing external, which would be held together by the strength of its style, just as the earth, suspended in the void, depends on nothing external for its support.

ZS: Christ. You need ambition for that.

IM: But I was writing tiny little stories, certainly not novels. Those kind of remarks impressed me, I liked them and there still is an element of that remaining. At the beginning of *Saturday* it's there in the idea of the character getting naked out of bed and standing unencumbered in the dark. It's as if he's just being born.

ZS: It does have that form, of the whole day being made with nothing taken for granted, no quick flashes into the past, every single block of it is built, as if by hand. You go through the day with Henry.

That's an enormous amount of work, I would think, to write.

IM: Yeah. But to go back to this business of roots and stories and what I didn't like in fiction—

ZS: Right, because I thought you meant Iris Murdoch at first and that kind of conversational fiction, "chattering classes" or Hampstead fiction, or whatever.

IM: There are many of them still alive, like Margaret Drabble, and I actually was inclined to change my view later, because there's good stuff there... but at the time, in describing a world about which I knew nothing and had no interest, I was impatient. I thought writers ought to be hippies. I did have a rather romantic sense of what it should be. I got a bit hot under the collar about all the politeness and the overstuffed quality.

ZS: Furniture everywhere.

IM: Furniture. All of it described, you know, the names of everything. But it was exactly this: too much already taken for granted. It was a world and the reader was meant to have already filled in a lot of the colors, assuming a bond between writer and reader— a class bond, often—and I didn't share it. Whereas with people like Roth there seemed to be an energy about the prose. It had this wonderful self-invented, handmade, watermark quality, and that's why I liked both Roth and Updike. They've loomed over my writing life, even though nothing in my stories reveals that.

ZS: That intrigued me, too, these influences of yours that can't quite be detected, or at least not directly.

IM: But it's about reading something while you're working and your heart is just longing for your project, and the joy of reading this book by somebody else is actually what makes you turn up at the desk the next day in the broader sense, you see. If I can just generate the same feeling in the reader that this writer generated in me then I'll have succeeded. And that is probably the biggest influence.

ZS: What about some of the things that have been said about your progression as a writer? Usually the story is from good to bad to worse, but you've moved forward and consistently got stronger and stronger and I've heard a lot of quite lame dinner party suggestions as to why that might be so. But I wondered how you felt about it yourself. My feeling is that being slightly outside a privileged literary class tends to make you more artisan-minded, the way Keats was, the idea of working and working and working until it's right.

IM: I had a long apprenticeship. I started writing in about 1970. It was 1978 before I published a novel and even that was just sort of an extended short story. As was my second one.

ZS: But you have always been a writer—I mean, you're working life has been a writing one. And this is a subject which honestly concerns me, not a little, because it's my life and it's likely to be my life for a really long time. And I'm terrified by the stultifying effects of being a writer and staying a writer. But you don't seem to feel it, or not as strongly as I do.

IM: No, not at all. Someone once asked me "If your life could be extended to 150 and you could start another career, would you?" And I said "No, thanks, I think I'll stick at this." And the reason I gave, I quoted Henry James on fiction. He said that the concern of the novelist, the subject material, is all of it, all of experience. And you don't run out of experience by being a writer.

ZS: That's true. Sometimes it feels endless. But to me I have other days where I feel like it's a corrupt, intellectually finite, and stupid way to live, with nothing real in it—I can feel myself cannibalizing my own life and I think "how long can this go on for?" There is a lot in *Saturday* of the details of your own existence.

IM: It is the first time I've really cannibalized my life.

ZS: It is the first time. And I wondered what happens next.

IM: Next, I will almost certainly have an entirely invented set of circumstances.

ZS: There's always a difference, though. Certainly I find the more I carry on at this lark the less I have time for imagined, physical detail. I just don't do it. If I need a sofa, I look across the room and there's a sofa. If I need a lamppost, there's a lamppost in the street. I can't conjure lampposts out of nothing. Maybe when I was fourteen. That's completely beyond me now.

IM: No, quite. And also how much furniture does one need any more? In answer to your question, having cannibalized my life for this novel, it makes the next one easier. I'm left with everything that's not *this* [*points around the room*], and that's a hell of a lot. I have no idea what it will be. There's also all the past which I've never really borrowed—my childhood. But I don't know. Naturally when people say "You've got better" I get a bit pissed off and say "Well, what was wrong with the others? What was I doing wrong before?"

ZS: Well, it's not that the earlier stuff was worse, but it's that the tools and machinery of this one work so very smoothly, one feels completely confident as a reader. You've no problem at all anymore with "making a novel." When I think of both my novels the second halves of both are rubbish because of basic, technical inability. When you're younger every page is still a struggle. And when I read *Saturday* I just felt: well, "making a novel" is the least of your bloody problems, mate. Same with Roth. There are other things that are being developed—ideas, themes, larger ambitions to do with a canon of work—but the "making a novel" bit feels like it's done effortlessly. Maybe that's not how it is at all. But I wondered whether the autobiographical stuff makes the composition process a slightly smoother process.

IM: I have to say I thought it would be. I made this decision, OK, I will blatantly use my life in this next novel so that will save me an awful lot of time. Actually it didn't. It was just as much a struggle. Even when I was actually using the internal layout of this house for the scenes, it rarely occurred to me as I walked about this house that this was the same house in the book. It's somehow a map of a parallel house.

ZS: Talking of parallels, there's a paragraph in *Saturday* about surgery, apparently, but it seems to me to be about writing.

IM: Oh, well done.

ZS: I read it and thought it can't be about anything else. You know the paragraph I mean? "For the past two hours he's been in a dream of absorption"—it's such an exact description of what it's like to write when it's going well. And my favorite line is when you talk about him feeling "calm and spacious, fully qualified to exist. It's a feeling of clarified emptiness, of deep, muted joy." The events you put next to it, as comparative experiences—the love-making and listening to Theo's song—are two human states which are often advertised as bringing similar pleasure: basically, personal relations and art. But the book seems to suggests that there is a deeper happiness that one can only find in work, or at least, creative work. And I felt that joy coming off the book in every direction. Joy at being a writer!

IM: I'm glad that you found that paragraph. I knew I wanted to write a major operation at the end but it would really be about writing, about making art. So it starts with him picking up a paintbrush. Or rather, I was *so* sure, when I went for the operation, that Neil Pritchard, the surgeon, when he paints the marks on the patient, was using a two-inch paintbrush. And when I sent him the last draft, just to check it one last time he said, "I don't use a paintbrush," and I said, "But surely surgeons do," and he said "No, no." I was so disappointed personally. He dips the paintbrush in yellow paint and as the Aria of the Goldberg Variations starts, he makes his first stroke and it is a moment of artistic engagement... But very, very reluctantly I had to replace it with a sponge on a flap.

ZS: The joy of the extended analogy is that it allows you to write about writing as work. Usually when you read books about being a novelist, all you really get is the character at lunches and his publishing routines, and that's nothing to do with the process of writing. It's so hard to sit down and write about that procedure, but I feel that metaphorically it's done here.

IM: The dream, surely, Zadie, that we all have, is to write this beautiful paragraph that actually is describing something but at the same time in another voice is writing a commentary on its own creation, without having to be a story about a writer.

III. "I'M NOT AGAINST RELIGION IN THE SENSE THAT I FEEL I CAN'T TOLERATE IT, BUT I THINK WRITTEN INTO THE RUBRIC OF RELIGION IS THE CERTAINTY OF ITS OWN TRUTH. AND SINCE THERE ARE 6,000 RELIGIONS CURRENTLY ON THE FACE OF THE EARTH, THEY CAN'T ALL BE RIGHT..."

ZS: I want to ask you about the optimism in *Saturday*. There's this recognizably Updikean enjoyment in the book, which I love; you seem to relish the things of the world. And you're right; it *is* an amazing thing to be able to go and get a glass of fresh orange juice in England—these supposedly normal things that would have been revolutionary even sixty-odd years ago. But surely one of the problems we have with all this progress is that it has been at the expense of foreign places and foreign people who do not partake of the progress, and that's kind of exactly the reason we're in this shitstorm/"war-without-end" nightmare scenario right now. So I found it hard to celebrate with Henry Perowne, knowing what his privileges are based on.

IM: Yeah. Well, I guess this is writing against the current in as far as I would take your view to be one of the conventions of liberal intellectual anxiety, one of the spectral opponents of the pleasures of life in the West. Perowne has these, too. He has all these mar-velous advantages and yet he finds himself in a state of anxiety—we have all the pleasures and yet we're looking behind our back. And the reason I wanted to make Perowne a wealthy man is because, actually, that's what the first world is.

ZS: But by any comparison, he's pretty damn wealthy.

IM: The fact that he's wealthier than some but not all journalists…

ZS: You knew you were going to be set up by that. Some people were always going to find the descriptions of Perowne's luxurious life distasteful.

IM: Yeah. That doesn't touch me at all. Because I know that these journalists are wealthy by any planetary standard. That's precisely why I had him gazing at the locks on his door, thinking about the bad people, the drug dealers who want to get in—there's an embat-tlement. They're on the other side. You block these people out of your world picture. It's a kind of framing. You cease to see a patient on the table because you only see the little square, the mole—

ZS: Exactly. But then you are saying that happiness is based on unreality or a bubble of unreality.

IM: It's a kind of framing, yes. But great things are achieved with-in that frame.

ZS: The other thing about championing progress is the danger that we go too far in the "celebration of all things Western" direction. I'm reading articles by Rushdie recently which rigorously defend Western thought, and because I've just reread *Black Dogs* (in which the character Bernard is a great defender of the principle of "rationality"), it did strike me that Rusdhie has become Bernard Extraordinaire. He's defending the Enlightenment against all com-ers now, bravely and viciously, but very strongly. I understand his emotion, exactly. But it's strange when you consider where we were fifteen years ago when some of the more confident Enlightenment assumptions, the quasireligious worship of the rational, for example, were being radically questioned. And now we're at this point where it's three cheers for Descartes because we've got these mad men in their planes. It's like we've all become radicalized in response to that.

IM: When the Enlightenment was being sort of undermined by the theorists in the academies, that was done with a general sense of security about the ultimate cultural victory of Enlightenment values, and now I think that victory is a lot less assured.

ZS: And so would you say you've lost patience, if you've ever had any patience, with the idea of religion?

IM: Absolutely. I agree with Salman about that. I have no patience whatsoever.

ZS: I suppose I feel the same, but I feel strange about feeling it.

IM: I'm not against religion in the sense that I feel I can't tolerate it, but I think written into the rubric of religion is the certainty of its own truth. And since there are 6,000 religions currently on the face of the earth, they can't all be right. And only the secular spirit can guarantee those freedoms and it's the secular spirit that they contest.

ZS: You were asked once what you believe, truly believe though you can't prove it, and you said: the absolute belief that there's nothing after consciousness. But something about *Saturday* and its joy in the world and, again, that kind of Updikean pleasure, made me wonder whether you'd ever imagined yourself moving in that vaguely Christian direction…

IM: No.

ZS: Never? No change as you've got older, no inching fears or hopes…

IM: No. I don't see any paradox in that which celebrates all things within the context of the extremely brief gift of consciousness.

ZS: See, for a lot of writers even the phrase "brief gift of consciousness" is enough to send them into a fit, and I'm one of them. As a breed, we tend to harbor quite severe death fears.

IM: And *gift,* by the way, is a metaphor because—

ZS: Nobody gives.

IM: Indeed, there's nobody there.

ZS: But I think amongst English writers it's quite unusual to have such a solid, non-death fear.

IM: I have an absolute death fear! I don't want this thing to end. [Philip] Larkin expresses that feeling so beautifully.

ZS: But I think with Larkin, he's the kind of man who would have taken any religion that seemed even vaguely convincing, he wasn't fussy. He'd take anything—he didn't believe in being brave… but as it happened everything was too stupid to be acceptable to him. Anyway: enough about death.

IM: Yes.

IV. "I WAS TRYING TO SAY… THE EROTIC IMAGINATION DOES NOT NECESSARILY NEED CRITICAL MANIFESTOS, THAT IT CAN'T BE GOVERNED IN THAT WAY."

ZS: I want to talk to you about sex and women. You said something once about *The Female Eunuch* being revelatory. I think that about that book a lot as well—as weird as it is to talk about that now, given all that's happened in the past six months. [Germaine Greer appeared as a contestant in Britain's *Big Brother* TV show.]

IM: Yeah. Is that the same Germaine?

ZS: It's hard to imagine. Anyway, I wasn't there in '75 to see the first book come out, but I would imagine the word "feminist" was not one often used much in the context of your short stories. But the women in them and the care and concern with women all the way through your fiction is really interesting to me. And there's a lot of honesty about the deep, masculine hatred for women.

IM: "About it." That's the key.

ZS: Right. Almost every dimension of it is looked at. Silent women, damaged women, sexually vulnerable women, little girls, everything.

IM: I got a good kicking over all that. I was trying to write about the very things that I felt the feminist discussion was involved in, and also to have some fun writing about them. The first story you get is of a man who falls for a shop window dummy and then I just let this man project every fantasy on to her, just see what happens.

ZS: There's an idea in those stories that sex is where things can go most right and most wrong. That seems to be a very McEwan idea. It'll save you and also completely destroy you.

IM: But also it seemed to me at the time, in the '70s, that there needed to be a huge realignment in the way men and women would talk to each other. And I'm absolutely certain if you were to get into some time machine and go back to the early '60s, the condescension and also the apartheid would completely amaze you.

ZS: It's like when I'm reading Kingsley Amis. Whatever the attitude is to women is not really the interesting thing, it's that the women are so *other*. It's as if they've come off a different planet. There's no communication at all. You want to say, "Go on, Kingsley, poke her with your finger, she's *real!*"

IM: There was no game about it, either. People lived it. I used to talk to Martin Amis about thinking of girls as real people and then he married Antonia and I think then he got it, he suddenly saw something he hadn't seen before and actually his books have changed. Meanwhile I was going in the other direction. I remember going to a conference on the erotic, I don't know why I'd been invited, it was a time when the left, they were tough cookies, there were many separatists. Anyway, I gave a very good talk and what I was trying to say was the erotic imagination does not necessarily need critical manifestos, that it can't be governed in that way. The erotic imagination can be very interested in unkindness, for example. In sadism. I was booed offstage. I said, until you take that on board, then your picture of this is not accurate. I said, let's talk about masochism for example, male *and* female masochism.

ZS: That's the basis of *The Comfort of Strangers.*

IM: Yeah. So that's what I then went on to write. I felt: Oh, well, there must be other terms for discussion about what takes place between a man and woman beyond sociology and critical manifestos. What about the sort of thrilling notion that you could test love, test trust, that you could experiment with un-freeing yourself?

ZS: So the stories are news in a way, news from the male consciousness. And the news is: male consciousness ain't always the happiest place to be. And it's news unattached to dogma, which in 1985 I would imagine was a pretty out-there thing to do.

IM: 1981.

ZS: Oops.

IM: But, yes, and actually within a year or two there were American feminists writing about the erotic in ways that were really much closer to what I was trying to write about. British feminism is very rooted in Marxism, so it was very much about wages and matters of real concern, but it sat very uneasily in any discussion about the erotic.

ZS: Certainly in the past ten years feminism has become much more willing to talk dirty. There's a kind of cheap, fetishized version that you get in the women's magazines, trumpeting women who are able to say, "Yes, I am a feminist, but I still quite like being tied to a doorknob for three days." It's easy to satirize that stuff, but I feel you really believe in the underlying argument that there's no point in feminism ignoring the female instinct for the perverse. And then you get the other side of the argument, typified by my husband, who believes masochism and sadism will always be found to have its root cause in some kind of emotional damage, that there's no other reason.

IM: No, he's absolutely wrong. Madonna famously said being tied down gave her the thrill and comfort of being strapped into a car seat when she was three. I thought, Ah! She's said it.

ZS: The quote at the end of *The Comfort of Strangers*: "She was going to tell him her theory, tentative at this stage, of course, which explained how the imagination, the sexual imagination, men's ancient dreams of hurting and women's of being hurt, embodied and declares a powerful single organizing principle, which distorted all relations, all truth."

I'm a writer who never writes about sex. It's so far from my own fictional world, and it unnerves me when you say "powerful, single, organizing principle." You mean that sex is the pole that everything else moves around—in which case, I'm really missing a trick. That seems to be what you were saying in 1981. And I wonder if you still feel that.

IM: No, I don't.

ZS: Because it's a very a big thing to say.

IM: That's a very big thing to say especially in a tiny novel. But it's something that someone who had just gone through what the character had gone through might well feel. But no, I have now reached the stage where as soon as anyone says life moves around a single, organizing principle I stop listening to them. I don't feel that life organizes itself around any single principle. It's a religious impulse to only grasp at one thing, one explanation.

ZS: I understand.

IM: That's interesting, though… I don't know where things stand now in the sexual debate. I've just started reading *Villages* [John Updike's new novel]… plenty of sex in there.

ZS: I know. It's unbelievable. I don't know how he stays interested. I find it amazing, not just purely technically, but the virility of the man, the continued interest.

IM: The virility of the man!

ZS: You know what I mean. He's still bothered. He loves women and he says, somewhere in that book, that he can't believe that women "tend to us" or "care for us at all" or something like that. As if to say: what a miracle it is. He doesn't seem to have ever gotten over the idea that women don't mind making love to men.

IM: I like the bit at the beginning when he's being shaved, the hero, and it's like: the girls all worship us but of course they don't have enough intellect to be able to worship us. *If only they knew how vast our consciousness is…* But seriously, it still remains difficult, more difficult now than it was, to understand what the true relation is between men and women. Back then everything was being stirred up, it was a blizzard, it was an argument you had to get involved in. Now it all seems to have slowed and settled. A sort of muffled silence.

ZS: In a lot of the chick lit, depicting women slightly older than me, the sexual maturity is that of a nine-year-old, maybe. The sex is just this giggly and ridiculous activity one is subjected to in order to make a man stay in your house and marry you. There's no honest expression of female sexual desire, the kind you find even in those old cheesy feminist manuals like *Our Bodies, Ourselves.* We've gone backwards. I mean, if you had a daughter who believed this stuff they're printing now, you'd be devastated.

IM: I keep hearing that song "Too Drunk to Fuck"—have you heard that?

ZS: Yeah. Things have not gone well in the past ten years.

IM: What a shame.

ZS: What about your two boys? Are you conscious of bringing up different kinds of men from the ones I had to date?

IM: Yeah, I think so. They're both very rapid in their development. When they got to the age of about sixteen or seventeen, they had their first girlfriends, and stayed with them for two or three years. I think it was enormously healthy. And they remained friends with them afterwards. And now Will is in his second long relationship and Greg has just finished his first, but they still meet and it's very touching. Three-hour phone conversations still go on and they seemed to have had lots of sex. Far more sex than I'd *ever* imagined at the same age. I find it deeply enviable.

ZS: One of the critical standards I remember being levied at all your generation of male writers was: *does he write women well? Can he write a convincing bird?* Do you think about that still? Does it concern you? Do you think you've improved?

IM: I think I'm sort of gender-blind on this. I think it was Fay Weldon who said that a man could never write a woman properly, which I thought was ludicrous. Taken to its logical extension, novelists could only write about themselves; you couldn't write about an old person, a young person, a person you didn't know. Henry James said that in the contract between writer and reader one thing we must accept as given is the subject matter. I accept that wholly. It's a great contract. There's nowhere you'll not let your imagination go.

V. "AS YOU GET OLDER YOU FEEL THE NEED TO MAKE YOURSELF CLEAR..."

ZS: Ah—I wanted to talk about the places you let your imagination go. Dark places. The most striking thing in *Saturday*, I think, is the final scene, in particular, the sadism of it. Now, either I'm an idiot or—well, I just didn't expect it, I was caught out complete-ly. I was having a lovely time in a lovely world with lovely people and I went upstairs to read the last hundred pages—Nick [Nick Laird, Smith's husband] was downstairs watching TV with friends—and was sitting alone with this book feeling like I was being attacked. My scalp was prickly, I was sweating, I kept want-ing to shout downstairs but then there's no point trying to explain what's happened in a book if somebody's not reading it... I felt physically assailed. And maybe there's a lot of fiction which does that and I just don't read it. I'm always reading this flowery liter-ary fiction. But I'd never had that feeling before. And I never expect that response from my readers, I never expect anything physical from them. I know I can't make them cry and I can't make them go [*sharp intake of breath*] like I was doing with your book, yesterday. So I wonder if you sit down and aim for that response and how you can possibly pace a novel, bargaining on that result? Because what if it didn't happen? What if I just read that scene and went, "Uh, yeah," and moved on?

IM: I knew what I wanted to get, I had no idea exactly how I was going to get it. I leave blanks in my planning, and there are bits it's best not to think about till you get there. I didn't know whether he had a knife nor did I know what he wanted. I had to write it to find out what was going to happen. I mean I knew that he would end up being thrown down the stairs, and that the opera-tion would happen but I was looking for my... well, to go back to where we started this conversation, to 9/11, and the sense of inva-sion, one can only do it on a private scale. If you say the airliner hit the side of the building, a thousand people died, nothing hap-pens to your scalp. So I, in a sense, tried to find the private scale of that feeling.

ZS: But what advice would you give regarding how a writer might *earn* that moment? Because when I finished reading I thought you'd done exactly what you needed to do, to earn that moment.

I didn't feel that you'd tried to scare me in a cheap way or you'd taken a backdoor. More could have happened in that scene, in fact. I was interested, in my mind, as to how far you could have gone with that narrative before I was angry with you for a manipulation. All the narrative decisions you make in a scene like that are ethical decisions, and also aesthetic, and you have to make them, they're serious. And someone who can't write makes them very badly.

IM: Especially if you're going to have a young woman with no clothes on, being looked at in that way. How long you dwell on it is key. And I felt I was taking a risk having Daisy naked. And the risk was—well, first I got it completely wrong, I didn't make it frightening enough and the reason I didn't make it frightening was I didn't want to humiliate her. But then it was unreal. So I had to go back and I made her defiant. But it just didn't stand up.

ZS: I would never be defiant in that situation.

IM: There's no way anyone could be defiant with this man holding a knife to your mother's neck. But again the question of the amount of time one dwells on the nakedness. And I thought if I was Updike now Perowne's gaze would be relentless and we would have to have Daisy's body described. And I thought: there Perowne cannot go. So I went to fear and fear did what I thought a brother and father would have to do in an emergency. Look to the floor, think of a way of attacking. And in a sense so did I, I looked to the floor. Apart from the swell of her pregnancy. The whole thing is four pages. It's narrative time enough but not particularly long to dwell.

ZS: In the past you worked more on the complicit nature of the reader-writer relationship. That story about the father with the two little girls, "In Between the Sheets," makes you complicit by constantly allowing—without authorial comment—these descriptions in which the father makes the children sound older than they are. Several times they're described as looking older, speaking like women, moving like women. This makes the reader complicit in the pedophile's idea, or potential pedophile's idea, that these girls could be his. And that's an incredibly uncomfortable experience as a reader.

IM: Yeah. I was very keen on making readers uncomfortable. I think I've lost that ambition now, it doesn't interest me so much as a project.

ZS: It's a kind of cruelty.

IM: Yeah. Leading the reader into siding with the murderous pedophile or rapist. It's not so interesting.

ZS: Or offering the reader an extreme, antihumanist perspective on a human being. In the story "Homemade" you describe a young boy running a race as a "tiny amoebic blob across the field... staggering determinedly in its pointless effort to reach the flags—just life, just faceless, self-renewing life..."

IM: Yeah. I was trying to be funny. Because he comes home thirteenth.

ZS: But the reader is also being forced to see people from perspectives the novel as a form doesn't usually encourage.

IM: Absolutely.

ZS: Do you think your taste for that has lessened a little?

IM: It has lessened a little. Because I think death anxiety or numbers-of-days-left anxiety make me keen to make sense of the human, rather than to distort it. I think there's a wonderful recklessness you have in your twenties and thirties as a writer, you can do terrible things because although intellectually you know your time will end, you don't yet feel it in your blood, in your gut. It's a recklessness I think one should really enjoy, relax into it, spread out. As you get older you feel the need to make yourself clear.

ZS: Right.

IM: There are a couple of things. One is you have children and as you age, there's some growing sense of wanting the human project to succeed. Not fail. Or you no longer wish to dwell quite so much on the possibility of it all going wonderfully, horribly wrong. You begin to wish it would go right.

ZS: So, in conclusion: what are you going to do about your mellowing coinciding with the world's hardcore radicalization and madness? That's a strange mix. You feel it in *Saturday*. The collision of somebody in that moment of their life where they're feeling satisfied and fulfilled and unfortunately that moment's happening on a planet that's losing the bloody plot entirely.

IM: Yeah, it is an extraordinary moment. It's like we've engaged ourselves in some medieval struggle. We had our Diderot and Voltaire and now you'd hope we'd at least now investigate the structure of DNA, and the origins of the universe, and the possibility of understanding more about ourselves with a new metaphysics—but that's not the focus right now. The struggle is a medieval one between faiths.

ZS: Yeah. It's all gone wrong. When I was in America around all these classic left-wing intellectuals, the feeling was one of literal despair. They just run through the streets screaming. That's basically their only reaction to the moment they're in, as if this moment were unprecedented. But that's the interesting thing—it's nowhere near unprecedented. I liked the fact that in *Saturday* you seemed to be saying, instead, what we were getting here is a madness that, in truth, has always accompanied progress.

IM: You know, twenty-five years ago or twenty years ago, all we talked about was the possibility that the Soviet Union and the United States were going to have a global conflict and do it in Europe. That was the unprecedented moment.

ZS: You wrote your own apocalypse story at the time as well.

IM: It felt like a real possibility. And we got very indignant, caught between two empires, we thought we might all die. Martin Amis famously said that if the war started he would drive home, shoot his wife, and then shoot his children.

ZS: He doesn't do things by halves.

IM: As a humane act. So the liberal Left went around saying "Dear sir, in your interview, you said you'd shoot your wife and children. Do you really think that's an appropriate response?" But anyway it was on our minds. And madness was in the air.

ZS: In *Saturday*, Henry Perowne wonders whether the madness and trauma of 9/11 will take a hundred years to resolve itself. Do you believe that?

IM: At the end of *Saturday*, I think of a figure like Perowne but a hundred years earlier, 1904, and of what terror lay ahead then. We've almost forgot the First World War, Stalin, and then the Second, the Holocaust—if we had a fraction of that we'd be very fortunate. At least we know what we're capable of. But the moment is not unprecedented.

ZS: Maybe everything takes a hundred years or more to play itself out. Look at the bloody Treaty of Versailles. Now: next question is utterly unrelated.

IM: Good.

ZS: I read your back catalog over a month or so and I felt very satisfied merely having "read all of McEwan." And then I thought, fuck, imagine *having written all of McEwan*. So I was wondering what it feels like to look at your own bookshelves and see this nice little backlog of work. This little stack. I don't know what that would feel like. Amazing, I would think.

IM: It's not amazing because you get there by very slow increments. If you think of Updike—*that's* amazing. Updike's "Also by" page is now a few pages long in itself. An insane amount of books.

ZS: That is insane. He has a condition I think. It's a disease with him—he can't stop.

IM: Graphomania. Well, it would be easier to dismiss if it wasn't so good.

ZS: Does it give you pleasure, though?

IM: It's like a family album, the consciousness of your own past—well, you must find this already. I certainly find it. People say what were you doing in such and such year, and I know exactly what I was doing. I know I was publishing a particular book, or halfway through one. These books are the spoonfuls with which I've measured my existence. ✯

SEAN WILSEY

TALKS WITH

HARUKI MURAKAMI

"WHAT THE NOVELIST NEEDS IS NOT
DIVERSE OPINIONS BUT A PERSONAL SYSTEM
OF STORYTELLING UPON WHICH
HIS OPINIONS CAN TAKE A FIRM STAND."

Interests that would seem to cancel each other out:
Kafka, baseball
Chandler, drinking in moderation
Dostoevsky, browsing used record stores

aruki Murakami has published thirteen books in
English, of which the majority are great, and two are
better—that is, deeper, funnier, lonelier, more life-
affirming and breath-taking and sleep-depriving—
than anything I've ever read.

    *A rough sketch of Murakami's pre-writing years goes like this: born in
1949, in Kyoto, his self-described uneventful suburban childhood was
enlivened by voracious reading of Dostoevsky and Raymond Chandler
(the latter in paperbacks left behind by American sailors). A few years as a
middling university student in Tokyo introduced him to the two loves of
his life, jazz music and his wife, Yōko; he married and opened a jazz club,*

called Peter Cat (cats being a third love), which was such a success that Murakami's life seemed set on its course—comfortable, bohemian—until, as he told an audience in 1992, "Suddenly one day in April 1978, I felt like writing a novel... I was at a baseball game... in the outfield stands, drinking beer... My favorite team was the Yakult Swallows. They were playing the Hiroshima Carps. The Swallows' first batter in the bottom of the first inning was an American, Dave Hilton. You've probably never heard of him. He never made a name for himself in the States, so he came to play ball in Japan. I'm pretty sure he was the leading hitter that year. Anyhow, he sent the first ball pitched to him that day into left field for a double. And that's when the idea struck me: I could write a novel."

So he wrote a novel. Every night after closing Peter Cat Murakami sat at his kitchen table, drank beer, and in six months produced the short, Vonnegut-like Hear the Wind Sing *(1979). He submitted the novel for a literary award, and when it won Murakami went to get Dave Hilton's autograph— "I feel he was a lucky charm for me"—then went back to the kitchen table and wrote another novel,* Pinball, 1973 *(1980). This book (coupled with a movie deal on the first) was successful enough to allow him to sell the jazz club and become a full-time writer at age thirty-two.*

Established, Murakami moved back to the suburbs and began work on A Wild Sheep Chase *(1982), technically the final book in a trilogy that began with the first two—the trilogy of the rat—though he considers it his first novel, because it's where he found his voice. (An unfortunate footnote to this success story is that neither* Hear the Wind Sing *or* Pinball, 1973 *will ever be available in the United States because, as Murakami bluntly told* Publishers Weekly *in 1991, they are "weak.")*

Style found, weakness behind him, lifestyle then changed. Murakami began exercising religiously, running marathons, eating meticulously, drinking moderately—living with a Shinto purity in order to maintain the rigorous work habits that have permitted him to be so consistently productive. He also began translating, mostly American writers, dividing his days between his own writing and the rendering into Japanese of Americans'. With his regime in place Murakami produced some astounding books, beginning with the hyper-experimental Hard–Boiled Wonderland and the End of the World *(1985, and still his personal favorite), and then, in pursuit of a wider audience, changing course to write what he described to* Publishers Weekly *as a "totally realistic, very straight" story, its title aimed directly at the mainstream:* Norwegian Wood *(1987). The novel was so huge that he fled Japan to escape the unprecedented, pop-star scale of his success. On the lam he wrote* Dance Dance Dance *(1988), a rollicking sequel to* A Wild Sheep Chase *(making a two-thirds-suppressed trilogy into a half-suppressed quadrilogy) and* South of the Border, West of the Sun *(1992), an elegiac version of* Norwegian Wood—*quieter and more mature.*

Then, working as a professor in the United States, he began his masterpiece, The Wind-up Bird Chronicle *(1994–1995), in which he took the best of his experimental and realistic voices, plus a new sense of history and morality, and closed in on what makes a writer immortal. The* Wind-up Bird Chronicle *was published in Japan in three volumes in 1994–1995, and in the U.S. in 1997, in a single abridged edition. Since then Murakami has returned to Japan. Short stories have always come naturally, and he has written some of his best in the past few years, collecting them in the 200-page tour de force* After the Quake *(2002). He's also written a nonfiction book,* Underground *(2000), about the poison gas attacks on the Tokyo subway, and two more novels,* Sputnik Sweetheart *(1999) and* Kafka on the Shore *(2005).*

For this interview we communicated by email; I wrote questions in English, and he responded in Japanese. Jay Rubin, translator of The Wind-up Bird Chronicle *and author of the indispensable biography* Haruki Murakami and the Music of Words *(2002), translated the answers into English.*

As an interviewee Murakami does not open up the deepest recess of his heart and soul. As a writer he opens up yours.

—*S.W. (Summer/Fall 2004)*

SEAN WILSEY: It occurs to me that the most malevolent figure in your work is a sort of professional interviewee (Noboru Wataya in *The Wind-Up Bird Chronicle*); and you equate his facility with the

media (and the slipperiness of his opinions) with his evil and soul-
lessness. You seem to be saying if a person is too good at opening
his mouth in public he's empty inside. Then again, one of the most
illuminating interviews I've ever read with anyone on any subject
was the *New York Times*'s interview with you on the subject of
9/11, and its similarities to the Tokyo subway gas attacks. There
you said, speaking of cult leaders, and their relationship with their
followers, "If you have questions, there is always someone to provide the answers. In a way, things are very easy and clear, and you
are happy as long as you believe." How does one speak publicly
without becoming a professional/Noboru Wataya, or stopping
people from thinking for themselves?

HARUKI MURAKAMI: I often get calls from newspapers asking
my opinion on some news event or other—for example, "What do
you think about Japan's decision to dispatch Self-Defense Force
troops to Iraq?" or "What's your view of the twelve-year-old girl
who cut her classmate's throat?" and such.

I do of course have my own reasonably clear personal opinions
about such events. But there is a definite difference between my
having an opinion as an individual and "novelist Haruki Murakami"'s having an opinion. Still, it goes without saying that any
personal opinion of mine appearing in the newspaper will be read
by the public as the opinion of novelist Haruki Murakami. And so
I make it a rule never to respond to questions from the media.

I am not, of course, saying that novelists must not express their
personal opinions. It is my belief, however, that, rather than expressing his views on a number of diverse matters, the role of the novelist would seem most properly to lie in his depicting as precisely
as possible (as Kafka described his execution machine in chillingly
minute detail) the personal bases and environmental forces that give
rise to those views. To put it in a more extreme manner, what the
novelist needs is not diverse opinions but a personal system of storytelling upon which his opinions can take a firm stand.

In that sense, Noboru Wataya's stance is, as you suggest, shallow and superficial. Precisely because his opinions are shallow and superficial, they communicate with great speed, and they have great practical impact. What I wanted to convey to the reader through my portrait of Noboru Wataya was the dangerous influence that contemporary media gladiators, who use such rhetoric as a weapon, exert on our society and our minds: the special cruelty they deploy below the surface. We are practically surrounded by such people in our daily lives. Often, the opinions we assume to be our own turn out on closer inspection to be nothing but the parroting of theirs. It is chilling to think that in many instances we view the world through the media and speak to each other in the words of the media.

The only thing we can do sometimes to avoid straying into such a sealed labyrinth, is to go down alone into a deep well the way the protagonist Watanabe does: to recover one's own point of view, one's own language. This is not an easy thing to do, of course, and sometimes it involves danger. The job of the novelist, perhaps, is to act as a seasoned guide to such dangerous journeys. And, in some cases, in the story we can simulate for the reader the experience of undertaking such a task of self-exploration. For me, the story is a powerful vehicle that performs many such functions.

What Shoko Asahara, the founder of the Aum Shinrikyo [the cult that released poison gas on the Tokyo subway], did was to undertake the deliberate abuse—and misuse—of such functions of the story. The circuit of the story he offered was oppressive and firmly closed off from external input. By contrast, the circuit of a genuine story must be fundamentally spontaneous and always open to the outside. We must reject all things Wataya-like and Asahara-like. This may well be the marrow of the story I am trying to write.

I responded to the *New York Times*'s request for an interview because I wanted to speak about my general view of the world and of the novel, not to give my personal opinions or to play rhetorical games. There is a major difference here. Wouldn't you say that

Noboru Wataya is less an interviewee than a commentator?

SW: Let me ask novelist Haruki Murakami about writing. You've talked about loving and being influenced by Carver, Chandler, Dostoevsky, and Kafka. I love Dostoevsky (*The Possessed* is one of my favorite novels), and I have always found him very funny; do these writers also make you laugh?

HM: I agree that *The Possessed* is one of Dostoevsky's funniest novels. Carver and Chandler, too, have wonderful senses of humor. Kafka's novels and stories are weirdly comical in their very structure. Humor plays a big role in my fiction, too. I suspect that you can't have genuine seriousness without an element of humor.

SW: What do you think about cuteness? Modern Japan, or at least the Japan we see over here, at its most extreme, seems like a nation swinging between its obsessions with either the extremely cute, or the extremely efficient (Hello Kitty; Honda Civic).

You've said that violence is the key to Japan. *The Wind-Up Bird Chronicle* is the book in which you wrestle most directly and harrowingly with Japan's history of violence, and the character you use to wrestle with it is called Cinnamon—a very cute name. What are you saying about cuteness? Is Japan's obsession with cuteness a means of wrestling with the violence of its recent history?

HM: I myself am not much interested in the cute and the efficient, so I can't really answer your questions. The commodification of the cute and the efficient is not something unique to Japan. Mickey Mouse is cute, after all, and the Swiss Army Knife is efficient. And nations are violent systems by definition. I feel it can be dangerous to explain whole cultures with buzzwords.

SW: The Japanese artist I most closely identify you with is Hayao Miyazaki, whose (sometimes cute) characters have to struggle with tragedy or loneliness or loss. As artists you both seem to know loss and deal with it in somewhat similar ways. Do you like or identify with Miyazaki?

HM: I have never seen any of Miyazaki's films. I don't know why, but I have never been much interested in *anime*. I like to keep a sharp division between things that interest me and things that don't in order to use the limited time allotted to me in life most economically, and anime just happens to belong to the category of things that don't interest me.

SW: I've noticed that female musicians in your work tend to be classically trained, and somewhat cursed (Reiko from *Norwegian Wood;* Miu from *Sputnik Sweetheart*), while the men are happy cads who play jazz, like Tony Takitani's dad [from the short story "Tony Takitani"]. Reiko and Miu possess great skill and dedication, but insufficient emotion, and, ultimately, following deeply scarring emotional incidents, which they are each incapable of translating into art, they give up on music. As someone who used to run a jazz club, and who has said in numerous interviews that "concentration" is the most important tool a writer can possess (rather than emotion), what are you saying about the creative process? Is music really that different from writing? (There's a great deal of music in your sentences.) Why do your female musicians always have such a hard time?

HM: Women often act as mediums in my novels. They guide the protagonist to "places out of the ordinary," and they make the story move. As you know, music (along with dance) is the art most deeply imbued with ritualism. In that sense, a woman with musical ambitions may be an important presence in my work. Both Reiko and Miu might be said to be "mediums who have been abandoned by the gods." For them, their having given music up (their having been forced to give music up) is equivalent to their having severed a special tie with the world. (Now, don't forget this is entirely my personal opinion, not the opinion of novelist Haruki Murakami.)

I believe that concentration plays an equally central role in both music and the creation of a novel. Only the outward appearance of that "concentration" is different. The performance itself is usually the final expressive form in the case of music, and so the appearance of that concentration inevitably turns out to be more short-term, more expressive, more tangible. In the case of the creation of a novel, the concentration has to be more long-term, more introspective, more enduring. The way I see it, emotion is more an ordinary part of everyday life. It exists in everyone. Human beings devoid of emotion simply don't exist (do they?). In order to get a firm grasp on an emotion and express it with precision in an objective medium, however, what is required is strong enough powers of concentration to bring time to a temporary standstill. And for that what you need is the physical strength and stamina to maintain that concentration as long as possible. This is not something available to just anyone.

At the same time, I think that having made my living through most of my twenties as the owner of a jazz club taught me a lot about music and played an important role in my writing of novels. It might be true to say that I imported my methodology as-is into my novels—the importance of rhythm, for example, the joy of improvisation, the importance of establishing empathy with an audience. This is not a metaphor. For me, writing and the performance of music (though I don't actually perform music) have a direct and literal link in the air.

SW: Your male narrators are often unemployed, or unconventionally employed, but they always make it clear that money is a non-issue. There are some meditations on money in your early books, but the subject dropped out of your fiction quite quickly. Why doesn't money interest you?

HM: For no special reason. I suppose I'm just more interested in other things. I grew up in a family that was neither over-supplied with money nor troubled by a shortage of money, so, for better or worse, I probably never had to think seriously about it. As an adult, of course, I had to start dealing with money problems as a practical matter, but I suspect that one's childhood experience plays a big role in these things.

SW: You get up early in the morning and write on a set schedule every day. How much note-taking do you do outside of this schedule? Does the writing part of your brain turn off when you finish writing, or are you always writing?

HM: As a rule, I don't think too much about my fiction when I'm not sitting at my desk. If anything, I try hard to think about something else (or about nothing at all)—to switch gears in my head by doing sports or listening to music or reading or cooking. Maybe, in some remote corner of my mind, I'm thinking about my novel. Not even I know how my brain works.

SW: Do you ever just decide to take a break and not write?

HM: For me, writing is like breathing. I'm always writing something. When it's not fiction, I'm translating or writing essays and stuff like that. Writing is like training for an athlete or practice for a musician. If you stop entirely, it takes a long time to get your pace back.

SW: But in your periods of less intensely sustained labor, how do you fill your time?

HM: I'm happiest when I'm making the rounds of the used record stores.

SW: You wrote your first novel at a table drinking beer, and there's a lot of beer in it. (In fact, by my informal count, there are an average of three beers consumed on each page of your first two books.) Do you still drink beer? Do you have a favorite beer?

HM: I still like beer and often have a drink. I like Bass Ale and Samuel Adams. I'm not a big drinker, though. I like a bottle or two in the evening, maybe with a little whiskey or wine afterwards.

SW: In addition to your medium-like women, your books often contain a cursed place or thing—in *Dance Dance Dance* it's the

Dolphin Hotel and the Maserati ("the curse of the Maserati"). In *The Wind-Up Bird Chronicle* it's the abandoned house. Where do these things come from?

HM: I don't know, maybe those places (or places like them) exist inside me. I really can't say much more than that writing about such places is entirely natural for me. Unnatural things occur quite naturally there.

SW: Can you talk a bit about where you might be going next? I've noticed that you seem to be writing in new ways, about both younger and older characters.

HM: What I want to do is write about lots of different characters in lots of different situations, and that way to create stories with greater breadth. New character types are beginning to appear in my books because I know now how to write them. *

NELL FREUDENBERGER

TALKS WITH

GRACE PALEY

"SOMETHING AMORPHOUS
AND FRIGHTENING IS ALWAYS
LURKING BENEATH THE ACT
OF WRITING. I HAVE AN ABIDING
TERROR OF WHAT'S IN THERE."

Locations of seats that inspired stories:
By the front window
At the American Academy of Arts and Letters ceremony
On the steps of the library
In front of a military parade

I *first met Grace Paley in 1996 in Prague, where she was the writer-in-residence at a summer fiction workshop. She was staying in a baroque apartment building near the university, where each student got to meet her; I remember especially the wide stone stairs and massive double doors. I think I first approached Paley's stories the same way I climbed those stairs: a little too reverently. I remember being surprised by the tremendous warmth and humor of her prose.*

Paley is a writer whose authority, both literary and moral, has put her firmly in the American canon—a funny position for a person whose politics and habit of speaking the truth as she sees it have gotten her into trouble with the establishment again and again. The week we met, in May of

2005, she attended a ceremony of the American Academy of Arts and Letters, where she is a fiction fellow and where, in the same grand auditorium in Harlem, in 1970, she had accepted an award for her short stories with an incendiary speech about the U.S. bombing of Cambodia and Laos. In 1969, she traveled to Vietnam as a representative of the peace movement, to bring back American P.O.W.s; five years later she went to Moscow as a delegate to the World Peace Congress.

"Two ears, one for literature, one for home, are useful for writers," Paley has written: a kind of explanation for stories that don't sound like anybody else's. Paley was born in 1922, to Russian immigrant parents in the Bronx, but her literary ear was tuned first and primarily to poets. I think it must be their precision, as much as her Russian-Yiddish-English childhood, that makes her storytelling voice so distinctive. Although she started as a poet, today she's best known for her stories, a fact that probably says more about contemporary American literary culture than it does about Paley. In a way she's tricked us, though: her stories are as demanding as poems. She reads aloud as she writes, refusing to accept the almost-right word, and her work requires a similar level of attention from the reader.

Paley has published three collections of stories, The Little Disturbances of Man *(1959),* Enormous Changes at the Last Minute *(1974), and* Later the Same Day *(1985), two books of poems, and one book of poems and prose pieces,* Long Walks and Intimate Talks *(1991). Her essays, reports, speeches, and notes about writing are collected in* Just as I Thought *(1998). People often bemoan or wonder at the fact that Paley hasn't written more; maybe what they mean is that she hasn't made more of a fuss about what she has published. Her friend and neighbor, Donald Barthelme, famously had to come across the street and encourage her to go through her files in order to find the material for her second story collection, published fifteen years after the first one.*

Today Paley lives primarily in Vermont with her husband, the writer Robert Nichols, but complains that she spends most of her income traveling back and forth to New York. She still keeps the apartment on West 11th Street where her children grew up; we conducted this interview in the kitchen, over tea with sugar that she'd "stolen" from a restaurant around the corner. Afterwards, she took me to the living room to show me the window where the "wild old woman" in "One Day I Made Up a Story" leans on her elbows and yells out at the street. Paley admired a lush ginko tree growing just outside the window. "It wasn't here when we moved in," she explained. "At that time there were no trees, except in the fanciest neighborhoods. The city was worried that the roots might crack the pavement or something." She laughed: "Look at it now."

—N.F. (Spring 2005)

I. MEANING

NELL FREUDENBERGER: In the short essay "Jobs," you say, "The whole meaning of my life, which was jammed until midnight with fifteen different jobs and places, was writing." When did you first know that?

GRACE PALEY: I think I always sort of knew that's what I was doing, because I made no effort to do anything else. Except have children.

NF: Well, and all the other work you did—the peace work.

GP: Yeah, well, that was just natural. That was part of how my family lived, and how I lived and stuff like that. I mean I said that, but actually: What is the meaning of my life?—it's stupid. It's a very stupid remark to tell you the truth, because to say at whatever age I was then, What is the meaning of my life?—you don't know what the meaning of your life is until you're just about done. You didn't come to hear Stanley Kunitz last night, did you?

NF: No.

GP: Well, everybody who ever wrote a poem in the world was there. It was at the Bronx Community College Auditorium, which is enormous, and utterly packed. And I thought of all these people going home and writing a poem…

NF: I've heard you talk about how your first stories were published, by your friend's husband Ken McCormick at Doubleday.

GP: Yes. That's what happened. One of the great accidents. People always—you know when I do readings—always ask about it, and I say, "It's just luck. I mean, I'm embarrassed by the luck of it all."

NF: Was that simply a good experience, or was there any anxiety about publishing them?

GP: Well, no, what happened—what happened was a very good thing, because if that hadn't happened, I would've written another story when I got around to it… and another story when I got around to it. You know, I would've been much slower—even slower than I am. But I was not slow in getting that book together. He said, "I want seven more stories, and then I'll publish the book." I had, actually, another one or two very small ones, and then, inside of two years, I finished the other stories. But if that hadn't happened, I would not have done it. I would never have written "In Time Which Made a Monkey of Us All," which is this long story, you know? Which I just read recently up at Dartmouth.

NF: It's a great story.

GP: Reading it aloud surprised me. There's stuff in it I would've thought that nobody would've gotten. Anyway, the point is, I never would've gotten to write that story. And probably not either the one or two before. So it was really just the luck of it. Because I'd been writing poems anyway, and never sending them out. I sent them out once, when Jess [Jess Paley, her first husband] came home from the army. I was about twenty, twenty-one then. And I published three poems in a magazine called *Experiment*— they took them. But then the war ended, and life got very thick, and we had to find a place to live, and it was very exciting—a young couple—well, you know that. So, that was good, but I don't know if I ever would've reached that point of experience in writing that I would've taken certain risks and stuff like that.

NF: You've said that the First Amendment has been useful to our country, and that "it has made our literature one of the most lively and most useless in the world." Do you think American literature, and fiction in particular, can be useful?

GP: Well, all of art is useful, isn't it, in that sense? You couldn't grow up and live without art. I mean, you couldn't live without story-telling, couldn't live without painting. It's just eternal. It's very old, it's a hundred thousand years old, at least, and you draw pictures in caves, and tell stories, and write the Bible—write all sorts of things. It's not helpful; it's not not-helpful. It exists, just like we exist.

NF: In the introduction to *Just as I Thought,* you make fun of Americans a little for their obsession with hunting down their ancestors. Why do you think Americans are so interested in genealogy, but not very interested in history?

GP: I think probably everybody is interested in genealogy to some extent. I mean, there are some cultures where the great-great-grandparents are like gods. Their bones are kept in an altar; all cultures are different in that respect. I think there really is a kind of normal curiosity, eventually, about where you come from. I mean, my parents didn't talk very much about it. And nowadays, with the tape recorder and all, young people are extracting stories like anything from their parents. They're not letting them sit there like a log and say, "Nothing happened. Oh well, that was nothing." [*Laughs*] "So why did you leave Daddy?" "Ah, well, we were just fighting, didn't know what to do—I thought I ought to get a job…"

But I think it's true that the technology exists, and that's one of the reasons that it's happening.

NF: You've said you used to worry your stories were "too personal." That they weren't about the kinds of things people would want to read about.

GP: No, I didn't say that. I said because they were about women's lives. But not personal. I never even thought about that. I just thought of how women I knew were living, and nobody was interested in that. It was after the war, after all—not too long after the war. Ten years or so. It was a men's literature. Simple as that.

II. EDUCATION

NF: The other day at the American Academy of Arts and Letters ceremony in Harlem, we heard Roger Wilkins talk about the progress we *haven't* made in American education since Brown v. Board of Education. Did you agree with him?

GP: Well, I'm not here. But I know that even where we live, in Vermont—as you can see [*Paley passed me two digitally printed photos of her grandchildren at the beach*] my grandchildren are African American children—my daughter was working with a group of people to get an antiracist statement from the school. There aren't more than five, six, seven kids, but still, as she said, it was about educating the white children. And she had a lot of trouble getting the word "antiracist" in. The school board kept saying, "That's too strong." [*Laughs*] "Say diversity." You say "diversity" and you sound like you had an iron and you smoothed everything out. As soon as I heard that word, I knew that it was going to be a warm iron that could just go over all the wrinkles. So even there where I'm living, the governor—who's not a bad guy, you know, he's a Republican, but the Republicans of Vermont, they're very relaxed mostly—he just didn't reappoint to the human rights commission the one black guy who was on it. So it's all white guys. It's as if you were talking about women's lives or something, and you only had men. So even there, in a place like Vermont, the lesson hasn't come through.

It's interesting, you know, if you look at television, they really have a lot of black people on television nowadays. That was a shock—since I don't have television—when I come here, I look at it. I'm astonished, really. But the black fathers all have very light wives. I mean, if I was a black person myself, personally, I would really be in a rage about that. Look at it sometime, you'll see.

Wasn't it *Cosby*? The men are black, you can see that. But the women are very light.

NF: You've said you're an optimist by nature. Have you maintained that optimism about American public education?

GP: No, I'm not optimistic in that sense. I think it's a characteristic rather than a thought-through position of any kind. It's a disposition almost—I have that kind of disposition.

NF: Well, you're friendly. It's nice.

GP: Well, I'm friendly to the world, yeah. I feel as long as people are acting in the world, there's hope. In areas like, say, the election: it didn't come out good. But the number of young people especially, who went door to door, who learned some political things. It was quite remarkable. I mean, those young people aren't going to disappear... yet.

NF: Do you have an opinion about single-sex education for women?

GP: Well, I think in general I don't like single-sex education. I think it's worse for boys than for girls, though. I think boys should not be corroborated at every turn. I taught at Sarah Lawrence for twenty-two years, so I watched it change. And the women—some of them were very powerful, and some of them were not—and some of them were aggressive and some were not—some of them were wonderful writers, strong and all that, and some were not. They ran the whole spectrum. Then the boys came. Well, the first thing that happened, in the theater: the boys began to be directors, and the girls were actors. Then the boys took over the paper for a while—I mean, whatever happened, the boys stepped in. On the other hand, there were very few, so they were in a state of constant embarrassment. But I saw that they were able to do that, and it really took a couple of years for the women to get back their power. But they did get it back. I mean, they got back a certain degree of their power.

III. VIETNAM AND CHINA

NF: Where was the "Women's House of Detention," where you were in prison for six days during the war in Vietnam?

GP: Oh, everybody knows it. It's right where the park is now.

NF: Do you remember what you did to get sentenced?

GP: We sat down in front of a military parade. I think that's what I did—I'm not sure.

NF: Were your kids curious about it?

GP: They were all for me. I have a photograph of Nora, when they're all about eleven years old or something like that. Her class from P.S. 41 right here. They all had banners of some kind—they were very into things.

NF: Writing about your trip to North Vietnam in 1969, where you went with other representatives of the peace movement to bring back prisoners of war, you say, "Of course, when you go to a foreign country where you don't know the language, you certainly can't see or hear too much 'for yourself.'" But then you say, "So if my understanding of Vietnam was imperfect, my understanding of my own country was growing daily."

GP: Oh, I said that? That was smart. [*Laughs*]

NF: I know that trip confirmed a lot of what you already thought about the American involvement in Vietnam. Were there also some surprises?

GP: You know—we don't know war. So any aspect of that is a shock. It's a great shock to see whole villages decimated. Just the sight of the women, cleaning up afterwards… those things were great shocks. It really gave me such a view of these P.O.W.s, because they were all officers and they were all pilots. They were all bombers. All these P.O.W.s had really committed terrible acts.

NF: And it seemed to you that they hadn't been treated very badly, once they'd been captured?

GP: Well, I shouldn't say that, because they said that to us. They sort of described what had happened when they were captured. There were people about to tear them apart, because they'd destroyed their village. The young militia stepped in between. The anger of the people—I couldn't understand why they didn't tear them apart. Look—if it was me, if it was my little corner here of 11th Street, I don't know what I'd do. The reason I say that, is I'm sure in many cases they succeeded in really harming those guys. The ones that I talked to described the anger of the people, but then said that people stepped in.

But what happened in prison, I don't know. If you went down and met the prisoners, and the guards, the sight was so scary because our guys were all so big. And if they were starving to death, they didn't look it. They didn't look fat—they were thin—but standing beside them were these small people, also very thin. So a thin, small person and a thin, big person, look—at one point I thought, they should have *two* small, thin people watching one big, thin person.

NF: And a lot of those guys ended up going back to flying after they were released?

GP: Well, that's what we heard, yeah. Or teaching flying. Very important things were happening that year, '69. In '69, as we were leaving, a reporter came and said, "When you go home, tell everybody that Cambodia and Laos are being bombed." And we did, but nobody listened. And then it was 1970 that I got this award from the American Academy of Arts and Letters, and a couple of guys who were getting art awards, painters, came to this very house to talk to me, and said, "You know, we have to do something. We have to speak up. We can't just sit and let them give us this stuff. We have to say something." And I said, "Yeah, I agree with you." Well, it turns out—I'm the writer, right? Well, I had to write the statement, and I had to take the statement [to the Academy]. So I was scared to death. You saw that place, right? And you saw the way it's all set up. I just remember coming in, and there was Muriel Rukeyser…

NF: I don't know her.

GP: One of the great American poets. You must read her, darling, you must. And she was sitting there, and I said, "Muriel, I'm going to say this thing." And she said, "Good!" And so I got up there, and they gave me—I forgot the name—a very lovely guy gave me this thing, a very important man, gave me this and made a statement. And I made this talk: I said, "You know, at some point institutions will have to take a position on this. Meanwhile, I understand that you can't do that right now, but certainly I can and many of the people here can." And I got such a lot of applause. And I got *such* abuse. Both. From the front, I got a lot of applause. From the seated—great men, you know—one of the guys, he actually taught at Sarah Lawrence, was screaming out, "Inappropriate! Get her off! Inappropriate!"

And they did get me off—I mean, they didn't push me or anything. They said thank you, and I walked off. But I had said it. I said thank you, and got off. And Norman Mailer in writing the history of what happened omitted that. And I felt really washed out, especially since he said that the guy who gave me the award he thought was so brave.

NF: Brave for what?

GP: After I spoke—trembling and terrified—he said, "Yes, it's true: we must not be doing this." Which is, I mean, great—it's lovely that he did it. Anyway, that's funny. Funny story.

NF: I love the story "Somewhere Else"—twenty-two Americans visit China "with politics in mind, if not in total command." You said you went to China in the '70s, right?

GP: We were invited there by China. We were called political activists, so we had a goodly number of Reds among us, you know. The one thing that neither the Chinese nor the Americans knew was that there were people with tremendous political splits in our group. I mean, they were forced to talk to each other, and never would have. There were real China guys, real Maoists a couple of them, and a couple of real Russia supporters.

And Barbara Ehrenreich was with us. She was the best. I understood what a reporter does. I mean, that was long ago—she hadn't written these books yet. She went around and she asked questions. I watched her; I was so impressed by the way she didn't let anybody off the hook. She would keep asking them these questions: "Why do you think Zhou Enlai has ruined your daily work with his political position," and so on and so forth. "In what way?" She really showed her very fine self.

NF: In that story, the characters are still "in love with the revolution and Mao Zedong"; by the time you wrote the story, would they have known more about the Cultural Revolution and everything that had happened?

GP: Well, we had to know more. I remember I went to Iowa to do a reading, and I met all these old poets who had just been released. They had been sent down to the country [during the Cultural Revolution]. And I met this guy, Wang Meng, who was very interesting, also a writer. I know him the best because I flew back in the airplane with him. He later became a cultural ambassador of some kind. He was very interested in the Uigur people; he'd been sent among them. And he became a translator with them. I just read about them now; they suddenly appeared in the newspapers, after not thinking about them at all for twenty years. But the old poets, they said, "It was all right; it was OK. We found out how the peasants lived, you know." That was their answer. But there are wonderful novels that show how terrible it was for people, to be sent down to work with peasants who didn't really want them.

NF: Did you start out with the idea that the story would happen both in China and the Bronx?

GP: No, that just happened. I just felt that I had to write about it. You know—the thing is this: if I just wrote about China, it would be a report, more or less. You have to have two stories to have a story. That's what I've been teaching my classes. You need two stories, at least. And for a novel of course, you probably need more. I couldn't find the other story. I mean, I wasn't conscious of this; my idea that you need two stories came long after I wrote everything. I said, "Oh, that's what I was doing."

NF: You went to the Soviet Union and Vietnam in connection with your work for peace. Have you traveled much without a political task to do?

GP: [*Laughs*] Well, it's more for literary tasks now. I go to England, and Ireland—I had to read—and to France, Germany, Italy, you know.

NF: I know the stories have been published all over the world, but was there one country where you felt they gave you special attention?

GP: Well, I've been told that they love me in Japan, but they didn't invite me to come, so I feel bad. But I've done better with royalties in Japan than almost anywhere. My books do all right abroad; if I paid more attention and went over there more, it would probably be better. I should've gone to Germany not too long ago. They were studying my stuff, and I really should've gone. Even just to sell books, but…

IV. DESCRIPTION

NF: New York City is everywhere in your stories. But you don't describe it physically very much. Why?

GP: I'm not a describer. I don't know why. I just feel like it's so described—they don't need me to describe it. There are so many books with descriptions of this street or that street. Every now and then I talk about the trees on 11th Street, but apart from that, I really don't.

NF: You've said that the difference between a story and a novel is "the amount of space and time any decade can allow a subject and a group of characters. All this clear only in retrospect. Therefore: Be risky."

GP: OK, I'll stand by that. Whatever it means. [*Laughs*] Read it to me again!

NF: What did you mean by that in terms of your own work? Was there something about the time you started writing that made stories more natural to you than novels?

GP: Well, basically, in terms of my own work, I worked as a poet first before I wrote stories. And the short story is very close to poetry.

NF: Yours are.

GP: No, but in general, it's closer to poetry than it is to the novel. When it's too close to the novel, it's not very good. It means it's being overdeveloped or something. That's what I think. But it seemed almost natural for me to begin to write short stories after writing poems. And I tried to write a novel, and couldn't—I really couldn't stay interested in those people, and every fucking thing they did, you know? It's a very different thing, and a lot of novelists can write good short stories, but a lot of them really can't, because they can't pick the thing up. It's like poems, you just sort of pick them up in your hand... and there it is.

NF: Does it have something to do with the "wild old woman" in "One Day I Made Up a Story?" She leans out the window to shout at the street, and then closes the window to play the piano for a while. And then she opens it again.

GP: Yeah, I'm a little bit like her. I sit at the front window. Exactly—there's the piano and there's the window.

NF: Is there a conflict between writing and worrying about the world, or are those two activities complimentary?

GP: Well, they are complimentary, but you're pulled at different times. People always say, "Well, how did you balance"—you know, I didn't balance *one thing*. I mean, everything was out of balance. Totally. But sometimes the kids were the most important thing. Sometimes the writing was the most important thing, and sometimes the politics. But at the same time they were all important, and sometimes I had to go to a demonstration, or I had to write a preface—that pulls you away. And there are writers that wouldn't be pulled away, I have to admit. My husband is a writer, and he works from five-thirty until eight-thirty in the morning, every morning, and he just finished his last novel. I think it's a masculine thing basically—he won't let anything pull him away from that. I'm glad I didn't have children with him. [*Laughs*] I mean, I'm glad I met him later.

NF: What's it like being married to another writer?

GP: I've been married to him for thirty-five years, so… hell, I like him a whole lot. I mean, I like him with my whole heart. He's published mostly by New Directions and by Johns Hopkins Press. And his short stories are so different than most people's.

NF: Are his stories pretty short?

GP: Oh—no. Not particularly. I don't think he'd do a two- or three- page story. I don't think he'd find it worthwhile. [*Laughs*]

NF: I love "Wants." I think that's my favorite of your stories.

GP: Is that the library one? That one I wrote sitting over there. [*Points in the direction of Sixth Avenue*] I mean, I was sitting on the steps of the library, and I saw this guy, and I thought he was Jess.

But he wasn't. So... I was thinking about it. I just walked home. I had that story pretty much in my head for several days, and I just sat down and wrote it.

NF: It sounds so good out loud.

GP: I love to read out loud, anytime, anywhere—anytime anyone asks me.

NF: And do you read your stuff out loud while you're working?

GP: Yes. I do. I went through a period when I didn't, and it showed.

NF: Did you make a conscious decision to switch to the first person to write "Faith in a Tree?"

GP: No. I had the first couple lines of that "Faith in a Tree" and I was thinking about it in the park—which they're now going to fuck up totally. Millions of dollars to move the circle so that it lines up with the arch. It's horrible—they want to take down the mounds, which kids loved.

NF: In "Faith in a Tree," she has a kind of political awakening on the playground, and she begins to "think more and more and every day about the world." Did you have a moment like that, or was it more gradual?

GP: It was more gradual for me. I'm not her, really. But she could be a friend of mine. I always say she works for me.

V. DEBTS

NF: You've said that you don't write your stories *to* anyone, but sometimes you write *for* someone. I think you mean telling someone else's story, in order to understand it. Is that right?

GP: Well, I think when I said that, it was early. I have a story called "Debts" and with "Debts" I felt I owed a story to my friend Lucia. I tried to be as accurate as possible, which made it very convoluted. Other stories I've written for people—my friend who was dying—a story called "Friends." I wrote it for them, not to them. Everybody thinks that they went with me to visit her, but they didn't. In "Friends," she's dying, and three friends come to visit her by train. We didn't all go together at all—but now people think we did.

NF: Your stories use very colloquial language, but they send me to the dictionary pretty often, too.

GP: Oh, really?

NF: Is there something about that combination of plain and fancy words that's important to you?

GP: Well, I love words—I love the language. It comes from poetry: every word is special. Which is hard to do in a novel, I know. But I feel that way. The wrong word is like a lie, jammed inside the story.

NF: Are there some writers you've admired your whole life?

GP: I mean, my whole life... [*Laughs*]

NF: You talk about loving Eliot, and then growing not to love him—are there some others like that?

GP: Oh, I never liked him that much. I loved him less than I loved other people—much less.

NF: You loved Auden.

GP: I loved Auden, I loved Robinson Jeffers. I loved these very strange men. This work—very different from a Bronx kid. But when I was quite young I loved those insane Robinson Jeffers poems about the West Coast, you know, quite crazy.

I loved Edna St. Vincent Millay. I loved all the poets, I mean, in general. I didn't get to love Whitman for a long time. I didn't need him until much later. But then I did get to love him, too. But as for books, the wonderful books you read when you're young and they stay with you forever. When I was about eighteen or nineteen all we read was *Ulysses* by Joyce. We'd walk up and down, saying it, saying those words. But I haven't read it in a long time; I don't know if I ever will again. But I know those were important language things for me.

NF: What about Virginia Woolf?

GP: I didn't love Virginia Woolf when I was very young. I don't think I loved her until I got to be middle-aged. I didn't have a feeling for her until I was in my '40s and '50s. I mean, I loved "Three Guineas"—I loved some of her political things, before I loved the novels. I loved the Russians, because they were around the house all the time. I didn't love Dostoevsky.

NF: But Tolstoy?

GP: I loved Tolstoy. I loved Chekhov, Turgenev. I loved all of those guys. Mostly, as time went on, it was Isaac Babel I loved the best.

NF: A character in one of your stories asks his father, "If you had it all to do over again, what would you do different? Any real hot tips?" Can I ask you that?

GP: Any hot tips? [*Laughs*] The only thing you should have to do is find work you love to do. And I can't imagine living without having loved a person. A man, in my case. It could be a woman, but whatever. I think, what I always tell kids when they get out of class and ask, "What should I do now?" I always say, "Keep a low overhead. You're not going to make a lot of money." And the next thing I say: "Don't live with a person who doesn't respect your work." That's the most important thing—that's more important than the money thing. I think those two things are very valuable pieces of information. ✷

CORNELIA NIXON

TALKS WITH

MARILYNNE ROBINSON

"A LOT OF HIGH-QUALITY INTELLIGENCE
AND SENSITIVITY IS MISSPENT
OR UNDERUTILIZED, BECAUSE WE
HAVE BEEN ACCULTURATED TO BELIEVE,
BY THIS GREAT VOICE AROUND US, THAT
WE ARE TRIVIAL PEOPLE, WHO WILL NOT
SAY ANYTHING THAT REALLY MATTERS."

Things Americans refuse to believe about England:
English people can do dumb things
It is not all green and pleasant
English companies dump toxic waste, too
In England, you can be sued for hurting people's feelings

hat first drew me to Marilynne Robinson's work was the beauty of her sentences. It is a rare kind of beauty that is clear and simple and intelligent, restrained and tentative as it tries to tell the truth, always aware of irony and how near tragedy can be to comedy. It does not strive for musical effects, but it is like the best lyric poetry, in that it questions itself and tries to get things right, often failing and trying again. It can be precise as anything by Hemingway, as in this sentence from the first chapter of Housekeeping (1980): "When they got the Ford back to the road she thanked them, gave them her purse, rolled down the rear windows, started the car, turned the wheel

as far to the right as it would go, and roared, swerving and sliding across the meadow, until she sailed off the edge of the cliff." This sentence asks nothing of you except to see what has occurred, the way things happen in life, though it is the narrator's mother who is killing herself here. This event is too unexplained and too ordinary to decorate with music. Instead the prose regards it with a distracted wonder that remains open to metaphysical nuance.

Marilynne Robinson was born in Sandpoint, Idaho, graduated from Brown University in 1966, and received a Ph.D. in English from the University of Washington in 1977. Her first novel, Housekeeping, *received the PEN/Hemingway Award in 1980. Her next book,* Mother Country: Britain, the Welfare State and Nuclear Pollution *(1989), was a finalist for the National Book Award in nonfiction and was followed by a collection of essays,* The Death of Adam: Essays on Modern Thought *(1998). Her second novel,* Gilead, *was published in 2004 and has so far been awarded both the National Book Critics Circle Award and the Pulitzer Prize.*

On May 2, I had the following conversation with Robinson in her living room in Iowa City. It helped me to see how all her works cohere around the complexity of human consciousness and her humane, democratic Calvinism. Listening to the tapes, I am struck by how much time we spent laughing together. —C.N. (Spring 2005)

I. GILEAD

CORNELIA NIXON: Both your novels so far have been generational, focused on two twentieth-century generations but with time given to several earlier ancestors. The narrator of *Gilead,* Reverend John Ames, is seventy-six and writing to his seven-year-old son in 1956. The timing allows for Ames's family memories to extend back to the Civil War, John Brown, Abolitionist fervor, and the war in Kansas over whether it would be a slave state or free, as well as two world wars and the Great Depression. Meanwhile, the story is told at the start of the Civil Rights movement, and the final plot turn concerns the racism of the 1950s. Was that a late inspiration, or the reason for the choice of the narrator's age and the time setting?

MARILYNNE ROBINSON: Basically, it grows out of my interest in the history of the Middle West, which is in a very great degree in its early stages a history of Abolitionism, which is a very much forgotten history, and the fact of its being forgotten is, was, concomitant with the loss of the cause itself. Oddly enough, the South is called the Lost Cause, but I think the North could have been called the Lost Cause also over the course of time.

CN: Abolition you think is a lost cause? I mean, slavery was abolished.

MR: Slavery was abolished, but these people had much more in mind than the abolition of slavery. They developed very integrated institutions. They created colleges where blacks were admitted on the same basis as whites, and it was very hard to tell unless they could confirm it otherwise that a student was black in one of these colleges, because they did nothing to signify the race of the student.

One of the things that is an important myth is that because the Abolitionists were Northerners, New Englanders, they had very little experience with black people or with the institution of slavery, but in fact of course they had what you could call the only normal contact with black people that probably any white person in the world was having at that time, because black people were actually their students and their fellow students, and so on. These reformers felt very strongly, most of them did, and this is something else that's misrepresented, that the races certainly were equal, and they believed it on the basis of experience which would allow this to be seen as true. That's all forgotten.

CN: Do you think we have not accomplished the aims of the nineteenth-century Abolitionists?

MR: I think to a certain extent we have. I'm not sure that we really have, because there was the long intervening period of Jim Crow and what was called Scientific Racism, which was the use that was made of Agassiz and Darwin during that period, in which there was a very strong quote-unquote "eugenic argument" against the equality of races, which is the same argument that led to the extermination of Jews and Gypsies and so on in Europe. It's exactly the same literature.

It's very pervasive, it's very trans-Atlantic. There's a mid-nineteenth-century book, *The Inequality of Human Races,* by a French writer, and though the South published almost nothing, they did publish annotated editions of that. So it was very influential in pre-war Southern thought. It was also at the same time extremely influential in the emerging racist thought in Europe.

CN: I am amazed by how well you channel John Ames, the preacher, born in 1880. How easy was it for you to inhabit him and his voice? How close is it to your own? Are his thoughts on the Bible and Christian doctrine the same as your own?

MR: Frankly, the book became possible because it suddenly seemed to me as if I knew that man, and it was a pleasure to write from that point of view, because writing a book is normally a kind of lonely misery sort of thing. But I would feel even after I've had a difficult day, I can go home and be with this old man. [*Both laugh*]

As far as his thoughts on the Bible and theology, he's within the same tradition that is my tradition. I would not have felt confident to try to write from another perspective. But at the same time, his religious thought is highly specific to his circumstance, and his circumstance is not mine. So, given his character and given his circumstance, I felt as if it were his thinking, in effect, you know? It was a strange experience. There were things that I absolutely knew about him, like he loved baseball. I've sort of been perfectly respectful of baseball, but I've never paid that much attention to it. And besides that, since he was so much older than anyone I've ever known, I had to find out what he would have known. So I hired a graduate student, Earle McCartney, the one who's credited in the book, and so he researched baseball for me. So, for example, Bud Fowler is an actual player.

CN: The great black player in the book? John Ames says he lost track of him after they started up the Negro Leagues, which I guess sort of sent him to obscurity. So that's another piece fitting together. I didn't realize that was where the book was going, but it's all about racism. Did you watch baseball when you were writing it?

MR: No. [*Both laugh*] I feel as though I've gotten as much of the idea of baseball as I'm likely to get in this life. [*Laughter*]

CN: I heard you say that you were inspired to write John Ames when you were writing a poem.

MR: I was actually working on another fiction, and the fiction had a character in it who, frankly, did nothing but sit on a bench. I mean, he was probably two pages of character. But he was a minister. Who knows where he was going. But he had written a poem, and a fragment of the poem—about "open the scroll of conch" [*Gilead*, pp. 45–46]—it was his poem, and it seemed appropriate, and also I felt as if I had to keep that acknowledgement of this other character, who had died aborning and for some reason vanished himself and left John Ames in his place.

CN: Do you write poems? Or was it just because of that character?

MR: It was just that character.

CN: Sometimes I realize that something I'm writing is just holding the place of something else that is going to have to be better. I love the character of the narrator's grandfather, the first of the three ministers named Reverend Ames. He lost an eye in the Civil War, fought beside John Brown in Kansas and came back to live with his son (the second Reverend Ames, of whom he more or less disapproves) and his wife and child (the narrator). He believes in giving away whatever is of value and steals items from his son's house and distributes them around the neighborhood, to whomever has need of them. Near the end, John Ames says, "I think he was a kind of saint," and I tend to agree. Was he based on anyone in particular, any real person?

MR: In a certain sense. See that picture up there, that little framed photograph?

CN: [*Fetches the photo, of a historical marker in front of a farmhouse. Reads the plaque, about a nineteenth-century Abolitionist minister in Iowa, named John Todd*] So is he John Todd?

MR: There were a surprising number of people more or less like him, radical clergy, often New England Congregationalists and Presbyterians, who came out and did that sort of thing. He was a graduate of Oberlin, and the people that originally settled that town were from Oberlin. A lot of them came from the old Divinity School. That was a very big headwater for the religious side of the Abolitionist movement, which was most of the Abolitionist movement. In any case, they were amazing people. The things they did were just astonishing.

These people founded a college in Tabor, that for a long time sent women—they educated women and men, as these places typically did—and they sent women graduates to Turkey and Korea and all sorts of places, where they started schools for educating women, and in many places they were the first schools to educate women in that country. And so they had this huge, I mean, really big ambition for creating enlightenment and equality and all the rest of it. And that's characteristic through the Middle West. Grinnell was founded in the same way, and Knox College, and Carleton College. You can just go on and on. It's a very beautiful tradition. These people were so enlightened and infinitely energetic, and they had beautiful prose styles, and they had magnificent educations. They all knew Greek and Hebrew and Latin and all the rest of it. The Congregationalists, after the Civil War, founded five hundred schools for educating black people in the South. They had this idea and they didn't stop. And then it's like they go *whap* into a wall. This huge kind of cultural overturning like an iceberg rolling over. And everything just gets lost and goes into abeyance. They get treated as fanatics.

You find this same rhetoric in H. L. Mencken, who thought they were ridiculous for trying to establish the equality of women and the equality of black people. It's one of the most powerful lessons that American history contains, that so much could be done so insistently and patiently by people of great idealism, and it can all be lost. One of the things that is most painful about it, and I think one of the reasons it was most effective, the turnover, is because it started from the top down, because racial theory, which is what evolution primarily was when it entered the country, came in through the universities. They would have their little charts, and it would show the ape, and the gorilla, and the black guy—

CN: And then the white guy—

MR: Yeah, and with a few other guys in between and no women at all. They had no role in evolution at all, you know. [*Both laugh*] You still can't find any women in those little charts. And then it was, well, look here, we have science to prove that you're utterly naïve to think these things can be accomplished. And because it was an intellectual culture that tried to establish equality, it was particularly vulnerable to this kind of supposed scientific rebuttal. I think it's not at all unusual in a war for the loser to win, in effect.

It's like the old paradox about the Romans defeating Greece and becoming completely subservient to Greek culture. There was the romance of the elitism of Walter Scott and so on. The racial hierarchy was very much reinforced from reactionary movements in Europe, which were also aristocratic movements, nostalgia for aristocracy. You find it in T. S. Eliot. You find it in those people that published *I'll Take My Stand,* Southern poets, Robert Penn

Warren. It's like the French Revolution and nostalgia for the beauty that was lost and the culture that was lost. And these people who were the first wave of Abolitionists were as cultured as anybody this country has ever produced, but it doesn't matter.

CN: Like the first Reverend Ames and his Greek Bible.

MR: Exactly. And because they were who they were, he had hard hands and a Greek Bible, you see. And these things cancel each other out. [*Chuckles*]

CN: In both your novels, you work often in the narrator's interior, rather than in scenes, especially in the new book. Both are in the first person and *Gilead* is one long letter, and though it does include scenes, much of it is summarized with direct statements that might not come up in dialogue. John Ames reflects philosophically as he ponders scripture, religious doubt, arguments to counter doubt. He does reveal things he may be unaware of, like his naïveté and long-standing prejudice against his best friend's son that at times seems to verge on sexual jealousy. But his blind spots are subtle, and some readers may miss them, while no one can miss the direct statements. How do you feel about the creative-writing dictum "Show, don't tell?"

MR: Oh, I think that dicta in general are to be eyed with suspicion. [*Laughs*] It's so strange. That one has such power, and even more we're told all the time that the problem with creative writing programs is that they conventionalize. I think this is not true, but when it is, it's because people are told things like "Show, don't tell." It depends absolutely what your character is, what your situation is, what your subject is.

I think, frankly, it's a little bit like behaviorism or something. I really wonder how much it carries over from science, I mean really crude science as understood in the late nineteenth century and the early twentieth century—that there's something illusory about thought, and that in fact it's behavior that counts, and only behavior, when in fact people's brains are buzzing all the time. People are to an incredible degree constituted of what they never say, perhaps never consciously think. Behavior is conventionalized and circumstantial. In many cases, the behavior that in fact would express what someone thinks or feels is frustrated, cannot occur. Here we are, basically organized to carry this big brain around, and [*laughing*] it's absolutely bizarre to act as if what goes on in there is not part of the story.

CN: I wouldn't believe in him as a minister if he weren't extremely thoughtful in presenting his thoughts fully flowered sometimes, and thinking them through again, right there on paper.

MR: I think of him as somebody who is very much in the habit of thinking on paper. I get a lot of mail from ministers. I may be the darling of the American clergy right at the moment. [*Both laugh*] But this mulling over is one of the things that they very, very much identify with.

II. HOUSEKEEPING

CN: Part of the phenomenal success of *Housekeeping,* published in 1980, was due to the contemporaneous burgeoning of feminist literary theory and the creation of Women's Studies programs, which embraced the book as a feminist statement about women's generational influences on each other and women's spirituality, which often is seen as including pantheist elements rather than conforming to any conventional church doctrine.

Now you have written a great second novel that in some ways parallels it, as a generational exploration of men's lives. *Gilead,* however, has no detectable feminist elements. Its main emphasis is on matters of faith, in terms identifiable with recognizable church doctrines, and on last things, the need to summarize a life and take account of it. Would you say your views have changed since *Housekeeping*? Or was your faith as well defined then as now and merely less recognized by critics then?

MR: I had less vocabulary for my faith, I suppose, because, frankly, I've read a lot of theology in the intervening years. I'm fairly firmly persuaded that the human species is made up of two genders and that they are more interesting in their aspect as human beings than they are in their aspect as either feminine or masculine. I think that the degree to which they are seen as different is highly suspect. The idea, for example, that at the level of what we might call mind, they are very different, is the thing that my dear Abolitionists were trying to overcome by demonstrating that women were absolutely as intellectually competent as men were, and I think that what they accomplished is another thing that we've forgotten.

There were very great women in the nineteenth century, and I'm afraid it would be hard to come up with their equivalent in this enlightened time, which is a frightening thought. But they were women who were well and optimistically educated with the assumption that they certainly could be great. Which I think is not really by any means characteristic now. Instead I think that women are very largely being educated, frankly, to plead a case against the world at large, as if what they have to do is be fascinated by what has happened that ought to disturb or anger them, rather than being fascinated by the possibility of doing something else. They're not making the space that other women I think in another two generations will want to occupy. I'm even afraid that categories like pantheist are anti-intellectual. And I don't think that men are—the whole Romantic tradition is "pantheist." I think that things are being ascribed to gender that are not gender-determined, and it's tending toward limiting distinctions in the same way that people were doing in 1810.

CN: The emphasis on women being different from men does sound to me like the literature of the late nineteenth century, some of it by ministers, arguing that women will damage their uteruses if they are educated, that it's physically bad for them and beyond their capabilities, and that they should be treated as children, essentially.

MR: Exactly. And I really do think that too much of that has been internalized and so that there is an infantilization of women's intellectual life now. It's very regrettable. One of those painful ironies, another iceberg turning over. My idea of feminism is that the world can be seen deeply and seriously through a woman's eyes, which does not mean only a woman's eyes. I wrote *Housekeeping* the way I did, because, frankly, whenever I tried to put a male character in, he didn't fit, so I took him back out again.

CN: [*Laughing*] There is a brief appearance by a Mr. Fisher, Sylvie's husband, but he doesn't ever quite come on stage. And the grandfather is there but not for long.

MR: [*Laughing*] In any case, I consider myself an excellent feminist, but I don't consider myself an ideological feminist. When I was writing *Gilead,* something of the same kind happened, in the sense that I felt that it was generational in the way that meant that certain cultural things were passed down through the male line, in the same way that in *Housekeeping* certain things pass down through the female line, the whole issue of nurturing and so on. You feel terrible pointing out things about your own novel. But an enormous number of the decisions in *Gilead* are made by the wife. She's the one who says he's writing the boy's begats, and she in a sense shapes the project from the beginning. She proposes to him, and he always defers to her, and she gets mad at him when she thinks he has not been fair to Jack [his best friend's son], which he has not been.

I just don't think that anybody ought to accept a restrictive definition of herself or himself, or certainly not encourage it in other people either. When you consider what a complex thing a human being is, and what a complex experience any human being has, you're going to come up with a new roll of the dice every time. This country is as diverse as any population has ever been, and why do we need these stupid generalizations? Everything tends toward a party platform these days. I do want to say that *Housekeeping* was at least as well received by men as by women. There are lots of papers and so on written by men, which are perfectly fine things.

CN: I think it was a man who first told me to read *Housekeeping*.

III. MOBY-DICK

MR: You know, I've always admired *Moby-Dick* very much, and I was sort of disturbed by the implications I heard from feminists that I ought not to like this book because it has only male characters. And so when I was writing *Housekeeping* and noticing that men kept going over the side every time I tried to write one, I thought that if I could write a book that had only female characters that men understood and liked, then I had every right to like *Moby-Dick*.

CN: I've noticed that. More and more as I read *Housekeeping*, I am struck by the parallels to *Moby-Dick,* which you signal in the very first line, which is roughly "Call me Ruth." I was pleased last year to hear that you were teaching a whole graduate seminar at the Iowa Writers' Workshop on *Moby-Dick,* right when I was telling my students that there is a certain Romantic view of nature in *Moby-Dick* that I was catching echoes of in *Housekeeping.* Were you conscious of the influence of Melville and other writers from that period, Transcendentalists, American Revival writers, when you were writing it?

MR: I was very aware of it, actually. I wrote *Housekeeping* and basically I didn't expect it to be published, but I was very interested in the extended metaphor. The extended metaphors that really interested me were nineteenth-century American, and like so much of the nineteenth-century American world, it seemed to me that the experiment they were making ended before it was finished. And so

I was sort of demonstrating to myself what I understood to be their mode of consciousness. They being Emerson and Thoreau and Dickinson, but above all, Melville. There is a transformative character in metaphor, when something is perceived and articulated in terms of what it suggests, how it might fit into a fabric of speculation, when you move through perception to idea. Not to say a closed idea, but an open idea, that makes you realize what you have not thought before.

The method of Melville is just opening, opening, opening. He sees something, he transforms it metaphorically, he in a sense takes in from it what can be comprehended, what the fabric has allowed him, and then he feels the insufficiency of the thought. So the process begins again. That's interested me very much. One of the things that it does is make demands on language that language is almost uncannily capable of meeting, demands that are almost never made under other circumstances.

CN: So the white whale is a metaphor he's using to get at something he's trying to understand?

MR: The white whale is the mystery that makes every intervening mystery seem as if it could give evidence about the ultimate mystery. All the sorts of things he does—the mapmaking and the coffin for Queequeg, and when they do the sperm thing and he talks about the angels—the rise of the giant squid—just over and over, these beautiful images. He has the metaphor of the masthead, when the sailor goes up there and begins thinking great Transcendentalist thoughts. It's the encapsulation of consciousness that is also the enlargement of consciousness. The analogy for it even historically is scientific method, which proceeds from the assumption that something is wrong with even the most brilliant idea. It can always be taken further, or it needs to be modified or rejected, and there is something beyond it, something beyond.

CN: I've reread *Housekeeping* a dozen times in order to teach it, with that special sort of attention you give a book when you know you have to come up with something to say about it the next day, or at least ask the right questions. The biggest reason I love it is what I see you saying in some passages, that there is what I call a sort of permeable membrane between life and death, through which living beings or their souls may pass back and forth.

The lake is identified with death early on, when the grandfather's train slides into it. It's called Fingerbone, clearly skeletal, not Finger, and the girls' mother drives her car into it to kill herself. Ruth says that if the dead apple trees in her grandmother's orchard were to burst into bloom, "It should be no great wonder," only "a small change." People see and hear dead children who are cold and hungry all around them, begging for food. When the lake rises and swamps their house, a kind of darkness seems to come in with it and open Ruth to clearer perception of their aunt Sylvie, who may have learned to pass through the membrane. She seems impervious to cold, and her version of housekeeping readies the place for bats, dead leaves.

It seems to me that Sylvie challenges the distinction between living and dead, and Ruth gets closer to her during the very dark night she spends out by the lake with Lucille, while Lucille recoils and moves in with her Home Ec teacher, whose housekeeping is conventional. Ruth eventually leaves with Sylvie to wander through realms that may be postmortal, since they burn down the house on their way out and may be run over by a train on the railroad bridge across the lake. That's what the local paper believes, and the final pages include ambiguous, ironic, almost funny statements about "after our death," and Ruth turns the coffee cold as a waitress in a coffee shop. My question is, am I right? Is that what you meant?

MR: [*Laughing*] Oh, I can't answer a question like that! I think that people, depending on their circumstance, live in a much larger continuum of experience than conventionally we allow ourselves to acknowledge. Part of it of course is the experience of loss that is simply the result of the passage of time, and we know that we are mortal, we found that out when we were very young children. I don't consider *Housekeeping* a realist novel in quite the way that some people do. One of the lines that was on my mind when I was writing it—all kinds of things were on my mind—it was much more allusive than I would have dared to be if I thought anybody would ever read it. [*Both laugh*]

I remember that line from the Yeats poem, "like a long-legged fly upon the stream / her mind moves upon silence," and that's a very lovely image, of the creature suspended on the surface of water. I consider the book a sort of poem about the mind moving. The mind moving in the ambiguities, the tides of memory and being, and time. I've said before, you probably know I've said this before—I don't think of these people as opposed. I think of them as arrayed—that one feels a yearning for darkness and woods and perhaps even death itself.

And then one also feels the yearning for the warm house, the lighted house. If you choose or are helped into the warm house—the benevolence of society sees to that—you never stop feeling I think the attraction of the other, if you've ever felt it. So that it's not as if you are simple, in the sense that you have made one choice or the other. One of the things that I think I say in the book, and that I wanted to say, is that the town itself understands this, but part of its sort of huddled quality is precisely the fact that it knows the attractions of dispersal—and entropy, call it that.

CN: Dissolution...

MR: Yes, exactly that! Part of the reason I wrote this book the way that I did was because, when I went to Brown, where I went to college, I was a curiosity, coming from Idaho. Anybody else was less rare. People considered Idaho just empty, like they'd been through and there was just nothing there. [*Laughs*]

In my own growing up I had always felt this intense, plangent emotional density about forests and mountains, hidden places and forgotten places. I wanted to evoke that sense of the landscape, which I think people often recognize as something they feel also. I think people that live in the Northwest understand what it is that I have tried to evoke. The myth of the West is so stupid, with all these cowhands and lumberjacks and so on, and my family actually homesteaded there, and I am the fourth generation to live there. So, the narratives I heard from my family were vastly different from that, which is another thing I wanted to evoke.

CN: I agree that it's not a realist novel. And yet it is also. It's a realist novel about consciousness and perception.

MR: Yes, exactly. Which is, like, 90 percent of reality. [*Both laugh*]

CN: *Housekeeping* has passages that remind me very much of Romantic poetry, especially Wordsworth's "Ode: Intimations of Immortality," about how we come from another world, trailing clouds of glory that we soon forget, and how sleeping, fainting, slipping away even toward death gets us back closer to the glory. There's been a lot said about dissolution in Romanticism, the attraction to dissolving, coming apart like something in water, including in Romantic fiction like *Moby-Dick*. But while water is important in both your novels, it is associated with death, dissolution, spirituality, and liberation in *Housekeeping,* and in *Gilead* it seems more recognizably Christian, since Reverend Ames calls it the purest liquid and therefore appropriate for blessing and baptism. This strikes me as a step toward doctrinal Christian thought and away from what feels like pantheism or the spirituality of the Romantic poets, perhaps. What do you think?

MR: I think they're on a continuum. Reverend Ames would have been a later representative of exactly the same religious tradition that produced people like Melville and Dickinson, certainly Dickinson, and also Thoreau and also Bronson Alcott and a lot of them. So they're analogous traditions. The minister because he's thought about these things in these terms his whole life, expresses them in terms that are specifically religious.

But the passage you quoted is from a famous atheist. That's Feuerbach. So he's stepping outside of that kind of language when he says that. You know, water is what makes this planet. Without water, forget it. It happens that there is a huge lake by Fingerbone, as there was by the town that I grew up in. In the Middle West, water is a big deal because we don't have enough of it often, which makes you aware of rain. And water is extraordinarily beautiful. I don't think anyone has ever thought otherwise. As Feuerbach would say, I don't think it's an accident that it is so strongly associated with ideas of the sacred.

CN: I've often thought that technique implies worldview, that writers' technical choices indicate assumptions about reality that they may not even know they have. In *Housekeeping* you use what I call provisional narration when you allow Ruth to imagine conversations and events she did not see or hear. This works with poignance in the last three pages ("after our death"), where Ruth says that in the future Lucille's "thoughts are thronged by our absence" and she "does not watch, does not listen, does not hope, and always for Sylvie and me." This seems like a sophisticated spiritual statement, in a section that begins "All this is fact. Fact explains nothing," as if spiritual truth can only be implied sideways, or in reverse, or slant, as Emily Dickinson says.

MR: It has to do with thinking about the mind in the way that I was talking about before—that when people choose against something, that doesn't mean they cease to feel it as a choice they have. I think a real problem for writers is the flatness of most characterization, that it comes nowhere near capturing the actual complexity of experience. When you are with somebody you love, that seems as it ought to be. But when they're absent from you, you are more aware of them because of their absence. Loss can create a more profound presence than presence itself.

IV. THE DEATH OF ADAM

CN: This wide-ranging collection of essays is primarily a critique of contemporary American thought. In "Darwinism," you dissect Darwinian theory, pointing out its reliance on discredited paradigms of its day and its unproven elements. And while you scornfully dismiss simple-minded Creationist views based on the Biblical account, your introduction argues for the superiority of John Calvin's ideas over those of our contemporary scientists. Have you received response to these arguments from any direction—Creationist, Calvinist, Darwinian?

MR: It's a delicate thing; as soon as you talk about Darwinism, you've stirred a hornet's nest. The thing about it is that Darwinism and evolution have been treated as if they meant the same thing, whereas evolutionary theories predate Darwin. There's a collection of essays called *The Fundamentals*—fifteen volumes of it—written by people who were trying to shore up American Protestant theology against the invasion of Darwinism and Agassiz's system, and they say, of course there was evolution.

The question is, what does it mean, how do we interpret it, does it imply the things that were claimed by people of that time that it did imply, for example, eugenics, racial inequality. You can read things about how these theories implied to people in the early twentieth century that they should prevent child-bearing among isolated populations in the, you know, in the Berkshires [*laughing*], whom they just took to be darn inferior!

CN: I thought you were going to say the Amazon Basin or someplace, not the Berkshires...

MR: [*Laughing*] The Berkshires! In places outside Pittsfield and so on. I mean, talk about a sword that turns every way. But in any case, the issue was never religion on one side and science on the other. It was the question of this science, in this cultural frame. It was doing the same thing all over the world, of course. It rationalized the extermination of the Tasmanians. It was again a basis for racial policy in fascist Europe. So it was a very serious issue, and it's been very much simplified. At first it was religion in a state of confusion against bad science. Now it's bad religion against bad science. So we're just in a complete swamp at this point.

But Calvinists think I'm a pretty good Calvinist, and that pleases me. People don't read him so they don't know what I mean, except the other Calvinists. One of the things that does please me is that I was cited in the Cambridge book of essays on Calvin, in the essay on metaphysics. So that was devoutly to be hoped. [*Laughs*] And I had a conversation with a scientist that was set up by *Harper's,* in the Rothko Chapel in Houston. He was a Nobelist, a physicist, who writes for the *New York Review of Books,* and he just joked about this kind of crazy contemporary evolution. He said, "You know what they call it, they call it Just-So Stories," which is what it is, if you read it. Nevertheless it has the imprimatur of science, which just knocks people over. If they read any scientific history, they would realize that it has bumbled along in exactly the same way that any other human enterprise has done, and perhaps taken as many victims.

CN: Freud, for instance, is considered to be scientific. You only have to read about what he was actually doing, which was getting his friend Fliess to operate on people's noses to cure their sexual hang-ups.

MR: [*Laughing*] Exactly! Exactly!

CN: What you're saying about how all human enterprise is bumbling reminds me of "Facing Reality," also in *The Death of Adam.* There you suggest that we need to forgive ourselves and each other for being fallible and mortal, as are all of our enterprises. I especially love the last paragraph, which I typed and taped to my office door for a year after a close friend of mine was killed in a plane crash along with both of her parents. There you say, "If the universe is only all we have seen so far, we are its great marvel. I consider it an honor to follow Saint Francis or William Tyndale or Angelina Grimké or Lydia Maria Child anywhere, even to mere extinction. I am honored in the cunning of my hand." What moved you to write "Facing Reality"?

MR: It was one of those interesting invitations that came in the mail. These are all occasional essays, except for "Darwinism." A great problem that we have is a kind of false consciousness that I talk about in "Facing Reality," that we've been sold a bill of goods, a thousand bills of goods. I think that to be a good writer, you have to put yourself on the line, you have to think deeply about what is meaningful to you and you have to make a good-faith effort to speak from the integrity of your own deep experience. There is a tendency to disallow deep experience, as if it were something that we twentieth-century Americans don't have. Nobody doesn't think of something in crisis or in deep difficulty. God help us, maybe there are some poor souls for whom this is not true. But virtually everybody has been acculturated to have some notion of the terms of ultimate human experience. It tends to be religious because that's the way that people generally do deal with these things.

I'm sure there are people who have been brought up to think in terms of returning into the great organism of being, or something like that. But for most people we have what our grandma told us. And people are not encouraged to consult those things, or to acknowledge the fact that they live in the same mythic landscape that the formulators of these difficult narratives lived in also—that the things that have been passed down as ways of understanding it have not ceased to be relevant. And there's a sort of a falseness in the consistent inability. People don't think about accessing what is the deepest narrative for them. I think that that's about 99 percent of the subject of literature. A lot of high-quality intelligence and sensitivity is misspent or underutilized, because we have been acculturated to believe, by this great voice around us, that we are trivial people, who will not say anything that really matters.

CN: I tell students to figure out what they believe in the way James Baldwin believes in racial equality. To find what matters deeply to them and write about that.

MR: Right. And also write *from* it. I mean, racial equality is not a pressing issue except to people who love justice, who understand the offense that inequality is, just on the face of the earth.

V. MOTHER COUNTRY

CN: What I was hoping when I found this book was that it would be a new novel by you, and I was surprised that it was an environmentalist statement about a nuclear power plant in the British Isles called Sellafield. The image I still have in my mind from it is of sheep grazing on a green hillside and this nuclear power plant right next to them.

MR: They have done that. They've grazed sheep by it, they've grazed cattle by it, they've put golf courses by it. They sometimes even use the phrase "Sheep may safely graze" [*both laugh*] out of Handel, when it's a real dodgy question whether they may or not. It's a very filthy plant that systematically releases radioactive materials and nitric acid in liquid tons every day into the Irish Sea and has done so for decades. It's in the Lake District, not far from Wordsworth's house. [*Laughs*] They consider it isolated. They've been doing it for so long now that there's really no turning back. They have another one, equally vile, in Scotland, called Dounreay, which was supposed to be a breeder reactor, but it had accidents, as they all do.

Europe has dabbled with that stuff and so has Japan, using British technology. They have built these reactors that are graphite-moderated like the reactors at Hanford that make bomb-grade material, and they consider them "dual use." They produce electricity and then they also produce plutonium and uranium, which

Britain sells, ships into Germany and into Japan by sea. And now the Irish Sea is the most radioactive body of water in the world. All this talk about nuclear proliferation, and people talking about Russia, but Britain is a much older and more important source of nuclear proliferation difficulties.

CN: Why did you choose Sellafield and not someplace here like Three Mile Island?

MR: Nothing to compare in scale.

CN: And you were living in England at the time.

MR: I was. And one of the articles that caught my eye was one that said they had discovered that it was more harmful for children to ingest plutonium than had previously been thought.

CN: So that's part of the bill of goods we've all been sold.

MR: Yes. That's a major bill of goods. And for me, many things go back to racism.

CN: Because the Lake District is considered full of lesser people?

MR: No, actually, it's quite the other way round. Many Americans who consider themselves extremely liberal have this sort of displaced patriotism, where they will not hear and cannot believe anything negative about Britain. And we liberals, we right-thinking people, can't believe that white people who speak English can do anything dumb. You can't believe how pervasive this kind of thinking is.

I learned a great deal from doing that book. And it was quite respectfully reviewed in general. But it didn't matter. People can't take it in. You say, you know, there's a television program where a British journalist is holding up a Geiger counter into the air, and the wind is coming in off the sea, and the Geiger counter is shrieking. It's nuts. "Well," they say, "but it's still a great place to vacation." I was in Britain and I was becoming aware of all of this because it was in the newspapers, it was on television. I know lots of Americans there. I would say to them, "What do you think about all this plutonium?" And they'd say, "What plutonium?" Our prejudice in favor of Europe is so profound, and it's going to have huge consequences. I think one consequence is that we can look forward to the construction of British and European reactors in this country. We don't know anything about the standards they apply, although the information is perfectly available.

CN: So the audience you're addressing is in this country.

MR: Yes, although it was printed in England. It was published by Faber and Faber. But it had to go out of print because I was sued by Greenpeace under British law.

CN: Wait—Greenpeace sued you? I would have thought they'd be on your side.

MR: One of the things that was very disturbing was that while Greenpeace was active about all this in Britain, there was no information about it in the United States. Or to the extent that there was any, it tended, as it does tend to be, very misleading. For example, they had a brochure that said that Greenpeace claimed that they had helped to create a ban on ocean dumping of radioactive material. But there still is ocean dumping of radioactive material all the time, a great deal of it done by Britain. They not only put this stuff down a pipeline into the ocean, but they dump radioactive waste off the coast of Spain. So, this rouses one's curiosity about what Greenpeace understands its role to be. They collect an enormous percentage of the money that's donated for environmental causes in the world.

There was one particularly ridiculous episode in which Greenpeace figured, and I couldn't get any satisfaction about what they were doing. So in the book itself I raise questions about why did this happen and what were they doing. I made it joking around a little bit, but basically they have this pipeline that since 1957 has been pumping radioactive waste into the sea, right? And according to Greenpeace, they had taken divers out and lowered them to block the thing. In the first place, it's been putting out corrosive material since 1957. How are you going to make a cover that fits the thing? Isn't that a little bit hard to imagine? Then they had lowered these divers to the mouth of what is the source of the most intense radioactive contamination in the world, pulled them back up again. There happened to be a Geiger counter in the boat, which pinned. [*Makes gesture of a dial going over to the max*]

Now, what's wrong with this story? You're going out to block something because it disgorges radioactive waste, and you don't take a Geiger counter? You only accidentally have one there? It only accidentally goes off when the divers come up? Who are these divers that you're going to put them into this intensely radioactive environment? It's all craziness. I simply ask in the book, what can this mean? So I got sued. And among the things that Greenpeace sued me for were hurt feelings.

CN: Did they win?

MR: They won. Well, you know, under British libel law, you can be found guilty of libel if you say something that injures someone's reputation.

CN: So that's why they sued you there instead of here.

MR: In England, yes. They couldn't possibly have sued me here. But the consequence of it was, when a book is *sub judice,* as they say, it can't be mentioned in print.

CN: So if it can't be mentioned in print, it couldn't be reviewed.

MR: Couldn't be reviewed. Just—poof, disappeared in England.

CN: But here it got attention.

MR: Yes. But here nobody wants to believe what you say about England.

CN: That explains the title! You're speaking about our mother country—

MR: Yeah, the colonized attitude that we basically have. It's like primitive patriotism. We cannot see the "green and pleasant land" people. People act as if I am hostile to England, when in fact I'm trying to say something that might perhaps alleviate a dreadful situation that is very much an English problem. I mean, it's everybody else's because they export the stuff and it flows around in the sea. But they are the primary victims.

VI. THE WRITER IN THE WORLD

CN: The role of the writer in this culture is no longer what it once was, when writers were routinely asked to make statements about public controversies. What do you think about the position of intellectuals in our culture now? How would you change it if you could?

MR: This is such a good question. This country is so various. I'm surprised to find, when I travel around, the cultural life of Minnesota, the cultural life of North Dakota, it's like going from one country to another. And you find people that are intense about where they are, and what is at issue in the place where they are.

One of the things that afflicts this country is that it is so large and so active that it cannot successfully generalize about itself. So it generalizes unsuccessfully. And the unsuccessful generalizations are usually very much to its detriment. One is programmed to think in certain ways, about how much cultural vitality there is, and it's a great privilege to be in a position where one can see it. We have a way of talking as if the intellectual life is something conducted in a drawing room, in New York probably, when it is vastly larger than that. I think that the people who are noticed as intellectuals, which is an artificially small group, tend to be in a certain sense influenced by the majority about the cultural deadness in this country. [*Laughs*] We continuously get misinformation about ourselves.

One of the ways in which perhaps one is acknowledged as intellectual is by being a spokesman for this misconception, that there is no intellectual life in this country. It is the classic posture of intellectualism, and it goes back to people like H. L. Mencken, "the boobocracy" and so on. And I think it has made an enormous problem, because there is at this point a fair consensus that the culture has failed, and that the public schools have failed, and the public universities need to be revamped, because they have failed. We can't acknowledge our own life. I don't think that people who speak about these things publicly are particularly encouraged to do that. And they should be, simply because it is better to say something that is true rather than something that is not true. [*Both laugh*]

CN: If you could say something to world leaders today, what would it be? Or to your fellow Americans?

MR: To my fellow Americans, I would say that I have the deepest admiration for their better potential and I would be so happy and relieved to see it expressed in public. There's nothing in the world that I love and admire more than the best impulses of this country. Nothing that breaks my heart more than seeing it betrayed. World leaders, in general I think I would tell them: Go home. Take a warm bath. [*Both laugh*] Pick a name out of the phone book, appoint him/her as your successor, and we couldn't be worse off.

CN: Including in this country?

MR: I'm not terribly impressed with the current leadership.

CN: That is part of what you were saying about the betrayal of our best potential? You mean who we elect to represent us and speak for us in the world?

MR: Nobody speaks for us. Every day in the newspaper, a new surprise, and I'm never happy with it.

CN: Yes. The image of America one gets from the mainstream media and the activities of our elected representatives—that's one vision of America. But I can't fit into it, say, this conversation we've had today. You are simply not represented there.

MR: I certainly don't feel represented. You know, I miss many things. I miss generosity. I miss magnanimity. I miss a loyalty to the future that makes people reasonable about how they conduct their lives in the present. The idea of a possibility, for ourselves and others—who is it who said that civilization is planting a tree that you will never sit under? That's what we need to do. We have all these great libraries and all these wonderful resources, museums and so on, because other people planted trees that they were not going to sit under. And now we feel no obligation to leave behind similar legacies, at least in the highest scales of public debate. ✶

DAN POPE

TALKS WITH

JAMES SALTER

"THE REAL OBLIGATION OF A WRITER
IS TO ENTHRALL, LIKE SCHEHERAZADE.
IT'S NOT THAT EASY."

Good times to write:
During a long drive
In the morning, hungover
In between jet-fighting

 once heard a writer say that she plays a sort of parlor game or bibliomancy with the work of James Salter. She opens one of his books blindly, then invariably finds two of three sentences on that page that blow her mind with their lyricism, their precision, their perfection. Try it yourself. It works every time.

James Salter was born in New York in 1925. He graduated from West Point in 1945 and served in the Korean War as a jet fighter pilot. His flying experience formed the basis of his first two novels, The Hunters *(1956) and* The Arm of Flesh *(1961), which he later substantially revised and published as* Cassada *(2001). After resigning his commission in 1957, Salter devoted himself to fiction, and to writing and even directing movies in*

Europe. *He wrote the screenplay for* Downhill Racer *(1969), which starred* Robert Redford, *and directed a 1962 documentary short,* Team Team Team, *which took first prize at the Venice Film Festival.*

His short novel A Sport and a Pastime *appeared in 1967 and was recently republished by the Modern Library. Salter is also the author of* Light Years *(1975) and* Solo Faces *(1979). In addition to the novels, Salter has published two collections of stories,* Dusk and Other Stories *(1988), which won the PEN/Faulkner Award, and* Last Night *(2005), and a book of remembrance,* Burning the Days *(1997). A compilation of his writings on flying,* Gods of Tin, *appeared in 2004, and a book about food,* Life Is Meals *(coauthored with his wife, the playwright Kay Eldredge) will be published next year.*

Salter is eighty now, and splits his time between Aspen, Colorado, and Bridgehampton, New York, where he lives with his wife and teenage son in the warmer seasons. We conducted this interview via the U.S. postal system—I would send him questions on separate pieces of paper, and he would type the answers and send them back. —D.P. *(Winter 2004)*

I. "EARLY REJECTIONS ARE THE MOST PAINFUL EXCEPT FOR LATER ONES."

DAN POPE: Can you tell a bit about your early years as a writer? The first inklings toward pen and paper? Where did it come from, that urge, do you recall?

JAMES SALTER: I began to write in prep school. A young English teacher, Richard Wooster, put his arm around my shoulder, so to speak. The impulse to write may be there, but also there's the matter of encouragement. He made me feel that I had some ability. That carried me for a while.

In college—I'm calling the Military Academy college—in the bleakness of it there was a series of witty and well-written pieces in the *Pointer* written by an upperclassman named Gordon Steele. I didn't know him, but reading his mock diary called *Ducrot Pepys*—"ducrot" was a generic address for plebes—helped to keep me interested in the idea of writing. I wrote a few stories during my second and third years. I had only a vague idea of how to go about it.

From the time I was twenty until I was twenty-five, I sometimes worked on a novel. I was in the Air Force and although there are examples of real writing by men under arms, they must have had a stronger spirit. I sometimes imagined myself as a writer, apart from being a regular officer, but there was no basis for it. The skimpy notebooks I kept at the time are banal. I wrote a few poems.

Finally, a year after returning from the Korean War, I completed the novel I had been carrying around so long—I had even written some pages of it during the war—and now came a significant event. I had been referred, I forgot how, to a literary agent, I think named James Oliver Brown, who in turn referred me to another one, a doughty old fellow who had been a pilot in the First World War. He took me on. Kenneth Littauer was his name. He had flown out of the same fields in France that I had. On freezing mornings they had made a big bonfire in the shape of a circle and stood inside it to get warm before taking off. "Weren't you afraid of getting burned?" his secretary asked. "No, we were going to be dead in an hour anyway, so what did it matter?" he said.

The novel was rejected, but I'd put a foot in the water. A few years later I wrote another, and it was accepted. That was *The Hunters*.

DP: And, as to those early years, what of the disappointments? Were any significant? You write, for instance, in *Burning the Days*, of the dozen or more rejections of *A Sport and a Pastime*—a novel that is now part of the Modern Library—before George Plimpton took the book on.

JS: There are writers who slip through without a bruise, but the chances are greater that you'll get rejections. *Light Years* was rejected, I should say dismissed, by Robert Giroux as well as by others. It recently won the Fadiman Prize after being in print for thirty years. I had a collection of stories, *Dusk,* that won the PEN/Faulkner and nearly every story had been rejected by the *New Yorker,* by the same editor. Early rejections are the most painful except for later ones.

DP: And what of the thrills of the writing game? Do any stand out? Early breakthroughs? Certain accomplishments? The first story accepted by the *New Yorker,* perhaps? Or something less obvious?

JS: There are few thrills like the first ones, but not long ago at a party a woman I was being introduced to said simply, "Did she really just read a magazine?" She was referring to a scene in *A Sport and a Pastime.* She assumed I would know. My God, all the things of inconsequence she might have said! I don't remember her name, but she was the unknown reader I sometimes say I imagine, the woman in her thirties or forties who perhaps lives in Buenos Aires.

When *A Sport and a Pastime* was chosen by Modern Library, my editor, Joe Fox, gave a small dinner to celebrate, or should I say, in honor of it. Alec Wilkinson, George Plimpton, and one or two others were there. I didn't tell them that as I approached the restaurant a woman's stockinged leg was extending from a limousine near the curb, and as she stepped forth I saw it was the French girl, twenty years later, whose life had been described in the book. She had gone on.

DP: Wait. You're saying it was her? The girl who was the model for Anne-Marie? She was there for the dinner? Or you just ran into her by accident? Did you say hello?

JS: It wasn't a girl. It was the woman she'd become, that Dean once knew. She wasn't living in Troyes with a French husband. She wasn't alone that night. It was sheer coincidence that she appeared at that moment. She never came into the restaurant.

DP: I've been told that the photograph of the woman on the cover of the first edition of *A Sport and a Pastime* is her. You can't see her face, of course.

JS: Yes, that's true.

II. "ONCE YOU REACH A CERTAIN POINT, MATERIAL IS LIMITLESS."

DP: *Burning the Days* contains poignant testaments to the writers of your generation who meant the most to you in a personal and literary sense: James Jones, Irwin Shaw. Your new collection of stories, *Last Night,* is dedicated to George Plimpton. You yourself seem as vibrant as any man your age, but does it take a toll, to witness the fall of these idols?

JS: It's not the fall of idols, it's the vanishing of a world. Everything you know, have known, becomes old, and an entirely new order of things appears.

It's like crossing a galaxy. After a while you begin to get the idea. You progress from the outside, from nowhere, towards the center or near it—stars are being born, stars are dying, and in the end you are heading for the outside once more.

DP: Whom do you miss the most, of those that are gone?

JS: Toni Ellis when she was young, Woody who I was in Korea with, Lane Slate, Robert Phelps, and mainly for what he represented, Irwin Shaw.

DP: Of that world that has vanished, or is it vanishing, what do you miss most? What has been lost? Cheever wrote of his prime that it was a time "when almost everybody wore a hat."

JS: I miss letters, ocean liners, New York when you could drive anywhere and park, and I miss the indifference that once existed toward popular culture.

DP: You came to speak at the Iowa Writers' Workshop a few times during the years I studied there. One thing you said, if I remember correctly, is "It is the writer's obligation to travel."

JS: Did I say obligation? The real obligation of a writer is to enthrall, like Scheherazade. It's not that easy.

DP: Well, then, how did your extensive travels influence your literary aesthetic, if at all?

JS: I'm not the first to feel that travel is a writer's true destiny. You don't have to go to Europe or the Far East. It can be Mexico or just a different part of the country. You see and understand things, maybe even your own life, in a new way.

DP: You also spoke about a certain sense of urgency, now, in your work. You said, if I recall correctly, "At one point it was a question of what to write about. Now, of so many stories, the difficulty is choosing which ones to tell."

JS: Once you reach a certain point, material is limitless. Perhaps that's because you come to understand what you are looking for or perhaps it's a matter of accumulation. John Cheever wrote stories in two or three days and Hemingway once wrote three, I think, in a single day. Novels have been written in six or eight weeks. For me, it always seems to take longer although I did write "Bangkok," the first version of it, in a morning. Sometimes you seem to get in a rhythm.

I also find that I am able to write more readily when freed from my usual self, as it were. It may be during a long drive or the morning after one drink too many. I'm a bit removed, looser. There is writing when you are intending to, and this other, less frequent, sometimes more beautiful writing that just comes.

DP: Regarding that sense of urgency, if you do in fact feel that now in your career, you have three books coming out in less than a year. If I'm not mistaken, you worked on *Burning the Days* for ten years or more, or at least you missed your deadline with Random House for that book by a good number of years. So, what's causing this sudden acceleration? Or have these works merely been in the pipeline for a long time?

JS: Well, I've been healthy, I suppose that's a warning. I realize it was an indulgence to spend ten years on something that could have taken far less time, but I was teaching for a living and we also had a child born to us, a son, which proved a blessing. I wrote some stories, so the collection that is coming out has been more or less in the pipeline, as you say. *Gods of Tin* was largely the work of two editors, William and Jessica Benton, although the words are mine. And the book that my wife, Kay Eldredge, and I have just finished was several years in progress. I don't know where it will be in Barnes & Noble, under Food, History, Autobiography, Non-Fiction, or Cooking, but I'm hoping not on the top or bottom shelf. Three books this year, none for the next five.

DP: One could say that you work slowly but surely. The books are adding up, ten of them now. Are you pleased—wholly—with your body of work, what has been published so far, or do you feel that a few pieces are missing, books perhaps you wanted or tried to write but didn't, for whatever reason?

JS: I suppose there are books I could have written. Perhaps it would have made a difference. I wrote things I was passionate about and didn't write other things. To say I am pleased or not… it's simply the way things turned out.

III. "THERE'S DESIRE, BETRAYAL, THE NECESSITY OF IT."

DP: *Last Night*, your most recent collection of stories, focuses upon those pivotal moments that make up a life—missed chances, wrong paths taken, that one great opportunity, which a character perhaps did or didn't take. I'm thinking about "Comet," "Bangkok," "Palm Court," "Arlington."

JS: "Comet" doesn't have a missed chance. It's about a wife who, at a dinner, begins trashing her husband's life, his past, but in a way she can't because (*a*) it was marvelous and (*b*) it belongs to him, he lived it, it can't be touched. "Bangkok," I would say, is about a woman's attempt at revenge. "Arlington" is really just a portrait with a kind of moral. No one I know of has been able to definitively say what a short story is or should be, what distinguishes it from an anecdote or an account—Mishima's "Patriotism" is an account but with a power that dismisses definitions—or a piece of description. I like stories that keep you reading until the line that makes it a story, as in, say, Carver's "Night School" when [the narrator's wife] says, "That's only writing.... Being betrayed by somebody in your own family, *there's* a real nightmare for you." Suddenly all of it, solid, with a click like steel, falls into place.

DP: Let me try again. Do you see any recurring themes in the stories in *Last Night*? Does the book function as a summing-up of sorts?

JS: Well, there's desire, betrayal, the necessity of it; these are things I keep circling around. I generally seem to be writing about men and women and what exists between them. Murder doesn't interest me, or greed, or the anatomy of family life, except in *Light Years*. But these stories don't sum anything up. They're a partial summing-up.

DP: You have a certain stature among fellow writers. Many writers, such as Richard Ford and Susan Sontag, have praised your sentence-making, your prose, your precision of language; such skill, though, is perhaps not as revered by the general reading public; does that matter?

JS: Obscurity is not so bad, especially if it is local. I can't brag that I beat Mr. Turgenev, I beat Mr. de Maupassant, and fought two draws with Mr. Stendhal. That's for fools. I didn't have the misfortune of great early success—I don't believe it would be dangerous to me now, but I don't see it coming. The bestseller list will bring you money, but it's never been much for glory. Of course, in those rare cases where it has been, that is the summit.

DP: When I read your work, when I read a story like "My Lord You" or "Comet" for the first time, there is a certain thrill. There is a first realization that, "Oh well, I'll never be that good, I might as well quit." But eventually that feeling translates into a renewed vigor, which makes me, as a writer, want to get back to my desk. I feel that with your work, with Shirley Hazzard, with a few others. Were there books or writers like that for you? You mention *Under Milk Wood* in *Burning the Days* as perhaps such a book. Were there others? Are there any now?

JS: Some fade, but not many. You can't write like Robert Lowell. You can't write like Saul Bellow or Anne Carson or W. G. Sebald or Isaac Babel. They're in a different class. The coach at San Pedro used to tell his team, "Play your position, you're not made of the stuff champions are made of." Maybe you think you are.

IV. "WHEN YOU READ SOMETHING WONDERFUL THERE IS NO AWKWARD AFTERWARDS."

DP: What's the worst part about being a writer?

JS: Having to do it. Anyone will tell you that. Or having done it and failed.

DP: The best part?

JS: The greatness of that world and feeling part of it. There is a reality in it that is greater than other realities even though it cannot replace them. When you read something wonderful there is no awkward afterwards or sense of having used something up. It's still there, it is still waiting for you, the thrill doesn't fade.

DP: Jill Krementz published that terrific book, *The Writer's Desk*. You get a peek into the writer's workroom. Saul Bellow bent over a portable typewriter. What does your desk look like? What's on the walls of your office?

JS: I don't have an office. I work on one table or another. The typewriter is thirty feet away, in another room. I don't need that until later. If I'm near bookshelves, there are some photographs leaning in them, mostly people I knew when they were younger. The best table I ever had was in New City, New York, in our bedroom which was on the lower floor of what had been a barn. I was in my thirties; I could work late at night or start at dawn, in the quiet. My wife was sleeping, the children, the dog. The table was made of narrow strips of pale oak glued together, and it had a row of books along the far edge, the ones that I thought were important.

DP: Tell me what your day looks like, at this time of your life, when you're at home and working, whether in Aspen or on Long Island.

JS: I avoid habit. I sometimes sit down to work in the morning. After a few days, I change to the afternoon or early evening. The dog likes to walk in the fields; I begin the day with him, that's at about 8:30, and we go again at 4. I almost never go out to lunch. Through the summer and into the fall, my wife and I usually go to the beach to swim late in the day. We have an old car we keep for that. There's a tennis court in the other direction, and we sometimes go there and play.

DP: Have your work habits changed over the years? The nuts and bolts, I mean.

JS: Since they were established they've stayed pretty much the same. I write with a pen, then I type and retype, two or three times, sometimes more. Given my veteran status, publishers have let me give them typescripts. If I were to start over, I'd change things.

DP: Your books are extremely popular in France and Germany. Why do you think your work fits with a European audience?

JS: They must know something we don't.

DP: You've answered this question before in interviews but I wonder now, at this point, which of your own novels or stories stand out for you?

JS: Of the novels, I like *A Sport and a Pastime* and *Light Years* best. Of the stories, "Comet," "American Express," and the section in the bedroom of "Last Night."

DP: Do you have readers you show your work to for comments or impressions?

JS: In the beginning, of course, you want praise and only praise, but later you want firmer stuff. I have my wife and a friend, both good readers. I don't let anyone read work in progress.

DP: How do you deal with writer's block, if that is an issue for you?

JS: I don't have that. I have inertia, lack of faith, things like that but nothing will won't defeat.

DP: How do you know when a story, or novel, is done?

JS: Oh, that makes itself known. When you can't do any more or any better.

DP: You once mentioned that you read a few passages from *A Book of Common Prayer* before starting your writing day. Is this something you still do? What does it do for you?

JS: *A Book of Common Prayer,* yes, it must be around somewhere though I haven't seen it for a while. If you could go to the Met in the morning and stand in front of certain pictures or sculptures, it would do the same thing, purify and more or less convince you that it can be done.

DP: What are you working on? Is it something you can talk about in any detail? Or does it harm the process for you, in some way, to discuss a work in progress?

JS: I'm writing a novel. I'd like it to be a littler longer than usual. It's more or less What Mattered to Me, though *me* is not really in it—I don't like the postmodern ego. I'd like it to have a little breadth, perspective.

DP: Can you expand upon that concept for a moment, of the post-modern ego? *Burning the Days,* when it came out, seemed to confuse some readers who wanted it to be a memoir in the current vogue, that is, confessional writing. The book, of course, is not.

JS: I think of the postmodern as long-winded, clever, egocentric, and self-pitying. I like Isak Dinesen, writers like that.

V. "WRITING ISN'T TAUGHT—IT'S ACHIEVED, LIKE SIN IN IRELAND."

DP: You went to West Point. Served as a jet fighter pilot in the Korean War in combat. Wrote and directed movies in Europe. Met or knew about everyone—Fellini, Irwin Shaw, James Jones, Kerouac, etc. Where did the writing come in? How did it fit? Was it some sort of distraction or drag? It's your life's work, of course, but you lived first and foremost, obviously.

JS: I wish I had put down what happened at West Point, but I only made a couple of pages of notes and stopped, I'm not sure why. In the Air Force I was writing undercover. It wasn't as shameful as cross-dressing but it was an odd thing to do. You want to be a man, and that isn't part of it. I didn't write *The Hunters,* which is about flying in combat, until two or three years after the war. As I've said, flying in the war was a big thing for me, the voyage of my life, and I wanted to somehow inscribe it. I imagined a book that would be famous although its author would be unknown, still struggling probably with the question of whether it was an acceptable thing to do.

When I resigned my commission to become a writer, it was like running way from home. I didn't know where to go or what to do. At the very beginning, in despair, I'd gone to talk to and perhaps be consoled by my ex-wing commander, a wonderful guy,

John Brooks. A couple of years ago, before he died, I went up to West Point with him and we walked through the cemetery. His father, like mine, had gone to West Point before him, they were stationed on Corregidor before the war, in the early 1930s. He was reading the names on the gravestones, General this, Colonel that. He remembered many of them, had delivered newspapers to them as a boy, and so forth. After a while I looked and saw that tears were running down his face. The military life. He'd flown on the Ploesti raid. His father had graduated in 1912. I left all that to become a writer—what was I doing? I remember what John Brooks said when I told him I'd resigned. You idiot, he said.

So, there it was. I was free to become a writer, but it had to be built from scratch. It had to replace the other and, in a way, erase it.

DP: And life? Did it get in the way of writing? Or does writing get in the way of life? You've lived so richly, it seems there must have been a balancing.

JS: There have been a lot of things I haven't been able to do. Write enough is one of them.

DP: You come from a generation whose writing grew out of your lives and experiences, like Hemingway. I'm thinking of James Jones and Irwin Shaw and Norman Mailer and the rest, even someone like Truman Capote. Today, there are the academics—writers who go directly from college to M.F.A. programs and back to college as teachers. The work, it seems, tends toward the cerebral, as opposed to the visceral. People complain about these programs, of course. You've taught at Iowa and Williams and other places. Where does this lead? How do you feel about it?

JS: I was lucky, but the same thing happens in film, directors come along whose reference comes from films rather than life. Does it make any difference? I don't know.

Writing isn't taught—it's achieved, like sin in Ireland. But there can be a favorable atmosphere and perhaps a trustworthy

309

guide. Also, of course, you meet people headed your way.

DP: You once said that you tend to write about, or perhaps just like, dogs and women. This is apparent in your new collection, *Last Night*. Are young women evocative because they have the power to shape a story?

JS: No, no, there are no dogs. One dog. There are women, not all of them young. You have to have women, unless you're Kafka. I don't know if they shape the story, but they're like a magnet, without them the filings just lie inert.

DP: I'm often astonished by the pacing of your short stories, the way you stay ahead of the reader, how you draw the story along through time and place. A story like "American Express," say. How do you do that? I can think of no other writer who handles time quite like you do. You invite the reader to reread, to uncover meaning on the second and third tries. It seems a story like "American Express" cannot be fully known except upon rereading, although the first reading is fully satisfying as well.

JS: I think you should get it all the first time and in a slightly different way or with different pleasure if you reread, knowing what it is. "American Express" didn't actually happen, but things like it did, and I knew the two men and two of the women in it. I thought it should gallop a little, it would read better that way. But it evolved, it didn't just set itself down. There were different versions of it and dozens of pages of notes. Maybe that helped.

DP: I'm also often amazed at the unveiling of secrets in your short stories. You pull aside the screens, one at a time, until the characters are wholly revealed, in a metaphorical sense. I'm thinking of, say, "Give" or "Last Night" or "Comet" or "Platinum" from the new collection. Is this part of your aesthetic, something you plan beforehand?

JS: Well, there's discovery in life, isn't there? You find out more about someone, they reveal more. Sometimes the reader should have that. Not every time, not as a formula—more like a painter, a series of paintings or a phase, then a change to something different. But the same hand paints it all, and the same sensibility.

DP: What about the phenomenon of the author tour? This is something relatively new. I've been told Jacqueline Susann invented it. Is this something you enjoy, or merely tolerate? I'm thinking more of going bookstore to bookstore, from city to city, that sort of tedium, not reading at, say, the 92nd Street Y.

JS: Readings, authors touring: that makes sense in the case of Dickens or poets going around to colleges, but it's an anachronism in the age of TV. If you're well known, it's a gesture to the public to appear in person, and if you're not well known, it won't change things. If you write something that everyone wants to read, that changes things.

DP: Last question. It seems to me there is a spine that goes through all your published work, having to do with living a certain type of life. Your characters are always seeking; they aspire toward something higher than what they have, whether it be beauty or heroism or courage or love, or even a better bottle of wine, as one of the characters says in "Last Night": "It would be nice to have always drunk it."

JS: You write about certain people and things because you know something about them and you want to tell it. Writing is the consequence of the desire to tell. I'm not one of those writers at the mercy, so to speak, of his characters in a novel. I know what happens to them and more or less how it happens, it's not a surprise.

I think the odds in life are against one, and I like people who go on despite the odds and who feel themselves held to or drawn to some standard, even if that standard doesn't really exist. Stoicism, I guess, is also involved. I don't often try to analyze it, that doesn't work for me as well as finding examples. Yes, go for the summit. ✷

BEN MARCUS

TALKS WITH

GEORGE SAUNDERS

"THAT, TO ME, IS ART'S HIGHEST ASPIRATION: TO SHOW THAT NOTHING IS TRUE AND EVERYTHING IS TRUE."

Things for which there is no time to be:
Bloatedly intellectual
Merely clever
Stupid
Programmatic
Cloying

e was born George Saunders and has kept the same name his entire life. Sometimes he moves through the streets beneath a great coat designed to keep himself from being killed. Otherwise he is fearless, naked in the evenings, a family man. There has been a moustache, a beard, a bald face. The area locale where he has chosen to live is brutal and cold and produces a large share of lonely people. He sleeps and eats and functions as any person might. But there the similarities end.

For part of each day, Saunders is a hero. He would never agree to this designation. But his modesty, his generosity, his expansive imagination, and his fully developed tenderness-generating technique are a large part of *his heroism. His heroism is fitted with a blind spot that keeps Mr. Saunders from knowing about, or being able to acknowledge, the ways that he has beautifully scoured and remade—through artisan-quality writing—the people in many countries. His writing appears in books and magazines and quickly subsumes them, explaining the appearance of horizon fires in the far Northeast. The books of fiction are called* CivilWarLand in Bad Decline *(1996) and* Pastoralia *(2000). The Suits call his writing "stories," but they are really soft bodies to wear for a larger experience of life, hollowcore person-shapes that one can slip on in order to attain amazement. Saunders writes bodies, and his readers wear them. Some of these readers are probably in your house. If they are glowing or trembling, now you know why.*

The following conversation took place on an old Toshiba calculator.

—B.M. (Winter 2003)

I. "PAY ATTENTION TO EVERYTHING AS IF THIS WAS YOUR LAST MOMENT ON EARTH."

BEN MARCUS: When I visited your city of Syracuse, New York, I was kept awake all night by crows, who raised such a terrible noise in my motel room that I thought I might get killed. I later heard from other overnight visitors that this had happened to them also. Explain.

GEORGE SAUNDERS: It's true, we have a lot of crows up here. It's part of a Municipal Program to become the West Nile Virus Capital of the Northeast. We actually "recruit" crows from all over the United States—bring them here on special Crow Interview Trips, construct special "GlamorNests" for them all over town, screen weekend-long *Heckle & Jeckle* fests at our local movie houses. And they are loud. We had one in particular around our house who used to sound exactly like he was calling my wife's name ("PauLA! PauLA!") until finally—in connection with the Crow Recruitment Program—we had a translator over, who informed us that what the crow was actually saying was, "I could sure use some freaking grapes! I could sure use some freaking grapes! If I don't get some freaking grapes, I'm going back to Cleveland."

BM: Where does the name George Saunders come from?

GS: It actually comes from the fact that my great-grandfather, who emigrated from Greece, was catching a lot of crap for his last name, Vlahakis, and his accent. I think he was working as a fruit seller at the time. So he went for something very British. The accent he couldn't do anything about. He was kind of a wild card—left my great-grandmother and their sons for two years to go back to Greece and fight the Turks. And then as soon as he came home, he ran off with a waitress, to Napa Valley.

BM: Rather than ask who your ideal reader is, since I have met your ideal reader and he hurt me physically, I wanted to ask you how aware you are of entertainment, as a specific gift to a reader, and whether or not there's ever a tension for you between what you feel you ought to do as a writer, and what you actually do. This is not a question about capitulation to a generic sense of what a reader might want, but rather a question of a potential discrepancy between what might please you and what you feel will please others.

GS: This question rattles me, because it makes me realize that I make no distinction between what pleases me and what might please a reader. That is, if I feel the reader will be pleased by a thing, I simply want to do that thing. Period. My feeling is something like this: The basis for literature is the fact that all of our brains are essentially, structurally, identical. First love in 1830, in Russia, beneath swaying pines, is neurologically identical to first love in 1975, back of a Camaro, Foghat blaring. That's why that wonderful cross-firing occurs when we read.

It is not the case, as we sometimes feel, that the writer is making us feel what she felt. It is, rather, that the writer is poking that part of our brain that already felt (or knew, or sensed) what the writer felt (or knew, or sensed). Without getting too Star-Trekky, there really is, I believe, one universal mind, but the basis for the existence of that universal mind is the structural similarity of all those individual minds. Because the brain is a machine, and all those individual minds are just slightly different versions of that machine, only so many mind-states exist, and therefore you can know what I think, because it is what you thought, roughly.

So when I'm writing, I am trying to move myself, or impress myself, or prevent myself from getting bored and walking away—in the faith that, if I succeed in this, the writing will have some equivalent effect on the reader. On every reader? No. On every reader, to some extent? I think so. I hope so. Anyway, that's what I assume. That, to me, is the really magical thing about writing: if I write toward my own best nature, I am also writing toward the best nature of others. It sort of doesn't make sense, and even feels a little fascist, but I think it's true.

Here I have to confess that I also believe that certain effects have more power in prose than others, and that this tendency is, at least in part, universal. I believe in efficiency, action, clarity, velocity. I think these qualities are responsible for the feeling of being "drawn into" a piece of prose. Also, maybe paradoxically, I think that constructing this hierarchy of preferred effects is what style is all about. If one writer prefers some other suite of effects, and energetically tries to construct a prose-world based on the pre-eminence of those effects, style will result.

I will also confess that, for complex reasons of background, etc., I really don't care much about anything but being entertaining—with entertainment, I hope, being defined as "ultimately interesting." Ideally, I aspire to write stuff that takes into account the fact that we are all dying. So there's no time to be bloatedly intellectual, no time to be merely clever, no time to be stupid, or programmatic, or cloying. That's the hope, anyway.

And as for that ideal reader of mine, sorry about that. "Max" is basically a good guy, but he doesn't get out much, and, for

him, his fists are his most expressive part. That is, what you con-
strue as "punching" is, for Max, sort of like kissing might be for
most people.

BM: Your theory of a universal mind suggests that Buddhism plays
a role in how you think about fiction.

GS: You bet. I find Buddhism inspiring in that it says: Everything
matters. Suffering is real. Death is imminent. Pay attention to
everything as if this was your last moment on earth. And then I see
writing as part of an ongoing attempt to really, viscerally, believe
that everything matters, suffering is real, and death is imminent. Chekhov said that art prepares us for tenderness, and I think
this is also what spiritual practice can do. On a practical level there
are also parallels. Buddhism emphasizes honesty and openness,
nonattachment. So if you thought your story was going to be a
biting satire of a nail-biting patriarchal brutalizer, but then, on
page three, a street vendor comes in and makes a really interesting
speech about his lifelong love of broccoli, and that speech has
more energy in it than anything that came before—openness
means admitting to yourself that your story needs to follow that
vendor out into the street. That sort of thing.

BM: A cross old man once announced to me that it was impossible to teach writing. I replied, just as crossly, that he meant *he*
couldn't teach writing. Nevertheless, nonteachers of writing seem
to love to declare its impossibility, to call writing programs scams
and money-wasters, and just to generally deride the whole enterprise. Book reviews frequently resort to a shorthand critique, ci-
ting "workshop" stories, and a *Village Voice* article claimed that
Jonathan Safran Foer's originality stemmed, at least in part, from
his outsider status, since he did not attend an M.F.A. program.
I was thinking of you and a few other writers—namely Charles
Baxter and Aimee Bender—who have a reputation for being extraordinary teachers of writing, not to mention obviously original

and productive writers. I'd be curious to hear your take on teaching, what its value might be, and why writing-instruction, unlike other artistic studies—painting or theater or music—seems so susceptible to criticism.

GS: I suspect that what your Cross Old Man was trying to say was: only one young writer in a thousand ever gets a book out, and of those books, only one in a thousand lasts in even the slightest way, so why are you writing-program teachers holding out hope to so many young people, when you know and I know that only one out of a thousand out of an original thousand have any hope of writing an enduring work of literature? And basically, I would agree with that. The chances of a person breaking through their own habits and sloth and limited mind to actually write something that gets out there and matters to people are slim.

But I also suspect that your Cross Old Man is too narrowly careerist. Because he seems to be neglecting the fact that, even for those thousands of young people who don't get something out there, the process is still a noble one—the process of trying to say something, of working through the craft issues, and the world view issues, and the ego issues—all of this is character-building, and god forbid everything we do should have to have Concrete Career Results.

I've seen, time and time again, the way that the process of trying to say something that matters dignifies and improves a person. I've seen it in my own failures, in writing and otherwise. I think it comes down to the motivation of the individual student. If the student writer wants to get over, become famous, dominate others with his talent—then no matter what, he's going to lose. On the other hand, if he wants to go deeply into himself, subjugate his own pettiness, discover some big truths about life— there's no way he can lose. And the thing is, we all have both of those motivations within us, every second that we're writing. So it's an ongoing, lifelong battle to write for the right reasons. There's a sort of instant karma always working, if you see what I mean.

Having said that, I do think it's possible to "teach writing," in the sense that an older, like-minded person can certainly speed some younger person's progress along that younger person's personal arc. I imagine it this way: The younger writer is racing through some snowy woods, wearing ice skates. The M.F.A. experience, ideally, is a frozen lake that suddenly appears. The writer just gets sped up. The way is easier. The trajectory is roughly the same, but the velocity is higher. The danger of a workshop environment is a kind of groupthink that can creep into even the most enlightened gathering. Since ultimately what we are trying to do as writers (let's admit it) is be iconic and undeniable and breathtaking, setting up a group whose function is to Thoughtfully Regard, then Rationally Critique, may be problematic. But then, I also think it's possible to take that into account—to undercut that tendency, to keep knocking the legs out from under it, so to speak.

Finally: I think the success of the M.F.A. experience is proportional to how closely such a program resembles a salon or a group of friends. So I think small numbers are important, a longer residence-time, financial support. I find that the best teaching moments happen when I know my students well enough, personally and artistically, to make certain intuitive leaps with them, leaps that aren't strictly dictated by the work sitting in front of me.

By the way, it may interest you to know that the Cross Old Man lives next-door to Max, my ideal reader. Because of the Cross Old Man's impertinence to you, I have just sent Max over to "kiss" the Cross Old Man. I'll let you know how it turns out!

Can I do a follow-up, to you? Because what I am wondering about, in reference to the workshop questions, is what your experience was as a student in a workshop. Did you workshop anything that later became *The Age of Wire and String,* and, if so, how was it received? If you had put some of those stories up, and they'd gotten resistance—would it have mattered? I guess I'm asking because of the extreme originality of that book, and the fact that one of its many charms is that it keeps insisting on abiding by its own new paradigm.

BM: The closest I got to workshopping pieces from that book was in a class that Robert Coover taught called "Ancient Fictions." He assigned us to write new mythologies, or creation myths, and a few of the earliest pieces in *The Age of Wire and String* were written in response. It was more of a literature class, with some fiction-writing options instead of critical papers. But it was by far the best course I ever took having anything to do with fiction-writing. The pieces we wrote weren't really discussed. I think we read them aloud and all nodded thoughtfully.

The workshop situation I was in with other teachers tended to err on the side of permissiveness, and actual teaching was more or less absent. It seems strange to say this, but in my own teaching I've tried to reverse almost everything I experienced as a student. Students now also seem to expect far more than I or my classmates ever did: extensive line-editing and lengthy written critiques, follow-up conferences, and then extra critiques of whatever revisions they've done. We were lucky if our teacher showed up or said much at all. At the time, the teacher's silence or reticence seemed like blinding intelligence, but I'm not so sure now.

II. "IT'S NOT A DRAMATIC ARC
SO MUCH AS A DRAMATIC VECTOR:
STRAIGHT DOWN INTO THE MUD."

BM: Even in your wilder stories, a current of deep ethics seems to run through your characters, an immense desire to do good, and it is this desire, the conflicts it creates, that seems to generate story for you. Big moments of grief seem to result, and these serve as epiphanies, revelations, or just incredible finales. Is this connected to a belief you have about character, or does it derive more from your sense of what might propel a story? Or neither?

GS: I like the kind of story where the reader comes away loving the character, feeling strongly identified with the character. And I think the way to make that happen is to make a character who is as good as the reader. That is, the reader feels the character is doing everything just as he or she would, if put in the same situation. So for the writer this means no slumming, no puppeteering—by which I mean, no manipulating your character to prove a point or illustrate something you believe or service some prejudice you have or fulfill some secret hope for the story. Don't make the character stupider or blinder or meaner than yourself. That is, credit the character with the same basic nature as you, albeit tempered or complicated by whatever is happening to him, or has happened in the past, that makes the character "you," but in a parallel universe. Even if your main character is Hitler, believe that there is some part of yourself that could swell into Hitleresque proportions. Another way of saying this is: believe that there, but for the grace of God, go you. So, in part, this ethical tendency you note is just a strategy to get more warmth into the story.

But to be another degree more honest, I think that's just the way I see the world—in fairly simple ethical terms. I always have. As a kid I was interested in philosophy and religion, and came to reading and thinking via Catholicism, had amazing early experiences in the Church, glimpses into what ideas such as compassion and self-sacrifice might mean at a visceral level, got the sense that life was big and painful and that the purpose of an individual life was to aid other beings in trouble, which runs counter to our instinct, which is protect our own ass. And then that beautiful heroic narrative of Christ sacrificing himself to save everybody, even when he didn't want to. I found that very moving. That naïve big-question sensibility ("What are we doing here? How should we behave?") stayed at the heart of my ludicrous, spotty reading life through college.

Years later, when I was first working on *CivilWarLand,* I felt like I turned an important corner in my artistic life by letting that sensibility back in, that feeling that things matter, and that literature exists to help us examine the big questions. That there are such things as power, as abuse, as bad luck, and it definitely matters which side of the fence you're on. It matters whether we're hungry, whether your love is returned or rejected, whether we walk into the room with a fireplace and the cheering crowd or are locked out of the room and have to stand out in the cold with wet sneakers, etc. I guess what I'm saying is when it comes to writing stories, I don't know any other way to proceed. As soon as I start writing, things start to unfold around some central moral vector, and that's that. So, sometimes to my frustration, my stories tend to be "problem" stories: will he or won't he do the right thing? And they also tend to be fables, although I didn't realize that until recently. So the tendency you mention is both a blessing and a curse: I have something to write about, but there is a sort of an implicit ceiling, a kind of limit of subtlety I can't get past. The dangers of this approach are oversimplicity, preachiness, and, eventually, fascism.

Can I ask about your relation to this ethical stuff? I feel your work is extremely "ethical," in the sense that I always feel opened up when I'm reading it. I am, in the Chekhovian sense mentioned above, prepared for tenderness. Is this part of your intent?

BM: I'm not sure that in attempting sympathy in fiction I can claim a connection to ethics. It's hard for me to link writing with good deeds, since most of what I wrote for so long was character-free, and then when characters did show up they were interested in killing or at least harming the other characters. Not very ethical. A kind of coldness used to appeal to me. Behavior, if present at all, was mechanized and described the way a tree might be: sort of the stubborn opposite of giving human properties to inanimate things. But if I ever do get lucky and spill out some peoplelike pieces of writing, they are inevitably cruel or pitiful, take your pick. Unfortunately it yields only minimal drama. The cruel people act cruel to the pitiful people, who become more pitiful. It's not a dramatic arc so much as a dramatic vector: straight down into the mud. I'm sure most people get over this narrative paradigm in third grade, but it's about all I can manage so far.

I'm interested in the trace fantastical elements that appear in your stories, as well as the occasional ghost. So much of your stories seem wedded to an emotional realism, yet your settings—the landscapes—are often, if not fantastical, then exceedingly odd or improbable, leading to real emotions in an unreal world. And then your stories, sometimes very slightly, leave the realm of physical possibility entirely (the dead awaken, for instance). Are these three distinct writing-spaces to you? Do you see a difference between "realism" and fantastical writing?

GS: I guess it's strategic on one level: if you're going to have some really crazy things happening, you have a better chance of being believed if you jump off from some believable ground. It maybe comes from a sales instinct: If I'm trying to hustle ten bucks from you, and I've invented a wild story to support my hustle, it's probably best not to sing that story in an operatic voice. Better if I tell it in my normal voice, eyes downcast, acknowledging all your doubts about the veracity of my story. That's how I see the realist touches. I think the fantastical elements are there as my lame-brained attempt to mimic the real strangeness and mystery of even the most ordinary day.

Realism is nonsense, when you think of it. I mean, there is no such thing. Nobody writes realism, if realism is defined as "fiction that is objective and real and not distorted, but is just, you know, normal." But I think that's what "realistic" has come to mean. The nature of all fiction is distortion, exaggeration, and compression. So what we call realism is just distorting, exaggerating, and compressing with the intention of alluding to, or hand-waving at—taking advantage of our fondness for—what I've heard called "consensus reality"—the sort of lazy, agreed-upon "way things are." Which, of course, is not at all how they actually are. How they actually are is: We are walking corpses. Ideas people die for fade within ten years. Murderers walk. The dead don't really die because they can sometimes continue to affect the actions of the living just as much as if they were still around. Et cetera. So realism, as beautifully practiced by Zola, Chekhov, Carver, et al, is a strategy—a strategy to elicit our emotional loyalty by doing some sleight of hand to make the distorted, exaggerated, compressed thing they've made remind us of consensus reality. Why? Power of effect. They want to make a powerful effect.

What I find exciting is the idea that no work of fiction will ever, ever come close to "documenting" life. So then, the purpose of it must be otherwise. It's supposed to do something to us to make it easier (or more fun, or less painful) for us to live. Then all questions of form and so on become subjugated to this higher thing. We're not slaves any more to ideas of "the real" or, for that matter, to ideas of "the experimental"—we're just trying to make something happen to the reader in his or her deepest places. And that thing that happens will always be due to some juxtaposition of the life the reader is living and the words on the page, no matter how unconventional or conventional the representation of those events is—the heart will either rise, or it won't.

I think it's interesting, though, that some writers of our approximate generation have a sort of queasiness around this issue of realism. I know I do. There's something about the normal approach ("Bob, age forty-three, pale blond hair—a senior-level accountant—felt good about his marriage. He got into his tan Lexus, thinking of Maribeth.") that makes me scared and sick. I am always trying to avoid it.

You've written two radically unconventional books. Do you ever feel that pull toward what we're calling realism? If so, what's stopping you? What do you think that pull is about? That is, what do you fear you're missing by not doing "realism?" What concessions/changes would you have to make to be "more realistic?"

BM: I do feel a pull toward realism, but there's always a hand waiting to smack me down off it. From afar, where I definitely am, realism looks like a place of readability, which I very much desire, by which I mean that inscrutability is not something I value. But I can almost watch my fiction turn generic as I attempt realism, and then the trade-off leads to work that is punishingly dull. So what stops me is a total lack of ability. For probably good although unfathomable reasons, a narrative framework, a skin of story-telling—which I equate with a writerly promise that time will pass and that people will move around in a made-up space—seems to justify many kinds of conceptual or innovative approaches to fiction, but I find that, in itself, a kind of fantastical notion. I've seen a few writers I hugely admire, such as Joe Wenderoth or David Markson, become marginalized or called "experimental" because they have forgone the typical narrative skins and pursued more conceptual or subversively informational fiction. Yet their realism is, for me, extremely high.

There are these soporific, safe phrases like "once upon a time" that make nonrealist writing much more OK, and so I'm at the point where I'm wondering if that's a good thing worth pursuing or if it's a capitulation.

III. "HAVE WE SUFFICIENTLY DESCRIBED THE WONDERS OF LIVING IN OUR TIME?"

BM: Several less-narrative pieces of yours ("Four Institutional Monologues," which was in *McSweeney's,* and "I Can Speak!" which was in the *New Yorker*) did not make it into *Pastoralia.* What was the process of selecting work for that book? The above pieces were far less story-driven. Did that play a role in your decision?

GS: If I remember right, "I Can Speak!" was written after the manuscript was finished. So I had all these story-driven pieces and the one monologue, and it didn't seem to fit. But both stories you mention, plus another monologue ("A Survey of the Literature") will be in the next collection. The monologue-like pieces feel different for me—easier, in some way. They don't depend on surprising myself as much as the more story-driven pieces. But I like them, and my thought for this next book is that they might add a little something—maybe offer a political or institutional angle on stuff that is covered more emotionally by the stories. I can picture a sort of a "spine" of these types of nonnarrative pieces running through the book. I like the way books like *In Our Time* or *The Coast of Chicago* use little spacer pieces that are different in tone and intent than the longer, more narrative pieces.

My usual approach so far has just been to put everything together that feels like it came out of the same aesthetic suite of ideas, which usually corresponds to a certain three-to-four-year time period—and then weed out the weaker links, or the anomalous ones. I usually have two or three pieces I start and don't finish, and another two or three that I finish but am not happy with, and then another couple that I'm happy enough with, but don't seem to fit with the rest. They make a sort of goiter on an otherwise smooth shape. And then I figure that, if each of the pieces represents an intense move in some direction, a move that I played out aesthetically, then if I put them all together, with attention to the order—the book should be more than the sum of its parts. That's the theory, anyway.

For this next book, there is a pretty strong nonnarrative presence and also, I think, a stronger political (or overtly political) feeling. This wasn't planned but was maybe a product of the time during which the book was written.

BM: There is a word sometimes used in connection to fiction—moral—that can scare the bread out of me because I use it too, and then must secretly admit that I don't really understand it, or what it means, yet it seems to me to be a word that is reached for when something called "serious fiction" is discussed, a word we'd like to assign to the fiction we care about. Does "moral" fiction mean

326

something to you that you can articulate?

GS: The short answer is: All good fiction is moral, in that it is imbued with the world, and powered by our real concerns: love, death, how-should-I-live. This is true, I think, of all great writers, regardless of their approach: Sterne, Chekhov, Barthelme, Morrison, Gogol, Bellow—whomever. But I think that word has taken on additional overtones since the Gardner-Gass debates of the 1980s, where the binary was: (1) Fictional effects are effects of language vs. (2) Fictional effects are effects of represented experience. My guess is, most of us who have ever tried to write a sentence in a story know that both (1) and (2) are simultaneously true. If I write, "The cow, ducklike, made a ducklike cow sound, then disappeared down the Shaughnessy Chute,"—we recognize that there is a pure-sound quality to that, but also that cows and ducks and chutes are somehow "appearing" in our reading-mind. So it's the confluence of these two effects that makes the heart-rise I mentioned above (or doesn't, in this case).

But somehow, at that time, there was this sense that the purpose of fiction was "moral" in the sense of "instructive." That I reject. I mean, it is instructive, it feels that way, but instructive in a deep way, and in a way that does not flow from a writer's desire to instruct, if you see what I mean. Rather, it flows from the writer's confusion in the process of writing, or at least the writer's sense of exploration. Writing can be a formal way of enacting Oliver Cromwell's plea: "I beseech you, in the bowels of Christ, think it possible you may be mistaken." When a writer does that, then I think the result is moral, in the sense of "accounting for all complexities." I think you leave the work of art not instructed, but baffled, baffled in a way that humbles you and makes you move more carefully (but fully) through your life, at least until the effect wears off.

For writers of our generation (and of course, using that expression means I am really talking about me), that phrase "moral fiction" seems to signify something else, though, some deeper fear, a fear that the assumptions "we" have made about writing are self-limiting, especially around the issues of being ironic/edgy/experimental—a feeling that maybe our approach is preventing us from reaching into the more profound aspects of our experience, especially as we get older and less jaded and the checks start rolling in and the grandkids have grandkids and we see that life is not so angsty after all, at least not all the time. That is, the fear that our approach may be omitting significant aspects of our actual experience. I sense a real feeling of discontent hovering over American fiction right now and maybe all American art forms, post-9/11, that has at its core questions like (and please excuse the *USA Today* "we" in what follows): Does what we are doing matter? Are we writing as big as we need to write? Are we just spoiled-brat sneering aesthetes who are masturbating while looking away from the big questions of our age? Have we sufficiently described the wonders of living in our time? Are we properly accounting for the good and the beautiful and the enjoyable? But also: Are we properly accounting for the fact that evil exists, and exploring the difference between this and not-evil? How much of the irony and cleverness of our experimental writing—and for that matter, how much of the earnest and uplifting We-reinforcement of our realist writing—is just knee-jerk and ultimately reactionary?

In other words, life came brutally knocking at our door, and now we are reconsidering the venture. And I'm not saying everyone should get busy on their Kosovo novel—I think there is a way in which even the most domestic story (or wild experimental story) can take into account the larger world. But one could argue that American fiction has ghettoized itself by insisting on a self-reifying view (humanist/materialist?) in which all answers are known, the political binary is carved in stone, we all have swallowed whole certain orthodoxies, and the purpose of the fiction is just to reinforce these. At the heart of this lies a selfish agenda, that has (one could argue) really ceased seeing the world as a unity, and has begun aggressively internalizing certain capitalist dogmas that say: Of course you are the most important thing, of course you exist separate from the rest of the world.

I'm not sure I actually believe all of the above—but I do find myself thinking about these kinds of things a lot lately. Does this make any sense? Do you feel any of this? It may just be that I am saying: I really really hope to, in the future, write better. By the way, I just came back from the Cross Old Man's house, and am happy to report that, after many many "kisses" from Max, the Cross Old Man has at last admitted that writing can be taught.

BM: I worry that if you smother an old man with kisses, crank up his sexual heat or whatever, he'll admit to anything. These lonely people are just waiting to tell us what we want to hear.

IV. "THAT VOICE OF HEMINGWAY'S CAN'T FUNCTION IN A WAL-MART, ON CHRISTMAS EVE, WHEN YOU HAVE AN STD..."

BM: You have a film project underway. Can you tell me about it?

GS: Back in 1997, Ben Stiller optioned *CivilWarLand* and so for the last year or so I've been working with him on a script. It's been interesting in that film writing is so much about structure and so little about language. You can just say, "Tens of thousands of chimps emerge from mobile phone booths, speaking French," and that's it. There are the chimps. In other words, you don't have to do what we usually do, which is convince with language. You can just make these little structural units, which will be de facto "convincing" because the viewer will be seeing them. So it changes the nature of the challenge, writing-wise. It forced me to use a different part of my brain; the part that says, if I put A, then B, then C— trusting that each of these will be done well—then I've made resulting Meaning D. Which is not how I think when I'm writing fiction—then, I tend to concentrate on the individual line, trusting that some worthwhile effect will come out in the end, but I don't necessarily know what it is.

It's also been interesting anthropologically—getting some idea of how movies get made, how the larger mass culture might get accessed, how finances play into the whole thing, etc. So much of our storytelling now takes place within this quasicorporate framework, and so it's interesting to see if there is a sort of de facto editing effect working, and if so, what the flavor of it is. Also it's been interesting for me to think about broad appeal—is it possible/ desirable for somebody like me? What is the difference between "literary" and "popular"? I've been especially interested to see, in myself, a sort of knee-jerk tendency toward the dark, the negative, the nihilistic—somehow, film-writing made this tendency more noticeable. When I do this knee-jerk thing, it's more apparent, feels more like flinching. In film, it seems like because there are actual people up there, somehow my urge to credit the noble, the good, the simply decent is more easily managed than in stories.

I'm not sure what to think of all that, but I've noticed it, and am sort of mulling it over. It goes back to something we talked about earlier: how much of the brooding cynical nature of our art-fiction is meaningful (i.e., is telling a deep truth) and how much of it is just limited technical ability and/or sloth? I think there are deep truths about our time that are dark and scary—but I also think that not every dark/scary move that is accomplishable via fiction necessarily has a real-life corollary. Sometimes they're just easier—as Montherlant said: "Happiness writes white."

BM: You've had two amazing and critically lauded collections of short stories. Do you feel pressure to write a novel?

GS: I sometimes do. I just finished reading *Appointment in Samarra* and *Revolutionary Road* and those really made me want to write a novel—they're such beautiful, complicated books, and they show America in so much wonderful detail. My main problem is a very small intersection-set between (1) the abilities it takes to write a novel and (2) the abilities I actually have. Working on a story, I have very strong and intuitive opinions. With novels, I have mostly

Ideas, which, in my case, are deadly. I seem decent at compressing, but not so good at elaborating. So for now, I'm just allowing myself to do what I love, which is write stories. The one thing I would love to do in a novel is show the world as a big, stunning contradiction: to show Truth A in all its glory, then show Truth B (which contradicts Truth A) in all its glory.

There's a beautiful story, which sounds like a joke, because it starts: "Once Tolstoy and Gorky were walking down the street." As Gorky described it (in a memoir piece he wrote about Tolstoy), this mob of hussars comes walking up the street, and Tolstoy launches into this brilliant bit of polemic about how that sort of young man—brutal, cocksure, militaristic—represents everything that is wrong with Russia. And Gorky was convinced. Then, as the hussars passed in a cloud of tobacco smoke and cologne and leather, etc., Tolstoy spun on his heel and delivered an equal-but-opposite dissertation on why that sort of young man—fully alive, masculine, passionate, spontaneous—was the hope of Russia's future. And again, Gorky was convinced. That, to me, is art's highest aspiration: to show that nothing is true and everything is true. To work as a kind of ritual humility, and ritual celebration, of all that is.

BM: Like Raymond Carver and Denis Johnson before you, your stories have served as an ideal model—an inspiration—for legions of newcomers. This may be an awkward question, but does being so widely emulated by younger writers change the way you approach what you're doing?

GS: I don't really see that. Every so often, someone will send me a story full of funny franchise names, or composed completely of acronyms. But to the extent that it's true, I'm honored. And it's funny how, as you get older, and look back at your own work—it seems young. In a good way, but... young. And you remember whom you were channeling or admiring at the time. So I say, anything that gets us going. I remember basically rewriting *Red Cav-*

alry by setting it in an oil camp in Indonesia, where I'd once worked. And also rewriting *In Our Time,* but set in Amarillo, Texas, and Nick had not just come home from war, but was on spring break. And what I felt most acutely, doing those little knockoffs, was how inappropriate and uncomfortable someone else's stylistic tics were, superimposed on my life.

In other words, those imitations helped me realize that there is no Real Life—there is no objective reality. There is just your version of it, and that version has to be in your language. I thought: that voice of Hemingway's can't function in a Wal-Mart, on Christmas Eve, when you have an STD and your uncle is drunk and trying to buy an O-Jays record to give to his new girlfriend, a speed-freak waitress. Hence the constant necessity for new voices. ✶

SARAH STONE

TALKS WITH

JOAN SILBER

"THE WORLD IS NOT REVOLVING AROUND
YOU—OR IT'S REVOLVING AROUND YOU
FROM YOUR POINT OF VIEW, BUT
THERE ARE A LOT OF OTHER REVOLUTIONS
GOING ON AT THE SAME TIME."

Things not always necessary in fiction-writing:
First drafts
Buddhist meditation
Weight
Scenes
The mechanics of sex

*hen something awful happens, people often say
that it builds character. More often than not,
though, those who endure tragedies and disappointments are likely to become aggrieved, self-
pitying, and sometimes vengeful. So it's a relief
to read Joan Silber's stories, which have an almost godlike perspective on
suffering, both self-inflicted and otherwise. Her characters endure pain, but
neither the characters nor the story seem to luxuriate in that pain. Silber
spent most of her teens looking after her sick mother, who died when Silber was in her twenties. In surviving adversity and loss, Silber herself has
developed the kind of character many of us would kill for: apparently endless cheerful helpfulness and patience, a focus on the world around her, a*

complete lack of self-importance. Silber's writing has a clean, brisk author-
ity that doesn't linger to congratulate itself over either its insight or its won-
derful details. "Time is moving," these stories seem to say, "so let's get on
with it while we still can."

In Silber's most recent book, Ideas of Heaven: a Ring of Stories
(2004), a variety of characters of different ages, genders, and historical
moments tell the stories of their lives and yearnings. Here is the sixteenth-
century poet Gaspara Stampa at a party:

> *We had just barely finished supper when people started playing the Game*
> *of the Blind Men, a good game, really, and popular with this group. Each*
> *of the players had to tell how he had lost his sight because of love. The idea*
> *was to make the story as tricky as possible, full of obstacles and unflinching*
> *sacrifice, a set of tests. Rescuing the beloved from a fire, climbing the spikes*
> *of a fortress, crossing the Alps through the glare of snow. Lover after lover*
> *was struck in the eyes. Oh, why do we like to hear this? I thought, as we*
> *applauded the Alpine saga. We were all smiling, as if love's wreckage were*
> *a shared joke, which I suppose it was.*

Silber is the author of five books of fiction; she won a PEN/Hem-
ingway Award for her first novel, Household Words *(1980), as well as*
fellowships from the National Endowment for the Arts, the New York
Foundation for the Arts, and the John Simon Guggenheim Memorial
Foundation. Her stories have appeared in the New Yorker, *the* Paris
Review, *and other magazines. For some years, though, after her early suc-*
cess, Silber endured a long struggle to publish her later books—the literary
equivalent of being dropped in the wilderness with nothing but a light
sweater and a stick of gum. Recently, things have been looking up again.
Her stories have been published in prize volumes and other anthologies,
and Ideas of Heaven *was a finalist for the National Book Award for fic-*
tion in 2004. Silber teaches at Sarah Lawrence College and has taught in
the Warren Wilson College M.F.A. Program for Writers. She lives in New
York City. We talked informally over dinner when we both happened to
be in Chicago, and then on the phone and by email for the interview.

—S.S. *(Spring/Summer 2004)*

I. "IF THE CHARACTERS' TROUBLES ARE TOO CASUAL, THE BOOK SEEMS TOO LIGHT TO ME. SOMETIMES I READ BOOKS AND WANT TO SAY, 'OH, YOU'LL GET OVER IT.'"

SARAH STONE: You describe your new book, *Ideas of Heaven,* as a "ring" of stories. Peter Ho Davies has said that the book "profoundly reinvents the short story collection." Can you describe how this book differs from the more usual groups of linked stories?

JOAN SILBER: The usual way of linking stories is with the same characters throughout or in the same place, and often they're in chronological order. What I wanted to do began gradually. I had written about a character who's a villain in one story and I wanted him to be a human being in the next story. This comes from my beliefs as a person *and* as a fiction writer, about how flipping sympathies is a good thing. And then I wanted to write about Gaspara Stampa, the Venetian poet who's mentioned in the second story, and I realized that this would string the three together.

I liked this linking so much that I wanted to keep doing it. I starting telling friends that I was writing about sex and religion: forms of devotion, forms of consolation—those were my catchphrases for what I was writing. And I realized that I was going to use Giles, who's mentioned in the first story, in the last story, and that would make a ring. The links got looser or more subtle as the thing went on, but I liked the idea that what's a little detail in this picture is a big deal from another perspective. It's a vision that you have automatically as you get older, that you're not the whole thing. The world is not revolving around you—or it's revolving around you from *your* point of view, but there are a lot of other revolutions going on at the same time. So it was a way of conveying that, of giving a broader canvas than fiction sometimes gives.

SS: The characters in *Ideas of Heaven* have so much perspective on their pasts and their lives. You've written about the idea of "weight" in fiction in more than one essay, writing about the work of Jane Austen, Alice Munro, Chekhov, and Flaubert. What is your current thinking about weight and complexity in fiction?

JS: I do complain that there's not enough of it; it disappoints me sometimes in books that I pick up. But you're asking what constitutes weight?

SS: These stories have so much depth. Has writing them taken your ideas about weight to a different place?

JS: My initial ideas about weight had something to do with depth of feeling and how much sorrow there is in a work. If the characters' troubles are too casual, the book seems too light to me. Sometimes I read books and want to say, "Oh, you'll get over it." But then when we talk about Austen—she always knows how small her world is. And in fact it's very frustrating to her characters a lot of the time, worse than frustrating. So there's a way of presenting "lightness" from that perspective.

And then there was an idea in a Chekhov story that was very important to me years ago. It's called "Strong Impressions"—he has a bunch of jurors on a murder trial sequestered together, and to pass the time they tell stories about the worst things that have happened to them. A few tell about near-deaths, but one man goes on about how he almost jilted his sweetheart because a lawyer friend argued him into not liking her. It's an almost-funny story about tricky lawyers. And then after they've all listened, they hear the clock tower strike, and they realize that the prisoner who's about to be tried for murder is also hearing it strike, and that everything in his life is on a whole different scale at this moment. And that's where the story ends.

I taught that story to an amazing class I once had at Boston University, which had in it Ha Jin, Jhumpa Lahiri, and Peter Ho

Davies, and another really good writer named Marshall Kli-masewski, who's finally getting a book out. It was just an amazing group. I was teaching that story, and I wanted to tell them something that had happened to me the week before. I had left the class early to get a plane to New York to go back to a dinner that was a big deal to me—my very fancy then-agent was having a farewell party for her assistant. My plane took off an hour late, my taxi in New York got caught in traffic, I was about to jump out of my skin. And it turned out that the taxi driver was from Beirut. This was in the early '90s when Beirut was just barely there anymore. And he was so impressed when he heard that I was a teacher that he wanted to ask my opinions about everything. And I thought, "I'm worried about getting to this dinner on time, and this guy's whole city isn't there anymore." So you know how you bring up your anecdotal stories to the class—I wanted them to see how this had made me think of the Chekhov story. And I remember Ha Jin nodding because of how his world had changed.

SS: Each of the stories is so full and layered that it could be a novel. How do you know when what you're working on is a story and when it's a novel?

JS: At the moment one person's life doesn't seem like enough for a novel to me. And I found I really did like covering long periods of time in short stories. I had once given a craft talk on it years earlier. So I thought, "I could just keep doing that. Why not?" This is a funny thing to say, my work has done OK, but I haven't been over-the-top successful by any means. So in a way that frees you, because no one's waiting for you to do the same thing. I thought, "I could do *this* now." And then I liked it; it felt right when I did it.

II. "THE THING WITH FICTION IS THAT IT'S NOT EXACTLY JUST ABOUT THE SENTENCES. IT TOOK ME YEARS TO UNDERSTAND THAT."

SS: What is your process in inventing or developing characters?

JS: Sometimes there's a core event that I have, a tale that someone's told me. And often in the early versions the characters are much dopier and shallower. And then I'm working against stereotypes. I think, "They can't just do that. That's so obvious." And that makes me pull at them more strongly, and I think that's how they get deepened.

SS: How much does your own sense of them come from the past, and what is invented? What was your own family like?

JS: My own family was much like the one in *Household Words,* my first book. My father died when I was five, and my mother died when I was in my twenties. For someone who had an otherwise completely middle-class, untroubled childhood, those are very big events. So a lot of what everybody else is told about how families work and how the world works was different for me. From a kid's point of view, the worst *could* really happen. So that was instrumental, and like a lot of kids who are disaffected without knowing the word for it, I read a lot. Reading was very important to me, and I wanted to write from the time I was quite little.

SS: What are some of the books that you're reading now, or that you've been reading recently, that are important to you?

JS: Alice Munro is the contemporary writer that I feel closest to, for obvious reasons. People that I know, like Charlie Baxter and Andrea Barrett, have certainly influenced me. And also my friend Kathleen Hill, although I didn't read her work until I had been writing for a long time. But she's a very meticulous, Proustlike craftsperson, and I think that her dedication and her fixity of purpose became important to me. By the time I'm reading stuff now, it's not influential, which is different from not loving it. It's not bearing on my own work exactly.

SS: Do you show people your very first draft?

JS: Well, I don't exactly work in drafts. I work the way you're not supposed to, which is that I revise each sentence as I go. By the time I'm showing it to someone, it's not really naked, even though the ending is usually a big mess or there's some lump in the beginning.

SS: Did you always work this way? How did your process change over time?

JS: I always worked very slowly, and for years I thought, "If I don't get over this, I'm never going to be a real writer." And then I just decided it was OK. And I did get faster, but my method is the same. I do take notes—I'm not moving in the dark. I have some sort of overview. Even at the end of the day, I'll sometimes make little notes on what's going to happen next. But I don't rough it out in sentences. There are other people who work this way, don't they?

SS: There are a lot of people who work that way: each draft is absolutely exquisite, and then they completely change it and throw most of it out.

JS: The danger is that you get so attached to your own sentences, but the thing with fiction is that it's not exactly just about the sentences. It took me years to understand that. I studied with Grace Paley. That's the only fiction course I ever took, because I wanted to be a poet in college. And she was a big sentence person, so that may be a part of it.

SS: What were your turning points as a writer?

JS: There were good and bad turning points. The first good turning point, obviously, was getting the first book published. That made all the difference in the world. I can still remember taking one of my friends out to lunch to celebrate. She had just stopped drinking, so I had a Bloody Mary instead of ordering champagne, but it was a gala lunch. Winning the Hemingway was a great thing and a great surprise. And then after the first two books were published, I couldn't sell the next one, which was a novel. There's a big jump in the publication times from the second book, in '87 (which then came out in paper in '88), to the next one, a book of stories, in 2000. I had a story in the *New Yorker* during that time—another great celebration, I was living in Rome that year—but I couldn't sell a book. So that's a lot of years. And I wasn't not writing—I was writing all that time. I think it's true that certain kinds of defeat really change you. I had to learn a kind of equanimity. And there's a difference in the writing between the first two novels and the last three books.

SS: Do you think that experience, the difficulty of it, affected them?

JS: A lot of time went by, so I got smarter from being old. But I think I stopped being what I would call a domestic realist—I just naturally moved away from closely paced scenes packed with social and sensory detail. And I began working much less from my own autobiographical material. I was always making some of it up, but by the time I was writing the third book, *In My Other Life,* those really were not my stories. Maybe two-thirds of them are based on people that I knew, but none of the characters is me. So I was getting out of my own skin more, and that's probably very significant.

III. "PEOPLE DO HAVE SEX IN MY STORIES, BUT SINCE THE MECHANICS ARE SORT OF BASIC AND FAMILIAR TO ANYONE, THE READER DOESN'T HAVE TO BE THERE FOR EVERY MOMENT IN A STORY TO GET THE IMPORT OF IT."

SS: So many of your characters take risks: they have illegal drug habits, run shady businesses, or take wild sexual risks. Can you talk about this theme of risk-taking or self-destruction?

JS: I did have a youth that partook of some of that. When I first came to New York, I waitressed in a bar for three and a half years. That was in the late '60s and early '70s, so everything was happening in those bars. So of course I knew I wanted to tap that material. That's the direct answer: I had the stuff, so I used it. I clearly am drawn to it. Sometimes I think, "Oh, my god, I'm still writing about these things all these years later, and thousands of other things have happened to me." There is something intensely interesting to me about characters getting swept into unexpected appetites, of not knowing they were going to do these things.

SS: The difference between the intentions people have and what they actually do.

JS: Yes.

SS: The other thing, in thinking about material, is that you take on two of the hardest things to write about—characters' sexual and spiritual lives.

JS: People do have sex in my stories, but since the mechanics are sort of basic and familiar to anyone, the reader doesn't have to be there for every moment in a story to get the import of it. I try to be subtle and discreet, but precise, and also connect it to character. The spiritual stuff was harder, I'd have to say. There's a whole realm of really soppy writing that you absolutely don't want to get into. So I was very proud when I was able to bring anything off, and there was a lot that got cut because it was too soppy. But during the writing I was getting very actively involved in Buddhism, albeit with a lot of qualifications. And now I go to a Buddhist group, a Vipassana group. I'm a terrible meditator; I'm not even sure that meditation is that important. But I love the ideas of it; they have been very important to me. So if you have this enthusiasm, you want to get it down as truthfully as you can. And also, it really does change the way you view the world, if you're involved with something like that. What a lot of the world cares about starts to seem like small potatoes. You think, "They're stuck on *that?*"

SS: Do you think it has affected the perspective you have in writing?

JS: Oh, yes. A lot of Buddhism is about perspective. They asked the Buddha if he could summarize his teachings in one sentence. It's like what publishers ask you to do, to sum up your book in one sentence. And there were questions that he wouldn't answer, but that one he said, "Oh, yeah, sure." And the answer is, "Nothing whatsoever should be clung to as 'me' or 'mine.'" It's a very staggering notion. And a comforting one, if you come at it from the right side.

SS: You've said that you're unhappy when you're not writing. It seems to be a freakish thing most of us share, and not something we develop, but something inherent. When did you figure this out about yourself?

JS: It hasn't always been true. There have been times when writing often made me miserable, I think. I don't have an answer for that.

SS: Then let me ask, how do you survive the hard times in writing, either internal or external?

JS: I suffer. [*Laughs*] I mean, there have been times… you always do think, "I've been through this before, so I'll get out of it another way." But you sort of don't believe it. And there are projects that are stillborn, so you don't know when you're on one that's never going to work. There was a time, in those years when I couldn't sell a book, when I considered stopping writing. I thought, "No one is making me do this. I don't have to do it." But I knew it was like saying, "I'm going to go eat worms." It wasn't real.

I certainly know people who have given it up. But some people have substitutes, and I don't think I have a substitute that serves. Although I do other things. At this point, though, I sort of believe in it. After 9/11, a painter friend, a wonderful painter, said he wanted to do something to help other people, that painting wasn't enough. And I actually want to help other people, too, but I feel that writing does good, that it has a purpose in the world. I feel what I do isn't aimless.

IV. "SO SOMETIMES FINDING A WAY TO AVOID WHAT YOU CAN'T DO CAN BE FRUITFUL."

SS: You've experimented with form in various ways, not just in this book, but with the list-making in *Lucky Us* and so on. Can you talk about the relation of form to subject matter or ideas?

JS: I think when I began, I didn't have a sense of form. And it occurred to me that I should. I lived for many years with a composer, and they talk about form all the time. Although I didn't always know what he was saying, invoking that word was really helpful to me. So I began to look more for it and to be more aware of it. In *Lucky Us,* I had to think of the road not taken and the different things that *could* have happened. To get something like HIV is to have had a weird kind of luck. It could have happened to any of us—certainly to me. So I wanted the structure to reflect that, to show the lines of alternate paths.

In *Ideas of Heaven* I knew I was talking about the ways things connect. And I also thought, "That's barbed, the way they're all linked together." It creates violence. If those missionaries in China in "Ideas of Heaven" had never left home, they would have been fine. It isn't just, "Oh, we're all together, why can't we all get along?" It's also that we *are* all together, and it's like the tigers chasing each other in the story where they turn into pancake batter. It's volatile. I guess I wanted to get some of that too.

SS: It's both a strength and a weakness?

JS: Or a danger. It's both a strength and a danger.

SS: How much did your volunteer work with people who were

suffering from AIDS affect *Lucky Us*?

JS: I had the idea for the book around the same time I started volunteering for Gay Men's Health Crisis; it came out of the same impulse. So I actually wrote most of it when I was a buddy—I'd visit a guy with AIDS once a week, to do errands or just hang out. He was an amazing guy—with great flair—who restyled his hospital room by taping vials of flowers to the needle-disposal unit. Friends told me that a day before he died, he lit up one of his Camel Lights and announced, "I've decided not to give up smoking." I knew him for the last two years of his life. Now I'm a buddy to a woman—she's my age, unlike the character in the book—who's great in a whole different way. So while I was writing *Lucky Us,* I was in the circle of illness—I was around people who were dealing with it—that certainly affected that book. I did it partly because I thought, "Oh, this is happening in the world, and I should think about it more," but I'd always dealt with illness because I had a sick parent growing up. I think illness is always in my mind as a possibility in life. My father died very quickly of a heart attack, but my mother was sick for a long time with a mysterious liver ailment that probably was from the doctors having screwed up a gallbladder operation, although nobody really knows. But she was ill with a liver that didn't work right for ten years at least. Or maybe twenty.

SS: Like Rhoda in *Household Words.*

JS: Very much like Rhoda. I did a lot of the caretaking, not in a really responsible way, but bringing her little trays. So that was a crucial part of my growing up. But even in that book, when I first started writing it, I was going to tell it through the mother, and then I was going to tell it through the two siblings. And then I just stuck with the mother. Already I wanted to get out of my own skin, I think. I was really quite young when I was writing that— I was maybe twenty-eight when I started. But that was the one good move that I made, and it got me out of the narcissism of my growing-up story.

SS: You really got very far outside your own skin in *Ideas of Heaven*. In what ways do you move into these very different characters?

JS: I go online to look stuff up. I know that's not exactly what you asked. But it helps because you can get details, and that vivifies the character. And usually I've been to the places, so that helps. I don't do anything that's completely outside my own experience, if that's the right word. I think it's like method acting, where you're always using your own experience to get inside the character. But the two historical stories that I did—I spent a year in Italy, and I did look at a lot of Renaissance paintings. When I started to write, I felt, I don't *really* know how to do this, but I can guess. And there was a really good book on Gaspara Stampa that I used. With the missionaries—I spent all that time reading Victorian literature. In graduate school, the things I loved were Dickens and the Brontës and Eliot. So I felt like I could get the missionary wife's voice because it wasn't a totally unfamiliar world to me. Whereas there was a lot of stuff I couldn't do.

SS: Is there anything you wish you could write that feels too far from your own knowledge or experience?

JS: I just finished work on a piece about an American woman who marries a Muslim from southern Thailand. The idea came from a woman I met traveling, and I assumed I'd tell it from her point of view, but then I saw I couldn't get close enough to what her marriage was—I live too far from that part of the world, in all senses. I'd be talking through my hat, no matter how much research I did. So I told it from the viewpoint of her second husband, who's jealous of the now-dead Thai, and it began to point to other issues I was interested in, about old attachments and new allegiances. So sometimes finding a way to avoid what you can't do can be fruitful.

V. "OFTEN WHEN PEOPLE ARE WRITING ABOUT THEIR OWN EXPERIENCE, THERE'S A KIND OF SPECIAL PLEADING, WHICH IS 'FEEL SORRY FOR THIS CHARACTER,' OR 'ADMIRE THIS CHARACTER.'"

SS: When you got your M.A., was it in Victorian Literature?

JS: No, it was just in English. But I did work on Arnold Bennett, whom I love, and I did my thesis on Fanny Burney, a precursor of Jane Austen.

SS: I think this inhabiting of the different characters is why your work reminded me, from the first time I read it, of Chekhov or Alice Munro. In creating these characters, you create a balance between objectivity and compassion or engagement.

JS: When I was *really* young and reading Chekhov, that's what I saw in him, that he did that. We had a book of his in the house when I was growing up, so I always loved him. I can remember a moment of reading a story called "At the Manor," where a boorish old man holds forth in a long, bigoted rant that drives away his daughter's only suitor, and Chekhov makes us feel bad for him anyway; he's a lonely old man who's a jerk, and I thought, I want to do that.

SS: I think I'm asking a perhaps unanswerable question here, but how do you find that balance in writing?

JS: You can't be too soft on your characters, right? You can't forgive them for doing unspeakable things. But you also have to understand how they felt when they were doing it. I think it's as basic as that. The one thing, and you must see this in teaching, too, is that often when people are writing about their own experience, there's a kind of special pleading, which is "Feel sorry for this character," or "Admire this character." So I think you have to know to avoid that. I may have learned to do that in writing the first book in the voice of a character who was like my own mother, whom I was so at odds with (and for good reasons). To inhabit her sympathetically, but see her the way I saw her, was probably an important thing for me.

SS: *Household Words* was actually the first book that you wrote. How long did it take you?

JS: A long time. I think it took me five years, something like that.

SS: Many writers, when they're learning, don't know how to do summary. When I was examining "My Shape," from *Ideas of Heaven,* I realized that there were only two scenes, that all the rest was summary so vivid that it felt like scene. How did you come to grips with scene and summary and the handling of time?

JS: I taught this class at Warren Wilson before I was really doing this myself. It was the year I was living in Italy, so I used a story by Natalia Ginzburg called "The Mother," which is a biographical story. My Italian isn't very good, but I could look at the story and see that a lot of it was written in the imperfect tense, which we don't have in English. We say "would go"—the conditional—or we start in a progressive tense and switch to an indicative. But I remember being impressed by the fact that habitual action was being rendered as scene.

And Chekhov does that a lot—I had always noticed that. Even though the stories are so short, there's often a sense, like in "The Darling," where she does this every day, she does that all winter, and then there's a little bit of a scene. So it's really treating summary as scene that is the technical secret. But when I was writing the stories in *In My Other Life,* I felt that I was going into summary too much, and I was worried. And I remember writing to Charlie Baxter about it. Charlie loves Lars Gustafsson's *Stories of Happy People,* and he told me to read it, and I thought, "Oh, it's OK. People do this."

SS: This is going back to the question of long stories and the handling of time. When you're covering, in your stories and your novels, almost an entire life, how do you give that shape and form? How do you focus it to give a sense of what's important?

JS: Sometimes it requires some commentary from the writer at the end, often in the mouth of a character. Sometimes I have trouble doing it! Sometimes I thought I was going someplace, and I didn't get there as strongly as I thought. I do my best. I have some sense of what the story's about thematically, usually. More and more as I work, I'm increasingly theme-focused. I think the last book made me more confident about that, so that's been helpful.

SS: Where does a story usually start? What's the initial kernel?

JS: It varies greatly. It used to be, like with *In My Other Life*, that I knew I was working with a certain reserve of material, and that I just had to choose the characters, and then I could tell their stories. Now there are ideas I want to talk about. In the last book, I knew I wanted to talk about the interface between spiritual and erotic longing. In this new book, I'm doing a lot about travel and the ethical discomforts of travel. Seeing other parts of the world is a great thing, but what about when you're a person of privilege in a poor place, or you're traveling merrily through a country where your country has done a lot of damage, or people are hostile to you for no reason you can get hold of? You can get *caught* in all kinds of things that don't have much to do with you. Now I'm actually looking for examples of what I want to talk about, from memory and from half-imagined things. So I'm really working from theme in this one. I've been traveling a lot in Asia in recent years—in China and Laos and Vietnam and Thailand.

SS: I'm looking forward to reading it.

JS: Thank you. I hope it gets written. ✶

ADAM THIRLWELL

TALKS WITH

TOM STOPPARD

"I SUSPECT THAT THE WHOLE TRICK IS
TO UNDERMINE THE AUDIENCE'S SECURITY
ABOUT WHAT IT THINKS IT KNOWS AT ANY
MOMENT. I THINK THAT ONE HAS TO TRY
TO DO IT ON THE SMALLEST SCALE
AS WELL AS THE LARGEST."

This interview takes place:
Driving on the motorway from London
In deckchairs, watching cricket
After cricket, at tea
Driving on the motorway to London

om Stoppard was born in Zlín, Czechoslovakia, in
1937, and came to England in 1946. His major plays
include Rosencrantz & Guildenstern are Dead
(1966), Jumpers *(1972) and* Travesties *(1974).*
Every Good Boy Deserves Favour *and* Profession-
al Foul *were performed in 1977.* Night and Day *came out in 1978,*
The Real Thing *in 1982,* Arcadia *in 1993, and* The Invention of
Love *in 1997. His trilogy,* The Coast of Utopia—*comprising the plays*
Voyage, Shipwreck, *and* Salvage—*opened in 2002. In 1998, he won
an Oscar for Best Screenplay for* Shakespeare in Love. *He lives in London, and quite likes cricket.*   —*A. T. (Summer 2004)*

I. TO CRICKET

TOM STOPPARD: You know, I'd like to present myself as some-body who's really on the case when he's writing a play, and I rather admire—hang on a minute, where do we go? We have to go to the M25, and turn off—rather admire the theoretical writer who has an objective in mind and shapes his material in order to convey it and resolve it.

Ages ago I started to do something different from my earlier practice. My earlier practice was to try to work out as much as pos-sible, and not to feel that I didn't know what I was doing while I was doing the writing. But I realized that I wasn't doing that very successfully, and without really understanding what was happening I was actually inventing things as I was coming to them. So I quite quickly became that kind of self-conscious writer—someone who has decided just to start and keep his fingers crossed. And I still think that I ought to do that. *The Invention of Love,* for instance, was really quite a frightening saga. I didn't know where I was going, and if I hadn't got to the point where I realized that I could have a real-ly good solid scene where the old man is literally talking to his young self, which is quite a theatrical attractive situation for the audience—they have fun with it—if I hadn't somehow blundered my way into that, I don't know what I would have done, frankly. When I look back on my plays I'm absolutely mystified by the fact that I ever began writing them, because I know that in the begin-ning I didn't know what I was doing, and I think that—OK hang on, yes quite right, M25…

ADAM THIRLWELL: There's a lane on the left.

TS: I do know the way, it's just that I forget to look for the road signs.

With *Arcadia,* I remember writing this academic arriving at this country house and I had to decide whether the manuscript letters from 180 years before were in his briefcase or in the house. I hadn't worked out how it was going to go—which was quite scary and probably beneficial in some way. I'm rambling. Go on. Oh yes, what I was actually trying to say about fifteen minutes ago was that I don't have a play to write at the moment but I have at least two subjects for a play so in a way I do have a play to write, it's just I have no idea what the story will be. And I just don't believe in the kind of theater which I want to write—which isn't a storytelling theater.

There are three or four things I thought, you know, might justify writing a play. I mean, they're all quite interesting, and still are, but I have no idea of any kind of narrative or characters. Usually the problems just disappear, at least somehow—I'd be off. I took it all to France recently and read it all again: I had a suitcase full of offprints and press cuttings, and subjects and God knows what I had. I had more sort of assembled them out of pure *instinct* and I just kept shoving these elements around, and came home not having actually achieved anything at all. So then I got neurotic.

And then I had the realization that there was no necessity for me to write a play, nobody was asking me to. So I then cheered up and stopped trying to, and had a very good period where I was equally nonproductive, writing no play instead of not writing one, if you see what I mean…

AT: Yes.

TS: That sort of exhilaration has now died away and I'm actually going to try again.

My main thing was actually to do with what's called "the problem of consciousness"—the very words sound like a death knell of drama, don't they? There's been a mild academic fight going on, for the last fifteen years, between people like John Searle and Daniel Dennett, who have different notions of what consciousness is and where it comes from. They all agree on one thing—it's just the brain, physics. And I was just an unreconstructed dualist, actually. So, I thought, that would be interesting to write about. That was one thing. And then there was Sappho. I had a period of getting excited about exploiting fragments as an art form. I mean, *faute de mieux,* one has these pages of Sappho, and most pages don't make any sense.

God knows whether it's anything to do with a *play* or not, but it's interesting in itself.

They used a lot of papyrus for bandages—so if you imagine one of your pages, or Shakespeare's sonnets, being torn longitudinally into three strips, and just the middle one remains... It looks very interesting on the page, and all kinds of people have tried to write the whole poem on the basis of the fragments left.

AT: There's an Ezra Pound one, isn't there?

TS: Yes. There is. So that was another thing, and there were a couple of other things... And, quite perversely, I mean, without any real rationale, I decided to somehow jam them all into the same narrative, like cats in a bag fighting. And I think probably I was overambitious, which is why I didn't even get anywhere.

I'd write a page and a half, six or seven times, the same page and a half, and then I began not avoiding cliché, and I began to think about Martin Amis's "war against cliché." I got sidetracked. I began to think that he was completely wrong about that because one of the things one uses is familiarity, it's actually a useful thing to have in one's locker. The phrase goes home better because you don't have to think, "Oh that's nice and new." So I began to look for clichés in things I liked, and I began to realize very quickly that there are a lot of things I like, where the only right word was the obvious word. That Betjeman poem about the girl in the inglenook, and he's such a thumping crook—if you had something besides "thumping" it just would not be as good.

AT: There are writers like Betjeman who use cliché—Joyce, Ionesco, Beckett, who also do this: they don't use the cliché without consideration; they arrange clichés musically, with care. I think

Betjeman's often the same, although he's not seen as an experimental writer like them. He's doing something quite clever...

TS: I don't know how clever it is, in the sense of being conscious cleverness, but I think his instinct is right. That the poem is not a clichéd poem, simply because it's using some cliché. But that was something else.

But the *fragment* thing—I began to visualize the madness. I think in the end I thought, "No, you can't, this would have to be a film." Then you could just cut into the middle of a conversation, and out of it—and then do it again, and then do the other bit of it, and so forth. I don't think you can do that on the stage: I think it would be terribly irritating, and pretentious.

Yes, well, my Sappho play: nothing exists. I'm going to try again. I'm so depressed. I'm just sort of full of self-disgust actually. This morning I weighed more than I've ever weighed in my entire life. Literally. And that's really a low point isn't it—just thinking, "I've never ever, in all these years, weighed as much as this."

AT: Gaining in gravitas?

TS: Eating sandwiches and rueing the day.

The fact that *The Coast of Utopia* turned out to be three plays was something I didn't plan until I was on the point of starting to write—it's just that I got addicted to the background reading. And ended up finding this enormous nine-hour saga. And I was really very fascinated by the people but I was also aware that I had to massage the historical narrative into something which had some sense of being a play, having the architecture of a play.

AT: In my arrogant novelistic way I had this theory that you were borrowing from the novel—in the matter of length. A play has two hours, whereas a novelist has 450 pages in which to explore minute aspects of character. Obviously, in *The Coast of Utopia*, one of the things you're interested in is irony, ironic undercutting—the way that a character's ideas can be undermined by their behavior, and it's intriguing that this kind of thing is more interesting and easier to do, on stage, if you've got more time to do it.

TS: I think that's right.

[*Pause*]

AT: I can give you an example.

TS: All right.

AT: One of the things I was thinking was the infidelity between Alexander Herzen and his wife Natalie in *The Coast of Utopia*—the way the entire theme runs throughout the play is very delicate. It's first mentioned actually in relation to Herzen, with Natalie saying to Herzen's best friend Nick Ogarev, "I suppose you're going to say it was only a servant-girl." But evidently she's not devastated by it. She's sad from it and hurt by it but it's not ruined their marriage. And then later Herzen announces: "Fidelity is admirable, but proprietorship disgusting." It's the naïveté of Oscar Wilde in his essay "The Soul of Man Under Socialism": "Jealousy, which is an extraordinary source of crime in modern life, is an emotion closely bound up with our conceptions of property, and under Socialism and Individualism will die out." But Herzen is devastated and proprietorial when he finds out that Natalie has been unfaithful.

TS: That was completely conscious on my part.

AT: Then I think what's lovely is that it's complicated further so that Natalie is flighty, romantic: she's not perfect. So that when Herzen sentimentalizes the affair after her death and says, "Her devotion to me, her remorse, her courage when she faced the madness that man infected her mind with…" that's a falsification after the fact. And the further irony is that when Natalie Ogarev is unfaithful with Herzen, Ogarev does not mind—and yet Natalie wants to believe that he does—"He's in pain. We've broken his heart. His worst enemy couldn't have hurt him more."

That's an example of a theme that runs the length of two plays, and the complications and mirrorings of that would just not have been possible in a play that only lasted two hours.

TS: I think it would be possible in a play that was about nothing else. I think you could write a two-hour play that was only about that. There is something very attractive in having this vast canvas, in which you can really balance things against each other when they're separated by all kinds of other but no less equally interesting events.

The thing you've just been describing became for me what I *had*, all I had by way of a story. That was really it. Because Herzen's intellectual and ideological development didn't really go very far after 1848. By 1851-'52, he's pretty much worked out what he'd been disenchanted by and where the future for Russia ought to lie—that people were just too corrupted and the answer had to be to go back home and do it with the unpolluted peasantry. So by the time we get to the beginning of the final play, *Salvage,* he doesn't have anywhere to go as regards changing his mind about things, which is why I felt myself in trouble.

AT: Writers who are stylists are often writers who dislike ideas. And one of the things that I was thinking, in *The Coast of Utopia,* is that essentially you're sending ideas up. Ideas are things which people take very seriously, and yet there is this area of ordinary domestic experience which somehow manages to upend them— which washes over and ironizes the theoreticians in *The Coast of Utopia.* So you get Bakunin, say, the prophet of libertarianism, who's simply a domestic despot.

In *The Coast of Utopia*, the same idea is uttered by more than one character, but in different contexts. I imagine that this is to show that ideas are like suitcases, as it were: an idea is a suitcase into which you pack your own clothes.

TS: Yes. It's interesting, actually. We have to look for a gate on our

right. It's to do with the bad fit between private and public de-
meanours. It doesn't spring from a sense of confrontation. I mean
what I write about—it doesn't spring from an urge to refute or to
detach oneself. It's much more to do with recognizing, or feeling
that I recognize, a displacement between public and private utterance, and public and private posture; that people find it quite difficult to match up the private arena and the public arena so their
emotional and domestic lives sometimes seem quite irrelevant to
their intellectual lives. Hang on. Hello. My name is Tom Stoppard,
is this the cricket?

II. AT CRICKET

AT: Where were we?

TS: Yes, where were we?

AT: Turgenev. Herzen and Turgenev.

TS: I think Turgenev had a good sense of what he himself was
capable of doing. He had a good sense of what he was put on earth
to do. And he also had a good sense of his ultimate usefulness
rather than uselessness. His fictions lived longer than Herzen's
essays; they didn't have an obvious and direct utilitarian function,
but they did have a function—Bazarov and so on became part of
the language of a crucial movement. Because he's clear-eyed and
honest, and an artist, people return again and again to the stories
he wrote: the mortar between the bricks seeped into people's
thinking. So Turgenev played a larger role than Herzen, the way
things went in Russia.

They were both people who enjoyed and liked having the
finer things in life, and they were aware of the anomaly. Herzen
was aware of it. Herzen was actually the rich guy among this
crowd: he inherited his father's estate, he never had any money
problems, and he was aware of some kind of contradiction and
referred to it occasionally. But his humanitarian and egalitarian

instinct was extremely strong: a sense of justice and fairness. He was willing to have it all taken away from him, because he could see that it was unfair, and that's rather wonderful, because he was working against his own class, ultimately. At that stage, he had a sort of faith in other people's humanitarian impulses. Turgenev looks a bit cynical compared to Herzen.

AT: I think it's Turgenev's brand of skepticism that I find interesting. A militant aestheticism, as it were, has to be completely skeptical at all points of political action or political ideology. It's constantly aware of all the contextual motives. It isn't idealistic. And certainly someone who believes in the value of politics is going to find Turgenev rebarbative. There's a toughness to Turgenev: a rigor in his relativism.

TS: Turgenev had an absolute horror and terror of violence. Turgenev was a monarchist if the alternative was violence. And when Turgenev was under some kind of suspicion by association, he absolutely panicked, and wrote to Moscow saying: "Look, you know, everyone knows I'm utterly against anything like that," and so on.

Herzen's possibly trying to dissociate himself from apparent shared values with the system of Turgenev—although he did share a certain level of living, he enjoyed the same things and valued the same things, and liked them to survive.

Oh, it's very difficult to get at this one.

Turgenev is a bit like that story about John Braine in the southern states of America, at a cocktail party, with an Episcopal bishop, having a glass of sherry. And Braine said: "This is the most wonderful country in the world—America." And the other man said: "Well, not if you're black." And Braine looked slightly bewildered and said: "But I'm not black."

I think Turgenev was saying: "Yes, but I *am* a Western liberal, who was brought up to enjoy opera. That's what I *am*. How else can I see anything? I'm not a Sandwich Islander. I can only function from this point of view." Whereas Herzen was not doing that, not saying that: he had a much wider view and a deeper view of the context. But in the end—it'd be cruel to say he was ineffective, as people continue to get inspiration from him, so it wasn't as if he were dead—but he got overtaken by the traffic, just sort of run down, it came up behind him and squashed him. Turgenev made sure he wasn't in the road.

AT: This relationship, or nonrelationship, between the political and the literary, is there in your work, too. It intrigues me, say, reading Kenneth Tynan's *New Yorker* profile of you where, although it's full of love and admiration, there is this tiny undertow of Tynan thinking: "Why isn't this guy writing Brechtian plays?"

TS: I know. The thing is that he had the bad luck to write his profile just before *Professional Foul*. And then a month later *Every Good Boy Deserves Favour* was published.

AT: Did you ever discuss those plays with him?

TS: No, I didn't really. The truth of the matter is that he was broke and was terribly glad to have a long profile paid for with a lot of money. He asked Harold Pinter to cooperate for a profile. Pinter said he wouldn't. So then he asked me. I found out later. His main motive was to write a profile of *somebody*. Having written it, I don't think he was that interested in the fact that I followed with two plays about politics.

AT: The argument in the profile seems to center on Wilde.

TS: I used to have these conversations with Tynan about Wilde's essays, particularly "The Soul of Man Under Socialism." I was slightly dishonest with him because I pontificated about Wilde on the basis of the plays I knew, and nothing else. Tynan would then say, "This is all nonsense, this wonderful essay 'The Soul of Man Under Socialism,' blah blah blah." So I would think, "Oh, Christ, I better read that." And then I'd read it, as it were, with demolition in view—to undercut any effect. I'd dismiss it as being simply another form of his pirouetting.

I think that 9/11 and the Iraq war are events which... You can't behave as though they changed nothing, you know? Everything has to be changed in some way: your thinking is changed, your thinking about what you should be writing about, certainly. Well, I'm thinking about it. Well, put it this way: while the emotion is at its height, while the consciousness is at its most acute about what's happening, while you're living in that kind of atmosphere, your view or your assessment of the purity and validity of that sonnet somehow... It doesn't mean you think, "Oh I have to stop, there's no point in writing sonnets anymore, that's all over." It's not that. But the decades which led up to the end of what Fukuyama would call "the previous history" went on for so long. Occasionally there'd be a bit of a *frisson* called Cuba, but generally speaking it just went on for so long that it became the climate. You felt that Max Beerbohm would have written what he'd written, in the same climate.

I kept very quiet after 9/11. Everybody sort of bounced into print in a self-questioning way—and I can understand why, I felt much the same—but I thought, "Don't say anything because the times are distorting: they're distorting your ability to think clearly at the moment."

AT: I think I feel that the two are perhaps incommensurate.

TS: Go on with that one.

AT: Well, there are things that I care about concerning art, and that is evidently, on one level, a very important concern, and on another level an absolutely minuscule and irrelevant concern. Evidently art is a luxury. And so were I to be reduced to living in fur, in Siberia, tomorrow, I would not be caring particularly about Oscar Wilde and style.

It seems to me that sometimes there is a melodrama of self-questioning about art: if you believed before 9/11 that it was important to care about not using cliché, say, then there's no reason why 9/11 might change that. It might make you think that sometimes you should be thinking about other things as well, but then it surprises me that it would take something like 9/11 to make you realize that: the actual concern seems to me to remain...

TS: It alters the emphasis you put on it, doesn't it? For a while.

AT: I just think that there can be a tough kind of aestheticism, a pragmatic type—which thinks that obviously these concerns are limited within their own sphere, but that doesn't mean that the entire sphere has to disappear just because there are other things of importance. It's evidently true that the other things of importance will always rise and fall—so that at some point suddenly it will seem imperative to be thinking about terrorism, or thirty years ago to be thinking about communism—but it seems to me also that in the end the really good writers do have a slight autism to them, an earned independence.

I think sometimes you can see this kind of problem where writers try to make a link between being a good writer and being a good person, or a good reader and a good person. But there's no reason why there should be a correlation between your ethical ability and your aesthetic ability—and that kind of statement is made by someone haunted by the unnecessary worry that art needs to be justified on a further, moral level.

TS: No, I agree with that. Things get more interesting when the artist uses the event as his subject matter. I mean, in the trenches of the first World War, there were tens of thousands of copies of Housman. There's an edition published in a size you could fit into a battle-dress pocket. That's a different thing from, say, David Jones's *In Parenthesis*, which was an attempt to bring his aesthetic values to the subject matter. And there of course nobody has a problem—basically they say, "Well that's what artists should do, that's what they're for, they must remember, and relive, and see more clearly." And what *you're* saying is, "What about the guy who wasn't there, and wants to continue perfecting his sonnets?" And what *I'm* saying is that whatever the values one invests in the work he's doing, the fact that he's doing it is a moral statement. It's not like saying, "I'm not actually committing myself here": in a way you *are* making a statement by detachment, by detaching yourself.

AT: The guy who makes bicycles—you would think it was rather odd if he were to say to you: "I've had to rethink everything I've been doing since 9/11."

TS: Yeah, that would be odd, wouldn't it?

AT: And I'm not sure how different that is from the idea that the guy who writes plays, say...

TS: But you see, this is exactly where one sees that artists are not bicycles. I mean, PEN doesn't have a committee for pastry-cooks in prison, or bicycle-makers in prison. So you think, "Well, what the hell is this? What's going on here? When did society constitute itself in such a way that this figure of the artist had some kind of special status? How far back does that actually go?" And the answer seems to be, it actually goes back to the beginning.

AT: I wonder how far this problem of art is really a category mistake, of people wanting a word to mean more than one thing.

TS: A lot of questions which present themselves as problems turn out to be a failure of vocabulary.
      Decent shot, wasn't it?

AT: There was one thing you said earlier. I said that style was the most important thing for me. And you said that the idea never grew on you. Do you mean that actually now you don't believe that style is all important, that you grew out of it—or that you instinctively knew that it was something you never had to ponder?

TS: The question is, what do I mean now, or what did I mean then?

AT: Well, it could be either. Either is fine.

TS: What I would say is that it's different for a novelist.

I thought when I was young, and I think now, that a style-signature is why you read somebody. And, when I was young, finding and keeping and impressing that style-signature led me into a liking for certain kinds of writing in an attempt to emulate or simulate certain kinds of style-writing—which maybe put a strain on what I was writing. I mean when I was starting off I remember a short story I wrote that had a one-legged person in it, and I remember some translation showing up and I was thinking, "Well, this actually says in English 'intrepid uniped'—what is the *point* in Lithuanian, there's simply no point in *saying* it, if you can't have fun with the language." And I think that there are writers for whom that's not an important issue. Writers who are possibly very great writers, writers I revere—Hemingway for example. I imagine Hemingway in German would be absolutely fine. But there are writers for whom that can't possibly be true.

And I still feel that a writer's style, if that's the word—tone, signature, whatever—is the reason for reading him. But, where it stops is you begin to realize that the way a play can work upon you—event, physical event—is very effective indeed. When you refer back to the source of all this—the page—it doesn't seem to be there. Furthermore, there's no authorial voice in a play, every single voice is a person—and how can it be, why should it be, that each of these people should have a style? People are not, on the whole, stylish speakers. So one has to be careful of the word. Although as you perceive a thought, there always seems to be one more corner to go around. You might then say, "Well, look at Mamet, for example." Yes, well, look at Mamet! I mean, the artifice in that! The care that goes into every utterance! I think that when I started off, I probably didn't have enough confidence in myself to suppose that I could capture and hold the attention unless there was something startling going on all the time—and the notion that the attention would be held by something deeper than that *struck* me, but I didn't know how to do it, or felt I didn't know how to do it. So I always turned, somehow without even willing it, into comedy. But I may have got the chicken mixed up with the egg, actually.

Oh that's a just *beautiful* shot. [*Claps*] I'm always mystified by drives, the cover drive, which hits the bat higher up than I feel I could cope with. A cover drive which comes off the bottom three inches of the bat I understand. One which comes off the middle of the bat I find very hard to work out.

AT: A comment I love about dialogue in the *novel* is a moment where Lampedusa is talking about Stendhal. He says that in Stendhal "the fault of so many novels has disappeared, this fault which consists in revealing the soul of the characters through their dialogue…" Whereas in Stendhal, "*there is no famous dialogue.*" It's just, "How are you?—I'd like some scrambled eggs please." And I was thinking this is impossible for a dramatist—if you didn't reveal the soul of the characters through their dialogue in some way, the play's going to be impossible.

TS: Yes, yes. But the power that a play has over its audience, I think, in the end is not in the dialogue. It's the situation. I've always envied playwrights who are knock-out situationists—Ayckbourn is, for example. Who probably would be delighted to be bracketed suddenly with Stendhal, but I say this equally as the same compliment: he doesn't write memorable lines, but you're absolutely gripped by the situation on stage. I recognized this very early on, and I've become aware that plays of mine which worked better are the ones where the style element just becomes a bonus. But it's good if you find that your wisecracking people are actually in a situation which has the audience agog, and not really feeding off the style of utterance at all.

AT: I think somewhere else you said that the problem with your plays was that for a long time everyone spoke the same.

TS: Well, I did used to say that: I used to think it.

AT: But I think it's arguable about even your early plays, and it's certainly not true of plays from even *The Real Thing* onwards...

TS: I think it was true early on in some ways. I have an African dictator, in one play—and I remember thinking to myself, quite cold-bloodedly, "I'm going to have to find a background for this guy, which will enable me to write his dialogue, because I sure as hell can't write African dictator dialogue. I can only write the dialogue for somebody who was at the LSE and then went back to Africa." Which is more or less what I did.

I think that it's a slightly out-of-date quote. I think I learned to do things as time went on, or perhaps I just discovered they weren't as difficult as I assumed that they would be.

AT: I think that realizing how little you need to create a character's voice is an interesting thing: I think I always believed that it requires an incredible ingenuity of invention, that you had to be able to think up seventeen things that this character—

TS: It requires an *ear*—it's not actually inventing, if you're remembering it. And some people are better than others. I'm very bad at it. I know that from the way that I can put on a record, an album, which I've heard fifty times—it's a long way into the track before I work out which one it is. Or something comes on the radio, and I think, "It's one of my favorite records, which one is it, *which* of my favorite records is this?" And I'm sure for writers there's a strength there or a weakness, and I simply don't think of it as being a strength of mine at all.

There's another way of putting this.

How do you avoid being boring when you're writing a boring character? Well, the answer is really that we don't have a boring person in a play unless the point is that he's boring, and then you've got a situation which is interesting or funny or whatever because the boring element is there for a particular reason. There's a Peter Nichols play I remember where people show up at somebody's house and there seems to be—in my memory—reams and reams of dialogue on how they got there, which road they took—"Oh, no, you should have taken the A35." This is a conversation without any redeeming interest, either in subject or phrasing. But of course it was hilarious because—it's to do with recognition, isn't it?

Let's go and have a cup of tea.

III. TEA

TS: I've got a nice after-lunch feeling now.

AT: What is it you think is charming about cricket? I think I like its unpredictability—that this is a game which is played as a game of skill, but is essentially a game of chance.

TS: I never think of cricket as being anything to do with chance. It seems to me entirely about skill. Yes, the weather might intervene. But that's not really about cricket, that only possibly impinges on the result of a particular match, but the actual cricket is something separate.

But *my* involvement with cricket came through playing, not through watching it. I'm not sure I ever found it terribly interesting to watch. But being inculcated from the age of eight or nine, cricket—no more than any other sport I played—became interesting from the point of view of doing it. I was never that good at it, but I did aspire to being a wicket-keeper.

There's something about the position of wicket-keeper which appealed to me very deeply—I was very bad-tempered if I had to play in a match where while fielding I wasn't allowed to keep wicket. Cricket seemed more or less pointless to me if you weren't actually a wicket-keeper. And I could see that it might be a viable game if you opened the bowling and continued to bowl for the entire course of the innings. That also could be interesting, I suppose. I loved being involved in every ball bowled—which is your situation when you're keeping wicket. It isn't *even* true, really, of somebody who's bowling, who gets a rest every six balls. And consequently I hero-worshipped, in succession, Godfrey Evans, Alan Knott—I suppose I was too old to hero-worship people by the time we got to Jack Russell. But I find when I'm watching cricket on television even now—I rarely go to cricket—I still find myself mostly fascinated by what the wicket-keeper's doing.

It's partly to do with the fact that every ball is frightening, if you're keeping wicket, because there's a very good chance that you'll have to *deal* with it if the batsman doesn't. And, as you know, when it comes to catches being offered, probably three out of five go to the wicket-keeper, generally. So you feel that there's a lot of responsibility on you, and one is constantly frightened of publicly shaming oneself—by dropping an easy catch or missing an easy stumping—which of course happened to me all the time, but nevertheless that's what I liked doing.

AT: Whereas for me the thing I hated about fielding was the knowledge that at any point this thing could come towards you.

TS: But, when fielding, somehow you feel that there are so many other directions that the ball may go in. Whereas with wicket-keeping, if the batsman doesn't hit it, it's yours. And I loved, I suppose, the gloves and the pads and all that, and the sound the ball made going into a glove. It's quite a complex little thing, keeping wicket. And this tremendous sort of pride in standing up to a bowler who wasn't particularly slow, if you got to know him very well.

AT: It reminds me—talking of weather and cricket and chance. In *The Coast of Utopia,* in the second play, *Shipwreck,* Herwegh says: "*Stoical* freedom is nothing but not wasting your time berating the weather when it's bucketing down on your picnic." And in *Salvage,* Herzen mentions "picnics ruined by rain" in his list of things he's moved beyond. And the final scene is of an outdoor party where it's starting to rain. Is this a deliberate pattern?

TS: No, it's not. It was unknowing, I think. I mean, even if it wasn't unknowing, it wasn't supposed to mean anything. But it's nice that there is a pattern. The thing is, Adam, that things that are sort of *spottable* in that way are, as it were, rare—and sometimes are conscious. But they're there like jokes for the attentive reader, they're not there to provide vital clues to the thrust of the play, or a vital piece of symbolism—not to me, I don't think.

AT: It's true that it's not the key to the play, but it does link up to a larger theme: things happen beyond our control, as it were, the future is not reliable. Herzen says that people mistakenly want to believe that they can own the future. That was the pattern that I thought it linked up to, you plan a picnic, but you have no idea if it's going to be pissing down.

TS: No, I completely see that, and I absolutely feel the same way about it as you do, but also from the same perspective as you do. These things emerge, and you think, "Oh, that's good because it's X, Y, Z." What it is *not* is somebody sitting down with a piece of graph paper at ten in the morning and thinking, "Now how can I plant something which will convey, perhaps, no no no..." So it's all true but it's not that significant, that's all. I think it's very flattering, I think it's a great compliment when you come across somebody in conversation or print who actually has remembered a detail in a play. It's hardly what one expects but it's very nice.

AT: You said you aren't the kind of writer who has an objective in mind and shapes the material in order to convey that. And I don't like that kind of writer, either, who simply has a thesis and wants to expound it. But there's still scope for artistry, for organization, for theme, for formal play—and it's as if you are also trying to shut that off as well.

TS: Well, I think I know where the truth lies. What I mean is that

I can sort of see why I'm contradicting myself. When you're writing the speech about picnics ruined by rain, you're not thinking, "Ah, I'll have a picnic later where it starts to rain." What is going on is that you find yourself at a picnic and you remember it would be a good fit if it rained. So, you know—it's true from one angle and untrue from another angle.

I actually rather relish—in other people if I can spot it, and certainly enjoy it in my own things—echoes which bounce back at you, or echo down the play. I like that happening, and in fact occasionally I stumble into something which becomes actually structural, like the penknife in *Voyage*.

The great thing about the penknife in *Voyage* for me is that I didn't know that I'd be able to do this, until things emerged, and then it becomes the nicest thing in *Voyage* for me. It's not premeditated, but it's very knowing when you do it.

AT: I absolutely know what you *mean,* that no good writer is going to be thinking in terms of a play's architecture as a whole, at every moment. And yet although some of the formal tricks that I love about your work are things that might be lovely flukes, some things are too intricate.

It's interesting, say, following the penknife. If you think about the structure of *Voyage*, progressing forwards in time, twice, filling in the gaps from the first half in the second half—I love that the first time you hear about the penknife is actually when you don't know you're hearing it—when Tatiana says, "Did you catch anything?" You assume she means a fish.

TS: Yes, it's backwards.

AT: The penknife is a lovely miniature of the play's structure.

TS: One has seen quite a few good documentary drama plays where you're just shown what happened and what people said as near as one can endeavour that way. And what I remember thinking and feeling and I still feel the same way now, is that there's

368

something disappointing, something missing, if that's all you manage to do. So, I'm intensely encouraged and cheered up by finding things which are not happening on the level of history, but which are happening on an entirely different level, like the penknife, because they seem to me to save the play. To put it another way, they *make* it a play. That odd bit of artifice, odd bit of shimmer in the silk, I think saves the situation for the writer.

AT: They also link to one of the main themes in *The Coast of Utopia*: the misinterpretation of the present.

TS: There's something about shuttling back and forth, through time in the case of *Arcadia,* which I adore. I just love things which aren't exactly written at all—that in *Arcadia* a twentieth-century apple is cut by a nineteenth-century knife and fed to a tortoise. I find that more theatrical than three-quarters of a page which took a week to write.

And although I always claim that I like to come out of a different box each time, actually I think that the things they have in common are greater than I've allowed for. Although there are no time threads in *The Real Thing*, the same thing's happening as is happening in *Arcadia*: there's a man in a chair, and he gets a present from a woman and he opens it up and picks up the box and that's the end of the scene—and it's different and the same each time. It's that layer which I think separates a play from its fellows. Because one thing for sure is you don't change very much as a *writer*: the actual jokes you make, the kind of metaphors you like, the way people talk, that doesn't change very much, frankly.

I sound as though this is a very interesting subject. I can see it's objectively quite interesting, but it's not something which I think about much. Is that true? I think that's the problem at the moment, probably. I mean, it's not true. I think the reason that I'm a mess at the moment is that I'm too conscious of the things I've just been talking about.

What I think I mean is that there is a distinction between talking about work, and presuming to explicate it in some way. The most famous question in modern drama is, "Who is Godot?" What a total and utter calamity it would have been if Beckett had said, "Oh, it's the collective unconscious," or, "It's the inspector of highways," or, "Jehovah." What an appalling thing to happen to that play, because it just shuts off what that play actually does—which is that it's about what happens to you while you're watching it, isn't it?

But the *actual* reason why I came back from France without having started—is that I didn't know what the plot was, or who the people were.

AT: I think sometimes that plot is a slight embarrassment, to a writer who cares about form. Without a genuinely interesting story, any amount of formal experiment is irrelevant.

TS: I could write a play tomorrow, no problem, if my take on it was that the audience would be so fascinated to know what I was going to do next that they would be very happy just to see what these people were talking about for a couple of hours. I'm up to here in cognitive science, no problem. But it's not possible. The gulf which is supposed to separate the next Hollywood film from the next fringe drama is actually quite narrow. Both of them need a good plot. Because, unless you want to turn the page, you're not really winning, are you? This thing of the page turner—it's true of *Hamlet*. So, however clued up I am, and however brilliant I am, having speeches about neurons, unless someone's saying, "Yes, but what happens next?," you're dead.

I don't think I used to realize that. I don't think I wanted to.

AT: But form can make something interesting, too: a lot of interest is the plot's form, not its content—the organization of the material.

TS: I suspect that the whole trick is to undermine the audience's security about what it thinks it knows at any moment. I think that one has to try to do it on the smallest scale as well as the largest. When I got going on *The Coast of Utopia,* I was very aware of this. I think I lost sight of it somewhat. The first scene ends with somebody saying: "One thing for sure, we're not going to let this marriage take place." And then, the first line of the next scene is: "The newlyweds are here." And then you think: "Oh, well, he was wrong about that." And then think: "Oh no he wasn't, it was somebody else." This thing of undermining the audience's sense of what's going on—I think it is drama, a lot of drama is that.

AT: I think it's in one of your conversations with Mel Gussow where he says to you, "I'm not suggesting that you should write like Hemingway. I'm just trying to understand the admiration."

But I have a theory why you like Hemingway. Which is in this kind of occlusion. There is the famous thing Hemingway says: "It was a very simple story called 'Out of Season' and I had omitted the real end of it which was that the old man hanged himself. This was omitted on my new theory that you could omit anything as long as you knew that you omitted and the omitted part would strengthen the story and make people feel something more than they understood."

His writing is based on occlusion. Is that something similar? You like presenting characters, and the audience, with a situation they don't quite comprehend? You like pushing things to the side, so the reader or audience has to infer the rational situation that is going on.

TS: It's true. But you must know the people you like really have very little to do with what you like to write yourself. And anyone who loves Hemingway the way I love him would be well advised to just get past it, you know: do your Hemingway pastiche and move on. I did mine actually—short stories and things, really embarrassing. I was at a Hemingway conference once, where they have a Hemingway library, and I read my Hemingway short story without telling them who'd written it. A self-humiliation.

AT: Do you believe there could be a good play with bad technique?

TS: I worked out once that technique was actually about controlling the flow or the trajectory of information—from the play to the audience—just controlling it, so it gets there in a certain order, in certain stages: a lot of it boils down to that.

IV. FROM CRICKET

TS: Do you think that most people are integrated and coherent about what they are as writers? The way it works with me is that I stumble across some kind of formulation which has a certain persuasive quality, and because I get used to how to say it, I get very good at delivering that line. And then after a while, time goes by, and I no longer think it—if I ever did think it. I was just delivering the line because I knew how.

Did you ever read the *New York Review* talk I gave in the *New York Review of Books*?

I just couldn't *do* it. I stood up there and did my usual thing, and they all said it was fine but I knew it wasn't. They sent me the proofs, and I sat down and wrote new stuff and gave it back to them. They printed that as what I'd said. So anybody who'd been present would have thought, "Oh, what a terrible memory I have, I don't remember him saying any of *this*"—and I hadn't said any of it.

But, in writing it, I discovered things I thought, completely new thoughts, which I've hung on to ever since, and think, "Oh, yes, that's what I think." Some of them were quite central. One of them was getting sick of the whole *dénouement* idea. I fell into this thing, and by the time I'd come out of it, I emerged with this completely coherent intact philosophy, of the anti-*dénouement* writer, and it hasn't actually collapsed yet.

I still think that's what I think.

AT: One of the things I love in your work is a running joke—it's there in *Travesties* and it's there also in *The Coast of Utopia*—where you use Wilde for revolutionaries. So that in *Travesties* Lenin says:

"Really, if the lower orders don't set a good example what on earth is the use of them?! They seem to have absolutely no sense of moral responsibility! To lose one revolution is unfortunate. To lose two would look like carelessness!" And then Bakunin says in *Salvage*—"Our first task will be to destroy authority. There is no second task." Which seems to me to point to a continuity. You're replacing political belief with paradox and contradiction: aestheticism replaces sincerity.

TS: Do you think writing something because you feel it invests writing with a quality that distinguishes it from the unfelt?

I'll try and pose this in a get-at-able form. To somebody who is unaware of either, is there actually a real difference between Henry James and Max Beerbohm's parody of Henry James? What actually distinguishes them? We know that in the case of James there is sincerity and in the case of Beerbohm there is no sincerity, but can you find that difference when you look at the two?

AT: I think the interest of a parody is that, like all works of art, it is and is not like the thing it's representing. A parody exists in the same relation to a work of art as a work of art exists in relation to reality. It's a joke on the same theme. When you read Beerbohm's James parody, would you really believe it was by James? I'm not sure you would. Because James's style has a subject but Beerbohm's subject is only a style.

TS: I think you're absolutely right—you know James wouldn't have bothered to expend his style on this.

AT: I suppose the reason why the parody works is that sometimes James is examining velleities of feeling that basically don't exist, or only exist to Henry James, and therefore Beerbohm has this space to work on: sometimes you feel that James is giving too much emphasis to things which no one thinks about really.

But on the other hand, he's also brilliant at showing people that actually they think far more closely about very minor things than they thought they did. You have to revise what you mean by important or unimportant when you read James.

TS: For me, the reason it's become more political, now… A desire for the play to be moving was not part of my thinking in any way. I was interested in abstract ideas and I liked making jokes. From the very beginning, even Rosencrantz talking about being dead [in *Rosencrantz & Guildenstern Are Dead*] wasn't an *emotional* moment. It was, as it were, just logic-fun or word-fun or think-fun. But for the last fifteen years, I found myself writing things which moved me at a certain point, and move other people, and *now* I don't want to write a play which doesn't.

So I sit in France and I've got all these bits, and I can manipulate them quite cleverly, for a couple of hours, and that's what I would have been doing I suppose—but *now*, I can't start because unless there's some kind of human pain here, or redemption, I don't want to do it, or don't want to bother.

In *Indian Ink* there is a moment about a woman brushing petals off her sister's gravestone, so she could read the name on the stone, and then she says goodbye to her dead sister, and I remember having a bit of a gulp when it was being acted, even though I'd written it.

And this is quite a good way to close one of these circles, because the actual phrase was, you know, *par excellence,* without style, without finesse. It consisted of three words, "Bye bye darling": that was it. But because of the situation—this is what we were talking about—because of the situation it sort of made one gulp a little bit, and, if I've made any kind of journey at all, it's the journey from discounting that—discountenancing, I suppose I'm trying to say, that—to a place where it's central to the point of writing a play, the desire to write a play.

I think that's the one thing which has emerged from the chaos of conversation, from all our very enjoyable chat, as something which I do recognize has happened. I understand why I can't be

bothered to write the play yet, because there isn't this emotion…
available in it.

AT: There's a lovely thing Nabokov says, defending Dickens's *Bleak House* against the charge of sentimentality: "I want to submit that people who denounce the sentimental are generally unaware of what sentiment is." The problem is that sentiment is so close to sentimentality.

TS: It's very close, it's a hair's breadth, isn't it? I'm always doubting myself when I think I've brought off a moment of sentiment—and I think, "Oh, God, this is actually TV."

AT: If you take *The Invention of Love,* say, the title's ambiguity refers to both sentiment and sentimentality. It's about the fact that literally you invent the love object, so that Jackson and Bosie are both inadequate to the emotion expended on them, and yet the love for them is entirely real, entirely irrational, and entirely right. And completely true.

And this is very similar to Housman as a scholar. Whether you're in love with Moses Jackson, or doing an edition of Manilius, both involve "useless knowledge"—but that doesn't make them wrong or invalid.

But the second sense of the title is brought out in the way you use Wilde at the end. Like Housman, Wilde is in love with a boy who is not worthy of him. But Wilde is also shown to be sentimental—when he says, "Once, I bought a huge armful of lilies in Convent Garden to Miss Langtry, and as I waited to put them in a cab, a small boy said to me, 'Oh, how rich you are!'… 'Oh, how rich you are! [*He weeps.*] Oh—forgive me. I'm somewhat the worse for cake.'" It's slightly theatrical—the sentiment has become sentimentality. And it links to the earlier moment where AEH describes "False nostalgia"—which he glosses later: "all the risks—archaism, anachronism, the wayward incontinence that only hindsight can acquit of *non sequitur*…"

This seems to me the core of the play: how far a genuine love, the sentiment, can somehow in retrospect get shaded into nostalgia, into sentimentality.

TS: It's not a bad interpretation.

If you think of love letters, other people's or your own, there's tremendous—there's a sort of, there's a, there's a, there's a tremendous, Jesus God—there's a tendency for them to veer off into the most embarrassing pathos and sentimentality which is all too evident in retrospect but which at the time of writing seems to be an accurate expression of feeling. So it makes one wonder whether there's something which is relative to the observer which is not the same thing which is relative to the writer. And I think when I said they always seem to be a hair's breadth apart, it's that difference between how it is being felt by the writer and how it is being received by the audience.

AT: The thing is—this examination of sentiment, of feeling, is there in all your plays. Often you're described as a playwright of ideas: but most of the people called playwrights of ideas are people with very definite ideas: their plays prove ideas. Whereas in your plays, although there are a lot of people coming up with ideas, the interest is never for the ideas—it's to do with the process by which they come up with them, the emotions which are creating the cerebral theories.

TS: It's also to do with how one might rebut those very same ideas. But you can see that there *is*—God help me I'm not wrong about this, am I?—that there is the ghost of a promise of a play if I... There's this poem written in roughly 600 B.C. about a woman looking at the woman she loves talking to a man, and she just actually describes the symptoms and they're very precise: there's this wonderful phrase about how thin fire races under the skin. There are all these physiological things which happen to the narrator of the poem. So you can see that to explore or undermine that by describing it in terms of what's happening in her brain at that moment, in purely physical terms…

I'm sure there's something quite strong in *feeling* being the refutation of thinking: that the feeling that she expresses—in some way—cannot be accounted for by the neurologist, cannot actually be fully described and accounted for by the scientist.

And this… So there's a play there. There… There must be. ✶

VENDELA VIDA

TALKS WITH

SUSAN STRAIGHT

"MY WHOLE LIFE IS ON THIS STREET."

AN INTERVIEW IN SIX PARTS

I. AC/DC
II. James Baldwin
III. Crossing the border
IV. Firefighters that keep showing up
V. The Great Social Novel
VI. Running to the game

I.

usan Straight *drives a minivan with a* Van Halen *tape in the cassette player. Neatly arranged on the floor, between the front seats, are her oldest daughter's overdue library book, a novel for one of Straight's students at UC Riverside, where she is a professor of creative writing, and a box of candy bars that she's helping her middle daughter's friend sell to raise money for a summer science camp.*

At forty-four, Straight is the author of Aquaboogie *(1990),* I Been In Sorrow's Kitchen and Licked Out All the Pots *(1992),* Blacker Than a Thousand Midnights *(1994),* The Gettin Place *(1996), and*

379

THE BELIEVER BOOK OF WRITERS TALKING TO WRITERS

Highwire Moon *(2001), which was a finalist for the National Book Award. She is also the single mother of three girls, who are between the ages of nine and fifteen and whose heritage is parts African, Creek and Cherokee, Irish, French, and Swiss. Among the protagonists of Straight's books are Marietta Cook, a large black basket maker who makes her way from South Carolina to California; Darnell Tucker, a black firefighter; and Serafina, a Mexican Indian woman who is deported from California and made to leave her daughter behind. Thus it's surprising when meeting Straight to discover she is a petite white woman with blond hair and blue eyes. And yet you don't for a second doubt her narrative command or the authenticity of the voices she captures.*

Straight's prose is tight and her metaphors striking: in the arresting opening of Highwire Moon, *Serafina is captured by the police while her daughter, Elvia, sits on the floor of a car, the "mouth" of which had "hit something hard, like a fist against teeth." Straight describes what lies beyond the daughter's vision with such singular descriptions as: "Branches and leaves covered the windshield, pressed tight like a blanket of black knives" and "a pair of white hands pressed up like a snail's underside against the glass." And then there's Straight's dialogue, which is so unerring, so real, that even after you've turned the page—and your attention— to a new scene in a new locale, you're aware that the characters from the previous scene are still carrying on, still talking. You can almost hear them.*

This interview took place over the course of one day in Riverside, California, which the National Drug Intelligence Center recently referred to as the "methamphetamine capital of the United States" and which Straight calls "Rio Seco" in her fiction. As Straight drives through Riverside and its surroundings, she points out warehouses, old vineyards, early strawberry fields, the hospital where she, her brothers, and two of her daughters were born, the Laundromat her stepfather owned, and the bank where her mother worked. "I would never bounce a check," says Straight. "It's my mom's bank. So if you bounce a check, that's who finds out. I've only bounced two checks in my whole life, and she found out and called me."

—V.V. (Spring 2003)

SUSAN STRAIGHT: This is the Inland Empire.

VENDELA VIDA: The what? Why?

SS: The Inland Empire was a name given to this area by civic leaders, I guess. I don't know. I think it was to make it sound attractive, acknowledging that we didn't have a coast or L.A. Then, when local rappers wanted to call it something, they called it the I.E. Cooler. Now people call it the 909, after Blink 182 and Alien Ant Farm's success. We're the three famous people to come out of the 909. People who are really young get it—the 909—but if they're over forty and they're like "the 909?" I have to explain it. I have to say, "You know, Blink 182." I'm in more trouble if I say "Alien Ant Farm." Then it's all over. But anyway, this is the landscape people make fun of all the time. They ask, "How can you stay there?" But I'll show you.

VV: So you grew up here until when?

SS: I went to USC. That's one of the elite private schools in California. And I had come on a full-ride scholarship from Riverside. I'd never taken a midterm. Totally clueless as to what a midterm or a final was. Everyone else came from private girls' schools and I show up wearing my T-shirt with gang letters on the back that say "Itsy Bits" and they're like, "What is that?"

VV: Yeah, what is that?

SS: It was my name. They knew everything. I knew nothing. My parents dropped me off and were like, "See ya." Some students thought I was there to help them move in.

These are old vineyards, by the way. These have been here since 1920. There's nothing sadder or scarier than an abandoned vineyard. Now it's all warehouses. But when I was little I would check out all the ground squirrels.

VV: So did you ever become friends with the girls?

SS: No, I'd come home to Riverside on the weekends, and when I was at school I'd stick with the people I felt comfortable with— the football players.

At USC, I was the second female to be a sportswriter for the *Daily Trojan*. I was a huge sports fan, and part of that was I had all these brothers, and my neighborhood was full of guys... I thought being a female sports writer, I'd always get a job.

VV: How'd you get into sportswriting?

SS: When I graduated from high school, my mother gave me a small blue Smith-Corona typewriter, and she showed me a *Parade* magazine article about female sportswriters. She thought that would be a good job for me, since I'd dated a basketball player for three years and spent all my spare time watching sports on TV. Also, I think she wanted season tickets to the Dodgers. She learned good English from listening to Vin Scully doing Dodger broadcasts.

VV: And now your daughters all play basketball? Did you encourage them or did they pick it up themselves?

SS: I started playing basketball with them in the driveway. Their dad had put up a hoop before they were born, always thinking he'd have a boy. We got divorced after the third girl—not because of that, of course. When the middle one was seven, I showed her how to steal the ball off someone's dribble, and how to shoot, and she fell in love with the game. She's short, thin, and fierce, like me. Now both of the older girls play, center and guard, and their father coaches them. I can't even attempt to play in the driveway with them. One blocks my shots and the other fakes me out of my shoes. It's sad.

VV: So with all the teaching and basketball games, when do you write?

SS: I like to stay up till one. I always think it'd be a good idea to write between five and six-thirty, before the kids get up. But please. I like to stay up till one because that's the only time when it's quiet. If I got up at five and I wrote until six-thirty, the kids would hear me, the dog would hear me, somebody would get up, and then everybody would be up. But when I get everybody to bed by nine-thirty, if I can have a cup of tea at ten p.m. then I can stay up till one. Then I know I have three hours when nobody will hear me.

If I'm really, really, really good, I can stay up till three. But if I do that now... I'm forty-two, I'm ancient. And then there are the Oprah terms [that a guest talked about on her show], where you have to add a certain amount of years if you're divorced, if you're a single mom.

VV: So how old are you, according to that model?

SS: Eighty-five. I'm a single mom. I have three kids. I have a dog. I have two jobs. Relatives who are dead.

VV: Well, you look great for eighty-five.

SS: Thank you. Well, I feel eighty-five.

VV: How similar is Rio Seco to Riverside? Why'd you change the name in your fiction?

SS: At eighteen, I walked around downtown Riverside and knew I wanted to write about a city like mine, forever. I changed the name because I wanted it to be a fictional place, even then, knowing I would change geography and time, and people. I thought and thought that day, and picked Dry River because it was summer, and hot, and our river had shrunk every year.

VV: So what's your favorite song on this *Best of Van Halen* tape?

SS: I listen to "Runnin' with the Devil" and think of my brother coming over and hanging out with my girls and saying, "Now, you don't want to look bad like me and my friends, with all these scars, do you? That's what happens when you run with the devil." Then he'd laugh and leave them a Lynyrd Skynyrd CD so they could learn some lyrics. I played two songs from that CD at his funeral service and now I can't touch the CD. It's on my dresser with an order form for steel-toed Red Wing boots, all he ever wore.

Before, I played his other favorite songs, "Highway to Hell," all the AC/DC, and drove around imagining I was someone like Larry in *Highwire Moon*.

II.

Susan Straight lives in a single-story teal-blue shingled house with a wrap-around porch and a fruitless mulberry tree in her yard. From one of its bare branches hangs a tire on a rope. Knowing she was expecting company, her mother, from Switzerland, came over to help tidy up what one can see is usually an orderly house, Swiss mother or no Swiss mother. All around her clean house, books are stacked, and photographs of Straight and her three daughters are displayed. Off the living room is Straight's office, with a window that faces the street. (At three in the morning, she claims that her light and those of people cooking speed are the only lights on.) In the living room, a basketball remains surprisingly still. Mini Christmas Coca-Cola bottles line the windowsills of her kitchen, and in the kitchen nook stands an artist's easel displaying a collage of small hands made by Straight's youngest daughter, Rosette. Toward the head of the kitchen table sits a green wicker chair, which proves to be invaluable to Straight's research as a writer: it's where friends and neighbors come for tea or cake and sit and tell her their stories.

VV: Were you in your twenties when you published your first book, *Aquaboogie*?

SS: Yeah, I started those stories when I was twenty… rewrote them like thirteen or fourteen times. I sold it when I was twenty-eight, maybe.

VV: So you started off college thinking you'd be a sportswriter?

What changed your mind?

SS: Geoffrey Green was teaching at USC. He'd had a story published in the *North American Review,* making fun of *Jaws.* And he
brought it into class. I was probably nineteen, and he brought it
and showed it to us that day, and I went to the library that night,
and I found a *North American Review,* and Louise Erdrich had a
story in there called "Scales," which was later in *Love Medicine.*
When I met her at the National Book Awards dinner—she was
there—I said, "Your short story, 'Scales,' that was it for me." 'Cause
that's what made me think I could be a fiction writer. Have you
read that story?

VV: I read *Love Medicine.* Which one was "Scales"?

SS: In "Scales," there's Dot. She's the short blond woman that's
pregnant by Gerry, the big biker guy. She works in this weigh station, and she knits these little baby suits so hard that they come out
like armor. And sitting there on the floor in the library, reading that,
I thought, OK, maybe this fiction thing is something I can do. Not
that sportswriting is a horrible thing, but it wasn't quite the thrill
of reading something like that was. So Geoffrey Green was really a
big deal. Just from introducing me to literary magazines. And
encouraging me to send stories to the *New Yorker,* which I did.

VV: Did you work with T. C. Boyle at USC?

SS: T. C. Boyle was teaching there at the time. But I was afraid of
him. I never took a class from him because he looked like all the
horrible guys who I grew up with in Riverside. I mean, he had a
goatee, and he had the long hair, and he dressed like a biker. And
I just know now he was such a nice guy. [But then] all I did was
look at him and go, I hang out with those guys on the weekends.
I'm not hanging out with him at school, 'cause I'm supposed to be
here to learn. I'm not supposed to be here to get in trouble. Never
took a class with him. How stupid was that?

Anyway, he was very kind to me when I met him. I was a

senior and applying to go to graduate school, and I went to his office to talk to him, and he was telling me about Iowa and these other programs. But I only took classes from people I wasn't afraid of at USC. So I took the same literature classes over and over. I mean, I took the same professor, his name was Eggenschwiler, because I thought his name was Swiss, and I thought he wouldn't hurt me. I was so scared. Of everything. I mean, I hung out with these gigantic football players, and they didn't scare me. But other students—and the girls—scared me.

VV: If I had read all your books but hadn't seen your author photo, I would think you were a large black woman. Did you ever second-guess your authority to write from the perspective of black men, or Mexican women, as you do in *Highwire Moon*?

SS: That's what I was writing in Geoffrey Green's class. And he said, "Well, where are you from?" And I said, "Riverside." And he said, "Well why are you writing about all these guys?" And I'm like, "I don't know." And he just looked at me and said, "OK." And then he said, "Well, send your stories here…." He was nothing but helpful.

He didn't say anything to me about, "You can't do that." At the time, I was coming home every weekend. So I was writing a story about a friend of mine who killed himself by standing in front of a train. He did that because he got mixed up in this bad drug deal. He was seventeen and I was eighteen and he was all paranoid because he thought someone was going to kill him, so he decided to do it himself. It's the train that runs right behind my elementary school. Like right past my house and behind my elementary school. I mean, I listened to that train twice a day, all my life. That was a phone call that I got when I was in college. So I was writing stories about that. I never thought anybody would ever buy them. Who would? At that time I was reading the *New Yorker,* and the literature books. When I saw that story by Louise Erdrich, I thought, "Wait a minute. She's writing about some scary things—maybe I can do this too." And I went and I looked up her picture, and I thought, OK. She's writing about this blond, German woman who's knitting this baby suit, and she doesn't look like her.

So that was it. And that's when I started doing short stories. And T. C. Boyle told me about these schools. I already knew I was getting married. My soon-to-be husband had just dropped out of school, quit playing basketball, and he had to get a job.

VV: When did you start dating your ex-husband?

SS: We met in eighth grade. But I don't think we started dating until I was fifteen. We used to play basketball together. I think I was fifteen before our first date. The first one where he had a car, and I could go out with him in the car. His dad had just bought the car the night before. Some guy had been shot in the car, and so, in the passenger seat, there was a big towel. But there was a bullet hole in the passenger window next to my head. It was a '61 Cadillac with fins, so they called it the Batmobile.

I was pretty scared... I was sitting in the car, going, "What if they don't know this person's actually already dead? What if they're still looking for this person?" And Dwayne's like, "I don't think so. He's dead." I'm saying, "Yeah, but we're driving around in his car and he was murdered last night."

Anyway, we were going to get married, but we didn't have any money. And I was headed off to graduate school. So I get into five schools: Iowa, Brown, Johns Hopkins, Stanford, and the University of Massachusetts at Amherst. These were the five schools [Boyle and Greene] told me to apply to. And I got in. And then I needed money; I had no money. So, I went and sat down and talked to Dwayne. Because we were engaged and he was like, "Brown? Where's that?" and I go, "Providence," and he's like, "No sports teams." And he says, "Johns Hopkins, where's that?" And I go, "Baltimore," and he's like, "No sports teams. No basketball teams." And I said, "OK." He said, "Iowa? There's no black people." I said, "You have a point." He's like, "I don't want to be the only black person in the whole state!" And I said, "Well, there are probably some others," and he said, "Yeah! Five, six." So Iowa was out. And Stanford didn't offer me any money or anything. So there was the University of Massachusetts, Amherst. They offered me a full ride and all that. And Dwayne said, "Cool. We can go to the Boston Garden and see some games."

He didn't come the first year. He stayed here and was working to make some money, so I was on my own the first year. I lived in a house with two other roommates. I had a mattress on the floor, a typewriter and one of those packing crates with my typewriter my mom had given me on it. And I had my little boombox that Dwayne had given me. And that was it.

And then, the second year, we got married. We lived in married student housing, and we had nothing. We drove my Honda across the country. And we had to go find furniture, but we had no money. We literally went out looking on street corners for furniture.

So it was really hard. It snowed. Well, that's how it was for us—hard, when we came from here, where it was 80 degrees. And we had the one car. It took Dwayne six weeks to find a job. And he found a job as a night counselor at a group home. So he worked graveyard—he's always worked graveyard—and I took classes during the day. And since he was gone all night, I stayed up all night and wrote. That was the beginning of my habit—of our habit—of writing at night.

I went to school in the day… and then I taught; I was a TA. Delivered papers too, at like, three in the morning. And then I would write. And it was cold at night in the house. And I finished all those stories. So a lot of those stories [in *Aquaboogie*] were for my senior thesis. After I graduated, we came straight back here.

VV: At the University of Massachusetts at Amherst you studied with James Baldwin. What was it like working with him?

SS: James Baldwin put together a class with two or three students from the schools in the Amherst area, and for once, I was around a workshop table with women of color. No one asked why I would write about young gang members in Southern California, or said I couldn't use the kind of language I was using. James Baldwin, sitting regally at the end of the long table, studied us very quietly, watching people show off or be afraid, listening and listening, and then he would say one or two lines that were so profound.

He liked Dwayne because Dwayne didn't want anything from James Baldwin. At that point in his life, Baldwin received hundreds of manuscripts a month, and countless invitations or imploring phone calls. But Dwayne would just ask him about the weather, or whether he was going to eat his brownie. Baldwin invited us to come to visit him in southern France, and I was sorry we didn't do it.

He had me come to his house one afternoon to talk about my story "The Box," and he was so quiet while I worried about everything. Then he said, "The heart of the story is in the scenes at work. That's where you need to do more." I was puzzled, because those work scenes seemed very minor to the story, but then, two years later, back in Riverside and feeling lonely and as if I would never write again, I looked at the story. He was right. And when I redid those scenes, and tightened up the ending, it became the first story I sold, to *TriQuarterly*. And when James Baldwin died, not long afterward, I was so sad, and I had a new baby, and I took her for a long walk on the sidewalk at night and told her about him, and what he'd meant to me. His picture sits on the shelf next to my desk.

VV: What's the greatest number of people who have sat in that green chair and told you their stories in one night?

SS: Four.

III.

Four years ago, with Eric Barr, Straight founded the Master of Fine Arts in Creative Writing and Writing for the Performing Arts program at UC Riverside. Today, in her creative writing class, Straight discusses Jamaica Kincaid's short story "Girl" with her twenty-two *students. "Do you think the mother in this story is a bad, nagging mom or is she just being a mom?" Straight asks the class.*

The students conclude she's just being a mom.

After class, Straight heads for the department office, where she tempts coworkers to purchase the science camp candy bars. A graduate student approaches. He hasn't finished the story he had planned on turning in to her, and offers no excuse. "I never say I didn't have time," he explains to Straight, "because I remember the first time I heard a student say that, you said, 'Do you have three kids and two jobs? You know you're better off telling me you were too busy drinking in Tijuana and throwing up than telling me you didn't have time.'"

IV.

For lunch, Straight drives to a Vietnamese restaurant on University Avenue. Straight recently wrote about the restaurant for a travel magazine, and the owner comes over to the table to half-brag, half-complain about how busy they've been since the article ran.

SS: My whole life is on this street. On this street is the university where I teach and the Mobil gas station where I used to work, and across the street is the Hacienda Motel that's a place for mentally ill people now. It used to be a motel, and my foster sister and brother who lived with us for four years, their mom was an alcoholic. She was there for a while and we brought them to the Hacienda to see their mom and I never forgot it. So in *The Gettin Place*, the Kozy Komfort Inn was something I modeled after the Hacienda.

VV: Darnell Tucker, a young black firefighter, first made an appearance in a story in *Aquaboogie* entitled "Toe Up and Smoke Dreaming," resurfaces as the main character in *Blacker Than a Thousand Midnights*, and has a walk-on part in *Highwire Moon*. I love that he keeps coming back. Was his reappearance a deliberate choice, or is he simply one of the characters in the Rio Seco landscape, and that of your mind, and thus it's only natural for him to continue to be present in your books as well?

SS: Darnell is one of my favorite characters, and he was in a story I wrote when I was twenty—"Safe Hooptie," which ended up in the *North American Review* [published as "Two Days Gone"]. I waited patiently for his novel to come to me, and it did, and then when I was writing *Gettin Place,* he showed up during a crucial riot scene, along with his workers from Oaxaca. Same thing happened in *Highwire Moon*—I was aghast that Michael was stuck up there in the palm tree—that was one of the first scenes I ever wrote, when I was nineteen and first wrote what two decades later became the seeds for the novel—and didn't know how to get him down, and Darnell drove up. I was hella surprised, as we say here. Anyway, readers always ask about three recurring characters: Darnell, Marietta, and Nacho. I think that they are part of the landscape of my novels and my mind, permanently, like people I still see at Target whom I know from kindergarten.

VV: When we were talking earlier this morning, you said that people just tell you their stories. Do you ever have to reinterview them to get more details? I'm wondering how your stories seem so accurate, so believable. For example, in *Highwire Moon* when Serafina crosses the border to America to try to find her daughter, it struck me as impossible that you hadn't experienced that first-hand.

SS: I remember standing at the border, where they call it the soccer field, and watching hundreds of people running, and helicopter beams searching them out, and I imagined what that would be like, to be careening through those mazes of arroyos in the dust.

VV: Some people would ask why you stay in Riverside, especially since many places you pass by on a daily basis are reminders of something unfortunate that happened—the sound of the train is a reminder of your friend who walked in front of it, and you've said that when you drive up one street, you see some relatives and childhood friends doing things outside the law, marketing schemes you don't like to think about.

SS: Why do I stay? This is my home, my landscape, the trees and sky and rocks that I know, and when I was gone for two years, in graduate school in Amherst, I kept thinking I would write about snow and maples and bleeding hearts.

Instead, I missed tumbleweeds and chain-link and date palms and even the rustling sound the palm fronds make in the wind. They glisten—that's the only way I can put it—when they're high above you at night. I missed the language I knew from birth, rather than the more academic language I was learning then. I'm just a big chicken, face it, and I couldn't stay away from home.

Even now, I love to travel, but I miss dumb things like big tumbleweeds green-blue in the vacant lots. Like a huge quilt made by the Jolly Green Giant. And my whole family is here, and my parents come over every day, and who else would cook?

V.

Straight *drives to her ex-husband's neighborhood to retrieve a pot from a soul-food potluck that was held there the previous weekend ("100 people came that day—even ex-spouses and girlfriends—all of us still tied together") and then continues on to pick her daughters and their friends up from school and take them back to the house. Sitting on Straight's porch is like a scene out of* Aquaboogie*— neighbors pass by, and Straight and her children comment: "He's the one who's a math whiz"; "He's the one who got in trouble for drinking…" At least fifteen people—Straight's stepfather, her daughters' basketball coach, her kids' friends' parents, and neighbors—come and go over the course of an afternoon. The temperature in Riverside is so perfect you forget to notice it. The palm trees rise and line the street, and above them curve a row of much taller, thinner palm trees. Straight's daughters entertain themselves by looking through Straight's 1978 North High School yearbook; they go to school with many of Straight's former classmates' children.*

VV: I heard Joan Didion, who, like you, I consider a great California novelist, say that before she starts a novel, she always re-reads Conrad's *Victory.* Are there any novels that you read over and over again?

SS: Yes. Every year I read [Leslie Marmon Silko's] *Ceremony* and [Toni Morrison's] *Sula.* Dwayne used to tease me about this, and I'd say, "Aren't you watching that same John Wayne movie you know so well you can mouth the dialogue when they say it?"

When I was sixteen I read *Sula,* and that's how I figured out about dialogue, that in a book people could actually talk the way people I knew talked. And in *Sula,* that was so transforming when she describes the birthmark that's sometimes like a snake, like a rose, and sometimes something else. Then it's just the way she describes how people look. The girls [in that book] look one way and then, at thirty, Nel's skin had taken on the sheen of a maple struck down and sanded at the height of its green. And I was like, Wow!

And *Ceremony,* I didn't discover until I was in college. I was seventeen years old. It's a totally nonlinear story; it's all about the storytelling. And I was just amazed at the way the story circles around, and it's like five or six different people's story, it wasn't just the one person's story. They have all these different points of view, and the way she talks about the landscape—it's amazing. The main narrator is Tayo, and he's wounded. He's coming back from World War II. And he comes back to Laguna, New Mexico. He goes out to the desert and just the way that landscape is described, and the weather, and the smells of it, were amazing. And I was so obsessed with it that when Dwayne and I got married, and we were headed out to Oklahoma, to Tulsa, to stay with his great-aunt and uncle, I had to stop at Laguna to see what it looked like, and how it smelled. We got a flat tire and spent hours waiting for a repair, and Dwayne said, "This is what happens when you get off a freeway because of a book." I spent a long time there. I walked around town imagining the book.

VV: What do you think the difference is between a so-called male novel and a so-called female novel?

SS: It's something I've given a lot of thought to. Do you have any idea how long my friend Holly Robinson and I have spent talking about this subject? Oh, fifteen years! How come a woman writes a novel about a family, it's a domestic novel, but if a guy writes it, it's a great social novel?

Even if it's a big huge sweeping novel, if a novel has, at its center, a family, and it has a woman's name on it, then it's called a domestic novel. One of my favorite novelists in the world is Pat Barker, from England. She wrote that great trilogy: *The Eye in the Door, Regeneration,* and *The Ghost Road.* They're all about World War I. And she's written a lot of other novels too. She's one of the greatest social novelists there is. She writes about war in a social novel, and she writes about this family disintegrating under the pressures of someone who's mentally ill. Is it a domestic novel, or is it not still a social novel? And Leslie Marmon Silko—look at all the social issues tackled in not just *Ceremony* but her second one, *Almanac of the Dead.* It was this huge, Tom Wolfe, *Bonfire of the Vanities*–size book. How come when Tom Wolfe writes *Bonfire of the Vanities* it's a social novel?

It's that same thing I told you earlier: if a woman has had children, it's just assumed that she's incapable of doing these other things. If I don't write about mothers and children, and why this happens, or how this happens, who's going to grow up and read these novels? How come children are completely useless things? Who's going to grow up and read all those novels in ten years? Who's going to grow up and make those tires for your car? It's the same thing as saying I'm not writing novels for somebody who works at Kaiser Steel. But you don't know what those people do at Kaiser Steel—they might be reading your novels on their lunch break.

One of my favorite writers is A. Manette Ansay. She was an Oprah pick. A lot of those Oprah choices were great choices. She

SUSAN STRAIGHT & VENDELA VIDA

wrote *Vinegar Hill* and *Sister. Sister* is this great novel about...
a family! It's a boy whose sister watches him be too feminine, in a
sense, for the dad. And the boy ends up dead. Because of that,
really. How is that not a great social novel? It's the Midwest. It's the
entire Midwest contained in this family, and how they fall apart.

VV: You told me earlier that your middle daughter, Delphine, told
you about a boy in her class who touched a girl, uh, where she
didn't want to be touched. How'd you respond?

SS: I asked her what she was going to do if that happened to her,
and she asked, with this trace of malicious glee, "Can I hit him?"
I said, "No, 'cause then you'll get in trouble for fighting." And
I showed her how to throw that mean elbow that catches them
in the jaw and ear. I gave her the line to say after: "Oh, you star-
tled me, and I'm sorry you're bleeding now."

VI.

After dinner, Straight and all three daughters ("We travel in a
pack," she explains) scramble to get her oldest girl, Gaila, to
basketball practice. They lace up shoes, zip up jackets, and put
the dog on a leash. The sky outside is the kind of blue that makes you
want to make comparisons, and the street lamps light the undersides of the
palm trees. "We've got to hurry," Straight yells out. Gaila's coach is a former classmate of Straight's and he scolds her when they're late. "What's
your excuse?" he'll say to Straight. At the crosswalk, mother and daughters and dog wait, impatiently. The dog runs in a circle around their legs,
and they have to untangle themselves from the web of his leash. "Come
on," Gaila says to the light, to the sky. The chirping sounds signal that
the lights have changed. "OK," Straight yells. "Run!" ✷

GARY ZEBRUN

TALKS WITH

EDMUND WHITE

"I'VE CONDUCTED MY SOCIAL AND INTELLECTUAL LIFE ALMOST BY ACCIDENT AND IN THE MARGINS OF MY SEXUAL AMBITIONS."

Intellectual mentors:
Paul Goodman (though not for his writing)
Susan Sontag (though later they became enemies, alas)
Michel Foucault (though they seldom talked about ideas)

he first time I met Edmund White, I was twenty-six years old and he was the fifteen-year-old nameless narrator of A Boy's Own Story *(1982). Until then, my only glimpses of forbidden homosexual encounters in literature were the plague-filled streets of* Death in Venice *or the room at Peter Coffin's Spouter-Inn where Queequeg and Ishmael shared a bed at the start of* Moby-Dick. *In 1982, White's novel was a rare example of a story about a gay character whose struggle with his sexuality was at the heart of a piece of fiction.*

For all his notoriety among gay literary circles in this country, White truly crosses over on the other side of the Atlantic. In France, for more than

a decade, he's been a Chevalier de l'Ordre des Arts et des Lettres. He's as well known there and in England and Italy as his American contemporaries are recognized here: Philip Roth, Norman Mailer, John Updike, and Princeton colleague Joyce Carol Oates.

He has a trail of astonishing books (nearly two dozen) which include the great trilogy, A Boy's Own Story *(1982),* The Beautiful Room Is Empty *(1988), and* The Farewell Symphony *(1997); the giant* Genet: A Biography *(1993), which won a National Book Critics Circle Award; the little gem of a biography* Marcel Proust *(1999); the anguished AIDS love story* The Married Man *(2000); and even* The Joy of Gay Sex *(1977). His book of collected essays—*Arts and Letters*—was published by Cleis Press in the fall of 2004. His memoir,* My Lives, *will be published in January 2006.*

Edmund Valentine White III was born in Cincinnati in 1940 and moved to Evanston, Illinois, with his mother and sister after his parents divorced when he was seven years old. He graduated from the University of Michigan in Ann Arbor in 1962 and moved to New York City. For decades, when he wasn't living in Paris or Rome, he was a writer for Time-Life Books, a senior editor at the Saturday Review, *and a teacher at Johns Hopkins, Columbia, Yale, Brown, George Mason, Temple, and New York universities.*

These days, at sixty-five, he lives in Manhattan's Chelsea district and teaches creative writing at Princeton University. He travels widely and voraciously explores a landscape of cultures that, at a time when America seems so obsessed with itself, makes him a marvel in the quest for passion and engaging art. —G.Z. *(Spring 2005)*

GARY ZEBRUN: In 1983, shortly after *A Boy's Own Story* was released, in an interview with Don Swaim, a New York City radio talk show host, you said that you sensed a thousand gay men struggling with their sexuality were watching over your shoulders while you were writing the novel. There was a touch of embarrassment in your voice. Now, more than twenty years later, how do you feel knowing that you are a literary icon?

EDMUND WHITE: You and I both know that literary celebrity, even when it's of a brighter magnitude than mine, pales beside that of movie stars, politicians, and television and sports personalities. If I'm an icon it's a very small, dark one in the corner of the chapel without even a single candle guttering before it. That said, I must confess that I have always felt it was the greatest good luck to be published at all much less read by my small band of patient, faithful, knowing readers. As for my status in the gay community, I am well known enough to be asked what I think of gay marriage, for instance, though I seldom have an opinion about politics that is more interesting than anyone else's.

What I do like is the feeling that gay people are still figuring out who they are and that fiction is the best—virtually the only!—public place for exploring questions of ethics and identity and destiny. My chance has been to be a part of that dialogue for three decades.

GZ: Well, shaping a dialogue, whether it's cultural or social, is pretty political, I think. Your nephew Keith Fleming recently wrote *Original Youth: The Real Story of Edmund White's Boyhood*. In the introduction, David Leavitt is struck by the young White to whom it was "self-evident that the world was very phony (as well as heartless, deluded, and selfish)," and how "this deep-seated distrust of humanity throws interesting light on his subsequent aloofness from political concerns." Funny, even though you say you seldom have an opinion about politics that's different from anyone else's, I don't see the detachment from politics in your fiction, even in the fiercely "autobiographical" work. And in *Fanny* one of its astonishing strengths is its political satire. So are you a "closet" political or social activist, even though you don't march in the streets?

EW: I guess I think of myself as political though I've never voted once in my life. In *The Farewell Symphony* the narrator isn't interested in Watergate since he thinks of the American government as "their" government, certainly not his as a gay man. I suppose it's difficult for young gays to understand, but in the '50s and early '60s, when I was coming out, there was very little sense of a coherent gay community. We used to say that if we were leaving a gay cruising place and it caught on fire we'd just keep on walking and not look back. That double alienation—from a cold, self-hating world of gay men and from a violently disapproving dominant culture—certainly scotched any nascent sense of political involvement and responsibility.

To be sure, at the University of Michigan I hung out with Tom Hayden and the authors of the *Port Huron Statement* and I thought of myself as a radical, at the very least a socialist. But by 1971 I had the brilliant Simon Karlinsky, a Russian expatriate, nipping at my heels and attempting to force me to face up to the horrors of the Soviet regime. He gave me Nadezhda Mandelstam's *Hope Against Hope* to read, although it took me another ten years to wake up to historical reality. Now we know that many more people were tortured and killed in the name of socialism than by the fascists, but that recognition was a long time coming. I was as guilty of blindness of that sort as other so-called leftists of my generation in America.

So much for politics in the old sense. In the newer acceptation of the personal-is-political I've certainly always felt that my books had a political dimension. I felt that I was showing in my trilogy, for instance, the deforming power of the Eisenhower years, the heady sexual liberation of the 1960s, the New York artistic effervescence of the 1970s, and the debacle of AIDS in the '80s—and in my case a flight to Europe. Since I am at least as interested in sociology and class analysis as I am in psychology, a "political" approach to styles of life comes to me naturally.

GZ: These days, I often feel like flying off to Europe and staying there, though I'm not sure, as an American, I'd be very welcomed. You're one of the few American writers of your generation who has spent enormous chunks of time abroad, and your affection for places such as France and Italy is a wonderful force in your fiction. In *The Farewell Symphony* the narrator on the eve of returning home from Rome says, "An English guy had tears in his eyes... He told me he was sad to be going home. As an American I was used to the idea that 'home' was superior to everywhere else (richer, more powerful, trend-setting)... Suddenly I saw that for an American travel abroad is always a form of slumming." Tell me a bit about your passion for places outside the United States and the necessity for you to return home.

EW: It's true that I've known Scots in Crete and Dutch in Spain and they would never dream of returning to their cold, rainy countries full of spotty countenances and tepid beer and limp french fries. To be sure, I've also known Americans in Paris who refused to speak English and who had thoroughly replaced their American with Gallic souls. But that sort of "traitor" is rare among Americans. We love our country or at least feel that it is setting world standards. These days, of course, the standards can be downward trends—towards isolationism, military intervention, a two-tiered society of very rich and poor getting poorer, of inadequate medical care, polluted environment, declining academic levels, even inadequate nutrition.

Even so, America for a working writer remains a great artistic environment. We may not worship art as Europeans do, but at least we make a lot of it; America has bad readers but great writers, just as France right now has great readers but few good writers. America is so complex, violent, inassimilable, raw, and religious that it never bores an observer nor comes entirely clean in any social analysis.

A punk kid once interviewed me on British television and said, "Mr. White, you are known as an American, a writer, and a homosexual. When did you first discover you were an American?" My answer: "When I moved to Paris." Like many cultured Americans of my generation I wanted to impress Europeans with how civilized I could be, speaking foreign languages, knowing how to kiss a hand, daringly sexual in conversation but otherwise markedly discreet, etc. We wanted to jump through all those golden European hoops. We wanted to be "polished." Now I feel most at home with other Europeanized Americans. We can laugh at French humorlessness and trumpeting American voices, remark on the lack of a French word for "name dropping" or an American word for "*frileux*" (sensitive to the cold), etc. Certainly living in two languages (French and English) made me much more self-conscious about language than ever before. The French insist on clarity, have an allergy to figurative language, appreciate a simple style devoid of slang, and some of those predilections have worked their way into my prose.

GZ: In many of your novels, as Robert Lowell or William Carlos Williams did in their poetry, you draw your characters and narratives from an autobiographical well. If anyone asked me, I'd say you're really a devilish manipulator. I'm always surprised when critics or book reviewers confuse your sources of material with plain confessional writing. In the essay "Nabokov's Passion" you write about his "particular delight to invent sinister or insane or talentless versions of himself, characters who are at least in part mocking anticipations of naïve readers' suspicions about the real Nabokov." I wonder, does this also describe the way you treat your own life in those novels, such as the trilogy, that appear so autobiographical?

EW: I'm a good deal less playful than Nabokov. A lot more prim and serious. More devoted to the truth as I conceive of it than to beauty. At the same time I am always conscious of the reader's response to my work, which means that in my autobiographical fiction I have made my first-person teenage stand-in a bit less precocious sexually and intellectually than I really was; I wanted people to identify with the young hero of *A Boy's Own Story*. At the same time I dared to end the book with the boy's betraying the only adult man who has accommodated his sexuality, and that stroke certainly turned off many readers, not to mention potential film-makers. I suppose at every moment of writing for me there is a trade-off between my desire to woo the reader and my debt to the truth (in real life I did betray a prep-school teacher, and I wanted to acknowledge that dark stain on my youth). As the trilogy moves through time I suppose I was willing to take on board more of my real experience and complex personality. For one thing a gay man who is thirty in 1970 will be entirely different from a gay man who is thirty in 2000. If childhood—at least middle-class suburban childhood—sometimes feels timeless and "universal," adulthood is far more inflected by the contemporary setting and moment.

GZ: Yes, I love the way you almost effortlessly portray the actual moment of your life in much of your work. In the Nabokov essay you discuss the philosopher Theodor Adorno's defense of the artist's attention to experience, to the concrete. You point out that Adorno said "the universality of beauty can communicate itself to the subject in no other way than in an obsession with the partic-ular." In *The Farewell Symphony,* the nameless narrator puts it this way: "The writer's vanity holds that everything that happens to him is material. He views everything from a distance and even when the cops arrest him for sucking a cock through a glory hole, he smiles faintly and thinks, 'Idea for Story.'" So talk about steal-ing parts of your narratives straight from life.

EW: Right now I'm living through the most painful moment in my romantic life that I've known since I was in my twenties. Even though I cry all the time, can't sleep and talk to myself, forget things and respond emotionally to the most inappropriate cues, nevertheless I'm taking notes of my moods and quirks, since in the past I failed to map out the shape of a broken heart—its strategies and lies and illusory victories. Probably when I'm lowered into the grave I'll still be writing, "Idea for Story."

I've been influenced by the theater and actors all my life, and the prevailing doctrine of my day (and still today) was Stanislavski's. He puts a great emphasis on the impossibility for an actor to body forth any emotion at all unless he can find a concrete example of it in his own memories. Maybe an actor has never lost someone close but he can still remember a devastating parting or the death of a pet or something. He must recreate that memory within himself not by going directly for the emotion but by feeling his way into the sensory recollections of the setting—the unclean feeling of the velvet upholstery, the depressing smell of carbolic acid, the look of a fluorescent light behind shutters.

In *Fanny* I wanted to write about Mrs. Trollope's affair with an escaped slave. Fortunately I've had the experience of submitting my aging white body to the frequent attentions of a black athlete I've known for the last three years—with a few substitutions, voila! There are things I wouldn't dare to describe (childbirth, for instance) unless I accompanied a woman friend through the whole process, *et encore...*

GZ: I'm shifting gears here, but I know you love the work of Marcel Proust and Jean Genet, one bourgeois and the other iconoclastic. Is this a tension that fuels your imagination?

EW: If Proust is bourgeois he's also gay and half-Jewish (Jews would say all-Jewish since his mother was a Jew). He publicly denied both affiliations; he fought a duel to clear his name of the slur that he was gay and when a newspaper listed him among promising young Jewish writers he stiffly reminded the editors that he was a baptized Catholic. In *Remembrance of Things Past* the Narrator is very Old France and Catholic and one of the few men left standing at the conclusion as an uncompromised hetero. I contend that Proust's constant lying to his friends and readers—his unending transpositions of men into women, Sodom into Gomorrah, illicit gay sex into illicit affairs with "butcher girls"—that all these lies trained his memory and imagination and made him a great writer. It's precisely in the ten thousand passages where he lies that he is most creative.

If Genet is iconoclastic (and he was), he inverts Catholicism to create his own devil-worship, he crowns his drag queens with a tiara of ripped-out dentures in a ceremony worthy of the Cathedral of Reims, he describes a thug's penis with words worthy of Racine. (Once, to a cute boy he was trying to pick up, he improvised a pun on Phaedra's line, "O Prince, I languish, I die for Theseus.")

GZ: Maybe that's why gays love to tell stories; like Proust, we've all lied about our sexuality at one time or another. God, I lied about it until I was forty. I'm curious: I've heard you say you were interested in reinventing, much in the way you reimagined Fanny Trollope, a gay companion piece that Stephen Crane had written to *Maggie: A Girl in the Streets* but was forced to destroy by his editor. I've read that some literary scholars believe Crane spent his life suppressing his homosexuality. You've been so utterly open about yours for so long. Why are you interested in Crane?

EW: Was Crane gay? I've never heard that before. It wasn't his editor but his friends who insisted he destroy the manuscript to *Flowers of Asphalt*. No, I'm more impressed by Crane's kind of naturalism that led him to want to document homosexual prostitution despite the social onus against it. In the end he chickened out, but even his initial attempt was very daring. I subscribe to the constructivist notion that homosexuality is invented anew by each epoch, and I'm eager to imagine what it could have been like in the suddenly burgeoning big-city excitement of New York in the 1880s, a moment when the old don't-ask-don't-tell silence about sodomy was giving way to a new sociological descriptiveness about "vice."

GZ: Well, you never chicken out about painting the vibrant underground of gay life. You celebrate it, even when it's touched by so much loss. The nameless narrator in *The Beautiful Room Is Empty* says, "The appeal of gay life for me was that it provided so many glancing contacts with other men." Some people, especially straight people, think the gay experience is filled with passionless promiscuity. That's garbage, isn't it? Can't a multitude of glancing contacts be a kind of love? Evanescent maybe, but still love?

EW: A key experience for me was when I was in my twenties and I'd go to the "meat rack" on Fire Island between the Pines and the Grove. It would be two or three in the morning, the surf was pounding on the beach just beyond the dunes, the stars would be swirling because I'd drunk too many gin tonics, a fog would be floating over the scrub brush and wind-trained trees, my calf muscles would be tired from walking so far off the path and into the sand—and up ahead someone would be sending signals with the pulsing end of his cigarette. Then suddenly there he would be, wrapped around me, my hands full of hard dick and soft skin, his finger pushing up inside me, our mouths exchanging smoke and saliva... Soon we'd be three or four but as the daylight began to crack the code of the night's secrets I'd be lying in the sand next to that first all-blond whose weary, happy face was now developing like a photo in the pan to reveal the little aerodynamic lines around his eyes, the sheen on his well-kissed lips, the scribble of blond hair around his absurdly small dark nipples...

Oh, those were the days, and if all that was anonymous sex (technically it was) then I can only say it was more powerful and poetic than what goes on in any marriage bed.

GZ: Yes, powerful and poetic and one of the loveliest pieces of erotic remembrance that I've heard. Proust would approve. I'm a bit jealous you celebrated your sexuality so young and made so many gay friends. Your fiction possesses a dizzying patchwork of friendships. In your latest novel Fanny Trollope obsessively wants to befriend others, particularly Fanny Wright, but she ends up disappointed and alone again. Can you discuss the importance of friends in your life and how they intersect in sustaining or melancholy ways in your work? And I suppose we're coming to a close, so let me ask one of those final, stupid interview questions, which you can ignore: If you could have dinner with three or four other writers long gone from this earth, who would be at the table?

EW: I've never been very interested in celebrities, not even in meeting celebrated writers. When I was in my twenties, however, there were two New York writers I longed to meet—Paul Goodman (*Growing Up Absurd*), who's now long dead and largely forgotten, and Susan Sontag, who much later became a friend for a couple of years before we became enemies, alas. In both cases I was hoping they'd help me to get published. In my daydreams they'd read me, see the merit, and miraculously open doors for me. In fact, when I did know Sontag fifteen years later she did help me to get a Guggenheim and an award from the American Academy of Arts and Letters, and she wrote a blurb for *A Boy's Own Story* (which eventually she demanded I remove from the cover of subsequent editions).

I wasn't particularly interested in Goodman's writing, though his diary *Five Years* was an early gay confession about the exciting artistic and sexual milieu that was developing in New York in the late '60s and throughout the '70s. Sontag's writing, on the other hand, always fascinated me, and thanks to her I became interested in Roland Barthes and Artaud. Her terse, impacted style—so different from the flowing, easygoing belletristic essays that preceded hers in America—demanded concentration and invited genuine intellectual participation from the reader.

Now I am well past the stage of having literary crushes of that sort. I don't expect anyone to take me up and make me better known. Foucault in the early '80s was perhaps the last vital intellectual idol of my life, though we seldom talked about ideas and I never wanted him to "help" me. Other French friends have meant a great deal to me: Marie-Claude de Brunhoff, one of my two or three best friends, who introduced me into all the closely packed circuitry of Paris social and cultural life. Albert Dichy, who helped me with the research for the Genet biography and who is one of the few people I've ever known who is always rethinking virtually every question. To listen to him is to hear a first-class mind at work. Nor does all this work exclude a wild and boyish sense of humor. He is the ideal companion. Then there is Chantal Thomas, a new friend whom I've met since leaving Paris though she is a Parisian. Chantal, who has written a remarkable novel about Marie-Antoinette (*Farewell, My Queen*), is someone who is a pure pleasure to be with. She is responsive as much as she is stimulating. She knows everything but is never guilty of pedantry—and she, too, like Albert Dichy, never repeats herself.

I have spent so much of my life pursuing handsome men, like a bloodhound led on by the odor of sperm, that I've conducted my social and intellectual life almost by accident and in the margins of my sexual ambitions. Nevertheless friendship has brought me as much pleasure as sex or love, though friendship is a mild pleasure, neither addictive nor a good subject for obsessiveness. Many of my friends, of course, are ex-lovers. I've seldom broken with anyone who was ever important to me sexually. Since my main erotic emotion is gratitude, even the dim remains of this feeling are a good basis for friendship, which combines complicity with admiration.

I feel I've learned nothing about "life," that is, how to have a good one. As a novelist I distrust general ideas and moral conclusions. The realm of fiction is all about morality—the testing of conflicting values, the staging of competing claims—but I would never want to reduce those conflicts to a message, an endorsement.

As for that dinner party—I guess I'd be most excited if I knew I'd be spending it with three or four (or just one!) young men who'd like me. Moody, difficult, affectionate guys. ✶

MILES MARSHALL LEWIS

TALKS WITH

AUGUST WILSON

"BLUES IS THE BEDROCK OF EVERYTHING
I DO. ALL THE CHARACTERS IN MY PLAYS,
THEIR IDEAS AND THEIR ATTITUDES,
THE STANCE THAT THEY ADOPT IN
THE WORLD, ARE ALL IDEAS AND ATTITUDES
THAT ARE EXPRESSED IN THE BLUES."

Favorite play topics:
Love
Honor
Duty
Betrayal
Ex-enslaved people who sell dog shit

n *May 10, 1988, I met my Bronx high school's black alliance club at the 46th Street Theatre, a shrink-wrapped copy of* Lovesexy *(released that day) tucked under my arm. Amazingly, Prince was the last thing on my mind after more than two hours of* Fences *(1986), August Wilson's Pulitzer Prize–winning play—a riveting treatise on a father-and-son conflict over their visions of black identity.* Fences *was my first taste of Wilson's ongoing drama cycle, which encompasses the black experience in each decade of the twentieth century. Enthralled by Wilson's blues-tinged voice, I followed his subsequent successes:* Joe Turner's Come and Gone *(1988),* The Piano Lesson

(1990), Two Trains Running *(1992),* Seven Guitars *(1996),* King Hedley II *(2005), and revivals of* Jitney *(2001) and* Ma Rainey's Black Bottom *(1985).*

Born Frederick August Kittel in Pittsburgh, Pennsylvania, in an impoverished neighborhood known as the Hill, the playwright was one of six siblings. Dropping out of high school after a teacher's racist accusation that he had plagiarized a paper, Wilson soon became a poet under the inspirational aegis of Dylan Thomas and Amiri Baraka. He began writing plays in the 1970s after a brief stint with the Black Horizons Theatre. Ma Rainey's Black Bottom *caught the attention of Dean Lloyd Richards at the Yale School of Drama in 1982, which led Wilson to the Great White Way. He swiftly kicked its ass: the playwright has been awarded a Pulitzer Prize and a Tony Award for* Fences *and another Pulitzer and Tony nomination for* The Piano Lesson *(1990).*

Outdoors at an Au Bon Pain in Boston, the fifty-nine-year-old Wilson took a break from rehearsing a pre-Broadway production of his latest play, Gem of the Ocean. *Lighting Marlboro Lights proved difficult under the chilly, gusty wind as we bound from the blues to hiphop, Bearden to Basquiat, and beyond.*   *—M.M.L. (Summer 2004)*

I. "I THINK THAT'S THE CORE OF BLACK AESTHETICS: THE ABILITY TO IMPROVISE."

MILES MARSHALL LEWIS: Despite the similarities between *Fences* and *Death of a Salesman,* and the art of playwriting as a predominantly white discipline, you've cited your greatest literary influence as poet/playwright Amiri Baraka. How would you say he influenced you?

AUGUST WILSON: I'm not sure what they say about *Fences* as it relates to *Death of a Salesman.* At the time I wrote *Fences,* I had not read *Death of a Salesman,* had not seen *Death of a Salesman,* did not know anything about *Death of a Salesman.*

My greatest influence has been the blues. And that's a literary influence, because I think the blues is the best literature that we as

410

black Americans have. My interest in Baraka comes from the '60s and the Black Power movement. So it's more for Baraka's political ideas, which I loved and still am an exponent of. Through all those years I was a follower, if you will, of Baraka. He had an influence on my thinking.

MML: Were you exposed first to his poetry or his plays?

AW: The poetry in particular. The book called *Black Magic,* which is sort of a collection of several books. That's '69—I wore that book out, the cover got taped up with Scotch tape, the pages falling out. That was my bible, I carried it wherever I went. So that in particular. I wasn't writing plays back then, so I wasn't influenced by his playwriting—although, to me, his best plays are collected in a book called *Four Black Revolutionary Plays,* with *Madheart, Great Goodness of Life, A Black Mass,* and *Experimental Death Unit 1.* They contributed a lot to my thinking just in terms of getting stuff on the page.

MML: How specifically was the blues an influence on your work?

AW: Blues is the bedrock of everything I do. All the characters in my plays, their ideas and their attitudes, the stance that they adopt in the world, are all ideas and attitudes that are expressed in the blues. If all this were to disappear off the face of the earth and some people two million unique years from now would dig out this civilization and come across some blues records, working as anthropologists, they would be able to piece together who these people were, what they thought about, what their ideas and attitudes toward pleasure and pain were, all of that. All the components of culture. Just like they do with the Egyptians, they piece together all that stuff. And all you need is the blues. So to me the blues is the book, it's the bible, it's everything.

MML: Baraka himself said that if you want to know where black people are at any point in our sojourn in this wilderness of America, listen to the music of that period.

AW: Yeah!

MML: Your characters also often riff off of each other like jazz musicians, particularly in *Seven Guitars*. Your work in general is like improvising on a theme: the life of Southern blacks who migrated to the North in the twentieth century. How has jazz impacted your creative process?

AW: I think that's the core of black aesthetics: the ability to improvise. That is what has enabled our survival. I came to jazz late, man. I wasn't interested in jazz. I remember guys walking around with John Coltrane, Archie Shepp albums under their arm and I go, "Aw, man, it ain't got no words!" If it didn't have any words, I wasn't that interested.

All that changed on an October night in 1966 when I came up on Kirkpatrick and Wylie Avenue in Pittsburgh and saw about two hundred people standing out on the corner, which was unusual. The first thing I thought was that somebody got killed. [*Laughter*] So I run down there and I say, "Hey, man, what's happening?" and they go, "Shhh!" And they were listening to John Coltrane out of the Crawford Grill, you see. And the people inside the Crawford Grill—cause the drinks cost ninety cents, in '66 that's a lot of money—the people inside, they don't even know how to spell John Coltrane's name. They inside talking about what they gonna do Friday night and so-and-so's cousin got a new Lincoln Continental, you see. John Coltrane ain't playing to them, man, he playing to the brothers out on the street, cause the music's coming straight out over their heads and out on the street. And the brothers outside, they prayin. This is their music. This is what has enabled them to survive these outrageous insults that American society has forced on them.

So when I saw two hundred niggas stunned into silence by the power of art in the music of John Coltrane and his exploration of man's relation to the divinity, that's when I got interested in jazz. And also, as a young man wanting to be a writer, I said, This is what I want my art to do. I want to accomplish that. I can't say I went out and found me some John Coltrane, cause I didn't have no record player. [*Laughter*] But I did perk up and I started paying attention at the jazz club. We had a guy named Kenny Fisher in Pittsburgh, he played saxophone. I just got more interested.

Other than just improvisation and being a master of the power of black aesthetic, I can't really say I've been influenced by jazz, although I've come to it late. I've been trying to catch up, man. Charlie Mingus?

MML: Mingus is a master.

AW: Yeah, baby.

MML: I got to see Miles Davis twice as a teenager, at the JVC Jazz Festival at Avery Fisher Hall. Seeing my namesake before he passed away was a very big deal. I know *The Piano Lesson* was directly influenced by the Romare Bearden painting of the same name, and that also his *Miss Bertha and Mr. Seth* and *Millhand's Lunch Basket* were on your mind in creating *Joe Turner's Come and Gone*. How did Bearden come to you?

AW: With Bearden, there was a book called *The Prevalence of Ritual*. Bearden painted a lot of collages. He was painting a collage of rituals attendant to everyday life: burials, funerals, and things of that sort. Bearden, I know he spent some time in Pittsburgh, his maternal grandmother lived in Pittsburgh then. I look at them collages, I know everybody in there! [*Laughter*] Ah, there's my uncle, yeah, that's Charlie, there's Dick over there. They even look like em. It was the first time that I'd encountered art that was black America in all its fullness, its richness. And it wasn't sentimental. It wasn't that "Aww, we sufferin." It was like, "We're the people, we're here, we're vibin and this here."

I said, I want to make my plays the equal of one of them canvases. Put Bearden here and put Wilson up there. I'm not a painter but I want to be able to hang in the same gallery with him, man.

And then someone asked Bearden about his art. He said, "I try to explore in terms of the life I know best those things which are common to all culture." So I go, the commonalities of all culture within the life I know best—which is black life, that's who I am— I'm gonna express that. That's what I want my art to be about. This is the way *we* do things. We all bury our dead, we all have parties, we all decorate our houses, but we do it different. And it ain't nothin wrong with it.

I watched, in a bus station in downtown St. Paul, these four Japanese guys have breakfast. They sat there and chatted politely among themselves. One of em got up and took pictures. Now I found out from their conversation that they were taking Greyhound across the country to California to go to college. They can all afford to fly first class but they takin a bus, they havin adventure, to have some fun. So when the bill came, they all reached for their American Express cards to pay the bill. They paid the bill and they left.

So I asked myself, if it had been four black guys in here having breakfast, what would be the difference? The first thing I noticed is that there's a jukebox there. It never occurred to any of these four Japanese guys to play the jukebox. But four black guys walk in, the first thing they do, *some*body going to go over to the jukebox and put a quarter in, right? The other guy gonna come and say, "Hey man, play so-and-so!" "I ain't playin with you, man. Put your own money in!" So he ain't gonna play his music, right? The second thing I noticed, nobody said nothing to the waitress. The four black guys, I don't care what she look like, somebody gonna say something to her. "Hey baby, how you doin?" "Look here, mama, what's your phone number?" They gonna do that, right? "Nah, nah, don't talk to him, he can't read, blah blah." And then the guy gonna get up to play another song, somebody gonna steal a piece of bacon off his plate, and he's gonna come back and say, "Hey man, I ain't playin with y'all, man, quit messin with my food." Other than that, when the time comes for the bill, it's that, "Leroy, lend me two dollars, man." Right? It's just the way we do it.

Now, somebody sitting over here would say, "They don't like each other. The guy didn't let him play the record, he stole some food off his plate, they harassed the waitress." So to them, the way you do things is all wrong. If you bring four white guys in, they'll do it differently than the Japanese and the black guys. What white America does, it accepts the way the Japanese does it. It accepts the way the Czechs from the Czech Republic might do things different. But blacks are supposed to act like them; they say, "Y'all still ain't learned how to do things."

MML: As a hypothetical, how do you think the artwork of Jean-Michel Basquiat might affect your plays?

AW: I suspect it would be closer to what we moving toward, which is [a] hiphop play. If he had been around in the '60s when I was twenty-three, twenty-four—a young man searching for the world—I'm sure I would've embraced that much more than when I was forty-five and coming to know his work. It's a different person coming to know his work, and I'm already trying to absorb these other influences. But I could see somebody being influenced by him, and the best way to say what it would be like is: it would look like them paintings. And I'm trying to make my stuff look like Bearden's paintings, the literary equivalent of that. I hear more and more hiphop plays being written. And they're written in poetry, they're written in verse, they're written in rhyme the same way you do a lyric. Only now, it's a larger canvas and we gonna tell the story; instead of using the three-minute thing here, we're gonna use a larger canvas. And I encourage that. There gotta be a future, and it can't be what it is now cause you gotta build on a present and keep moving and going down. It's supposed to be something that you can't think of now. That's part of life, man.

II. "TO ME, HIPHOP IS WHAT I CALL THE SPIRITUAL FIST OF THE CULTURE. THAT'S PROOF THAT THE [BLACK] CULTURE'S STRONG, ROBUST, INVENTIVE."

MML: What do you imagine the influence of hiphop might be on your work?

AW: I don't think it's any different than a blues influence or a jazz influence, because it's just an extension of music. It's just another way of doing it. You couldn't have hiphop unless you had Charlie Patton and Skip James and Sun House and all the rest of them. Although it is different; I recognize that, man. I recall when Baraka and the Black Power poets of the '60s tried to wed jazz in poetry. And, see, that didn't work, because it didn't have the beat. You have to have the beat. The blues and poetry are closer than the jazz and poetry. To me, hiphop is what I call the spiritual fist of the culture. That's proof that the [black] culture's strong, robust, inventive. That's not saying we ain't got some problems. I mean, it's the way we used to do with some of them lyrics and whatnot… [*Laughter*] But I look past that and I go, yeah, now we're here, we're strong, we're alive, we're robust, we're inventive, and we still doin it. That's proof of that. So I embrace it.

MML: Whose decision was it to put some Public Enemy into your last play, *King Hedley II*, which took place in the '80s?

AW: That's the director, Marion McClinton, that was his choice. I think it was not so much they were big in the '80s but what that particular song ["Fight the Power"] said as a relationship to the character, King.

MML: I've got a quote from you here that says, "If I were going to write a play set in 1980, I would go and listen to the music, particularly music that blacks are making, and find out what their ideas and attitudes are about the situation, and about the time in which they live." What music did you eventually listen to while writing *King Hedley II?*

AW: Blues. [*Laughter*] I said that, but I did not do that. All the ideas and attitudes that hiphop generation people in the '80s had, that's where they got it from. They got it from they daddies, it was rooted here. So I really didn't have to do that. I listened to Tupac. Relative to my blues collection, I got a small hiphop collection, or what I call "rap collection." It's not my favorite music; blues is favorite. I pay attention, keep my ear to the ground. I do recognize what's going on. I'm trying to think: I know I listened to Tupac back then, but still, basically, I thought the core impulse of people is still coming out of the blues. So I tried to make the other elements of my play reflect the '80s more.

People say, "Well, you writin a play in 1911 and you weren't alive in 1911. Did you do any research?" I say, I don't do research. They say, "Well, how do you know?" Because the plays ultimately are about love, honor, duty, betrayal—what I call the Big Themes. So you could set it in the '80s and make use of various things, but you're telling a story that is using the Big Themes. It's a love story, *King Hedley II.* It's a lot of things. It's really jam-packed, with King as a Christ figure, there's a lot of little ideas that I was working on in there, or echoes and suggestions of.

MML: What else is in your rap collection?

AW: Wu-Tang Clan. I got Snoop, his first album. People give me some over the years. I got some Biggie.

MML: There was a controversy in 1990 over an article you wrote about turning down director Barry Levinson to direct a film of *Fences.* You wanted a black director, which raised the question: can whites master a black style? That said, what's your opinion, if any, of Eminem? Do you think he's capable of mastering the black aesthetic of hiphop?

AW: Yeah. He's imitatin, he ain't creatin. There's a very big distinction. He's not an innovator. He can't create in that style, so everything he do is just imitatin. Anybody can imitate anybody.

MML: I've read someone say, "Sure, whites can box like Muhammad Ali, once they see him do it."

AW: The same thing with jazz. Benny Goodman could play jazz, but they ain't creatin no music, they not innovators. So the music, it's gotta be there for you to step into it. I wanna see you create it; it would be something different. Different aesthetics at work. But you can be influenced by, you can imitate anything. Got some Japanese guys that play some great jazz. Man, they really good, too! It's already been done, man.

MML: Many of your plays deal with the disconnect between the vantage point of different generations, in their respective ways of reading society. Do you find a correlation between that and this year's controversial comments from Bill Cosby that were critical of black youth?

AW: Let me say, first of all, I did not hear the comments, I hear people talking about them. My understanding of it is that he went on a tirade against poor black people. I say, if you want to go on a tirade, there's a whole lot of things to go on a tirade about other than poor black people, starting with the systemic conditions that create these poor black people. I have an uncle who lived in America and died in America, seventy-three years, was born a poor man and died a poor man. How is this possible when they comin over with two cents and become multimillionaires?

There's a reason why. Of course, the reason is he's black, and the opportunities, truncated possibility, etc. Let's go on a tirade about the United States Department of Agriculture, which admittedly discriminated against black farmers by denying them loans over the course of sixty years. So it's not one individual secretary of agriculture. It happened to be the same sixty years while this other hand [of government] over here is signing laws against discrimination, this other hand over here is fighting war against poverty, while they over there systematically denying these black farmers loans until the farms come down from $1,200,000 to $3,000. They go, "Oh, we've been discriminating against you, here's what we'll do: we'll offer you a settlement," which the *Washington Post* called a mere pittance, of $50,000. The average value of the farm is $500,000. And then, you look up two years later, they gotta fight like hell to get their $50,000. They've denied over 50 percent of the claims, they spent over $12,000,000 fighting the claims. Let's go on a tirade against *that*. Let's see what happens. Because you take the white farmer who was given the loan and track him down: his farm is now worth $5,000,000, he's now a productive member of society all them years. The black guy has to go drive a truck, drive a cab, do something to stay alive, and all because of discrimination.

Now was the secretary of the Department of Agriculture fired from his job? No. Was there an outrage about this? No. When they said they were gonna change the anchor on NPR, 17,000 people called up and they were mad about it because they're getting a different anchor on the goddamn radio. It's America—why didn't 17,000 Americans step forward and say, "No, we don't want that in America, we don't want discrimination"? Let's go on a tirade about that. And after we finish going on all these tirades, eventually we goin to get to wanna tirade about the way niggas act and the way they don't speak correct English and etc. My point is, there are systemic causes for that, so let's look at the causes. I have a special problem with a billionaire beating up on people because they poor.

III. "I CAN'T APPROACH [MY FEMALE CHARACTERS] ANY DIFFERENT THAN I HAVE, MAN, CAUSE ALL MY WOMEN ARE INDEPENDENT."

MML: What is *Gem of the Ocean* about?

AW: Love, honor, duty, betrayal. [*Laughter*]

MML: Well, how about a "plot synopsis"?

AW: There was a man who arrives at Aunt Esther's house seeking. He's in spiritual conflict. Then you find out that there's a man accused of stealing a bucket of nails from the local tin mill; he runs and jumps in the river and stays there till he drown. The people in the mill is upset about it, right? The whole plot point is about this bucket of nails and why the man drowned in the river rather than to come out the river and take his thirty days and admit to something he didn't do. He'd rather die in truth than live a lie.

Then we come to find out that the guy who arrives at the house of Aunt Esther, Aunt Esther takes him on a journey on a magic boat to a place called the City of Bones in the middle of the Atlantic Ocean, which is a half-mile by half-mile. It's a beautiful city unlike anything you've ever seen. The city is built of the bones of the Africans who were lost in the Middle Passage. So he traces his journey back on a boat, essentially on a slave ship, to the City of Bones, where he discovers a way for him to redeem himself. He takes that road to redemption. I don't want to say any more cause I don't wanna give the plot away [*laughter*], but that's what it's about.

MML: You set *Joe Turner's Come and Gone* in 1911 to take advantage of the African retentions of the characters. How do those retentions play out in *Gem of the Ocean*?

AW: When I set *Joe Turner* in 1911… In school, I was taught to start counting [decades] at one. So I put 1911, I'm working on my 1920s play, and my wife said, "What about the aught years?" And I go, "What?" And she say, "The aught years, the zero years." Then I realized I had another decade to do [*laughter*] and it was even prior to 1911. That would be the one that was closest to Africa, so I had to find a way to do that, and that's where Aunt Esther—who is 285 years old at that point—and the City of Bones come from. Because anyone who was like forty-seven years old in 1904 was born in slavery.

For instance, one of the cats is a runaway slave and he made it up to Canada. Instead of staying up there, he joins the Underground Railroad. He took sixty-two people there and now he's walking the streets of Pittsburgh trying to find something to do. He actually collects dog shit and he sells it, it's called "pure." The shoemakers use it to patent leather and all that kind of stuff too. He found a way. So this is what's happening in 1904. You got a lot of people wandering around who were ex-slaves, born in slavery—he was twenty years old when he ran away—so it's very close.

MML: Is that true? Did Africans escaping enslavement sell dog shit?

AW: The pure collectors? Well, in Europe they did that. There were pure collectors in Europe. I don't know about the United States, but I figured...

MML: Do you have an opinion about hiphop actors on Broadway? In the past few years we've seen Sean Combs in the revival of *A Raisin in the Sun,* Mos Def in *Topdog/Underdog,* and Mary J. Blige off-Broadway in *The Exonerated.*

AW: They were actors, right? They were actors who were hired to do the role and they did that, right? I don't have any problem with that. As a matter of fact, they did the *Def Poetry Jam on Broadway.* So when you look up there's gonna be like forty, fifty of em. Somebody should put them in the same play.

MML: Somebody should. [*Laughs*]

AW: I am aware that some of the actors have a problem: "They're in our thing and they just come in and do this..." That's who they hired to do it, man. Let him stand or fall based on his talent, not on who he is.

MML: What's your opinion of playwright Suzan-Lori Parks?

AW: I like Suzan-Lori Parks, I like her work, man. I saw *Topdog/Underdog.* I was on a panel once that selected an award for her, wrote her a citation and everything. It was the Laura Pels Award that's given by PEN.

MML: Essayist Sandra Shannon has criticized the women in your plays, saying, "His feminine portrayals tend to slip into comfort zones of what seem to be male-fantasized roles." Feminist critic bell hooks said of *Fences* that "patriarchy is not critiqued" and "sexist values are reinscribed." I was wondering if you've given thought to this in relation to approaching the final play in your cycle, which takes place in the 1990s, a time when women are arguably their most liberated and independent.

AW: I can't approach them any different than I have, man, cause all my women are independent. People can say anything they want, that's valid, they're liable to say anything they want. I don't agree with that. You gotta write women like… they can't express ideas and attitudes that women of the feminist movement in the '60s made. Even though I'm aware of all that, you gotta be very careful if you're trying to create a character like that, that they don't come up with any greater understanding of themselves and their relationship to the world than women had at that time.

As a matter of fact, all my characters are at the edge of that, they pushing them boundaries, they have more understanding. I had to cut back and say, "These are feminist ideas." My mother was a feminist, though she wouldn't express it that way. She don't know nothing about no feminist women and whatnot but she didn't accept her place. She raised three daughters, and my sisters are the same way. So that's where I get my women from. I grew up in a household with four women.

MML: My grandfather was a numbers runner in Harlem; Amsterdam Earl they called him. You wrote a numbers runner into *Jitney*— I wondered if you had any numbers-runner stories from Pittsburgh.

AW: At a bar, a guy put a gun to his head and was gonna shoot him unless he paid him fifteen dollars. And the guy didn't have no

fifteen dollars, so Harvey stepped forward—he's a number runner—and said, "Man, here's your fifteen dollars." "No, Harvey,
I don't want it from you. I want it from him." And Harvey said,
"C'mon, what kind of sense that make? He don't have anything."
Finally he say, "OK, Harvey, I'm doin this for *you*." So he took the
fifteen dollars and he kicked the guy, he didn't shoot him. The
police are standing across the street watching the whole thing.

I wrote a poem about a friend of mine, Ahmir Rashid. Ahmir
is like everyman. I'ma try to say my poem. "Ahmir has big days /
Standing on the corner of 125th and Lenox / Thin lips curled
around a reefer / He is waiting for the number man / So he can
go to Hackensack to see the woman in the red dress / The edge
of impatience rides his upper lip / The loaded .45 tucked in his
pants." Aw, shit, something about the loaded .45. [*Laughter*] "Makes
a soft bulge under his coat / The number man is late / Ahmir
knows he will either be in Hackensack tonight / Or booked for
murder in the 4th Precinct / The number man knows this also /
Which is why he is, right now, on a train to Atlanta." I hope it was-
n't Amsterdam Earl. [*Laughter*] That was "Ahmir Rashid #1." I just
got an idea. I might write about twenty more Ahmir Rashid
poems and put me out a book, man.

IV. "YOU CAN WORK SO HARD AND REWRITE SO MUCH THAT YOU GET CONFUSED OR CAN'T REMEMBER WHAT'S IN HERE, AIN'T IN THERE, OR WHY THIS PARTICULAR THING IS IN THERE. THEN YOU'RE LOST."

MML: What ever happened with the film of *Fences*?

AW: In 1987, when I wanted to make the movie, I told them
I wanted a black director. In 1990 they agreed to hire a black
director and then for a long time we battled over who that black
director should be. Once it was a black man, "It can't just be anyone. Now let's find the *right* one." So we stood there awhile. Eddie

Murphy was a producer and then they got another someone to take over from Eddie Murphy. I just finished a rewrite, a draft of the script. We ready to do it whenever we ready to do it but I don't sit by the telephone, man. [*Laughter*] I just keep moving, doing my things. If it happens, it happens. It's gotta happen the way I want it to happen because I gotta look in the mirror, face myself.

At the time, they told me there were no black directors, and about a month after that the *New York Times* put about thirteen new black directors in a photo. I sent it to them after I told them it was criminal that the guy didn't know no black directors. At the time, there was Gordon Parks, Bill Duke, Spike Lee. There were a bunch of black directors; he didn't know any. Marion McClinton, who is the director of this play, Paramount Pictures actually hired him and I've been working with Marion on the script. When we get the green light, we'll go ahead and do it.

MML: Baraka told me that Bill Duke directed *Hoodlum*—about Harlem numbers runner Bumpy Johnson—from a screenplay he'd written, but he went uncredited. Will you eventually write some screenplays for Hollywood?

AW: Yeah, I got ideas for about four of em. When I finish writing my plays, then I can do that. I'm not gonna do that and interfere with what I'm doing. If I did that, I would only have three plays written, man. When that's done, I'll write my book of poetry, do my paintings, I might even start singing, I don't know. [*Laughter*]

MML: Black playwright Woodie King, Jr. told me that poets make better potential playwrights than prose writers because of their mastery of the economy of language. He was criticizing Toni Morrison's play *Dreaming Emmett,* saying that fiction writers' plays tend to be too verbose. As a poet, do you agree?

AW: I would agree with him, but I wouldn't say that's the reason why. I think poets deal with ideas of metaphor, they deal with the idea of story. Every poem is a story but it's condensed in a small space. What's lacking mostly in American playwriting is the idea of metaphor, storytelling, etc. It's the way poets think that would lend themselves to dramatic structure. They're used to condensing ideas into small spaces, that's true.

I read somewhere that poetry is the enlargement of the sayable. In other words, the impulse to write the poem, that impulse is a great dramatic impulse. But hell, anybody could write a play. [*Laughter*] I do know this: All writers are not dramatists. You may be a great writer, but that doesn't necessarily mean you're a dramatist. Very few people have done both. I'm writing a novel when I finish my plays and then we'll find out. I know I'm a dramatist; we'll find out if I'm a novelist.

I always say that any painter that stands before a canvas is Picasso until proven otherwise. He stands before a blank canvas and he takes his tools. Paint, form, line, mass, color, relationship—those are the tools, and his mastery of those tools is what will enable him to put that painting on canvas. Everybody does the same thing. His turn out like that because he's mastered the tools. What happens with writers is that they don't want to learn the craft. That is your tools. So if you wanna write plays, you can't write plays without knowing the craft of playwriting. Once you have your tools, then you still gotta create out of that thing, that impulse. Out of necessity, as Bearden says: "Art is born out of necessity." Most writers ignore the very thing that would get them results, and that's craft. And how do you learn craft? In the trenches. You've got to do it. You got to get in there, you got to write. I say write and then write and write and write some more and go write some more.

Charles Johnson is a friend of mine in Seattle. Charles threw away 2,500 pages! It blows me away to this day. I said, How many? That's like ten books, just to get to that one. And that's work, but he wasn't afraid to do the work. And that's how you learn it, in the trenches. Do it, do it, and do it.

MML: I know you do a lot of rewriting—your plays may change

substantially between their first production and the Broadway run. How much rewriting is excessive/obsessive? How do you know when it's done?

AW: First of all, let me say, I'm blessed to have the opportunity to go back into rehearsals with a play and get it right. Sometimes you sit there opening night and go, "Oh, man." You don't see it until you see it. You can't make yourself see it, but when you see it... Sometimes opening night, I see something I could've done that could've improved the play. I don't write with a hammer and chisel. It's not set in stone.

How much is too much? At a certain point, you can overwork something. I've seen painters overwork a painting. I've done some drawings and my wife, I'll go show her the drawings, she'll go, "It's overworked." I'll go, yeah, I worked real hard on that. And working hard, I missed my original idea that I started with. That can happen in the plays, too. You can work so hard and rewrite so much that you get confused or can't remember what's in here, ain't in there, or why this particular thing is in there. Then you're lost. That's too much. But as long as you can have control of your material and you're working to make the story clearer, working to improve it... As long as you don't get lost up in the rewrites, you're OK. Once you get lost and you don't know why you're doing what you're doing, you're in trouble.

MML: The *New Yorker* once reported that you'd only seen two movies between 1980 and 1991: *Raging Bull* and *Cape Fear.* From 1991 to now, have you managed to hit the cinema?

AW: I just don't enjoy movies. It's not my thing. Even when I was a kid, I went to movies and stuff but I never became a movie person. That's true, I didn't step into a movie theater in them eleven years, but during them eleven years there was this invention of this thing called the VCR. So that doesn't mean I haven't seen any movies. I saw a few. To this day, I got DVDs now, I still don't see that many movies cause it's not my thing.

One year, I went twenty-three times. Me and my wife said we'd go every Wednesday. [A young black man staying in a homeless shelter approaches with quarters for dollar bills. I give him the dollars, Wilson gives him some more. He walks off and we don't mention it.] *Amores Perros,* I liked that. *Memento,* I saw that too. *Master and Commander*—a piece of junk, man, I didn't like nothin about that. I saw *Sankofa* in a movie house in Baltimore with my daughter. I loved that. I've seen Spike's stuff. I saw *Barbershop,* that was fun. I just would rather read a book or listen to some records.

MML: When I was four years old, my mother took me to *The Wiz* on Broadway, and at thirteen, my grandmother took me to *The Tap Dance Kid.* But seeing *Fences* at seventeen really helped cultivate my love for theater. It seems my peers don't really bother. So thanks a lot, Mr. Wilson.

AW: You're welcome. We're gonna change that with your peers, man. We workin on it. I think Puffy had a lot to do with that. He brought a lot of people in there that otherwise wouldn't have went to see the play. And if they come to see him as opposed to the play, that's OK. They come to see him and *discover* the play. People came to *Fences* to see James Earl Jones and they discovered the play. "This is a good play, too, but I saw James Earl!" All that helps, man. ✯

JULIE ORRINGER

TALKS WITH

TOBIAS WOLFF

"AS A WRITER YOU BEGIN WITH INFINITE
FREEDOM, AND THEN YOU MUST IMMEDIATELY
START HEMMING YOURSELF IN. PART OF THE
BEAUTY OF WRITING ABOUT THE ARMY, OR
SUCH WORLDS, IS THAT THEY OFFER YOU AN
ENCLOSED THEATER OF HUMAN FOLLY, OF
HUMAN ASPIRATION AND FORMATION."

Recommendations from Tobias Wolff:
When guessing a woman's weight, aim low
Never land a helicopter in a confined space
If you want to sweet-talk a girl, say you're into Ayn Rand

Tobias Wolff *is a short story writer, a memoirist, a novelist,
a father, a husband, a jazz aficionado, a hiker upon remote mountain trails, a neophyte pianist, and the mentor of many young writers. He was born in 1945 in
Birmingham, Alabama; grew up in Florida, Utah, and
the Pacific Northwest; attended Concrete High School in Washington, the
Hill School in Pennsylvania, Oxford University, and Stanford University, where he was a Stegner Fellow and a Jones Lecturer, and where he is
now the Ward W. and Priscilla B. Woods Professor in the School of
Humanities and Sciences. He is the author of short story collections, memoirs, novellas, and novels, including* In the Garden of the North Amer-

ican Martyrs *(1981)*, The Barracks Thief *(1984)*, Back in the World *(1985)*, This Boy's Life *(1989)*, In Pharaoh's Army: Memories of the Lost War *(1994)*, The Night in Question *(1996)*, and Old School *(2003)*.

Wolff's writing makes us recognize those aspects of ourselves that are hardest to acknowledge: our selfishness, our pride, our cowardice. But he also brings to light our potential for self-understanding and compassion—the knowledge that comes from years of honest introspection, from the desire to make sense of the decisions that shape our lives. For his rigorous intelligence and his deep empathic understanding of humanity, he has been compared to Chekhov; his writing is Chekhovian, too, in its gorgeous simplicity and in the way characterization gives rise to the shape of his narratives. He is a tireless reviser, a believer in the process of writing. In answer to an anxious question of mine a couple of years ago, he told me, "The only way to learn how to write a novel is simply to do it."

This interview took place at Wolff's office at Stanford, where he and I had spent many an office hour hashing through drafts of my own stories when I was a Stegner Fellow. —*J.O. (Summer 2004)*

I. WORLD'S FAIR

JULIE ORRINGER: In the time I've known you, I've known you only as a writer and teacher. But I understand you've also been a waiter, a night watchman, a busboy; you've guessed ages and weights for a living, you spent several months as a reporter, and of course you spent four years in the army, which we'll talk about later. So I'm wondering if you can guess my age and weight.

TOBIAS WOLFF: [*Laughs*] What I've learned to do with women is to go low. But I'm not going to do that today.

JO: Go high.

TW: I would say… stand up.

JO: Is it always standing up?

TW: Oh, yeah. This was at a booth at the World's Fair. [*Takes a moment to assess, and then guesses interviewer's weight and age.*]

JO: Close!

TW: I'm out of practice. Was I at least within three pounds?

JO: Nearly. Did you always give yourself a window of three pounds?

TW: Yeah, that was the range. Which actually allows you seven pounds, three on either side and the one in the middle. You really had to win when you were doing this, because otherwise people were just buying the prizes, which were cheap-ass little things. If you lost, they'd start looking at the prizes and thinking, "This isn't worth my fifty cents." So you had to win in order to get a crowd—or, in carny speak, a "tip." When you get a tip, people keep gathering to see what's going on. If they sense a real challenge, they'll play and pay. It's like having your own private mint. They can't wait to come up and give you money, but only if you're already winning. I was good at it. And it was clean; there was no way to cheat.

JO: Was there a scale?

TW: Yeah, there was a big scale. What you'd do to get going every night is have a couple of plants in the crowd. And you'd have a line of patter. If there was a pregnant woman, you'd say "Come on in, we'll weigh the both of you for the price of one!" You lay down a steady line to bring the crowd towards you and get a nice tip built up. It was hard to get it going during the day. Sunlight is not conducive to the mob mentality you need to create. But at night, under the carnival lights, with people screaming on the rides—it was a snap to pull in a crowd. I had a blast that summer. I'd lied about my age and was hanging out with all these old carny types.

JO: How old were you?

TW: I was sixteen.

JO: Where was it?

TW: Seattle's World's Fair. The rather squalid carnival section, not the World of Tomorrow, the culturally edifying part of the fair.

JO: Were you home on break from school?

TW: I was between years at boarding school at the time. When I got home I needed to scrape some money together to make up the shortfall of my scholarship and also to come up with my train fare back East. I started off working at a coin toss. Very quickly I figured out that the age-and-weight gig was much better. I had a friend over there and he segued me into the age-and-weight-guessing business. After the fair broke up in the fall, the carnival was headed on a big swing through the country, attaching itself to various state and county fairs. I was sorely tempted to stay with it; I'd met so many characters and was having so much fun. But I had just enough sanity to know that was probably not a good idea.

II. THE THEATER OF HUMAN FOLLY

JO: When I read the initial excerpt of *Old School* that appeared in the *New Yorker,* I thought back to "Smokers," your first published story, which appeared in the *Atlantic Monthly* in 1976. In both stories you perfectly portrayed the ways in which we manipulate the truth to our own advantage. What was it that pulled you toward that material?

TW: When I went off to boarding school, I already knew I want-ed to be a writer. This might sound unlikely or at least oppor-tunistic, but when I got there I knew that someday I would write about that place. It was so different from anything I'd experienced before, and it was such an intense wash of experience that at the time I could hardly parse it out. But I knew that someday I would. I remember discovering Salinger in my first year at that school because everyone was passing him around, still. The school he'd based his own recollections on was just down the road from us—we used to play them in sports—Valley Forge Military Academy, which he calls Pencey Prep. The book was forbidden there. The students were not allowed to have it, so of course all of them had read it. It was like a required text. I thought, "What idiots!" Can you imagine that?

Anyway, it had a local notoriety in addition to being interesting on its own. I laughed my ass off at the book when I read it. I enjoyed it so much. Of course I saw certain facets of life at my own school pictured there, but I was also very aware of some fundamental differences. By and large, the masters and boys at my school were not phonies. There was a sort of strange high-mindedness there, which I now understand to have grown out of a certain Anglophile tradition, and which was easy to satirize. Nevertheless, it was different. Salinger could not have written his novel about my school. But by the very act of reading it and correcting for it even as I read it, the seed of *Old School* was planted.

I have always loved reading school stories. I don't know why, exactly, but I do. I love William Trevor's school stories; he's got one in every collection, sometimes two. And there's the section in *Eminent Victorians* where Strachey talks about Dr. Arnold, Matthew Arnold's father, who was the headmaster of Rugby School. It's fascinating as an essay on education, and also very funny. Orwell's "Such, Such Were the Joys." School is a fantastic theater. A lot of writers certainly have found it so.

JO: It must have something to do with being in transition between childhood and adulthood. That's fertile ground for narrative. But in a way, being at boarding school also seems akin to being in the army. Both situations are bound by strict rules and codes of conduct.

TW: Exactly. They're both closed worlds.

JO: How does that affect the writing?

TW: It's akin to the advantage a poet has in consenting to work-ing within a form. As a writer you begin with infinite freedom, and then you must immediately start hemming yourself in. You have to choose a genre, you have to choose a voice that precludes using other voices. You have to choose a time that precludes other times. Part of the beauty of writing about the army, or such worlds, is that they offer you an enclosed theater of human folly, of human aspiration and formation.

JO: One of the particularly notable aspects of your school's culture was its focus upon the literary world, its love of writers, and its idea of the writing life as something to aspire to. Did you know that about the school before you went there, or was it a fortunate coin-cidence?

TW: It was a fortunate coincidence. I hadn't been there two months before Robert Frost came. He was revered in the wrong ways by the teachers I'd had up till then, because they saw him as a Hallmark card writer, which, I'm afraid, is what we were taught good writing was—uplifting sentiment.

JO: He is actually quite a dark poet. "From the time when one is sick to death, / One is alone, and he dies more alone."

TW: Oh, God, he sure is. He's a tough poet. And complicated. Not overcomplicated or perversely complicated, but he is complicated. And yet there is that face of his work which is deceptive, and can allow you to read him simplistically, and that is a great mistake. Before a visiting writer came to the school, the masters had us read this person's work, and they introduced me to a different Frost than I had been reading before. So when he arrived, it was an extraordinary experience, really. I had never seen a real writer before—certainly not one of that Olympian stature. He was the great American poet then. And indeed he went on to read at Kennedy's inauguration, as you know; he traveled to Russia on a goodwill mission, met with Khrushchev. It attested to the position

a poet could have in society—bringing the vision of the world of
poetry into the world of affairs. You just don't see that anymore.
Is there anyone like that now? I guess Robert Pinsky would come
about as close as you can get. Frost was very interested in politics.
If you read his letters, you find he had lots of ideas about education, too; he'd been a schoolteacher. Some of his ideas were really
cranky and mischievous. He would advise young people to leave
school and go off to strange places like Brazil and Kamchatka.

JO: Did he talk about that at the Hill School?

TW: Not to my knowledge. I ran across that in a book, a little
monograph called *Robert Frost as a Teacher*. Then there was something in the Lawrence Thompson biography that confirmed it.
Frost was very, very mischievous, and manipulative. But I've taken
the long way around the barn here: no, I didn't really know about
the literary nature of the Hill School.

It's funny—I just met a guy the other day who said, "That
school you wrote about—was that the Hill School?" and I said,
"Well, I did go there, and it was partly drawn on my experience."
And he told me how he went to be interviewed after a hockey
game at Hill—he wanted to do a postgraduate year there. Our
headmaster was the hockey coach, so he went to talk to the headmaster after the hockey game. He'd had his nose broken by one of
our hockey players. They were very rough, even then. And I said,
"Well, he would have loved you if you'd gotten your nose broken
by one of our players. That's your badge of honor. You're in." But
when he went up to the headmaster's study, William Golding was
there and the two of them were talking and drinking, just totally
shitfaced.

He did indeed get in and chose not to go, after all—he got
into some good college and went there instead. But here's William
Golding lying back with our headmaster, who's a very literary
guy—used to publish essays about education in *Life* magazine and
places like that. He taught the senior honors English seminar every

year. A very smart guy, widely read, advised the school literary magazine. If a kid was disgruntled about not getting his work published he could submit it to the headmaster, who would look it over and give him some comments, to help him do a little better next time.

JO: Did you do that?

TW: I did. Boy, I didn't like what I got back. He really gave it to me. He was right. I didn't want to know it at the time, but I certainly recognize the truth of his criticisms now.

JO: What were his criticisms?

TW: Lack of specificity. This woolly idea that the less you say about a person or a place or a situation, the more universal it will seem.

JO: We're really drawn to that idea as young writers.

TW: Yeah, because it's so easy. We like the symbolic. It's very seductive when we're young.

III. THE COMPANY OF OTHER WRITERS (OR, THE COMMENTS THAT DISTURBED ME MOST WERE THE ONES THAT WERE TRUE)

JO: One of the ideas I found particularly compelling in *Old School* was the notion that as young writers, we have some need or desire to be taken up by more established writers, to be introduced into their society—to shake the hands of writers who have touched the hands of other writers. Can you talk a little bit about how you developed that idea in the book, and also about how that was part of your own experience as a young writer?

TW: I was certainly conscious of the lore of writers. Even before I actually read anything about it, I was aware that Hemingway had been brought along by people like Gertrude Stein and Ezra Pound and F. Scott Fitzgerald. I mention Hemingway because he was the focus of my interest at the time. As I read writers' biographies later on, I noted that many of them met other writers and received help from them. Maupassant was a writer I loved; I read a biography that talked about how Turgenev took him up and put him through his paces. It's a natural enough thing.

Part of what my novel concerns is the way this boy is trying to move away from the orbit of his own father. He has decided—rather unfairly—that it isn't satisfactory, and he is looking, as you do when you abandon one father, for another. That blessing touch he's after gets embodied for him in literature. He's looking for that hand to fall on his shoulder, that anointing. Of course we discover as we get older that it doesn't work that way.

JO: In your experience, how does it work?

TW: Seldom the way it seems. For example, it's known that Sherwood Anderson helped Faulkner along. Well, yes, he did—he sent a novel of Faulkner's off to his publisher, but did so only under the condition that he didn't have to read it. He didn't read the book! He didn't *want* to read it. He never read it. A funny story. Anyway, writers when they're young tend to seek the company of other writers—some community of writers with whom they can share their work and get a response to it. I would imagine that the competition between Greek playwrights served as a kind of workshop. They were certainly aware of each other. They lived in the same town, or *polis*. Literature has always been written under the scrutiny—in the presence, if you will—of other writers. This idea of the writer as the *figure isolé,* it simply doesn't ring true to experience. You will feel the discipline and presence of other writers through the books you read, if nothing else. Influence is inescapable.

JO: In your own development as a writer, you spent some time as a Stegner Fellow and then as a Jones Lecturer at Stanford. How did that affect your work?

TW: I was thirty when I came here, and I'd been writing on my own. I had never given my work to a roomful of other people and had them mark it up and tell me what they thought of it. It was kind of a shock, really. Some of what I got back was silly stuff, I thought. But the comments that disturbed me most were the ones that were true—the ones that pointed out things I was doing that I wasn't aware of, for good or ill.

There were some good critics in that workshop, foremost among them Allan Gurganus, who is also a wonderful writer. Allan was very humane but truth-telling as a critic, and very good at catching tics he could tell you weren't aware of—tics of language, of manner. We had the same standard of writing, which was that every word should count, but I wasn't as far along in living up to that standard as I'd hoped I was. The workshop was very useful in helping me see what I was doing, making me more self-aware, to the point that I kind of had a hard time writing for a time after I got here. I did it, but the self-consciousness has a constipating effect at first. Then you drop those habits and you're off again. I wouldn't undo that experience for anything. It was infinitely useful to me.

JO: I think there's something essential about learning the nitty-gritty, the craft of writing—it helps you make rather large leaps in your work. But it does sometimes have a stymieing effect. I felt that very much at Iowa, when I was in Frank Conroy's workshop. He taught us so much about craft all at once that every time I sat down to put words on the page I felt a barrage of rules descending upon me. But eventually the craft becomes second nature, and the work becomes stronger for your having learned it. People talk about whether or not writing can be taught—that seems like one of the things that *can* be taught.

TW: I came to Stanford with some very ambivalent feelings about joining a workshop. For one thing, before I came here, I often wrote as a kind of subversive activity, something done in spite of the distractions that life presented, other jobs obviously being among them. Then there were personal relationships that seemed to represent a kind of obstacle to writing. At the Hill School and later at Oxford, writing was obviously valued, but they didn't do workshops—you wrote on your own, as an individual expression, something done almost in spite of the school. Because they asked so much of you in other ways, you had to steal the time to do it. I wrote even when I was in the army—not in a disciplined way, of course, considering the life I led.

JO: You were working on a novel.

TW: Yes, I was working on a novel. It wasn't any good, really, and probably couldn't have been, considering the halting way in which I was forced to write it. Nevertheless, I always felt as if I was getting over on them when I was writing, you know what I mean? I wasn't *supposed* to do it, and that made me want to do it. When I went to Oxford, after I got out of the army, the university had no interest in creative writing at all. They would have laughed at the idea of a creative writing workshop as part of the university curriculum. I wrote a novel when I was at Oxford, and I did it in spite of my studies. And I did it again when I was working at other jobs. I always wrote outside of the realm of what anybody expected me to do. It wasn't an approved activity. And I liked that about it. It gave it a flavor—let me put it that way.

In some ways, that flavor was essential to the activity itself. So to suddenly enter a world where it was the expected and approved and institutionally encouraged thing! I was really worried that I wouldn't be able to write at all. In some ways that happened, but more because of the self-consciousness than because of anything else. I was old enough to know that I didn't have time to waste, so when I was given the gift of time I used it. Nobody taught me lessons in craft as such. It was more a question of learning to be a good reader of my own work, and of other people's work as well. Not just the writers in the workshop, but more canonical writers. I think the great use of the workshop is that it teaches you to be a good, close reader. Not to read through the lens of an ideology, or the theory of a self-enclosed world of language, but what's here, what's right in front of you. Attend to it. What does it say? What are these words doing? What is the form of this piece? Why this form rather than another?

And the workshop also teaches you to think about human problems. It's not about craft for me. If it were, it wouldn't be interesting. When I'm talking with my students I'm really interested in the human springs of a story—what is there in the necessities of this particular character that produces this narrative? What has mattered to the writer in the writing of this story? We try to understand those things because craft without them is exercise. As you know from having been in a workshop of mine, I don't assign exercises. I think that each time out should be a swing for the fences. Don't do base-running drills. You can do those on your own time. The experience of reading other people's work with that kind of attention, and then having your own work read with that kind of attention and reported to you in detail, even by voices you don't agree with—even in your resistance to criticism you are educating yourself about writing and about your own writing. And if you don't end up becoming a writer, it's still got to be good for you.

JO: Because it increases your understanding of how the human world works.

TW: Absolutely. And how all our experiences and memories, in order to become intelligible and useful to us, must be shaped in some way. We impose a form on experience; there's no other way to live. We don't have a choice about it. We do it. But why do we do it the way we do it? Why do we choose one form rather than another?

IV. ONE HAS TO FACE THESE THINGS

JO: A number of critics have mentioned that there's a certain moral structure embodied in your work. How would you describe the way you arrived at your own sense of morality in fiction writing, and how did it affect the way you tell your stories?

TW: Well, I'm not sure, but the experience of reading and writing fiction is what gave me a sense of morality, more than anything else, because it helped me think out and objectify the question of character. In our everyday lives, we're mostly lost in the soup of ourselves. Where are we going to stand to see ourselves? We have to achieve some vantage point, and the continual experience of being inside oneself doesn't give you that. The vantage point must be different for different people. For some it's religion. I wouldn't equate religion and literature—I wouldn't want to make a religion of literature, it doesn't function well as a religion, but it does offer a place to step outside yourself, as much as one can, anyway.

So much of what I've come to think of as my character has been the result of my recognizing in other stories aspects of my own experience and my own inclinations, bad and good. That kind of heart-rising-to-heart you feel sometimes when you read, even if you're embarrassed to admit what it is that you're recognizing—you achieve in that way an escape from the imprisonment of the self.

JO: I was thinking about *In Pharaoh's Army*. The narrative tone throughout the book is self-effacing and often very self-critical. The scene I keep coming back to is the one in which you're about to be released from service and your replacement has come in—he's very self-important, a real jerk, and he thinks you've failed in your duties in Vietnam—and he's trying to direct a helicopter to land in a space that's too small, and you decide not to deter him, and the result is that a lot of people's homes are destroyed.

TW: Yeah, these little makeshift shelters they've thrown up.

JO: In that scene, and throughout *In Pharaoh's Army*—really, throughout all of your nonfiction—you avoid one of the dangers inherent in memoir, which is that the memoirist will portray himself as being larger or more humane than we suspect he actually was, or that he'll draw a veil over his failings. It seems to me that in your work, in a sense, you do the opposite of that.

TW: You know, that's a really astute point—when you say "the opposite of that." I think that, indeed, I may have sometimes exceeded what was required in self-revelation, especially of weakness and vice. I wanted so much not to do the kind of thing Lillian Hellman did in her memoirs, which was to constantly show herself in the most heroic light: always the smartest person in the room, always the one with the integrity. There are any number of memoirs like that. They seem written to show what a wonderful and superior person the writer was. Well, I know I'm not.

On the other hand, sometimes I wonder if in doing this—in making a vow to myself that I would not be any easier on myself than I was on anybody else I wrote about—if I didn't sometimes go too far in the other direction. That is, I think if I were writing such a book now I would be a little more understanding of myself, as I try to be of other people. Not in a sappy way, not in an exculpatory way; one has to face these things. But I think, perhaps particularly in *This Boy's Life,* the hand may have fallen a little too heavily on the narrator. Anyway, in my anxiety not to make a special pleading for myself, there was a danger—I might have been a little harder on myself than I needed to be in the interest of being truthful.

JO: Do you think that the tendency to be hard on yourself in your memoirs translates to the tendency to be hard on the protagonists of your fictional narratives?

TW: I hope not. I do write, as indeed most writers do, about things that have gone wrong. There's not much of a story if things have gone right. Stories are about problems, and not the kinds of problems that result from a safe falling out of a window, but from somebody having a choice and having a problem with that choice, and then the series of consequences that follow from making that choice. To portray that honestly is to show the way people parse out their choices, and self-interest naturally comes into play. It isn't so much a matter of wishing to be hard on people as wishing to be truthful. If there's a moral quality to my work, I suppose it has to do with will and the exercise of choice within one's will. The choices we make tend to narrow down a myriad of opportunities to just a few, and those choices tend to reinforce themselves in whatever direction we've started to go, including the wrong direction. Our present government likes to lecture us on the virtue of staying the course. Well, maybe it's not such a good idea to stay the course if you're headed toward the rocks. There's something to be said for changing course if you're about to drive your ship onto the shoals.

JO: *Old School* seems to a large extent to be about evasions of truth—about the characters' evasions of the truth with regard to religion, social class, and personal connections. I was fascinated by the way that theme developed across the various narrative threads of the novel.

TW: It's not so much about the evasion of truth, which has an active quality. A lot of what happens to this narrator grows from an accumulated sense of fraudulence. For example, you mentioned the question of religion. He doesn't really lie about that at all. What would be his lie, anyway? He feels like he's lying because he's not telling people his father was Jewish—something he's just discovered himself. Yet he has no Jewish relations that he knows, and he hasn't been brought up at all in this faith; he was brought up in another faith altogether. Even under Jewish law he's not Jewish. Mostly he feels himself to be Jewish because he's not saying anything about it. It's what he keeps secret that he feels to be truest about himself. His sense of holding something back gives it an obsessional character and, in that sense, confers an imaginary identity upon him. He does this with other things too. He doesn't really lie—and in fact no one would be that interested anyway.

THE BELIEVER BOOK OF WRITERS TALKING TO WRITERS

They may not be as fooled as he thinks they are, either. When he finally publishes his story it's no big deal to anybody. It's kind of like, "I thought that all along." It really doesn't seem to come as a great revelation to anybody.

JO: When he publishes his story—

TW: —that isn't his story—

JO: That isn't his story, yes; that's when it comes out that his father was Jewish. And it seems there must be a connection between this suppression of his Judaism and his sense of the unacceptability of his social class, too.

TW: That's right. But again, he's not entirely to be trusted in this matter. He intuits that there is something, some spirit in the school, that does not fully accept Jewish boys or boys of a different social class. But then he admits that never once has he ever heard anyone say anything to that effect or behave in that way. So where is that coming from, really? I mean, it probably is, in fact, partly coming from the school—but I think it's also coming from him. He's conspiring with the school to produce this feeling.

JO: Did you understand that aspect of the character when you began the book, or was it something that came out of the writing?

TW: I understood it when I began the book, though I didn't understand just how pervasive it would be. Certainly this character takes it farther than I ever did, but again it's a question of recognition. In writing a book, you can use things you recognize in yourself as points of inspiration. He's playing out on a large scale aspects of myself that I played out on a smaller scale.

JO: And you chose to write the book as a novel rather than as a memoir.

TW: Oh, God, yes. I always knew it would be a novel. First of all, nothing interesting happened to me at my school. Yeah, we had

Frost come, but Ayn Rand never came, and Hemingway certainly didn't—nor did he ever agree to. But these were the writers who were most influential on me. The writing competitions in the novel were largely an invention, too. I wanted to write about vocation, and I wanted to write about influence, and since I'm a writer, the influence I wanted to home in on was literary influence, and how it works—the omnivorous, ruthless way we consume and reject influences when we're young, the trail of dead writers we leave behind us as we progress.

Most of the boys at Hill had read Ayn Rand. At the girls' schools, they were even more into it than we were. At the dances we would have, I remember endless conversations with girls about Ayn Rand—they were really big-time into her. After all, she was writing about women who ran railroads, and nobody else was doing that. I mean, look at the women in other fiction at the time, popular fiction. And at that age, you know—it's a rare reader of fifteen or sixteen who is aware of the cheesiness of Rand's style. You're quite apt to get caught up by its very partisanship and by the heat of her own beliefs, which so animates all her fiction.

JO: Were you in high school when you began to reject those ideas?

TW: More just after. The narrator comes to his senses before I ever did, because you accelerate things in a novel. Again, it's the sense of form that compels it. It can't just be "and then, and then, and then," endlessly. There has to be a decisiveness to achieve literary form. You're giving an impression of life, but you can't actually record it just as it happens or it dissolves into mush.

JO: I'm curious to know more about your experience of writing the novel—how it was different from writing those early longer, novelistic memoirs, and perhaps even from writing *The Barracks Thief*, which is sometimes classed as a novella but which feels to me like a novel.

TW: *The Barracks Thief* is a short novel, but it was originally written at novel length. I'd also published another novel much earlier. It was never my wish to represent *Old School* as my first novel; I always have to set the record straight on this. Back in 1975 a novel I'd written at Oxford was published in England and was going to be published over here by Macmillan, but for reasons that I still don't know, it fell through at the last minute and was never published in the U.S., thank god, because after it was published in England I withdrew it from circulation. When it came out, I realized it was awful. I had thought it was good, but somehow the light came on when I actually read it again.

JO: What was awful about it?

TW: Oh, it was just terrible, just an embarrassing book. It's like a first draft of a novel. I learned something, no doubt, in writing it—made a lot of mistakes I wouldn't repeat. I do indeed wish it hadn't been published, and I never name it on my list of publications, and that was thirty years ago. My next book didn't come out until six years later, a collection of stories. I've always considered that my writing life really began with that collection of stories, not with the novel. I never mentioned it to my publishers; it was never listed in any of my books. I never thought to mention it to anybody. My own editor didn't know I had done it, so when they made up the publicity for *Old School* they said it was my first novel. In each interview I've had to correct that.

Having said all that, I don't know how to characterize the difference. I could give you a trite answer about how when you're working on short stories you do know they're going to end sometime, and how when you're writing a novel you spend years deepening your experience of the characters and the world you're writing about. But also a kind of anxious wonder sets in as to whether or not you'll really finish it, whether it will be any good, whether all this time will have been wasted—and we all hate to waste our time.

Everything I've written, including this book, has seemed to

me, at one point or another, something I probably ought to abandon. Even the best things I've written have seemed to me at some point very unlikely to be worth the effort I had already put into them. But I know I have to push through. Sometimes when I get to the other end it still won't be that great, but at least I will have finished it. For me, it's more important to keep the discipline of finishing things than to be assured at every moment that it's worth doing.

JO: Sometimes it seems so hard to hold off the skepticism.

TW: You just learn to do it.

VI. WRITING ABOUT WAR

JO: You've taken on the subject of war in both your fiction and nonfiction; what were the challenges it posed for you?

TW: The hardest thing about writing about a war you've been in is that you're terrified of getting it wrong, because of the people who have suffered such losses—and I'm not just talking about Americans. I'm talking about the Vietnamese, too. There were around five million Vietnamese killed, most of them civilians. You're aware that whenever you write anything about war, even with the intention of showing what it's really like, you're covering it with that inevitable glamour that war has for people except when they're in the middle of it. This last April, when those troops headed across the desert in their tanks, doing those "We're gonna go get these guys" interviews, like kids going to the next town to play a basketball game or something—those were the same kinds of things we were saying when we first went over. And now—talk to them now.

JO: A lot of people have drawn comparisons between what's going on in Iraq right now and what went on in Vietnam.

TW: It's very different, really. I don't think the comparisons work except in the folly of the enterprise and the mendacity of those who led us into it, and the willful blindness to reality, and the failure to appreciate anything about the country that we were going into, and the failure to seek out people who knew what the situation actually was, people who could plan reasonably for it, and maybe even decide not do it on the basis of what they learned. To start off with their minds made up, and to allow only those things into consideration that further strengthened decisions made in utter ignorance—in those ways, yes, it's similar.

But on the ground, in the place itself, they could not be more different. To begin with, there was no civil war going on when we went into Iraq. There was not a legitimate movement, a nationalist liberation movement we were going in to oppose. There was a despot, an evil regime in charge, unambiguously so. That didn't mean that we should've gone in. There are a lot of despots and evil regimes in the world. I don't know why, for example, we didn't take measures against Charles Taylor before we did, while he was slaughtering his fellow countrymen by the hundreds of thousands. If that really is the reason we went into Iraq, we should have been doing it elsewhere, with others.

JO: Of course, that wasn't really the reason.

TW: No, it wasn't, and it's not even the reason we were given. For them to appeal to that as their justification now is very dishonest. They fudged it, and now they're paying for it. At this point, we are actually creating a resistance that was not there before. In that way, I guess it could come to resemble Vietnam, but it will be a Vietnam of our own creation. Won't that be ridiculous?

JO: The ways in which we've managed to make ourselves villains in this war are just astounding. They're happening both on a very high level and on a personal level. We Americans used to be able to defend ourselves in the face of our government's actions overseas by arguing that those acts were coming down from our leaders, rather than from the people themselves. But the atrocities committed at Abu Ghraib made us question that defense.

TW: They did, absolutely. And people kept supporting the war in the face of those revelations. There was a piece in the *Times* by a guy named William Broyles who was the editor of *Newsweek* for a while, editor of the *Texas Monthly* before that, and a marine in Vietnam. He was ruminating about the polls that show that support for the war among Americans is still pretty high. He was saying this is only possible because most of these people don't have anybody at hazard over there, and that if you brought the draft back, those statistics would evaporate overnight. And he's right. We've created this mercenary army, essentially, made up disproportionately of people from minority and economically disadvantaged backgrounds. If our own kids were at hazard our feelings about the war would change very quickly. I hate the idea of the draft; I've got two boys who would be eligible. But the truth is, to make these things real, we need to share the danger.

JO: In a way, it brings to mind one of the things we're always trying to do as writers: to help people understand the humanity of others, the importance of other lives.

TW: Absolutely. That is exactly right. I think that's the greatest thing literature can do, and it is a very great thing indeed.

JO: In light of what's going on in Iraq right now, what kind of responsibility do you feel we have as writers? Do you feel like we have special responsibilities as writers?

TW: We have responsibilities as citizens. I don't think we have special responsibilities as writers. All you can do is try to humanize people's imaginations. I don't know any better way to do it than to just keep on writing as you write. What is a fiction writer to do? I don't know, except to insist on the value of what you do by continuing to do it. Because this world is continually trying to negate the value of what you do. That's your resistance. And then, to act as a citizen in other ways—to vote, to try to get other people to vote, to protest, to boycott, to do whatever a good citizen does in support of one's beliefs—yes, absolutely, all that. But not to turn your work into propaganda, because then you've become what they are. It will suck the humanity right out of your work.

JO: And in what direction do you see American fiction writing going now? What are some of the things you're noticing about the work that's different from what you were seeing ten or twenty years ago?

TW: I guess I'm seeing a little less interest in literature as a game. There's a tremendous faith in narrative, I think—a sense that maybe it isn't just a piece of criminal naïveté to believe that something valuable can come out of the telling of human stories. Postmodernism has forced tremendous self-consciousness upon us, perhaps against our will at times. After such knowledge, what forgiveness? You can't ever escape what you know. We're very self-aware as writers now, but it's interesting to see that narrative has been reinvigorated by that, rather than abandoned. It's given writers a new arsenal of forms, a new sophistication with which to tell their stories. Aside from that, I'm infinitely respectful of, and always in wonder at, the variety of ways that people tell stories and keep making them new. ✷

CONTRIBUTORS

Daphne Beal is at work on a novel. Her nonfiction has most recently appeared in *Vogue* and *McSweeney's*.

Robert Birnbaum was born in Germany, grew up in Chicago, and lived for too many years in Boston. He is editor-at-large at *Identitytheory.com,* a contributing writer at the *Morning News,* and regularly contributes to *Bark* magazine. He lives in New Hampshire with blond Labrador, Rosie.

Susan Choi is the author of two novels, most recently *American Woman* (2003), which was a finalist for the Pulitzer Prize. Her first novel, *The Foreign Student* (1998) won the Asian-American Literary Award. She teaches fiction at Brooklyn College, among other places, and lives in Brooklyn, New York with her husband and son.

Dave Eggers, the editor of *McSweeney's,* has written books and lives in California.

Ben Ehrenreich is a journalist and novelist who lives in Los Angeles. His work has appeared in *L.A. Weekly*, the *Village Voice,* the *New York Times,* and many other publications. His first novel, *The Suitors,* will be published in the spring of 2006.

Nell Freudenberger's first book, *Lucky Girls,* won the PEN/ Faulkner Malamud award for short fiction and the Sue Kaufman Prize from the American Academy of Arts and Letters. Her reviews and journalism have appeared in the *New York Times*, the *New Yorker*, the *Sunday Telegraph, Travel and Leisure,* and the *Nation.* She lives in New York City.

Novelist Tayari Jones is the author of *Leaving Atlanta* and *The Untelling.*

Jonathan Lethem's most recent book is a collection of essays, *The*

Disappointment Artist. He lives in Brooklyn and Maine.

Miles Marshall Lewis is native to the Bronx and currently lives in Paris with the love of his life and their baby boy. Lewis is editor of the urbane urban lit journal *Bronx Biannual* and author of *Scars of the Soul Are Why Kids Wear Bandages When They Don't Have Bruises*, an essay collection.

Ben Marcus is the editor of *The Anchor Book of New American Short Stories*. His books include *Notable American Women* and *The Age of Wire and String.*

Thisbe Nissen is the author of *Out of the Girls' Room and into the Night, The Good People of New York,* and, most recently, *Osprey Island.* She also coauthored and collaged *The Ex-Boyfriend. Cookbook* with Erin Ergenbright. Nissen lives in Iowa.

Cornelia Nixon's books include two novels-in-stories, *Now You See It* and *Angels Go Naked,* plus a book on D. H. Lawrence. Her awards include two O. Henry Prizes (one of them a first prize), a Nelson Algren Award, two Pushcart Prizes, and fellowships from the NEA and the Bunting Institute. She teaches in the M.F.A. program at Mills College.

Julie Orringer is the author of *How to Breathe Underwater,* a collection of short stories. She is a graduate of Cornell University and the Iowa Writers' Workshop, and she was a Truman Capote Fellow in the Stegner Program at Stanford. Her stories have appeared in the *Paris Review, McSweeney's, Ploughshares, Zoetrope: All-Story, The Pushcart Prize Anthology, The Best New American Voices,* and *The Best American Non-Required Reading.* She is working on a novel set in Budapest and Paris in the late 1930s.

ZZ Packer is the author of the short story collection *Drinking Coffee Elsewhere,* and was a 2004 PEN/Faulkner Award Finalist. Her stories have been published in the *New Yorker, Harper's,* and *Zoetrope All-Story,* and have been anthologized in *Best American Short Stories*

2000 and *2003*. She lives in the San Francisco Bay Area.

Dan Pope is the author of a novel, *In the Cherry Tree* (Picador 2003); his stories have been published in *McSweeney's, Gettysburg Review, Iowa Review, Shenandoah,* and other places.

Zadie Smith was born in northwest London in 1975, and continues to live in the area. Her first novel, *White Teeth,* was the winner of the Whitbread First Novel Award, the Guardian First Book Award, the James Tait Black Memorial Prize for Fiction, and the Commonwealth Writers' First Book Award. Her second novel, *The Autograph Man,* won the Jewish Quarterly Wingate Literary Prize and was long-listed for the Man Booker Prize. Her third novel, *On Beauty,* will be published later this year, and she is working on a book of essays on ethical thought in twentieth-century fiction. She is a fellow of the Royal Society of Literature.

Sarah Stone is the author of a novel, *The True Sources of the Nile* (Doubleday 2002/Anchor 2003), which was a BookSense 76 and *Detroit Free Press* book club selection and has been translated into German and Dutch, and a textbook, cowritten with Ron Nyren, *Deepening Fiction: A Practical Guide for Intermediate and Advanced Writers* (Longman 2004). She codirects the M.A./M.F.A. program in Writing and Consciousness at New College of California in San Francisco.

Michelle Tea is the author of four memoirs, including the illustrated *Rent Girl.* Her edited anthologies include the collection *Without a Net: The Female Experience of Growing Up Working Class.* She is a curator of literary events and performance tours, most famously the all-girl road riot Sister Spit, and San Francisco's Radar Reading Series, featuring underground performance and homemade cookies. In 2006 MacAdam/Cage will publish her first novel, *Rose of No-Man's Land.*

Adam Thirlwell was born in 1978. His first novel, *Politics,* was published in 2003; it has been translated into thirty languages. In 2003,

Granta magazine placed him on their list of the Best Young British Novelists. He lives in London.

Sean Wilsey is editor at large for *McSweeney's,* and the author of *Oh the Glory of It All.*

Gary Zebrun is an editor at *The Providence Journal.* A graduate of the University of Notre Dame and the Brown University writing program, he is the recipient of Yaddo, MacDowell, and Bread Loaf fellowships. His first novel, *Someone You Know,* was a finalist for a 2005 Lambda Literary Award. He has just completed a second novel, called *The Usher.* He lives in Newport, Rhode Island.

ACKNOWLEDGMENTS

Heidi Julavits, Ed Park, Andrew Leland, Alvaro Villanueva, Sarah Manguso, Marc Holcomb, Barb Bersche, Heidi Meredith, Dave Kneebone, Eli Horowitz, Sam Potts, Dominic Luxford, Jim Fingal, Alex Carp, Chris Ying, Jennifer Carr, Rachel Bolten, Melanie Glass, Juliette Linderman, Matt Werner, Polly Bresnick, Greg Larson, Soo Oh, Jacquelyn Moorad, Mac Barnett, Elise Winn, Jordan Bass, Brian McMullen, Aran Baker, Sydney Goldstein, Carolyn Gan, and Rebecca Goldman: Thank you.

NOT INCLUDED IN THIS VOLUME: INTERVIEWS WITH WILLIAM GASS DAVID SEDARIS LORRIE MOORE RAY BRADBURY
AND SCORES OF ILLUSTRIOUS OTHERS

Published ten times a year, every issue of the *Believer* contains conversations, like the ones in this book, between excellent writers—alongside interviews with artists, ninjas, musicians, philosophers, and spelling-bee judges. Each issue also features columns by Nick Hornby, Amy Sedaris, and Javier Marías, plus essays by writers like ZZ Packer, Rick Moody, Zadie Smith, and Jim Shepard. Subscribe with the form below and, in addition to a special discount, you'll get Nick Hornby's collected writings from the *Believer—The Polysyllabic Spree*—free of charge!

visit us online at
www.believermag.com
and fill out the below form for a special discount.